MULTINATIONAL ENTERPRISE AND ECONOMIC ANALYSIS

CAMBRIDGE SURVEYS OF ECONOMIC LITERATURE

Editors:
Professor Phyllis Deane, University of Cambridge, and
  Professor Mark Perlman, University of Pittsburgh

Editorial Advisory Board:
Professor A. B. Atkinson, London School of Economics and
  Political Science
Professor M. Bronfenbrenner, Duke University
Professor K. D. George, University College, Cardiff
Professor C. P. Kindleberger, Massachusetts Institute of Technology
Professor T. Mayer, University of California, Davis
Professor A. R. Prest, London School of Economics and Political
  Science

The literature of economics is expanding rapidly and many subjects
have changed out of recognition within the space of a few years. Perceiving the state of knowledge in fast-developing subjects is difficult
for students and time-consuming for professional economists. This
series of books is intended to help with this problem. Each book will
be quite brief, giving a clear structure to and balanced overview of
the topic and written at a level intelligible to the senior undergraduate. They will therefore be useful for teaching, but will also provide a
mature yet compact presentation of the subject for economists wishing to update their knowledge outside their own specialism.

Other books in the series
E. Roy Weintraub: Microfoundations: The compatibility of
microeconomics and macroeconomics
Dennis C. Mueller: Public choice
Robert Clark and Joseph Spengler: The economics of individual and
population aging
Edwin Burmeister: Capital theory and dynamics
Mark Blaug: The methodology of economics or how economists
explain
Robert Ferber and Werner Z. Hirsch: Social experimentation and
economic policy
Anthony C. Fisher: Resource and environmental economics
Morton I. Kamien and Nancy L. Schwartz: Market structure and
innovation

Multinational enterprise and economic analysis

RICHARD E. CAVES

Harvard University

CAMBRIDGE UNIVERSITY PRESS

CAMBRIDGE

LONDON   NEW YORK   NEW ROCHELLE

MELBOURNE   SYDNEY

Published by the Press Syndicate of the University of Cambridge
The Pitt Building, Trumpington Street, Cambridge CB2 1RP
32 East 57th Street, New York, NY 10022, USA
296 Beaconsfield Parade, Middle Park, Melbourne 3206, Australia

First published 1982

Printed in the United States of America

Library of Congress Cataloging in Publication Data
Caves, Richard E.
Multinational enterprise and economic analysis.
(Cambridge surveys of economic literature)
1. International business enterprises.
I. Title.
HD2755.5.C395   1982   338.8′8   82–4543
ISBN 0 521 24990 2   hard covers   AACR2
ISBN 0 521 27115 0   paperback

HD
2755.5
.C395
1982

CONTENTS

Preface   *page* ix

1 **The multinational enterprise as an economic organization**   1
   1.1 Horizontal multiplant enterprises and the MNE   3
   1.2 Vertically integrated MNEs   15
   1.3 Portfolio diversification and the diversified MNE   24
   1.4 Summary   29

2 **The MNE and models of international economic activity**   31
   2.1 Foreign direct investment and international capital flows   31
   2.2 The choice between exporting and foreign direct investment   36
   2.3 Foreign investment and resource allocation in the world economy   45
   2.4 Distribution of foreign investment among countries   56
   2.5 Summary   65

3 **Organization and growth of the MNE**   68
   3.1 Expansion processes in the firm   68

v

3.2   Organizational structure   74
3.3   Effects of organization: new venture or
      acquisition?   81
3.4   Effects of organization: joint ventures and
      control of subsidiaries   85
3.5   Summary   91

4   **Patterns of market competition**   94
4.1   Foreign investment and oligopoly   94
4.2   Market behavior with MNEs present   103
4.3   Competition policy and national welfare   113
4.4   Competitive processes with vertically
      integrated MNEs   118
4.5   Summary   128

5   **Income distribution and labor relations**   131
5.1   Income distribution in general equilibrium   131
5.2   Employment and wages: short run and
      long run   137
5.3   Labor-management relations and collective
      bargaining   147
5.4   Summary   158

6   **Investment behavior and financial flows**   160
6.1   Capital formation and foreign direct
      investment flows   161
6.2   Long-term financing decisions and
      financial-asset markets   168
6.3   Foreign-exchange rates and short-term
      transactions   178
6.4   MNE finance and public policy   188
6.5   Summary   192

7   **Technology and productivity**   195
7.1   The MNE as producer of technical
      knowledge   196
7.2   International transfer of technology   200
7.3   General-equilibrium and welfare aspects   212
7.4   Summary   223

8	**Taxation, MNEs' behavior, and economic welfare**		226
	8.1	Corporation income taxes, market distortions, and world welfare	226
	8.2	Tax conventions and national welfare	229
	8.3	National tax policies: empirical patterns	237
	8.4	Effects of taxation on MNEs' behavior	242
	8.5	Summary	249
9	**Multinationals in developing countries**		252
	9.1	Determinants of MNEs' activities	253
	9.2	Effects on economic development	261
	9.3	Summary	276
10	**Public policy**		279
	10.1	National and international welfare	279
	10.2	National policies: a behavioral approach	286
	10.3	International regulation	295
	10.4	Summary	298
Bibliographic essay			300
Bibliography			306
Index			336

PREFACE

Given the flood of literature on the multinational enterprise (MNE), the author who would further drain the world's scarce resources by writing another book on the subject carries a heavy burden of proof. My justification is that there has been no real synthesis of the MNE as an economic actor, modeled and interpreted in the light of economic theory. There are many books about how to run an MNE, many more about how it robs the poor and inflames nationalistic passions. A number of economists have, from vantage points of their choosing, applied economic analysis to some facet of the MNE's behavior. But those facets have not, as it were, been assembled into a well-articulated structural shape. That task is attempted in this volume. Chapters 1 and 2 investigate why the multinational company exists – why this particular economic organization represents a viable coalition of economic resources. With that question addressed, we turn in Chapters 3 through 9 to the comparative statics of the MNE. Given the reason why the MNE exists, how does its presence affect the operation of various parts of the economic system? Finally, Chapter 10 briefly addresses the implications of these two questions for economic policy.

This book is in part a literature survey, but it does not attempt the hopeless task of a comprehensive survey. Rather, its emphasis falls on the rather small amount of economic theory directly applicable to the MNE and the larger amount of systematic evidence that sheds light on economic hypotheses about the MNE's behavior and its consequences. Analytically useful evidence often lurks in a study that itself puts forth no tests of hypotheses, and so I have searched extensively in the descriptive literature on the MNE. But I cannot claim to have dredged up the last case study, and research published in languages other than English is sorely neglected.

Another incompleteness of this volume derives from the nature of the subject, in that the economic analysis of the MNE, its causes and consequences, spans the whole range of the standard fields of economics. The intellectual traveler must therefore pass from the fertile valleys of his scholarly specialty into the featureless plains of general scholarly acquaintance, and thence to the forbidding wilderness of Not My Subject. The balance of material doubtless reflects my preoccupation with the fields of industrial organization and international economics, although it does so in the conviction that the theoretical tools and research methods of these fields have more to contribute to an understanding of MNEs than do those of other branches.

This book is intended to serve not only the economist seeking an analytical survey of the literature on MNEs but also the advanced undergraduate or other student wishing a textbook-type treatment of the subject. Any experienced teacher will recognize that these objectives are importantly inconsistent with each other. The student does not care greatly about who are the players in the game, and the professional reader does not need an exposition of simple theoretical concepts. In trading between these two conflicting objectives, I have leaned toward the student audience to the extent of including expositions of some simple general-equilibrium concepts (especially in Chapter 2) that will be familiar to professional economists but that have not percolated to the principles course. I have also tended to place some smallish technical points in footnotes that might otherwise have gone into the main text. In trying out the manuscript in my undergraduate course (which requires only the principles course as a prerequisite), I found that students bogged down seriously only in passages drawing on general-equilibrium tools, which required extra classroom exposition. Teachers making classroom use of the book will need to develop the general-equilibrium analysis more fully in class or, alternatively, require a conventional undergraduate course on international economics as a prerequisite. Another strategy would be to delete from required assignments those encapsulated subsections of Chapters 2, 5, and 7 that make use of general equilibrium. As another aid to users of the book, I have included a bibliographic essay that designates, more candidly than the text, what I consider the most valuable items in the literature for both professional research and student reading.

An analytical survey of the MNE has trouble making peace with the vast literature on public policy. I know no subject in economic policy in which the issues that excite public discussion bear so little relation to the welfare issues identified by normative economists. Therefore, my strategy in Chapters 1 through 9 is to take up the policy issues as they devolve from economic analysis rather than from governmental pronouncements and Sunday-supplement musings. In Chapter 10 I do attempt an interpretation of the public-policy dialogue over MNEs. But rather than survey the actual issues, which are hopelessly numerous, diffuse, and variously defined from country to country, I attempt an end run by inquiring why the political process in many countries casts up policies and attitudes toward MNEs that sometimes seem to have so little to do with maximizing national (or anybody else's) economic welfare.

Polonius to the contrary notwithstanding, an author is necessarily a borrower. My earlier research on MNEs, which led up to this book, benefited greatly from discussions with Thomas Horst. We once planned to write this book jointly, and it is the poorer because that did not come to pass. The task of revising my first drafts was greatly aided by the hospitality of the International Centre for Research on Economics and Related Disciplines at the London School of Economics and Political Science, and I am indebted to the Centre's director, Professor Michio Morishima, and staff for their hospitality. I am grateful to Stanley Engerman, David J. Teece, and Louis T. Wells for comments.

R.E.C.

1

The multinational enterprise as an economic organization

The multinational enterprise (MNE) is defined here as an enterprise that controls and manages production establishments – plants – located in at least two countries. It is simply one subspecies of multiplant firm. We use the term "enterprise" rather than "company" to direct attention to the top level of coordination in the hierarchy of business decisions; a company, itself multinational, may be the controlled subsidiary of another firm. The minimum overseas "plant" needed to make an enterprise multinational is, as we shall see, judgmental. The transition from an overseas sales subsidiary or a technology licensee to a producing subsidiary is not always clear cut, for good economic reasons. What constitutes "control" over a foreign establishment is another judgmental issue. Not infrequently a MNE will hold a minor fraction of the equity of a foreign affiliate, and we shall see that what fraction of equity a parent holds in its foreign subsidiary is itself an economic decision. Countries differ in regard to the minimum percentage of equity ownership that they count as a "direct investment" abroad, as distinguished from a "portfolio investment," in their international-payments statistics.

The purpose of this study is not to sort the MNEs from the national firms in the world's enterprises. However, the definition does have the valuable function of identifying the MNE as essentially a multiplant firm. We are back to Coase's (1937) classic question of why the boundary between the administrative allocation of resources within the firm and the market allocation of resources between firms falls where it does. In the environment of a market economy, entrepreneurs are free to try their hand at displacing market transactions by increasing the scope of transactions handled administratively within their firms. In the Darwinian tradition we expect that the most profitable pattern of enterprise organization will ultimately prevail: Where more profit results from placing plants under a common administrative control, multiplant enterprises will predominate, and single-plant firms will merge or go out of business. In order to explain the existence and prevalence of MNEs, we require models that predict where the multiplant firm enjoys "transactional" advantages from displacing the arm's-length market and where it does not. In fact, the prevalence of multiplant (multinational) enterprises varies greatly from sector to sector and from country to country, affording a ready opportunity to test any models of the MNE that we develop.

The models of the multiplant firm potentially relevant to explaining the presence of MNEs are quite numerous and rather disparate in their concerns. It proves convenient to divide them into three groups: (1) One type of multiplant firm turns out essentially the same line of goods from its plants in each geographic market. Such firms are common in U.S. domestic industries such as metal containers, bakeries, and brewing. Similarly, many MNEs establish plants in different countries to make the same or similar goods. We refer to these firms as horizontally integrated. (2) Another type of multiplant enterprise produces outputs in some of its plants that serve as inputs to other of its plants. We then describe the firm as vertically integrated. Vertically integrated firms, MNE or domestic, may make physical transfers of intermediate products from one of their plants to another, but that practice is not required by our definition; they need only be producing at adjacent stages of a vertically related set of production processes. (3) The third type of multiplant firm is the diversified company whose plants' outputs are neither vertically nor horizontally related to one another. As an international firm, we refer to it as a diversified MNE.

1.1. **Horizontal multiplant enterprises and the MNE**

We start by equating the horizontal MNE to a multiplant firm with plants in different countries. Its existence requires, first, that *locational forces* justify spreading the world's production around so that plants are found in different national markets. Given this dispersion of production, there must be some *transactional advantage* to placing the plants (some plants, at least) under common administrative control. This is the abstract, static approach that provides the most general and most satisfying avenue to explaining the multinational company. The locational question – why plants are spread around the world as they are – we postpone until Chapter 2. We assume at first that plant *A* was located in southeast England because that was the lowest-cost way to serve the market it in fact serves. We also assume that this locational choice was not essentially influenced by whether the plant was built by an MNE, bought by an MNE, or not owned by an MNE at all. The static approach also puts aside the vital question of why a company grows into MNE status – something we can explain much better once the static model is in hand.

The transactional approach asserts, quite simply, that horizontal MNEs will exist only if the plants they control and operate attain lower costs or higher revenue productivity than if the plants function under separate managements. Why should this net-revenue advantage arise? Some of the reasons have to do with minimizing costs of production and closely associated logistical activities of the firm. The more analytically interesting reasons – and, we shall see, surely the more important ones empirically – concern the complementary nonproduction activities of the firm.

Intangible assets

The concept that has proved most fruitful for explaining the nonproduction bases for the MNE is that of intangible assets belonging to the firm. Successful firms in most industries possess one or more types of intangible assets. An asset may represent technology – knowledge about how to produce a cheaper or better product at given input prices, or how to produce a given product at a lower cost than competing firms. This intangible asset might take the specific form of a patented process or design, or it might simply rest on know-how shared among employees of the firm. Or the intangible might take the form of a marketing asset. The firm may possess special skills in styling or promoting its product that make it such that the buyer can distinguish it from those of competitors. Such an asset has a revenue productivity for the firm because it signifies the willingness of some buyers to pay more for that firm's product than for an otherwise comparable variety of the same good that lacks this particular touch. Assets of this type are closely akin to product differentiation, a market condition in which the distinctive features of various sellers' outputs cause each competing firm to face its own downward-sloping demand curve. Once again, the intangible asset may take the form of a specific property – a registered trademark or brand – or it may rest in marketing and selling skills shared among the firm's employees. Finally, the distinctiveness of the firm's marketing-oriented assets may rest with the firm's ability to come up with frequent innovations; its intangible asset then may be a patented novelty, or simply some new combination of attributes that its rivals cannot quickly or effectively imitate.

An intangible asset yields a rent to the firm[1] and makes the firm appear successful. But why should that cause it to be multiplant and multinational? The answer lies in the problems of market failure associated with arm's-length transactions in intangible assets. These failures deter a successful one-plant firm from selling or renting its intangible assets to other single-plant firms and thereby foster the existence of multiplant (and multinational) firms. Intangible assets are subject to a daunting list of infirmities for being put to efficient use by conventional markets:[2]

---

[1] Assuming, of course, that the firm itself owns the full equity in the intangible asset. Suppose, instead, that the firm works a patent that it licenses from an independent inventor. If the inventor bargains cleverly enough, he may be able to collect from his licensee all or nearly all of the net revenue imputed to his innovation, leaving little or no surplus for the firm.

[2] Williamson (1973) provided a convenient brief description.

1.   They are, at least to some degree, *public goods*. Once a piece of knowledge has been developed and applied at a certain location, it can be put to work elsewhere at little extra cost and without reducing the "amount" of the idea available at the original site. From society's point of view, the marginal conditions for efficient allocation of resources then require that the price of the intangible asset be equal to its marginal cost, zero or approximately zero. But no one gets rich selling his bright ideas for zero. Therefore, intangible assets tend to be underprovided or to be priced inefficiently (at a net price exceeding their marginal cost) or both.

2.   Transactions in intangibles suffer from *impactedness* combined with *opportunism*. This problem is best explained by examples: I have a piece of knowledge that I know will be valuable to you. I try to convince you of this value by describing its general nature and character. But I do not reveal the details, because then the cat would be out of the bag, and you would be free to use the knowledge without paying for it.[3] But you therefore decline to pay me as much as the knowledge would in fact be worth to you, because you suspect that I am opportunistic and overstate my claims. With these conditions present, I cannot collect in an arm's-length transaction the full net-revenue productivity of my knowledge. I will underinvest in the knowledge, or I may try to earn the most I can from what knowledge I do acquire by putting it to work myself.

3.   An element amplifying the problem of impactedness is *uncertainty*. If the knowledge were the recipe for a truly superb chocolate cake, I could bring about an efficient arm's-length transaction by letting you taste the cake and guaranteeing that (once you have bought the recipe and executed it properly) yours will taste just as good. Conversely, if neither of us can predict accurately how well the knowledge will perform when you use it, and if we are both risk-averse, too small a volume of transactions will take place in the intangible knowledge.

Consider what these propositions imply for the MNE: There are

---

[3] Unless, of course, I have established a property right in the knowledge that allows me to exclude those users who have not paid my asking price. Patents, copyrights, and trademarks are just such property rights.

seven soap factories in seven countries – each an independent firm. One discovers a way to make its product especially attractive to buyers at little added cost, and its rivals, by assumption, cannot imitate the innovation simply by copying it. The innovator could license its discovery to the other six firms, but would (for reasons set forth earlier) probably be able to collect less than the full net-revenue productivity. It could expand its output and export to the other six markets, but that would incur excessive transportation costs if the plants were all efficiently located at the start (as we assume). The most profitable solution for the seven plants (firms) jointly is to band together into one MNE in order to share the intangible asset. This analysis generates the empirical prediction that we should find a greater incidence of MNEs in industries where intangible assets are important. Tests of the proposition will be reviewed later.[4]

The intangible-assets approach yields certain extensions and variants that we can usefully develop here. When the MNE puts an intangible asset to work in its subsidiary abroad, it is, in a sense, making use of an excess capacity in its roster of assets. An intangible asset, because of its public-good nature, does not have a maximum "capacity" that limits its use. But the ongoing firm also employs many tangible assets that are discontinuous or "lumpy" and that may, as a result, be underutilized at a particular time. A new activity becomes a likely bet for the firm if it requires the services of the asset in question and can in fact fill up its excess capacity.[5] Some writers have suggested that the top management of a successful firm may

---

[4] This approach has developed through the hands of a number of authors, including Eastman and Stykolt (1967), Hymer (1960), Kindleberger (1969), Johnson (1970), Caves (1971), McManus (1972), Buckley and Casson (1976), Dunning (1977*a*), and Magee (1977*a*). For early antecedents, see Southard (1931, Chapter 3) and Pennie (1956). Ragazzi (1973) and Rugman (1980*a*) have provided surveys.

[5] This model of the firm's expansion process is quite a general one, capable of explaining product-market diversification as well as multinational expansion. See Penrose (1959) and Rubin (1973). Notice that the model denies the economic concept of long-run equilibrium, in which all assets possessed by the firm can be hired or fired, expanded or contracted. It supposes, not unrealistically, that the firms we observe are always operating in the short run, with some discontinuous and lumpy assets under their contractual employ. The coalition of inputs that make up the firm cannot be efficiently assembled and dismantled on short notice.

find itself in this position and that foreign investment may serve to utilize its top managers' capacity to the fullest.

Another asset of the ongoing firm is its capacity to generate investible funds beyond what it can profitably use for expanding its current activities. One view of the ongoing firm's financial decisions holds that it attaches different opportunity costs to funds from various sources. Externally secured funds – debt and new equity – have a high cost because of transactions costs and the reduced independence they entail for the managers, as well as the direct cost of paying additional interest or dividends. Internally generated funds – profits not paid out to current shareholders – have a lower opportunity cost, and managers will put them to work in a new activity with an expected profit rate (internal rate of return) lower than what would be needed to warrant external borrowing. Thus, excess capacity in internally generated funds can also motivate foreign investment.[6]

A third extension of the intangible-assets concept pertains to the way in which firms possess and apply collective skills that add up to "going-concern" value. The firm utilizes its assets, intangible and tangible, through the coordinated efforts of an ongoing team of managers and employees. Information shared by these individuals and habituated modes of coordination among them make the firm more effective than it would be if they were replaced by other persons with equal qualifications. Even if the firm could market its intangible assets effectively, it could not disentangle them from the skills and knowledge of the managerial team. This basis for multimarket firms appears in mirror image when we examine the market for transfers of technology at arm's length (Chapter 7).

Scale economies and cost minimization

The theory of multiplant operation (Scherer et al., 1975) has also indicated a number of economies more directly relating to the firm's production activities, and these could apply to the MNE if

---

[6] The financial model of the firm that underlies these propositions has less than universal acceptance among economists. The financial behavior of the MNE will be considered in Chapter 6.

they do not stop at the national boundary. There may be transactional economies in the procurement of raw materials that go beyond the input needs of the single plant. Economies may arise in the transportation network for outbound shipments of finished goods that extend beyond the single plant's output. Localized demand fluctuations may call for pooling plants' capacities so that several plants' outputs can be flexibly shipped wherever the peak demand is occurring. If the industry's output consists of a line of goods, it may be efficient for each plant to specialize in some items rather than for each to turn out the whole array. It is an empirical question how fully these economies are available to a multiplant firm operating across national boundaries, because they depend on the free movement of goods (inputs or outputs) among plants or the common use of managerial resources. But the hypothesis is there to be tested.

Empirical evidence

These hypotheses about horizontal MNEs have received rather extensive statistical testing. The usual strategy of research involves correlating the prevalence of MNEs in an industry with structural traits of that industry: If attribute x promotes the formation of MNEs, and successful firms in industry A have a lot of x, then MNEs should be prevalent in industry A. One can analyze the shares of sales held by foreign subsidiaries in a national market such as Canada or the United Kingdom to determine whether or not high shares occur in industries marked by the traits that should give rise to MNEs. One can perform the same exercise by examining interindustry differences in the relative sizes of foreign assets held by companies based in the various manufacturing industries of the United States or Sweden. One can compare the activities of national companies to those of MNEs. Let us summarize the conclusions that have emerged from these studies.

The presence of intangible assets as an encouragement to foreign investment has been affirmed in many studies. Although intangible assets by their nature resist any direct measurement, their prevalence is revealed by the outlays that companies make for the purpose of producing them. As indicators of these assets, economists have seized on the outlays for advertising and research and development (R&D) undertaken by firms classified to an industry. That the share of the foreign-subsidiary assets in the total assets of U.S. corporations increases significantly with the importance of advertising and R&D outlays in the industry has been confirmed statistically in many studies: Gruber et al. (1967), Horst (1972*a*), Wolf (1977), Pugel (1978, Chapter 4), Bergsten et al. (1978, pp. 242–5), Goedde (1978, Chapter 2), Parker (1978, Chapter 8), and Lall (1980). Goedde, whose analysis covered a sample of large U.S. companies, also showed that the influence of advertising appears most strongly in the food and chemicals sectors (the latter includes pharmaceuticals, soaps and detergents, and some other consumer goods), whereas the influence of the industry's research intensity appears strongest in the machinery sectors. This pattern closely matches one's sense of the apparent importance of different sorts of intangible assets in those industries.

Some investigations, both statistical and case studies, have invoked these same factors to explain why firms in some industrial sectors differ in their propensities to invest abroad. Horst (1974*a*, Chapters 4 and 5) explored the effects of various corporate assets on the foreign-investment behavior of firms in the U.S. food-processing sector. The strategies followed by these firms divide roughly into two classes. Some succeeded on the basis of extensive national advertising, others with extensive and intricate distribution systems for bringing their products to the local consumer in good condition. The latter class has taken part less extensively in foreign investment, because these complex distribution systems are a drain on managerial resources and are not themselves an exportable intangible asset. The advertisers, on the other hand, are heavy foreign investors. The firms with intensive distribution systems also display less extensive multiplant development within the United States, indicating that the diseconomies of scale in extending their empires constrain them geographically within the United States as well as internationally.

Outflows of foreign investment from countries other than the

United States have not received similar statistical treatments. Sweden is the exception: The extent of Swedish firms' foreign involvement is significantly related to their R&D activities in Sweden (Swedenborg, 1979, Chapter 5).

Other statistical investigations have dealt with inflows of foreign investment to countries such as Canada and the United Kingdom. Once again, R&D and advertising levels, especially when measured in the United States – the principal source country for the foreign investors – are significantly related to the shares of the local market held by the subsidiaries (Dunning, 1973*b*; Caves, 1974*b*; Baumann, 1975; Saunders, 1978, Chapter 7; Parry, 1978). Owen (1979) also found sales-force expenditures to be a weakly significant predictor.

The importance of managerial talent and skills has provided another empirical approach to the intangible-assets hypothesis. One line of thought suggests that managerial skills – especially those of large U.S. companies – are the sole explanation for foreign investment (Servan-Schreiber, 1968). Close analysis of this proposition makes it sound somewhat shallow beside the intangible-assets model; it might explain the international success of U.S. management consulting firms, but hardly operating companies. And the proposition's popularity has waned along with the fortunes of U.S. multinationals in their competition with large companies based abroad. Properly interpreted, however, the managerial-skills hypothesis converges on the intangible-assets model. We have suggested that intangible assets may not get marketed outside the firm, not just because markets for information work badly but also because the asset cannot be disentangled from the firm's managerial team. Team production involves a linkup of managers with sophisticated and specialized skills. Therefore, managerial skills give rise to foreign investment because they have become combined in effective teams to develop and utilize intangible assets that themselves cannot readily be marketed separately. Thus, the level and extent of managerial skills required in an industry should contribute to explaining its FDI activity (even after controlling for its intangible assets). Caves (1974*b*) did not find much support, but Pugel (1978), Jarrett (1979, Chapter 3), and Swedenborg (1979) – using more suitable variables

– did find a statistically significant influence for the extent and quality of managerial skills.[7]

Less conspicuous in the statistical research is the hypothesis that MNEs are merely a category of multiplant enterprises and that the advantages in plant coordination giving rise to the one will give rise to the other as well. Eastman and Stykolt (1967, Chapter 4) developed the original hypothesis and found some statistical support for it. Both Caves (1974b) and Saunders (1978, Chapter 7) tested and confirmed a simple version of this hypothesis – that industries whose leading firms have extensive multiplant operations in the United States will be the same industries in which MNEs hold large shares in the Canadian markets. Interestingly, Caves found the hypothesis confirmed for Canada, geographically cheek by jowl with the U.S. homeland of the major MNEs, but not for insular Britain. The economies of coordinating multiple plants through a single firm may stop at the water's edge.

Although horizontal manufacturing investments have held the attention of researchers, horizontal MNEs have expanded vigorously in banking and other services as well. The descriptive literature indicates that the intangible-assets hypothesis again makes a good showing – especially when expanded to take in an ongoing semicontractual relationship between the service enterprise and the nonfinancial MNE with which it does business. A bank, advertising agency, or accounting firm acquires a good deal of specific knowledge about its client's business, and the two firms may sustain an ongoing relation based on trust that lowers the cost of contracting and the risks of opportunistic behavior. If the service firm has such a quasi-contractual relation with a parent MNE, it enjoys a transactional advantage for supplying the same service to the MNE's foreign subsidiaries. But the service must be supplied locally, and so the service firm goes multinational to follow its customers.

---

[7] There may indeed be something in the original (Servan-Schreiber) version of the hypothesis insofar as the international success of U.S. firms after World War II rested partly on U.S. innovations in managerial techniques and the organization of the firm. These innovations were ultimately copied by foreign competitors, and the innovative rents to American multinationals eroded away. See Franko (1976) and Chapter 3.

Much casual evidence reveals this intangible asset of a quasi-contractual customer relation behind service industries' foreign investments (e.g., Safarian, 1966, p. 210; Behrman, 1969, pp. 3–4). The banking sector's case is particularly well documented (Grubel, 1977, and references cited therein; Pastré, 1981). Grubel affirmed the transactional model but also pointed to two other factors. Some banks may acquire particular product-differentiating skills analogous to those found in some goods-producing industries; although these cut little ice in most banking markets, they may explain banks' foreign investments in less-developed countries (Baum, 1974). Also, national banking markets often appear somewhat noncompetitive because of cartelization or regulation or both, and foreign banks are well-equipped potential entrants. The Eurocurrency markets can be largely explained on this basis. The traits of foreign banks' operations in the United States affirm these propositions (Lees, 1976; Terrell and Key, 1978). Their assets include proportionally more commercial and industrial loans than those of their domestic competitors, reflecting the primacy of business with their foreign-MNE customers. As they age, they develop other business from this base – drumming up other loan and deposit customers, undertaking large interbank transactions to balance their foreign parents' dollar positions.

Dynamics of the MNE

The transactional approach to the MNE has the advantage that it can explain the dynamic course of development of the firm over time, as well as the prevalence of MNEs at a given time – the approach we have explored thus far. If the MNE can sometimes seize an advantage to displace a market and reduce transactions costs, the firm itself faces costs of securing information and arranging transactions that shape its behavior. Here we shall set forth some propositions that arise from this fact; others will turn up in later chapters.

The dynamic transactional approach first makes an elementary point about why MNEs are not ubiquitous. Each person is normally a citizen of some particular country and brings to his business a general knowledge of the legal and social system, the "ways of doing things," peculiar to that nation. The business firm, unless already a mature MNE, has a clear-cut national base and identity, with its internal planning and decision making carried out in the context of that nation's legal and cultural framework. When the entrepreneurial unit extends itself to found or acquire subsidiaries in foreign lands, it must incur a fixed transactions cost of learning how things are done abroad. If it sends home-office personnel to run and develop the subsidiary, they will (for a time, at least) be less effective than at home for this reason. Foreign nationals can be hired to run the shop, but then a similar fixed cost must be incurred to teach them the firm's way of doing things. Either choice leaves the potential MNE facing a virtual disadvantage in the foreign market with respect to its local competitors, who are steeped in that social and cultural milieu and need incur no such fixed transactions cost. The transactional advantages of the MNE are necessary to get it over this intrinsic transactional disadvantage.

The transactional approach also implies that intangible assets are developed by firms in some national market. These assets influence a series of investment decisions taken over time by successful firms, including decisions to begin and expand foreign investments. The approach helps to predict how these decisions will be made. First, the firm that comes to possess some rent-yielding skill or intangible asset cannot overnight undertake all the profitable projects it can find utilizing that asset. Various constraints limit the firm's growth, because there is a limit to how rapidly it can expand its management cadre and its equity-capital base.[8] The firm ponders various strategies for using its distinctive assets so as to maximize the expected present value of its future profits. Suppose that its decisive advantage over (at least some of) its rivals becomes clear when it is a single-nation firm holding 10 percent of its national market. For its next big investment, does it expand into foreign markets, or does it go for another 10 percent of the domestic market? The answer could go either way, but information costs do create a bias toward contin-

---

[8] Penrose (1959) first emphasized the constraint on growth due to the firm's limited ability to expand its management; Horst (1974*b*) summarized the literature on financial constraints on the firm's growth in the context of MNEs.

uing domestic expansion. This is "more of the same" and does not require the firm to incur new information and search costs associated with going abroad.

If fortune continues to smile on the firm and its share of the domestic market grows, the marginal returns to additional expansion there eventually decline. Given the elasticity of the market demand curve, the higher our expanding firm's market share, the lower the demand elasticity that it perceives. Also, its increasing market share comes at the cost of dislodging stronger and stronger competitors. Expanding to serve overseas markets becomes more and more attractive.[9]

Once investments abroad rise to the top of the list of profitable investments for the firm, the choice of destination should be affected by information costs as they vary among foreign destinations. The first overseas investment is likely to be made in the national market where the entrepreneur faces the least disadvantage of language and culture.

The empirical evidence on patterns of expansion by multinational firms strongly supports these propositions. Horst (1972*b*) compared firms within industries to see what traits discriminate between those that go abroad and those not yet holding MNE status. The only significant difference he found was in the size (market share) they had already attained in the domestic market. This result supports the hypothesis that the successful firm runs out its successes in the domestic market before incurring the transactions costs of going abroad.[10] Another strong pattern of evidence bears on the countries that firms pick for their first ventures abroad. For example, U.S. firms tend strongly to make Canada the first stop. Evidence to be discussed in Section 2.4 shows that each source country's MNEs pick their debut foreign markets so as to minimize the information and transactions

---

[9] In Chapter 2 we stress that the firm might garner the rents from foreign markets by foreign investment, by expanding its domestic plant and exporting, or by licensing an independent foreign producer. For the moment, we simply assume that foreign investment is the preferred choice.

[10] Caves and Pugel (1980, Chapter 2) confirmed Horst's result but also found that the advertising outlays of different firms within an industry are associated with their foreign-investment activities. Also see Wolf (1975) and Swedenborg's findings (1979, Chapter 6) on Swedish MNEs.

costs associated with foreign investment. The new MNE can easily accommodate to the familiar environment while it is learning the ropes – acquiring knowledge that reduces the cost (or risk) of future expansions into more alien terrain. And its intangible assets provide it with some offsetting advantages at the earliest stages. It can work its plant at designed capacity sooner than a comparable independent firm (Forsyth, 1972, pp. 60–2), and a product innovation borrowed from its parent involves fewer shakedown difficulties for the subsidiary (Dunning, 1958, p. 120).

1.2. **Vertically integrated MNEs**

It is now an easy step to identify the vertically integrated MNE as simply a species of vertically integrated firm whose production units lie in different nations. Our quest for models to explain the vertically integrated multinational immediately turns to the economic analysis of vertically integrated firms. Again, we suppose that production units are placed around the world according to conventional locational pressures – the bauxite mine where the bauxite is, the smelter that converts alumina into aluminum near a source of low-cost electric power. The question is, why do they come under common administrative control?

Until recent years the economic theory of vertical integration contained only a small and unsatisfying inventory of models. Some dealt with the physical integration of production processes: If you make structural shapes out of the metal ingot before it cools, you need not incur the cost of reheating it. Such gains from physical integration explain why sequential processes are grouped in a single plant, but they hardly explain the common ownership of far-flung plants. The other group of traditional models proposed that vertical integration might be preferable to a stalemate between a monopolistic seller and a monopsonistic buyer. The deduction is reasonable enough, but it hardly explains vertical integration in the many markets that do not represent bilateral monopoly (even if they are less than purely competitive).[11]

---

[11] Of course, vertical integration might develop because a buyer wants to avoid paying the monopoly seller's price and so integrates backward into

Transactional explanations of vertical integration

The great source of enrichment to the theory of vertical integration has been a transactional approach of the same genus we employed to explain horizontal MNEs. Vertical integration occurs, the argument goes, because the parties prefer it to the contracting costs and uncertainties that would mar the alternative state of arm's-length transactions. The vertically integrated firm internalizes a market for an intermediate product, just as the horizontal MNE internalizes markets for intangible assets.[12] Suppose that there were universal pure competition in each intermediate-product market, with large numbers of buyers and sellers, the product homogeneous (or its qualities readily evaluated by the parties), information about prices and availability in easy access to all parties in the market. Neither seller nor buyer would then have any reason (other than personal esteem) to maintain a long-term relation with any particular transactor on the other side of the market. When these assumptions no longer hold, however, both buyers and sellers acquire a variety of motives to make long-term alliances. To retain our emphasis on transactions costs, suppose that parties in the market incur a substantial fixed cost if they shift from one transactions partner to another. Each seller's product may be somewhat different, and the buyer incurs significant costs of testing or adapting to new varieties, or merely learning the requirements and organizational routines of new partners. The buyer and seller have an incentive to enter into some kind of long-term arrangement.

If buyers and sellers are still numerous, however, why should these switching costs impair the operation of a competitive market? The disappointed transactions partner can always switch in the long run. Why does that consideration not keep everyone honest? The answer is that under plausible assumptions it can pay to be opportunistic and try to improve one's deal with an ongoing transactions partner. If everyone knows this, there is an incentive to enter into long-

the seller's activity; symmetrically, a seller might integrate to avoid a monopsonistic buyer.

[12] Williamson (1971) deserves credit for popularizing this approach. For an excellent survey of models of vertical integration, see Kaserman (1978).

term contracts with terms fully specified in advance so as to avoid any uncertainty and entrapment.

But that effort bumps into another problem with arm's-length vertical relations. Suppose the parties sit down to work out a contract that specifies how each will behave under all possible contingencies and provides policing and enforcement mechanisms that avert the problem of opportunism. Well and good, but the bargaining sessions may be prolonged indeed. The alternative to the uncertainty about how one will fare in an ongoing bargain is the high cost of negotiating in advance a contract that will anticipate every uncertainty and close every loophole. Careful definition of the agreement in advance bargaining saves on the costs of monitoring the agreement and haggling over unexpected developments after it is signed, of course, but only at the expense of greater negotiation costs. There is, as usual, no free lunch.[13]

Internalizing the market through vertical integration at that point becomes an attractive option. Although internal coordination of a vertically related MNE is not without its costs and strains on managerial capacity, it does allow adapting to the flow of events without concern for who benefits more.

To summarize this somewhat complex argument, intermediate-product markets can be organized in a spectrum of ways stretching from anonymous spot market transactions through a variety of long-term contractual arrangements at arm's length to vertical integration. Switching costs and durable, specific assets discourage spot transactions and favor one of the other modes. If, in addition, the costs of negotiating and monitoring arm's-length contracts are high, the choice falls on vertical integration. These are the empirical predictions of the "transactions" approach to vertical integration.

One other aspect of the theory of vertical integration holds promise for explaining MNEs of this type. Vertical integration can occur because of failings in markets for information, as analyzed earlier in

---

[13] Economists like to make the point that the uncertainties impelling vertical integration could be averted by resorting to comprehensive forward-contract markets, if they existed (Buckley and Casson, 1976). Because they do not exist for the same reasons that vertical integration emerges, the point has no operational significance.

the context of intangible assets. A processing firm must plan its capacity on some assumption about the future price and availability of its key raw material. The producers of that raw material have the cheapest access (and perhaps exclusive access) to that information. But they may have an incentive not to reveal it accurately to the prospective customer; the more capacity those customers can be induced to build, the higher the price they are likely to bid in the future for any given quantity of the raw material. Therefore, vertical integration may occur in order to get around impacted information coupled with opportunism (Arrow, 1975).

Empirical evidence

The available literature testing these hypotheses has included far fewer statistical studies than has the literature concerned with horizontal MNEs. Pugel (1978) did conclude that American manufacturing industries having greater involvement with natural resources invest larger proportions of their assets abroad. However, his indicator was nothing but a dummy variable designating the ferrous and nonferrous metals industries. McKern (1976) provided the only comparative examination of the extractive industries themselves. He was left unimpressed with the unimportance of monopoly/monopsony market structures for explaining foreign investment in Australia's extractive industries. Also, he could not accord much importance to the foreign MNEs' motive of assuring themselves access to supplies, because in many cases they did not transfer Australian raw materials directly to their own refining facilities but instead sold them on the open market. Accordingly, he argued that an important motive for vertical integration is the use by MNEs of the knowledge they have acquired about the international market for the raw materials in question. This basis for vertical integration in MNEs adds up to an intangible-assets explanation, analytically similar to the one that proves so fruitful for explaining horizontal MNEs.

A great deal of information exists on individual extractive industries in which MNEs operate on a worldwide basis, and this case-study evidence merits a glance in lieu of more systematic findings. For example, Stuckey (1981) found the international aluminum in-

dustry to contain not only MNEs integrated from the mining of bauxite through the fabrication of aluminum projects but also a network
of long-term contracts and joint ventures. All of these indicate a
general unwillingness of market participants to settle for spot transactions in bauxite (the raw ore) and alumina (output of the first processing stage). Stuckey likewise did not assign much importance to
the small number of market participants worldwide. Rather, the
problem is that switching costs are extremely high. That is, alumina
refining facilities need to be located physically close to bauxite
mines (to minimize transportation costs), and they are constructed to
deal with the properties of specific ores. Likewise, for technical and
transportation-cost reasons, aluminum smelters are somewhat tied to
particular sources of alumina. Therefore, arm's-length markets tend
to be poisoned by the problems of small numbers and switching
costs. And the very large specific and durable investments in facilities also invoke the problems of long-term contracts that were identified earlier. Finally, Stuckey gave some weight to Arrow's model
of vertical integration as a route to securing information: Nobody
knows more about future bauxite supplies and exploration than an
existing bauxite producer.

A good deal of evidence on vertical integration also appears in the
vast and contentious literature on the oil industry. The more ambitious investigations of vertical integration have addressed the U.S.
segment of the industry, but there appears to be no central difference
between the forces traditionally affecting vertical integration in national and international oil companies.[14] These studies give considerable emphasis to the risks faced by any nonintegrated firm in petroleum extraction or refining. Refineries normally operate at
capacity and require a constant flow of crude-oil inputs. Storing
large inventories of input is quite costly, and so backward integration
that reduces uncertainty about crude supplies can save the refiner a
large investment in storage capacity. It also reduces risks in times of
"shortages" and "rationing," when constraints somewhere in the in-

---

[14] By "traditionally" we mean before the OPEC cartel became fully effective in the early 1970s. See Penrose (1968, pp. 46–50, 253–9), Greening (1976), and Teece (1976, Chapter 3).

tegrated system (crude-oil supplies are only the most familiar constraint) can leave the unintegrated firm out in the cold. The reduction of risk is quite important for this industry, and vertically integrated firms have been found to be able to borrow long-term funds more cheaply than those with more exposure to risk (Greening, 1976, Chapter 1).[15]

Finally, country-based studies of the foreign-investment process have also underlined vertical MNEs as the outcome of failed arm's-length market transactions. Japanese companies have tended to become involved with extractive foreign investments only after the experience of having arm's-length suppliers renege on long-term contracts, and they have also experimented with low-interest loans to independent foreign suppliers as a way to establish commitment (Tsurumi, 1976, Chapter 2).

Vertical integration: other manifestations

The identification of vertically integrated foreign investment with extractive activities is traditional and no doubt faithful to the pattern accounting for the bulk of MNE assets. However, it gives too narrow an impression of the role of vertically subdivided transactions in MNEs.

First of all, it neglects a form of backward integration that depends not on natural resources but on subdividing production processes and placing abroad those that are both labor-intensive and footloose. For example, semiconductors may be produced by capital-intensive processes and assembled into electronic equipment by similarly mechanized processes both undertaken in the United States. But, in between, wires must be soldered to the semiconductors by means of a labor-intensive technology. Because shipping costs for the devices

---

[15] The international iron-ore market in the 1970s provides a neat example of the attraction of vertically integrated MNEs for reducing risk. Mostly because of nationalization of iron-ore mines, the degree of vertical integration in the international iron and steel industry had been declining. The nationalization and dis-integration had been encouraged by a period of high prices for iron ore. However, as the situation changed in the 1970s, the prices declined and the nonintegrated ore producers began scurrying to secure long-term contracts and restore some of the dismantled integration. See Vernon and Levy (1980).

are low relative to their value, it pays to carry out the labor-intensive stage in a low-wage country. The relationship of the enterprises performing these functions in the United States and abroad must obviously be a close one, involving either detailed contractual arrangements or common ownership. This subdivision of production processes should occur through foreign investment to an extent that depends again on the transactional bases for vertical integration. Some theoretical models (Stigler, 1951) have suggested that this type of vertical dis-integration proceeds as an industry enlarges, permitting real gains from an expanded division of labor as more and more separable processes are carried out by firms specializing in them. The model probably is applicable to the type of foreign investment just described. The gains from an expanded division of labor that Stigler (and Adam Smith) had in mind may depend on the geographical dispersion of production processes to specialized establishments and may have little to do with the form of transactions between the specialized establishments (spot, contract, or vertical MNE relationships).

Writers on the rapid expansion of offshore procurement and the associated international trade always refer to the role of foreign investment in transplanting the necessary know-how and managerial coordination (Helleiner, 1973; Sharpston, 1975). Jarrett (1979, Chapters 7 and 8; also see Helleiner, 1979) has explored statistically both the structural determinants of this type of trade and the role of MNEs in carrying it out. His data pertain to imports under a provision of the U.S. tariff whereby components exported from the United States for additional fabrication abroad can be reimported with duty paid only on the value added abroad; his statistical analysis addresses both the total value of imports and such articles and the value added abroad. Furthermore, the analysis explains how these activities vary both among U.S. industries and among countries taking part in this trade. His results confirm the expected properties of the industries that make use of vertically dis-integrated production: Their outputs have high value per unit of weight, possess reasonably mature technology (so are out of the experimental stage), are produced in the United States under conditions giving rise to high labor costs, and are easily subject to decentralized production.[16] Among overseas countries, U.S. offshore procurement favors those not too far distant (transportation costs) and with low wages and favorable working conditions. With these factors controlled, there is a positive relation of the component flows to the extent of U.S. foreign investment, both among industries and among foreign countries.[17]

A considerable amount of vertical integration is also involved in the "horizontal" foreign investments described earlier in this chapter, and we shall see that the behavior of horizontal MNEs cannot be fully understood without recognizing the complementary vertical aspects of their domestic and foreign operations. Often the foreign subsidiary does not just produce the parent's good for the local market; it processes semifinished units of that good, or it packages or assembles them according to local specifications. Pharmaceuticals, for example, are prepared in the locally desired formulations using basic preparations imported from the parent. The subsidiary organizes a distribution system in the host-country market, distributing partly its own production, but with its line of goods filled out with imports from its parent or other affiliates. Or the subsidiary integrates forward to provide local servicing facilities of information and customer service. These activities are bound up with the development and maintenance of the enterprise's goodwill asset, as described earlier, through a commitment of resources to the local market. The firm can thereby assure local customers, who are likely to incur fixed investments of their own in shifting their purchases to the MNE, that the company's presence is not transitory; because the MNE has sunk some costs locally, it will continue even in the face of some adverse disturbances. This consideration helps explain foreign investment in some producer-goods industries for which the

---

[16] Jarrett measured this last by the extent of multiplant operation of companies in the United States and by the extent to which U.S. producers depend on inputs purchased from other establishments in the same industry.

[17] If the presence of foreign investment is associated with offshore procurement, it should also be true that the factors influencing the proportion of U.S. imports that come from overseas corporate affiliates should include these same determinants of offshore procurement. This proposition is confirmed in Jarrett's analysis (1979, Chapter 2) of related-party imports to the United States.

intangible-assets hypothesis otherwise seems rather dubious (Tsurumi, 1976, Chapter 4).[18] All of these activities represent types of forward integration by the MNE, whether into final-stage processing of its goods or into ancillary services.

The evidence of this confluence of vertical and horizontal foreign investments mainly takes the form of casual descriptions rather than systematic data. It is emphasized in the study of foreign investments by West German enterprises by Fröbel et al. (1980, Chapter 12). It is implied by the available data on the extent of intracorporate trade among MNE affiliates – flows that would be incompatible with purely horizontal forms of intracorporate relationships. We can, for example, turn to data on imports of finished goods by Dutch subsidiaries from their U.S. parents (Stubenitsky, 1970, p. 102). These were high as percentages of the affiliates' total sales in just those sectors where imports might complement local production for filling out a sales line – chemicals (24.9 percent), electrical equipment (35.4 percent), and transportation equipment (65.5 percent). The prevalence of intracorporate trade in engineering industries also suggests the importance of components shipments (U.S. Tariff Commission, 1973, pp. 284, 314–20).

Recently, some statistical evidence has appeared on U.S. exports and imports passing between corporate affiliates that sheds light on this mixture of vertical and horizontal foreign investment. Lall (1978b) analyzed the factors determining the extent of U.S. MNEs' exports to their affiliates (normalized either by their total exports or by their affiliates' total production). He could not discriminate between two hypotheses, although he concluded that they jointly have significant force: (1) that trade is internalized where highly innovative and specialized goods are involved and (2) that trade is internalized where the ultimate sales to final buyers must be attended by extensive customer engineering and after-sales services. Jarrett (1979, Chapter 2) (see also Helleiner and Lavergne, 1979) con-

---

[18] Also, Jarrett (1979, Chapter 3) found that the extent of foreign investment by U.S. industries increases with the percentage of their product lines deemed to require frequent or extensive sales or technical services to customers. This influence is significant with other influences such as advertising and research intensity taken into account.

firmed these hypotheses with respect to the importance in U.S. imports of the interaffiliate component, which in his data includes exports by foreign MNEs to their manufacturing and marketing subsidiaries in the United States as well as imports by U.S. MNEs from their overseas affiliates. Jarrett also found evidence that interaffiliate trade in manufactures reflects several conventional forms of vertical integration: More of it occurs in industries populated (in the United States) by large plants and companies, capable of meeting the scale-economy problems that arise in the international dis-integration of production, and in industries that carry out extensive multiplant operations in the United States.

The entwining of vertical and horizontal relations has important corollaries for the behavior of MNEs that will emerge in later chapters. For example, it suggests that the expansion of output by foreign subsidiaries may coincide with expansion of the parent's production for export to the same market. A purely horizontal relation between parent and subsidiary implies that their outputs will be substitutes for one another, whereas the confluence of horizontal and vertical relations raises the possibility that they are complementary within the MNE. Evidence lending some support to this proposition will be reviewed in Chapter 5.

1.3. **Portfolio diversification and the diversified MNE**

The formal purpose of this section is to complete the roster of international multiplant firms by accounting for those whose international plants have neither a horizontal nor a vertical relationship. An obvious explanation of this type of MNE (though not the only one, it turns out) lies in the goal of spreading business risks. Going multinational in any form brings some diversification gains to the enterprise, and these reach their maximum when the firm diversifies across "product space" as well as geographical space.

The hypothesis that companies act to avoid risks may seem obvious, but it requires some explanation. The risk-averse investor generally must choose between investments involving greater risks and higher expected returns and those involving lesser risks and lower expected returns (somebody else has already seized any high-return low-risk options). Because foreign investment itself usually is supposed to be a risky activity,[19] the risk-averse business would be expected to avoid it. However, that conjecture neglects the process of diversification. Pool the cash-flow streams from two risky projects, and the uncertainty of the combined stream is almost always less than the uncertainty of either stream separately. The reduction demands only that the expected returns of the two projects be imperfectly correlated: Among various possible states of nature, *A* and *B* do not always have their ups and downs at the same time. *A* has the greatest diversification value for *B* if *A*'s ups coincide with *B*'s downs and vice versa, but some diversification is achieved whenever they are not perfectly correlated. As an explanation for MNEs, this analysis suggests quite simply that the risk-averse corporation may find that plants operated in different countries offer good prospects for diversification.

Some economists object to this hypothesis because the assumption that economic agents are risk-averse, surely applicable to most individuals, need not obviously apply to business firms. Individuals surely avoid putting all their financial eggs in one basket and hence hold diversified portfolios of financial assets. Indeed, a good deal of research suggests that wealth holders diversify away a lot of the risk inherent in individual securities, so that a holder of a portfolio of U.S. securities faces only a residual systematic risk associated with the uncertain prospects of the American economy as a whole. But if investors have diversified their risks, is it reasonable that profit-maximizing companies that issue the shares contained in individuals' portfolios should also behave in risk-averse fashion? Suppose that a company makes a risk-avoiding choice of investment projects, thereby earning a lower profit rate (and also a less variable rate) than it otherwise could. The shares that it sells to fully diversified portfolio holders will be depreciated in value as a result, because the securities buyers place no value on the lowered variability for its own sake if they already hold shares in companies that should do

---

[19] In addition to normal business risks, foreign investment encounters the political risk of hostile action by a foreign government. Also, because of the high information requirements of foreign investment and the costliness of information, we generally expect foreign investments to be undertaken with less complete information than those close at hand. (In a sense, riskiness and the absence of information are the same thing.)

well when this one suffers. A corporate management that does not act in ways that maximize what the public will pay for its shares is courting trouble.[20] Specifically, a MNE should embrace foreign investments only if they offer the highest expected profit and should stay away from those justified solely for their diversification value.

This argument against risk-avoiding diversification by the MNE is likely to fail for at least three reasons. The first, to be explored in Chapter 6, is that portfolio holders apparently find it costly or otherwise difficult to diversify across national boundaries. Therefore, MNEs can claim a reward for doing that job by offering the public an asset with international diversification built in. Another objection is that the business manager himself faces nondiversifiable risks if his company does badly. He cannot be 1/20th of a vice-president in 20 companies; when his firm fails, other potential employers may take it as adverse testimony regarding his competence. Finally, apart from the understandable concern of any business manager for risky outcomes, those managers who run enterprises owned by widely scattered and passive shareholders may simply have room to pursue a number of personal goals, including risk avoidance, at the expense of the owners' wealth. (This last hypothesis is referred to as "managerial utility maximization.")

Now we can assess diversification as a motive for the MNE. Within national economies, many shocks affect all firms rather similarly – recessions, major changes in government policy. Between countries, such disturbances are more nearly uncorrelated, creating opportunities for international diversification. Also, changes in exchange rates and terms of trade tend to favor business profits in one country while worsening them elsewhere.[21] Statistical evidence confirms that MNEs enjoy diversification gains: The larger the share of foreign operations in total sales, the lower the variability of the

---

[20] Specifically, it would pay a "corporate raider" to buy up a controlling proportion of shares in this company, kick out the risk-averse management, and run the company in a way that maximizes expected profits for the fully diversified stock-owning public. For a formal description of profit-maximizing behavior by a firm whose owners are fully diversified, see Greenberg et al. (1978).

[21] See Rugman (1979), especially Chapters 2 and 4.

firm's rate of return on equity capital (Cohen, 1972; Rugman, 1979, Chapter 3; Miller and Pras, 1980).[22] Jacquillat and Solnik (1978) investigated the degree to which large MNEs based in Europe and America can be regarded as "walking mutual funds" that are diversified across national economies. They found that the rates of return on the market values of their firms' equity shares are still quite closely tied to economic conditions in their national home markets, excepting only the MNEs based in the smaller European countries. In general, their evidence weakly supports the hypothesis that the MNE attains appreciable international diversification, but it is also consistent with MNEs existing primarily for other reasons (those reviewed in the two preceding sections of this chapter).

The ultimate diversification gain would accrue to the MNE that acquires a foreign subsidiary diversified in product line as well as geographical space. If diversification motivates foreign investment, we should find some of this "double diversification" in MNEs' structures. Earlier surveys (Barlow and Wender, 1955, p. 159) asserted that diversified foreign investment was a rare phenomenon. Also, Caves (1975) and Dubin (1976, Chapter 6) found statistical evidence that MNEs' activities are more diversified on their national home ground, confirming the impression from surveys (Dunning, 1958, pp. 115–18; Safarian, 1966, p. 211; Saham, 1980, pp. 172–5). Apparently the extra costs and risks of adding activities abroad look unappetizing to the firm that merely wishes to diversify;[23] also, minor related products in the firm's line probably get made at the home base. However, there is some evidence that diversifying in domestic

---

[22] Miller and Pras (1980) found that the variability of operating income for U.S. MNEs is negatively related to both their sizes and the numbers of foreign countries in which they have subsidiaries; they also concluded that being diversified among heterogeneous regions offers more stabilization than being in closely similar countries. Oddly, with these influences controlled, they did not find significant stabilization of profits due to the companies' exports and their product-market diversifications in the United States.

[23] If foreign investment typically had diversification value that offset its specific risks, we should expect MNEs to accept lower expected rates of return on foreign investments than on domestic investments. But survey evidence, such as that of Barlow and Wender (1955, p. 114), points to a higher minimum for foreign investments.

product markets and investing abroad are alternatives for mature companies (Caves, 1975; Wolf, 1977). And, indeed, specifically diversified foreign investments are growing more numerous. By the 1960s, U.S. Treasury data began to indicate that substantial proportions of the overseas assets of U.S. firms were diversified relative to the U.S. parents' principal manufacturing industries. Data on the distributions of controlled foreign assets in 1962 and 1968, summarized by Kopits (1979), indicate that the diversified proportion was 14.1 percent in 1962, rising rapidly to 22.3 percent in 1968. The share of forward vertical integration also rose, whereas that of backward vertical integration fell sharply (see Chapter 4) and that of horizontal foreign investment fell slightly. Kopits (1979) found that the extent of diversified foreign investment in 1968 was positively related to the extent of R&D activities in the U.S. base industry of the parent and to the rate of growth of foreign-subsidiary assets over 1962–8 (company size and seller concentration were also controlled in this regression analysis but did not prove significant). The statistical role of growth may do nothing more than affirm that diversified foreign investment was expanding rapidly, but the influence of R&D affirms one's expectation that a firm's research activities often produce intangible assets useful outside its base industry; these should lead to international diversification, just as they promote diversification at home.

Some other hypotheses not covered in this statistical analysis also help to explain MNE diversification. The data show a somewhat larger proportion of diversified foreign investments by U.S. MNEs in less-developed countries (LDCs) than in industrial countries. This is probably due to controls imposed by many LDCs on the remittance of profits by MNEs operating within their boundaries; restricted from repatriating its profits, the MNE's best alternative may be to invest in some diversifying activity within the country. Another explanatory factor is the large wave of conglomerate mergers that took place in the United States in the 1960s. Suppose that firm *B*, either a horizontal or a vertical MNE, is now acquired by the larger firm *A*. If *A*'s base industry remains the principal activity of the merged firm, *B*'s overseas assets will appear to be a diversified foreign investment of the merged firm. Or if *A* diversifies domestically, whether by merger or otherwise, its diversified domestic division may later sprout a horizontal foreign subsidiary, making the firm as a whole appear (to the statistician) diversified internationally.[24]

None of this evidence, it should be stressed, directly affirms the hypothesis that diversified foreign investment has a premium value for risk spreading. However, risk spreading is not inconsistent with any of the positive influences on diversified foreign investment that have been uncovered. And those influences account for only a small proportion of the observed diversified foreign investment, leaving plenty of room for risk spreading and other influences yet unidentified.

1.4. Summary

The existence of the MNE is best explained by identifying it as a multiplant firm that sprawls across national boundaries, then applying the transactional approach to explain why decentralized plants should fall under common ownership and control rather than simply trade with each other (and with other agents) on the open market. This approach is readily applied to the horizontal MNE (its national branches produce largely the same products), because the economies of multiplant operation can be identified with use of the firm's intangible assets, which suffer many infirmities for trade at arm's length. This hypothesis receives strong support in statistical studies, which also identify an influence of other "excess capacities" in the firm, such as managerial skills.

A second major type of MNE is the vertically integrated firm, and several economic models of vertical integration stand ready to explain its existence. Once again, the transactional approach holds a good deal of power, because vertical MNEs in the natural-resources sector seem to respond to the difficulties of working out arm's-length

---

[24] For evidence, see Horst (1974*a*, pp. 110–11). That overseas diversification represents some kind of optimizing global calculation is suggested by Gorecki's finding (1980) that the diversification levels of Canadian domestic firms can be explained by Canadian market variables, whereas the diversification levels in Canada of foreign subsidiaries operating there cannot.

contracts in small-numbers situations where each party has a durable and specific investment at stake. Evading problems of impacted information also seems to explain some vertical foreign investment. The approach also works well to explain the rapid growth of offshore procurement by firms in industrial countries, which involves carrying out labor-intensive stages of production at low-wage foreign locations. Although some procurement occurs through arm's-length contracts rather than foreign investment, the foreign-investment proportion is clearly large. Finally, numerous vertical transactions flow between the members of apparently horizontal MNEs as the foreign subsidiary undertakes final fabrication, fills out its line with imports from its corporate affiliates, or provides ancillary services that complement these imports.

Diversified foreign investments, which have grown rapidly in recent decades, suggest the use of foreign investment as a means of spreading risks to the firm. Foreign investment, whether diversified from the parent's domestic product line or not, does apparently offer some diversification value. Diversified foreign investments can be explained in part by the parent's efforts to utilize its diverse R&D discoveries, and certain other influences as well. But the evidence at hand does not specifically tie diversified foreign investment to the corporate motive of spreading risks through diversification among both products and national markets.

2

The MNE and models of international economic activity

In Chapter 1 we offered a relentlessly microeconomic view of the basis for MNEs, explaining their existence through the theory of economic organization. Yet foreign direct investment was traditionally a concern of international economics, a branch disposed to use general-equilibrium tools for explaining economywide or worldwide phenomena: nations' patterns of commodity trade, the allocation of their endowments of factors of production, and the functional distribution of income. Does international economics have a distinctive and sufficient explanation of MNEs to place against the organizational explanation from Chapter 1? If so, which has the more explanatory power? If not, how can organizational models of the MNE be consistently embedded within models of international production and exchange?

2.1. Foreign direct investment and international capital flows

The key junction point between international economics and the MNE arises from the export of equity capital to the foreign nation that occurs when a company starts a foreign subsidiary. International flows of capital are a central concern of international economics, and economists working in this field have long tended to explain the MNE as simply an arbitrager of capital. The MNE pursues profits by moving equity capital from countries where its return is low to countries where it is high. The firm's profits thus result from an arbitrage activity. If the differing rates of return to capital that induce these movements correspond to differences in the social marginal productivity of capital, then the MNE's activity also raises the world's real income.

This approach, if accepted, serves to tie the MNE to a considerable body of general-equilibrium theory about the interrelationships of international trade, international movements of factors of production, and the distribution of income (see Section 2.3). Furthermore, this body of theory has a variety of empirical implications: We should expect MNEs to be based mainly in the countries best endowed with capital (where its domestic marginal productivity is therefore the lowest). They should move capital toward the countries least well endowed with capital (with, presumptively, the highest marginal products of capital). But the theoretical role of the MNE as a capital arbitrager was never developed analytically, nor were the empirical implications of the hypothesis given careful tests. This tranquil if unsatisfactory situation was disturbed by Hymer (1960), who argued that the capital-arbitrage hypothesis was inconsistent with several obvious patterns in the behavior of MNEs:

1. The long-standing pattern of capital flows to and from the United States has shown net exports of foreign direct investment but net inflows of portfolio capital. How can equity capital be cheap and portfolio capital dear in the United States, relative to the rest of the world, unless American investors are exceptionally keen to take risks?

2. MNEs move in all directions across national boundaries, and some countries (United Kingdom, for example) are both home bases for many MNEs and hosts to many subsidiaries controlled abroad. If MNEs merely arbitrage capital, then rates of return to capital must be high in some industries in each country and low in others. How could this pattern arise unless national capital markets are balkanized to an unlikely degree?

3. If foreign direct investment is purely an arbitrage of capital, we should expect large financial intermediaries to be prominent participants. However, nonfinancial companies, instead, make up most

of the crowd, and the profits that they seek in particular markets hardly have an intimate relationship to the long-term rate of interest – what the international economist generally has in mind as representing a nation's marginal product of capital.

Hymer not only decked the capital-arbitrage explanation with these propositions but also laid the foundations for a microeconomic explanation of the MNE by pointing out that they are not randomly distributed among industries and that competitive conditions in particular product markets clearly influence foreign investment (see Chapter 4). His and subsequent microeconomic explanations of foreign direct investment still maintain that the MNE goes abroad to raise its total profit (perhaps along with other goals). But they also recognize that empirically this incentive cannot be neatly associated with differences between countries in some overall marginal product of capital. Specifically, the capital-arbitrage hypothesis runs into trouble on two points.

First, if an international difference in expected profits is necessary to induce foreign direct investment, it still may not be sufficient. Suppose that we find a given industry in two different countries, organized in both places according to the classic model of pure competition. Now allow demand for the industry's product to increase abroad, so that the price rises there and the existing firms make excess profits in the short run.[1] Do the firms in the domestic industry now turn themselves into horizontal MNEs? The intangible-assets model for Chapter 1 says no. Because the industry is purely competitive, there is no shortage of potential new local entrants to the foreign market to compete down the windfall profits. And in the purely competitive industry, firms by definition lack any unique rent-yielding assets that distinguish them from their fellows and offset the intrinsic disadvantages and transactions costs of operating in a foreign environment. As Hymer (1960, Chapter 1) and Kindleberger (1969, Chapter 1) argued, MNEs are logically incompatible with purely competitive organization of an industry. There must be some-

---

[1] Assume that the industry's output incurs transportation costs when it moves in international trade, so that the demand increase does not simply increase imports or reduce exports.

thing else to account for the rise of MNEs, and therefore the capital-arbitrage hypothesis by itself is not sufficient. Hufbauer (1975, pp. 261–3) showed formally that foreign investment depends on demand elasticities and production-function parameters, not just capital-cost differences.

The second problem with the capital-arbitrage hypothesis flows from the first. Under what circumstances is it appropriate to assume, as that hypothesis does, that capital earns a single rate of return in common among all economic activities carried on in a country? The hypothesis requires that the national economy behave in the long run as if all its markets were purely competitive – that any differential between the returns to capital in different activities gets competed away by domestic entrepreneurs. There must be no distortions that allow the return to capital in one sector to differ permanently from that in any other. There can be no barriers to entry into product markets, no imperfections in the market for capital itself, and no distortions that allow any factor of production (such as labor) permanently to earn more in one activity than another. A nation's stock of capital at any one time is embodied temporarily in many fixed uses (machinery, buildings, inventories, persons' educations, etc.), and in these locked-in forms capital may not be earning a normal rate of return even if all markets are purely competitive. Of course, one can save the capital-arbitrage hypothesis by applying it only to the competitive sectors of the economy and the capital not embodied in fixed forms. But that maneuver empties the hypothesis of most of its content, because we cannot readily determine that capital is "cheap" or "dear" in a given country, a necessary step in testing the capital-arbitrage explanation of foreign investment. The hypothesis dwindles to the correct but trivial hypothesis that people move capital in search of higher returns. The models set forth in Chapter 1 are consistent with capital arbitrage in that form, but they emphasize that foreign investment transmits capital internationally as an adjunct to transactions that occur for other reasons and that this capital is merely part of the "team" of assets shared within the international multiplant enterprise. The transactional explanation requires no appeal to a long run in which all capital can be disentangled from its uses.

For all these reasons it seems fair to conclude that the capital-arbitrage hypothesis has been swept from the field by the transactional hypotheses developed in Chapter 1. As postscript to this conceptual debate, it is also worth noting that empirical investigations resting solely on the arbitrage hypothesis have not fared well. The flow of foreign investment from the United States to Europe increased considerably from the 1950s to the 1960s. D'Arge (1969) and Bandera and White (1968), among others, sought to determine whether or not this increase corresponds to an increase in the profit rate on U.S. investments abroad relative to that at home. Their statistical results were insignificant or even perverse; the foreign profit differential seemed to fall just as foreign investment was increasing. The transactional approach does not, of course, say that firms go abroad in order to lose money. But it does point out (1) that they are after the present value of long-term expected cash flows and not short-term current profits and (2) that subsidiaries in their early years may run substantial shakedown losses, tribute to the knowledge disadvantages that face the entrepreneurial unit operating in a foreign market.[2] The second factor, in particular, can explain the seemingly perverse result: When foreign investment is rising rapidly, growing numbers of the population of subsidiaries are young and still in the shakedown period, and average accounting profits will appear to be falling. More carefully controlled studies of foreign-investment behavior have confirmed the expected positive relationship to profit differentials; at the same time, theoretical research on corporate finance has shown that the risk-averse MNE will not do all its borrowing in the cheapest place (see Chapter 6). In sum, the capital-arbitrage hypothesis, without something more, is neither satisfying theoretically nor accurate empirically.

So far we have heaped calumny upon the contribution of international economics to understanding MNEs. However, once we accept

[2] This has been suggested by many surveys and demonstrated statistically by Lupo et al. (1978).

the necessary role of the transactional approach, international economics provides several valuable forms of assistance for explaining the existence and behavior of MNEs. The remaining sections of this chapter will develop that complementary relationship. The next section is concerned with the relationship between exporting and direct investment at the level of the individual enterprise. The third section takes up that same relationship in general equilibrium and develops the foundation of some general-equilibrium models that are useful for understanding the causes and consequences of MNEs, and the final section considers the relevant empirical evidence.

2.2. The choice between exporting and foreign direct investment

This section develops an important extension of the intangible-assets model from Chapter 1. The firm blessed with such an asset enjoys several possible ways to claim the rents that it will yield in foreign markets. The product embodying the asset can be produced by foreign subsidiaries for local sale. It can be licensed for local production by an independent firm. Or it can be produced in the asset-holding firm's base location and exported. The intangible-assets model thus identifies exporting and direct investment as alternative strategies for the potential MNE. An immediate corollary is that forces restricting trade encourage foreign investment, at least in those sectors where the intangible-assets model identifies some potential for MNE status. Tariffs protecting a national market from imports therefore become at the same time an encouragement for foreign investment.

Theoretical models of the firm's decision

The behavior of the profit-maximizing MNE in the face of tariffs has been worked out by Horst (1971) (see also Copithorne, 1971), and a simple version of his analysis is presented here (based on Horst, 1973).[3] Assume that the MNE is able to sell its product in two countries, Home and Foreign, and faces a downward-sloping

---

[3] Also see Hirsch (1976) and Rugman (1980*b*, Part I).

demand curve for the product in each market. Its costs of production in each country depend on the amount produced there, and we are interested in both diminishing returns (marginal costs increase with output) and increasing returns (marginal costs decline as output increases). The firm is assumed to maximize its total profit. Home is the MNE's base, and the graphic analysis in Figure 2.1 is constructed so that the firm will always maintain production there; the question is whether it supplies Foreign by export or local production. Panel A of Figure 2.1 shows the market in Home and the firm's marginal cost (c_1), demand (p_1), and marginal revenue (r_1) curves. If it sold only in the domestic market, it would produce the quantity indicated by the intersection of r_1 and c_1. Panel C similarly shows demand conditions in Foreign and the firm's marginal cost function (c_2) if it becomes a MNE and undertakes production. Panel B contains a construction that serves to bring this information together. First, if the firm starts to export from Home, it will incur rising marginal costs as output expands and higher marginal revenue as the number of units sold to Home's buyers contracts. Suppose (contrary to assumption) that the firm faced a fixed price of M at which it could sell abroad. Then it would choose to produce Q_1 in 1, selling S_1 of it at home and exporting S_1Q_1. The domestic price would become P_1 instead of the lower price that would prevail if there were no exports. Curve c_x in panel B is what Horst calls the marginal cost of exporting from the home country, and it illustrates the quantity that would be exported for each price like M. From panel C we derive an analogous construction by allowing the firm the (imaginary) possibility of importing various quantities of its product for resale at prices such as M_t. If M_t is less than the firm's no-imports level of marginal cost in local production, it transfers some imports, cutting back its local production and expanding its sales. Given M_t, the firm would produce Q_2 locally, sell S_2, and import Q_2S_2. The lower is M_t, the larger are its imports, and the more does its production in Foreign contract (eventually disappearing). By experimentally varying M_t, we construct the schedule r in panel B, which is the marginal revenue from importing into Foreign.

Only one more step is needed to complete this construction. We

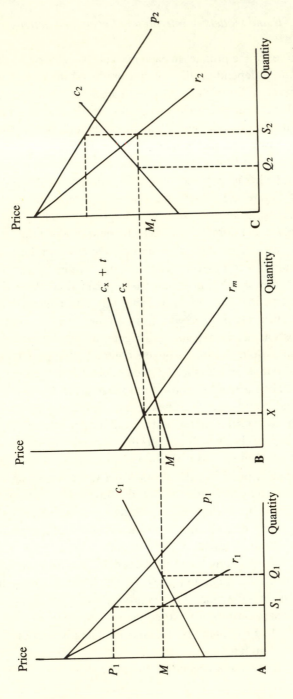

Figure 2.1. A: Revenue and cost functions in Home country. B: Intrafirm trade. C: Revenue and cost functions in Foreign country.

assume that Foreign imposes a tariff that elevates the delivered price of imports over their foreign price by an amount indicated by the shift from c_x to $c_x + t$ in panel B.[4] Now we have constructed a schedule showing the firm's marginal revenue from importing (r_m) and its tariff-adjusted marginal cost of exporting ($c_x + t$). Just as it sets its domestic price in each market by selling the quantity that equates marginal revenue and marginal cost, so does it determine the amount of intracorporate exports. Equilibrium exports are X, and the quantities sold (S) and produced (Q) are shown in the Home and Foreign markets.

In Figure 2.1 as drawn, the firm serves Foreign partly by local production and partly through exports from Home. If Foreign raises its tariff, the MNE responds by increasing its local production and reducing its exports. But the MNE's locational decisions also reflect the difference in real costs between the two markets – the classic forces of comparative advantage (as costs affect the production pattern for the country as a whole) and absolute advantage (as these costs appear to producers in a particular industry). One other factor influences the outcome: The MNE cannot set prices in the two national markets so different that other parties find that it pays to arbitrage between them.

Horst also explored the case in which the MNE enjoys scale economies in production, so that the marginal cost curves slope downward rather than upward (as in Figure 2.1). In that case the firm will never both produce in a market and transfer exports to it. It might produce only in Home and export to Foreign, produce only in Foreign and export to Home, or produce in both but not export. Suppose that the firm initially produces only in Home. Foreign then imposes a high tariff. The firm might find that it could most profitably serve Foreign's market entirely by local production. Indeed, it could even

---

[4] This potential flow of exports, of course, is trade within the MNE, and so there may be no identifiable market price. That may be a problem for the tariff collector if t is expressed as an ad valorem tariff. We are not concerned here with how the tariff is set, but we can note that the company has an incentive to understate the value of any goods it exports if the tariff is in fact set on an ad valorem basis. Transfer pricing will be discussed in Chapter 8.

find that it would then pay to shift *all* of its production to Foreign, serving Home's market with imports from Foreign (this would depend on Home's tariff). Another striking influence of scale economies is that where the MNE locates its production depends not just on tariffs and absolute advantage in production costs at any given scale. It also depends on the sizes of Home's and Foreign's national markets. Make Home a large market, Foreign a small one. The firm could rationally locate all its production in Home, serving Foreign through exports, even though Foreign has an absolute advantage in production costs at any given scale. For this pattern to emerge, Home must impose a tariff high enough to discourage the location of all the firm's production in Foreign.[5]

Evidence on tariffs and foreign investment

A great deal of survey and anecdotal evidence confirms the influence of tariffs on MNEs' locational decisions. Earlier in the nineteenth century, countries such as Canada and Australia often adjusted tariffs upward to encourage the growth of local production. Foreign exporters who had established markets in those countries then found it more profitable to establish production facilities within the tariff wall than to write off their investment in the local market or continue to serve it from lower-cost locations abroad. This pattern has been confirmed in numerous studies, such as those of Marshall et al. (1936, Chapter 4), Brash (1966, Chapter 3), Deane (1969), and Saham (1980, pp. 69–70). Wilkins (1974, pp. 172–3) noted that the effect operated even in the depths of the depressed 1930s, when tariffs were elevated enough by a number of foreign countries to cause many U.S. MNEs to create or expand subsidiaries behind the tariff barriers. The influence has been confirmed in some statistical studies by means of the following procedure: Find the shares held by MNEs, both through exports and through local production by their subsidiaries, in the various industries of some national market. By comparing shares in different industries, test the hypothesis that

---

[5] Accordingly, research on production scales in Canada often has blamed the small scales prevailing there in part on the U.S. tariff (Wonnacott and Wonnacott, 1967).

the higher the country's tariff protecting the industry, the larger the fraction of MNEs' sales accounted for by local production. Horst (1972*a*) reported this result for U.S. exports to Canada,[6] and Swedenborg (1979, Chapter 5) confirmed the finding for Swedish exports and foreign investment.

More recently, many less-developed countries have followed the policy of attracting MNEs first with tariff protection and quantitative restrictions on imports, then inducing them to expand their investments by means of domestic-content requirements and other such devices. For example, Reuber et al. (1973, pp. 120–32) found that substantial proportions of the foreign investors they surveyed had benefited from tariff or quota protection on their outputs and tariff concessions on their imports of inputs or machinery.

This relationship between trade barriers and foreign investment has also been explored through the analysis of changes over time – especially in the formation of the European Community, whose members eliminated trade restrictions among themselves while maintaining a standardized set of trade barriers against imports from the rest of the world. For potential multinational companies based outside the Community, the creation of this enlarged internal market should have increased the desirability of producing within the Community relative to exporting to it. That is because the enlarged market permitted some firms to attain efficient scale in European production and thus lower net costs of goods sold in Europe, even if the tariffs charged on imports from outside the Community were unchanged (their average level in fact did not change). Scaperlanda

[6] However, Horst's results were not confirmed in a replication by Orr (1975). Several other studies have failed to confirm the hypothesis; however, these failures probably were due to the research designs used, constrained in turn by the data available. They examined only sales levels of foreign subsidiaries, not the subsidiaries' share of the MNEs' total foreign sales (local production plus exports). Also, there is a problem of timing with these cross-sectional studies, which analyze tariffs and foreign-investment levels at a single point in time. The tariffs may have changed and affected foreign investment far in the past. Yet with general economic growth and many other changes occurring in the economy, subsidiaries' activity levels may lose any close relationship to the current level of tariff protection, even if that relationship was originally a potent one.

and Mauer (1969, 1962) did find that the book value of U.S. direct investment in the Community rose in harmony with the Community's gross national product, but their statistical analysis did not confirm that direct investment was displacing U.S. exports. Their test does not, however, directly capture the effect of enlarging the Community's overall market size, because the time-trend relationship picks up inducements to invest that were associated with economic growth in the European nations that might have occurred without the Community's formation. Schmitz (1970) got somewhat more positive results. Schmitz and Bieri (1972) devised a more effective test by examining the *share* of U.S. foreign direct investment going to European countries that took part in such tariff-preference arrangements. They did find appreciable statistical evidence that the creation of these preferences had induced an acceleration of the upward trend in U.S. foreign direct investment and a deceleration of the trend in U.S. exports.

If tariffs affect foreign direct investment, exchange-rate movements under certain conditions should have the same effect.[7] This corollary pertains especially to the years before 1973, when the industrial countries maintained pegged exchange rates and changed them only occasionally when large disequilibria had arisen. Suppose that the U.S. dollar has become "overvalued," meaning that U.S. money costs and prices are too high relative to those abroad for the current exchange rate to maintain an equilibrium in international payments (that is, the United States tends to buy more abroad than it sells). These unfavorable cost conditions encourage multinationals to shift their production out of the United States. Not only do they enjoy lower costs of production abroad, but also they acquire nondollar physical assets abroad that will appreciate relative to dollar assets when the dark day comes and the dollar is devalued. Enlarged capital outflows add to the trade deficit that the disequilibrium produces (Makin, 1974). Although this proposition has received sur-

---

[7] Batra and Hadar (1979) have shown that a devaluation of the MNE's home currency causes it to expand production at home and contract abroad, even if (as could be the case) it operates under conditions of diminishing marginal cost in one location.

prisingly little statistical testing (but see Goldsbrough, 1979), many have noted the coincidence of large outflows of direct investment from the United States and the dollar's overvaluation before 1971, as well as the accelerated growth rate of direct investment in the United States that followed the dollar's sharp drop during 1971–3 (see Arthur D. Little, 1976, especially p. 59). The U.S. inflow similarly rose sharply in 1979 after the 1977–8 depreciation (and a stock-market slide that encouraged foreign acquisition of U.S. companies) (Chung and Fouch, 1980).

Exports and foreign investment: joint determinants

The effect of tariffs (and exchange-rate levels) on foreign investment is really just one piece of a system of causal relationships. If we think that the (potential) MNE chooses the cost-minimizing way to serve any profitable foreign markets, then we expect it to take simultaneous account of all the factors favoring the one or the other. Anything that favors foreign investment (such as tariffs) discourages the use of exports, and vice versa. Researchers have therefore regarded exports and foreign investment as jointly determined variables, or they have simply analyzed what determined the *relative* use of exporting and local-market production through affiliates.

Horst (1972*a*) originated this methodological approach, and Swedenborg (1979) used data on Swedish exports and foreign investment to provide its most thorough application. She found that those Swedish industries with high levels of foreign investment tended also to have high levels of exports. However, the ratio of exports to total production for Swedish industries and the ratio of foreign production by subsidiaries to Swedish domestic production were influenced in opposite ways by certain forces. Notably, she found that industries whose plants are capital-intensive and exhibit extensive economies of scale tend to export rather than invest abroad. She also concluded that both exports and foreign production are positively related to R&D activities and workers' skill levels in Sweden – indicators of the importance of intangible assets. This finding agrees with various studies summarized in Chapter 1.

Other studies have confirmed and extended these results. Horst (1972*a*) found that the ratio between U.S. MNEs' exports to Canada and the local sales by their subsidiaries was higher the smaller was the Canadian market relative to that of the United States. This he took to indicate indirectly the deterrent effect of scale economies on local production in Canada. Buckley and Pearce (1979) analyzed the exports and foreign-subsidiary sales of the world's largest manufacturing enterprises, noting that those most active in exporting and least active in foreign investment are based in sectors with the greatest apparent scale economies. Their data also confirm a theoretical finding of Horst (1971, 1973) – that scale economies may pull the MNE's production abroad rather than concentrating it at home. MNEs in some small countries (Benelux, Switzerland) exhibit high ratios of foreign-subsidiary sales to total sales. Numerous studies have confirmed this finding indirectly by demonstrating that minimum efficient scale puts a lower bound on the size of the foreign-investment transaction.[8] Lall (1980) found that the ratio of U.S. MNEs' exports to the sum of their exports and foreign-subsidiary sales increased with the importance of their R&D expenditures but was negatively related to the importance of advertising expenditures; high advertising levels indicate traits of buyers' behavior that encourage local production and discourage serving the market from abroad. Caves et al. (1980, Chapter 4) analyzed imports into Canada and subsidiaries' shares in the Canadian market as jointly determined parts of a larger cross-sectional model. They reported at least weak evidence that advertising discourages imports and encourages direct investment; scale economies (as they appear in the United States) favor imports, whereas tariffs and transportation costs discourage them (the statistical significance of these last findings is somewhat questionable). However, the R&D level is positively related to both exports and foreign investment, a finding echoed by Buckley and Pearce (1979), Owen (1979), and Lall (1980).

---

[8] For example, in the smaller industrial countries, foreign subsidiaries are on average larger than their national-firm competitors (Caves et al., 1980, Chapter 4, on Canada; Deane, 1970, pp. 64–5, on New Zealand; O'Loughlin and O'Farrell, 1980, on Ireland).

In summary, we have combined the transactional model of the MNE from Chapter 1 with locational forces identified by international economics to deduce that exports and horizontal foreign investment should be substitutes for one another, and the evidence confirms the proposition. Two concluding comments are in order. First, this substitution should be related to the analysis of interaffiliate trade in Chapter 1. In this chapter we conclude that tariffs and other influences may sway companies away from exporting and toward investing abroad to become horizontal MNEs. In Chapter 1 we found that foreign investment generates some interaffiliate trade because the subsidiary does the final processing of components or serves as the parent's sales and service organization. Could foreign investment *on balance* increase trade, rather than replace it? The studies cited here imply that interaffiliate trade may weaken the substitution between exports and foreign investment but not reverse it. We shall take up the issue again in Chapter 5 because of its relevance to the effect of MNEs on income distribution.

Second, we are still in fact missing an alternative among the ways in which foreign markets can be served. Besides foreign investment and exports, there is the possibility of licensing the firm's intangible assets to an arm's-length producer in another country. Therefore, in principle we should roll the study of the determinants of technology licensing in with those of exports and foreign investment. Although we know a good deal about the traits and limitations of the market for arm's-length licensing, shortcomings of the data have blocked the right kinds of research design. The evidence will be considered in Chapter 7.

2.3. **Foreign investment and resource allocation in the world economy**

International economics does not offer a fundamental explanation for MNEs, but it does contribute substantially to explaining their scope of operation through the trade-off between exports and foreign investment. More than that, the general-equilibrium models of international economics provide a framework for understanding certain causes and consequences of the MNE's international movement of resources that are not apparent if we stick to the partial-equilibrium tradition of an industry-by-industry analysis.

Basic general-equilibrium tools

Most of the model building that allows us to pursue the MNE into the context of general equilibrium comes out of the Heckscher-Ohlin (H-O) model, a textbook staple in international economics (e.g., Caves and Jones, 1981, Chapter 7). The great advantage for this purpose of the Heckscher-Ohlin model is that it concentrates on the interrelationship between a nation's pattern of international trade and its endowment of factors of production (including capital). It can therefore be used to explore quite deeply the consequences of international movements of factors of production – the MNE's transfer of capital – by identifying them as changes in the factor endowments of the sending and receiving countries. The relationship between trade and foreign investment can be treated more fully, and propositions can be established about how foreign investment affects the rewards of factors of production and thus the distribution of income.

In its simplest form, the Heckscher-Ohlin model assumes that the world consists of two countries, Home and Foreign. Only two commodities, food and clothing, are produced and traded. Each nation has a given endowment of two factors of production, labor and capital. A crucial assumption of the model is that the production functions of food and clothing differ in their requirements of capital and labor; let us suppose that for any given prices of these factors, food production requires proportionally more capital per worker employed than does clothing. For some of its most interesting results, the Heckscher-Ohlin model also assumes that production functions are the same in each country: A given number of units of capital and of labor produce the same number of clothing (or food) units, both at home and abroad. Markets for products and factors of production are assumed to be perfectly competitive, and transportation costs are ignored.

Some key features of the model's treatment of the domestic economy can be reviewed in terms of the transformation (or production-

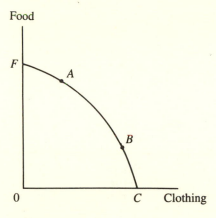

Figure 2.2

possibility) curve for the home country, shown in Figure 2.2. That curve shows all combinations of food and clothing that can be produced efficiently with the home country's assumed stocks of labor and capital – "efficiently" meaning that any increase in the output of one good can be accomplished only by cutting production of the other. One condition for efficient production is that the value of the marginal product of labor in food be the same as the marginal product of labor in clothing, and the same for capital. In the absence of international trade, the amount of each good produced equals the amount consumed, and demand conditions determine which point is chosen on transformation curve *FC*. Let us suppose that it might be either *A* (much food consumed, little clothing) or *B* (much clothing, little food). In order to see how output and factor use are interrelated, assume that equilibrium was at *A* but now shifts to *B* because of a change in consumers' tastes. The shift in preferences toward clothing raises the price of clothing relative to that of food. Output declines in food, the capital-intensive sector, and expands in labor-intensive clothing. Whatever wages (to labor) and rentals (to capital) levels prevailed at *A* will be thrown out of equilibrium by the change, because the contracting food industry discharges a lot of capital, whereas the expanding clothing industry seeks to hire a lot of labor. Therefore, wages rise relative to capital rentals. This link

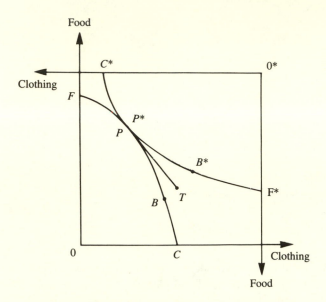

Figure 2.3

between production (product prices) and factor rewards obviously has some significance for the incentive to undertake foreign investment.

If the home country in fact trades with the foreign country, equilibrium in the model resembles Figure 2.3. Each produces at some point P or P^* on its own transformation curve, but the processes of international exchange determine some equilibrium point T that describes the (different) bundle of goods that each country consumes. As Figure 2.3 is drawn, the transformation curve for the foreign country F^*C^* is shown upside down, with its production point P^* superimposed on P for the home country. The home country produces a lot of food and a little clothing (P), exporting food and importing clothing to achieve the bundle of goods consumed depicted at T. Likewise, from the foreign country's viewpoint, a high level of domestic clothing production (P^*) is converted through trade into the consumption bundle T.

We have not explained exactly how the equilibrium associated with P, P^*, and T got established; we simply assume it is an equilibrium and note some of its properties. A sufficient reason for an equilibrium with this trade pattern would be that the home country is relatively well endowed with capital (used heavily in food production) and the foreign country in labor (used heavily in clothing). Home has a comparative advantage in food, Foreign in clothing. If P and T represent an equilibrium for Home, consumption with international trade absent would have been at a point like B (Home consumes more of both food and clothing at T than at B; those are the "gains from trade"). When production shifts from B to P, as trade is established, the relative price of food rises in Home, and therefore capital rentals rise relative to wages. In Foreign, the opposite process takes place: At B^*, clothing was cheaper than in equilibrium with international trade at P^*, and the shift of production from B^* to P^* raises wages relative to capital rentals. Indeed, with a suitably heavy freight of assumptions, it can be shown that introducing trade not only pulls factor rewards in different countries in opposite directions but also can bring them into absolute equality – that Home and Foreign wages become equal in equilibrium with unrestricted international trade, as do Home and Foreign capital rentals. If foreign investment took place in such an equilibrium, it would leave world output unchanged.

These fundamentals supply the basis for some propositions about international factor movements and the MNE. Suppose that no international trade exists, so that both countries are consuming outputs indicated by B and B^*, and factor payments are in equilibrium accordingly. Now allow for the possibility that capital can move internationally. Without trade, we know that capital will earn less in capital-rich Home than in capital-short Foreign. Therefore, foreign investment is induced to flow from Home to Foreign. Because the transformation curves depend on the factor endowments, the capital transfer will shift them as shown in Figure 2.4, from FC to $F'C'$ and from F^*C^* to $F^{*'}C^{*'}$. The discrepancy in capital's earnings between the two countries will be reduced, possibly eliminated. The shift

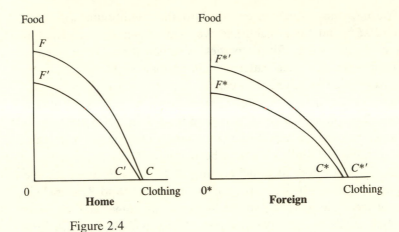

Figure 2.4

provides a real-income gain for whatever companies move their capital from Home to Foreign, and it indeed raises the rentals accruing to *all* capital in Home. But the erstwhile scarce units of native capital in Foreign lose – the inflow from abroad bids down their reward. Labor is also affected in both countries. Home's labor finds less capital to collaborate with in production, and so its wage falls; Foreign labor finds more capital clamoring for its services, so that wages there rise.[9]

We could have investigated international factor movements by starting not with the complete absence of trade but rather with equilibrium with free trade (*T* in Figure 2.3). Assume that sufficient conditions hold in this trading equilibrium for absolute factor rewards to be equalized in the two countries. Now suppose that Foreign imposes a tariff on imports of food from Home. That reduces its international trade (and Home's) and shifts its production point from *P** some distance toward *B**. The reward to capital rises in Foreign and falls in Home. Capital tends to move from Home to Foreign, and trade between them continues to diminish as its factor-endowment

[9] This brief summary omits a number of refinements to the analysis; in particular we ignore the role of demand conditions as they are changed by international factor movements, although demand could in fact affect the result importantly.

basis is eroded.[10] Eventually trade ceases, except for exports from Foreign needed to repatriate the profits from Home's foreign investment. Thus, this model shows in dramatic form the substitution between trade and foreign investment. Just as we saw (Section 2.2) that the individual firm chooses between exporting and investing abroad, so are trade and capital movements alternatives for the economy in the large. In general equilibrium, though, they are not always substitutes. Suppose that factor-endowment differences were extreme, with Foreign having very little capital and therefore specializing completely in the production of clothing in the free-trade equilibrium. Purvis (1972) has shown that a movement of capital from Home to Foreign can then lead to a new equilibrium, with more trade between the two countries. That is because the marginal product of capital in Foreign may then be much greater than in Home, so that the capital transfer increases Foreign's gross domestic product much more than it reduces Home's.

Foreign investment and specific factors of production

The Heckscher-Ohlin model offers dramatic conclusions about the relationship between international capital movements and trade, but does it really apply to the MNE? We have tentatively concluded that capital arbitrage is not the MNE's main business. Also, the intangible-assets model is at best shakily consistent with the assumption of perfect competition. Can general equilibrium and the MNE be pushed closer together? Some economists, making the attempt, have seized on the horizontal form of foreign investment, in which the firm based in the source country's food industry transplants its capital to that same industry in the host nation. The assumption is therefore made that capital is *specific* to that sector: It may move from country to country, but it does not move between the food and clothing industries in either country. The assumption on its face seems extreme. But it does approximate the notion that

---

[10] Mundell (1957) developed this analysis. Once again, we are not strictly specifying the full structure of the argument. It matters, for example, whether or not Foreign's terms of trade (shown by $P*T$) are affected by the tariff that it imposes.

the MNE transfers a bundle of assets when it invests abroad; the capital itself may not be tied specifically to that sector, but the managerial skills and intangible assets are. Furthermore, all types of capital are specific in the short run, and several modern contributions to international-trade theory have argued that the assumption of short-run sector-specific capital gives theoretical results far more reasonable than the contrary assumption that capital is continuously mobile between industries.[11]

Labor, however, is still assumed to be immobile between countries, although freely mobile between each country's food and clothing industries. If labor markets are purely competitive, the marginal products of labor should be equal in the Home food and clothing industries, and also in the Foreign food and clothing industries, but not in general between countries. Similarly, if MNEs move capital between countries until no more arbitrage is profitable, the marginal products of capital should be equal in the Home and Foreign food industries, and in the Home and Foreign clothing industries, but not between the two sectors.[12]

Specific factors change some properties of the simple international-trade model introduced earlier. Suppose that a MNE moves some capital from Home to the Foreign clothing industry. As before, the rentals to clothing capital are driven down in Foreign, and labor's wage is raised. Capital specific to Foreign's food sector also loses. That is because Foreign's expanding clothing sector attracts labor from Foreign's food sector, raising the marginal product of labor there and hence reducing the marginal product (and rental) of food-specific capital. Even though capital is sector-specific, an increase

---

[11] See Neary (1978) for a synthesis of these contributions.

[12] Suppose the assumptions are satisfied that we require for the strong result mentioned earlier – that trade flows alone will suffice to equalize factor prices between countries when there are two factors and products, no specific factors. Now, with specific factors we need make only *one* industry's specific capital mobile between countries, and that – along with free trade in commodities – will suffice to equalize wages, rentals to food capital, and rentals to clothing capital between countries. If *both* types of capital are made mobile, there is in general no longer an equilibrium with incomplete specialization in international trade: Either production of one good ceases or all international trade ceases except for international factor payments. Amano (1977) took issue with this conclusion of Caves (1971), but Neary (1980) showed it to be correct.

in Foreign's stock of clothing capital drives down the rentals there of food capital as well as clothing capital. Indeed, the rental of food capital in Foreign could fall more than the reward to clothing capital there. The effects of the capital outflow on factor rewards in Home are the opposite of those in Foreign: Labor loses and specific capital gains in both sectors. One prediction cast up by these relationships is that direct investment will be cross-hauled between countries. If the MNE transfers some clothing-specific capital from Home to Foreign (an exogenous disturbance), the rentals to food-specific capital in both countries change so as to encourage it to migrate from Foreign to Home.

In the specific-factors model, a tariff once again will serve to attract foreign investment. Suppose that Foreign imposes a tariff on food imports. Rentals to food-specific capital rise, food capital flows in, and Foreign labor shifts toward the food sector. But clothing-specific capital suffers. A good deal of tariff policy in practice seems designed to protect or enhance the rentals received by factors of production specific to that sector.[13]

Batra and Ramachandran (1980) have developed a slightly different version of this model in which multinational capital is freely mobile between countries in one sector, but local capital in the other sector is immobile between countries as well as between sectors. Many of their results deal with corporation income taxes and hence will be postponed to Chapter 8. Their other conclusions closely echo those just set forth. For example, make the Food sector the one occupied by MNEs and Foreign the net importer of MNE capital as well as the importer of food. Foreign's tariff on food imports attracts more MNE capital, raises wages in Foreign, and lowers the return to local capital in Foreign's clothing sector. Wages fall in Home, and the returns to local capital in Home's clothing industry rise. They show that the returns to MNE capital may either rise or fall as a result of this tariff-induced capital movement.

Another modification of the model comes from Burgess (1978),

---

[13] The analysis of the preceding paragraphs is based on the work of Caves (1971, pp. 17–19) and Jones (1971). It requires the assumption that Home and Foreign are merely two small countries in the world economy whose actions do not affect world prices of food or clothing.

who introduces goods that do not enter into international trade (non-traded goods). Suppose that Foreign's economy contains two sectors. Its clothing sector produces an internationally traded good – perhaps primary fibers used as an input by textile-based MNEs elsewhere in the world. Its other (food) sector is now assumed to produce a good consumed domestically and not entering into international trade. Once again, a disturbance takes the form of an inflow of direct investment to the traded-goods (clothing) sector. The resulting shift in factor rewards tends to follow the same pattern as before – capital loses in both of Foreign's sectors, and labor gains. However, a new element enters into the adjustment process in the form of a rising price of food, Foreign's nontraded good. That rise must occur because labor is drawn from the food sector to the clothing sector, while demand remains basically unchanged. This improvement in the relative price of food can offset the initial fall in capital rentals for food – indeed, more than offset it, leaving this specific factor better off. And the rise in the relative price of food creates at least the possibility that the workers are not better off after all. The smaller is the increase in wages relative to the increase in food prices, and the more of their incomes workers spend on food, the more likely is their real-income gain to be erased. Thus, Burgess usefully reminds us that the clear conclusions about the effects of foreign investment on factor incomes can be upset when product prices are also affected.

So far we have assumed implicitly that the presence of internationally mobile capital (through the agency of MNEs) leaves the basic pattern of comparative advantage unchanged. That is, Home exports food, Foreign exports clothing, and this pattern persists no matter how capital is reallocated internationally by MNEs. But that assumption could be false! Let us change the model slightly to bring out the reasoning, by making sector-specific capital a necessary input to food production, along with labor, whereas clothing production requires only labor. Workers do not move internationally, but capital moves freely to wherever it can earn the larger rentals. Now, David Ricardo would have said that the question which country exports clothing and which exports food depends only on comparative labor productivity. That factor still weighs in, but also relevant is the absolute advantage that mobile capital has for producing food in the two countries. Home labor may be relatively more efficient in textile production than in food, and yet the food productivity of capital in Home may be so high that all or most capital locates in Home, co-opting enough of Home's labor supply to make food Home's export good.[14] In general, the more mobile are factors of production, the less does comparative advantage have to do with patterns of production. If all factors were more productive in the United States than in Iceland and nothing impeded their international mobility, all economic activity would be located in the United States.

In the original Heckscher-Ohlin model (no specific factors), similar results emerge when we allow technology to differ between countries, so that a given bundle of capital and labor produces more clothing (or food) in one country than in the other. Make Foreign's food industry technically more efficient than Home's (no difference in clothing). Even though factor endowments favor Foreign to export clothing, the technology difference makes it possible that Foreign will be the food exporter, as well as attracting more MNE capital. If *both* of Foreign's industries are more efficient, the capital transfer from Home is further enlarged, and Foreign definitely exports food if her efficiency advantage is as great in food as in clothing (Jones, 1970; Purvis, 1972).

The basic specific-factors model has been generalized greatly in ways that clarify its general significance. Neary (1980) pointed out that its basic distinction is between factors of production whose stocks are fixed and prices flexibly determined (so that they stay fully employed) and factors whose prices are fixed within the individual country – either because they migrate freely to and from a much larger world economy or because they are subject to a minimum wage. Neary also demonstrated that the presence of these "fix price" factors affects the economy's responsiveness to disturbances. Product outputs become more elastic with respect to changes in their prices, but the rewards to factors in fixed supply (labor, with its

---

[14] This model has been developed extensively by Jones (1980).

wage competitively determined) become less responsive to changes in their supply. If the population falls, some internationally mobile capital flees the country, curbing the rise in the real wage.

2.4. **Distribution of foreign investment among countries**

The final section of this chapter takes up an empirical question not at all thoroughly researched in the literature but logically central to the concerns of Chapters 1 and 2: What factors explain the distribution of MNE activities among nations? The distribution among sectors, as we saw, can be explained quite well by the transactional factors developed in Chapter 1, with an assist from the locational forces introduced earlier in this chapter. Do other models help to explain the international distribution of foreign direct investment? General-equilibrium theory of international trade suggests two central propositions:

1. Just as patterns of international trade depend on comparative advantage and the factors underlying it, so should the distribution of MNEs. The MNE arises when an enterprise finds itself with transactional opportunities to start or link up with an establishment in another country. Some countries may be relatively well endowed with conditions giving rise to these opportunities, just as they are well endowed with capital, forests, or sunshine.

2. The general-equilibrium theory of international trade, briefly sketched in the preceding section, shows how factor endowments and trade flows are interrelated. It offers some specific propositions for testing and provides a framework for thinking about how everything goes together.

The first of these points needs some elaboration. One can imagine industry characteristics completely explaining the differing presence of foreign direct investment among countries. A certain proportion $p(i)$ of industry i's activity is carried out in establishments linked to MNEs, and $p(i)$ varies among countries only because of random factors. The proportion that industry i makes up of country j's economic activity (call it $v_j(i)$) depends only on classical comparative-advantage and locational forces. Then the MNE activity in j would be fully explained by $v_j(i)$ and the $p(i)$ values, which do not depend on j.

Notice that the proportion $p(i)$ does not distinguish between j's role as a home base for MNEs and as a host to their foreign subsidiaries.

This scheme, which denies any relationship between country characteristics and the extent of foreign direct investment, is not broadly inconsistent with any of the preceding analysis. The firm-specific transactional factors giving rise to foreign investment unquestionably bear a significant relationship to industry characteristics, so that the prevalence of MNEs varies systematically among industries. But these assets could be distributed among a world industry's successful companies randomly with respect to their national origins. However, the most casual evidence declares that national traits do directly affect the local prevalence of MNEs. Consider these possibilities:

1.   Some countries have endowments of real resources or culture that provide a yeasty environment for the development of potential MNEs. Others' endowments may lack just these traits. The former countries become disproportionately important as home bases for MNEs, the latter as hosts of their subsidiaries. The identities of these natural source and host countries may not be independent of one another: Given that country j is endowed to be an important source for MNEs, transactional and locational factors may make country k a natural place for its MNEs to alight. In formal terms, the $p(i)$ now vary with country traits and, furthermore, must be disaggregated into source and host components.

2.   The mixture of activities carried on within a country may not be independent of the extent of MNE activity in its various industries. In the notation used earlier, the $v_j(i)$ may not be independent of the $p(i)$, and are causally influenced by them.[15]

---

[15] We can note some statistical evidence that bears directly on this point and the underlying approach to the international distribution of foreign investment. Dunning's (1980) study of the international distribution of U.S. foreign investments found that the share of U.S. sales in foreign markets (whether through exports or subsidiary production) is larger the larger is the foreign market. If there are substantial fixed costs to each bilateral international transaction (whether trade or investment), one would therefore expect the $p(i)$ to be higher in larger countries. Caves (1980*b*) found grounds for rejecting the hypothesis that the extent of foreign investment in a national industry is independent of the scales and productivity levels of the establishments operating within it. Because these variables in turn affect an industry's overall size, these relation-

Empirical evidence on international distribution

It is handy to start with the studies that have sought statistical explanations of the distribution of foreign investment among countries at one point in time, in the spirit of the many studies of interindustry distribution cited earlier. Swedenborg (1979, Chapter 5) developed this approach, and Nankani (1979) provided a comprehensive investigation of the foreign investments of the leading industrial countries in the various less-developed countries (LDCs). Nankani did not possess data on exports, and so he could not analyze their determinants jointly with direct investment, but he did take the exports/foreign-investment trade-off into account in formulating his model. Nankani (1979, Chapter 3) found that both tariffs and non-tariff barriers to imports seem to promote foreign investment in the LDCs. He also found that foreign investment is enlarged between those pairs of industrial nations and LDCs that were formerly connected by a colonial tie. Not only did the colonial ties offer political protection and lower transactions costs to MNEs, but in his view their termination (generally after World War II) posed a threat to the industrial nation's remaining exports to her former colonies, as the independent LDCs erected high tariff barriers. Strong statistical support for this "export-threat" hypothesis was taken by Nankani to demonstrate the trade/foreign-investment trade-off. However, that interpretation is questioned by Svedberg's (1981) finding that the former mother country's predominance in a LDC's foreign investment was less in 1967 than it had been prior to independence.

Nankani found that the extent of an industrial country's investment in a given LDC is, other things being equal, negatively related to the geographical distance between the two countries; the transactional approach implies that distance increases communications and transactions costs and discourages foreign investment, whereas a purely locational approach to the relationship between trade and foreign investment would suggest that foreign investment increases

ships can be taken to mean that the $p(i)$ and the $v_j(i)$ interact with each other.

with distance (to avoid the high costs of shipping exports over long distances).

Nankani controlled for the industrial composition of the developed nations investing in the LDCs by assigning each sector a value for each structural trait relevant to MNEs (such as the advertising/sales ratio) and calculating for each investor country a weighted average of the trait for its sectors. (This control is exactly in the spirit of our no-national-effect model set forth earlier.) These variables, which describe the investing country's potential for MNE activity, prove statistically significant when interacted with the variable indicating former colonial ties.[16]

Two studies have investigated the intercountry distribution of flows of direct investment cumulated over time. Root and Ahmed (1978) concluded that the foreign investment attracted to LDCs increases with their gross domestic product per capita, extent of urbanization, strength of transportation and communication infrastructure, political stability, and trade balance. Consistent with this, Lubitz (1971*b*) found that the lower the LDC's level of human resources development, the more American professional and technical employees must U.S. MNEs send abroad. Dunning (1981) showed how gross inflows and outflows of foreign investment per capita vary among countries with income per capita. Gross outflows are high for the highest-income countries, but then drop off sharply. Gross inflows also decline systematically with income per capita, but not as fast as outflows. As a result, only the richest countries have net outflows, and countries with middling incomes per capita exhibit the highest net inflows. What causal factors lie behind these patterns is not clear from his statistical tests.

---

[16] Casual inspection of the data on source countries' stocks of foreign assets reveals a related effect. Small countries tend to have more "unbalanced" industrial structures than do large ones – some industries proportionally large, others missing. This is a natural result of scale economies in production. Depending on its particular complement of industries, we therefore expect that a small nation may have a very large foreign-investment stock (as do The Netherlands, Switzerland, and Sweden) or a very small one (Belgium, Denmark, and Norway).

Swedenborg's (1979, Chapter 5) investigation of the international distribution of Swedish exports and foreign investment confirms that low tariffs attract exports and discourage the MNE, but otherwise her results are full of puzzles. Swedish foreign investment is attracted to large countries – reasonable on account of scale economies in production – but so are Swedish exports. And Swedish exports are attracted to high-wage countries – reasonable because Swedish firms would tend to enjoy lower production costs at home – but so are Swedish foreign investments.[17] These results and Nankani's perverse finding about the influence of distance suggest that mechanistic hypotheses about cost-minimizing behavior do not serve very well to explain intercountry patterns of MNE activity.

However these puzzles may be resolved, qualitative evidence from less formal studies does nominate other national characteristics as substantial influences on the gestation of MNEs. Krainer (1967) and Franko (1976, Chapters 2 and 3) have argued that the paucity of raw materials in the European industrial countries, coupled with their high levels of industrialization, brought into being a large stock of MNEs integrated backward into the acquisition of raw materials. High raw-materials costs and risks to the continuity of overseas supply also promoted the rise of chemical firms specializing in man-made substitutes for natural materials; their discoveries then provided the intangible assets that floated subsequent foreign investments (also see Davidson, 1976). Franko (1976, Chapter 4) also argued that the small national markets of some European countries induced heavy foreign direct investment because the narrow domestic-market base provided successful firms with only limited opportunities to diversify their risks.

Japan, a latecomer to foreign investment, is also a strategic case for testing hypotheses about national characteristics. The cultural distance of Japan from the Western industrial countries and her substantial net dependence (until recently) on foreign technology left successful Japanese companies with little basis for going multinational. Indeed, the important intermediary role of the Japanese gen-

---

[17] Her procedure controls for industry-mix effects because her regression is run across country-industry cells, not just on country totals.

eral trading companies in economizing on the country's scarce skills for business transactions with foreigners – foreign investment included – clearly identifies cultural distance as a negative predictor of a nation's participation in foreign direct investment.[18]

A final line of analysis for explaining countries' prominence as parents of MNEs concerns the well-known product cycle (Vernon, 1966, 1974*b*), which predicts both the point of origin for MNEs and something about the pattern of their international spread. It starts with an assumption about where innovations are most likely to occur. Innovations tend to labor saving and thus are more valuable the higher is the cost of labor, whether the production labor saved by a process innovation or the household labor time saved by a new consumer durable good. Innovators perceive the needs and opportunities in their immediate vicinity, and so innovations are made in the countries with the highest labor costs and incomes per capita. Initial production also takes place near the point of innovation because of communication costs within the innovating enterprise and uncertainty about the production process in the early stage. Thus, proprietary intangible assets resting on innovations fall into the hands of firms in the highest-income countries. The model continues by tracing the diffusion of the innovation to foreign markets, first through trade, then through foreign investment, on the basis of forces discussed earlier in this chapter. Because innovative goods' attractiveness increases with countries' wages and per-capita incomes, foreign investment in a sense trickles down from the richer to the poorer countries. The latter are reached last by the innovation, perhaps after it has lost its proprietary character and escaped from the hands of the originating MNEs.

The obvious strength of this model lies in its ability to explain the manifest prominence of the United States as a progenitor of MNEs, especially in the two or three decades following World War II. The explanatory power of the model for that period is shown by the recent reversal of the United States's predominance as a source country, because the decline coincides with a loss of any significant ad-

---

[18] See the work of Yoshino (1976), Tsurumi (1976), and Ozawa (1979*a*). Exchange control may also have been a deterrent.

vantage in income per capita over the other major industrial countries (Vernon, 1979). The model's original version missed the point that if labor-short countries make labor-saving inventions, materials-short countries should equally make materials-saving innovations that then underpin MNEs. Davidson (1976) showed that innovations in the European countries are substantially more materials-saving than those in the United States.

This second-thoughts version of the product cycle also seems to reveal itself in some results of McClain's (1974, Chapter 6) discriminant analysis of the differences between subsidiaries placed in the United States by foreign MNEs and subsidiaries that they place in third countries. The foreign parents of U.S. subsidiaries are more research-oriented than are the foreign parents of subsidiaries in other countries. However, operating in a high-technology industry (by U.S. standards) disposes the subsidiary to be located in a country other than the United States. This odd-sounding pair of results is consistent if the research-intensive foreign parents specialize in a somewhat different mix of industries than do large research-intensive firms domiciled in the United States. McClain (1974, p. 273) also found that subsidiaries in the United States tend to steer clear of industries in which U.S. MNEs' stocks of subsidiaries abroad are particularly large; Swedenborg (1979, p. 147) reported a similar result. Thus, the international distribution of foreign investments seems to reflect some international specialization in creating innovations and disseminating them through foreign investments.

Host countries and diffusion processes

Although we lack persuasive statistical analyses of why countries differ in their tendencies to spawn MNEs, one nonetheless feels that quite a bit of the explanation is within reach: the product cycle, the distribution of natural-resource supplies, intercountry differences in the mix of industries and comparative advantage in commodity exports, and inability to communicate inexpensively with other countries. Can the importance of countries as hosts of foreign subsidiaries be similarly explained? An array of case studies and Nankani's statistical results, summarized earlier, immediately suggest the following hypothesis: The distribution of foreign investment among countries as hosts depends strongly on their national characteristics *relative to* the countries that are principal sources of MNEs.

This proposition requires that information (and its analysis) be quite costly to the firm and be accumulated largely through experience. Most of the direct evidence supporting the costliness of information will be discussed in Chapter 3, but it is useful here to summarize Davidson's (1980) research showing statistically the effects of information costs and uncertainty on the destination of foreign investment. He pointed out that low-information-cost countries like Canada, Mexico, and the United Kingdom bulk disproportionally large as destinations for U.S. MNEs, and they are even more prominent as one goes back in time. This aggregate pattern is consistent with Davidson's conclusions about the sequence of moves in which a MNE expands its foreign activities among countries and product markets. If a MNE is already turning out one product line in a given country, that increases the chances that it will add another product line in that country rather than in another country where it has no current operations. Furthermore, the effect of this learning process is more potent in unfamiliar and "far out" countries (Japan, Spain, the Netherlands) than in more familiar ones. Davidson was also able to establish the existence of a typical sequence of moves that starts with Canada (also see Horst, 1972*b*) and proceeds with the United Kingdom, West Germany, Mexico, Australia, France, Brazil, etc. The sequence shows a significant rank correlation with total GNP and with GNP per capita for the countries – factors predicted, respectively, by production scale economies and the product-cycle model. But, even so, culturally congenial countries like Canada, the United Kingdom, and Australia are out of line on the high side. Kravis and Lipsey (1980) similarly pointed out that the ranks of destination countries by the numbers of U.S. subsidiaries they contain vary too little among industries to reflect perfectly informed cost-minimizing decisions by MNEs – that the same countries should in the long run be the cheapest places to produce everything flies in the face of comparative advantage.

Stopford (1976) found a similar pattern among British MNEs.

Most of them began in English-speaking Commonwealth countries, although those industries long on assets suitable for foreign investment (see Chapter 1) later tended to become global. But those MNEs based in less congenial industries tend to remain pastured in the Commonwealth, where risks and transactions costs are low. O'Loughlin and O'Farrell (1980) similarly noted that Ireland, which provides public services that reduce risk and transactions costs for the MNE, has thereby attracted MNEs that are smaller than typical of the breed.

Casual evidence on other source countries confirms the general impression that the bulk of their foreign investments go where the transactional and information-cost disadvantages are least: Japan to Southeast Asia (Yoshihara, 1978, pp. 24–31; Tsurumi, 1976, Chapter 3), Australia to New Zealand (Deane, 1970, pp. 61–2), Sweden to neighboring European countries and the United States (Swedenborg, 1979, pp. 56–60), France to French-speaking lands and adjacent European countries (Michalet and Delapierre, 1976, pp. 8–9).

Although this evidence is quite congenial to the transactional model of the MNE set forth in Chapter 1, it runs the danger of understating the degree to which foreign-investment activities do rest on well-informed cost-minimizing decisions about where to locate economic activity. The locations of export-oriented foreign subsidiaries should and do provide the strongest affirmation of cost-minimizing locational choices. Kravis and Lipsey (1980) hypothesized that the exports of majority-owned foreign affiliates of U.S. MNEs tend to be concentrated where unit labor costs are least and access to material inputs is easy.[19] They also expected some scale-economy effects: More exports would come from larger countries. Their results confirm the hypotheses about access to materials and economies of scale; for unit labor costs, the sign of the relationship is correct, but the coefficient is not significant. Jarrett (1979, Chapter 8) analyzed the distribution among foreign countries of U.S. imports

---

[19] Their proxy for this is "residual openness": A country is assumed to have better access to material inputs if the ratio of its total trade (exports plus imports) to its GNP is higher than its population and density would suggest.

under tariff provisions allowing for goods of U.S. origin processed abroad to pay duty only on the processing.[20] He found that this activity favors countries close to the United States (lower shipping costs) as well as those with low wages and low incidence of labor disturbances. Riedel's (1975) findings on foreign investment in Hong Kong are similar. Lastly, one negative finding in this literature on host-country patterns: It provides, overall, very little support for the capital-arbitrage hypothesis. The extensive cross-hauling of foreign investments between countries cuts against it. So does the lack of any difference in capital intensity between foreign-investing sectors and others in either source countries (U.S. Tariff Commission, 1973; Juhl, 1979) or host countries (O'Loughlin and O'Farrell, 1980, did find MNEs in the more capital-intensive Irish industries, but they are no more capital-intensive than Irish firms in those industries). To reconcile this conclusion with the copious evidence that MNEs choose locations to minimize their production costs, one merely notes that other inputs than liquid capital seem to show much more variation in cost from country to country. For example, Tsurumi (1976, pp. 112–14) stressed the influence on Japanese foreign investors of low costs of industrial real estate and the smooth-functioning markets for skilled personnel and business services in the United States.

2.5. Summary

If the field of international economics offers a sufficient explanation for the MNE, it would seem to lie in the arbitrage of capital between countries where its marginal product is low and those where it is high. However, this is inconsistent with many obvious facts about the distribution of foreign investments, as well as superficial when compared with the transactional model of Chapter 1. Nonetheless, foreign investment generally does involve some net transfer of capital; so it is desirable to draw on the relevant theory of international capital movements.

At a microeconomic level we can model the choice that the MNE

---

[20] Recall that the foreign processor often is an affiliate of the U.S. importer, but need not be.

faces between investing abroad and exporting from the home base. Horst's (1971) analysis shows how the MNE makes this decision when it faces a downward-sloping demand curve in each market. If its production is subject to scale economies, the MNE chooses to concentrate production in one location, unless trade restrictions block this choice, and it can wind up producing only in a large national market even though it would enjoy lower costs in a smaller one. Historical evidence strongly confirms the effect of a tariff to lure the MNE's production behind the barrier, and the market enlargement effected by the European Economic Community had the same consequence. Exchange-rate changes also affect foreign investments when they are expected to be long-lived (i.e., to change the real terms of trade). The most sophisticated empirical studies regard MNEs' exports and foreign investments as jointly determined. Foreign investment is raised by the intangible assets described in Chapter 1, whereas scale economies tilt the firm's choice toward concentrating its production and exporting.

General-equilibrium concepts from international economics also help us to understand the causes and consequences of foreign investment, even though they presume perfectly competitive markets and equate the MNE's activity with capital arbitrage. The Heckscher-Ohlin model establishes a link among the factor endowment of a country, its structure of production, and the rewards to its factors of production. A capital-rich country tends to export goods that use capital intensively. When its exports expand, the rentals to its capital rise and workers' wages fall. In a free-trade equilibrium, under specialized assumptions capital rentals will be the same at home and abroad, leaving no incentive for MNEs to move capital internationally. Conversely, where trade is restricted, capital flows can effectively substitute for it; trade and foreign investment thus are alternatives in general equilibrium as well as for the individual company.

Efforts to bring general-equilibrium theory closer to the MNE have centered on the concept of specific factors of production, sector-specific capital that is mobile between countries but not between industries. The sector-specific model has its own implications for foreign investment and income distribution, and it has attractively realistic properties such as an ability to explain the cross-hauling of foreign investments. One broadly important implication of sector-specific mobile factors is that they tend to locate wherever in the world their reward is greatest, causing absolute advantage to determine patterns of commodity trade, not classical comparative advantage.

We can put these elements of international-trade theory to empirical use for explaining the distribution of foreign investments among countries. As a point of reference, that distribution might depend on nothing more than the differing affinities of industries for MNEs and the different mixes of industries found in national economies. However, national economic and cultural traits do weigh in. Nankani's (1979) analysis of investment in the developing countries emphasized defensive investment prompted by the cutting of colonial ties, while controlling for national differences in the industry mix. More casual studies have suggested certain traits that dispose countries to be sources of MNEs: short "cultural distance" to likely host countries, strong innovative performance (the product cycle), scarcity of raw materials, large size (some small countries are big foreign investors, but that depends on their mix of industries). Because MNEs seek to minimize transactions costs and uncertainties, countries become important as hosts because they provide easy access for MNEs based in countries that are natural sources, and the country-by-country expansion of a MNE reflects an incremental process of learning and risk minimization. But long-run cost minimization also wields its influence: Countries become important hosts if they are the low-cost locations for doing what MNEs do.

3

Organization and growth of the MNE

Economic analysis often treats the firm as a single decision-making center, as if one mind were absorbing all relevant data and making all decisions on the basis of well-considered objectives. In fact, decision making is decentralized within firms, and the decisions reached may be colored by the structure of internal organization chosen by the firm and the incentives and resources that it provides to its various groups of functional specialists. This coloration arises from precisely the informational and transactional considerations that we discussed in Chapter 1. There we urged that the MNE enjoys certain transactional advantages over the arm's-length market. But the obverse of this coin involves the organizational costs and constraints that the MNE encounters in going about its task. Therefore, an examination of the MNE's internal structure is a logical extension of our transactional model of the MNE's underlying rationale. More important, for policy making we need to assess how efficiently the MNE makes and executes its internal decisions. This assessment is also needed to predict how the firm will respond to stimuli.

3.1. Expansion processes in the firm

In Chapter 1 we outlined some implications of the transactional model of MNEs for the processes of the firm's growth and expansion. Whatever fixed assets the firm acquires shape its future expansion path by attaching to it "capacities" that affect the returns it expects from various expansions of its activities. The use of these capacities and the minimizing of information costs and risks are strong influences on the path of expansion, determining which firms go the multinational route and which do not. We shall now consider the organizational side of this expansion process.

Corporate organization and the foreign-investment decision

Many observers have stressed the haphazard nature of the typical firm's decision to undertake its first foreign investment. That appearance is understandable, and indeed conforms both to our knowledge of organizational behavior and to the emphasis already placed on transactions and information costs in the genesis of MNEs. A large firm (or division of a firm) consists of many functional departments. Each has its own responsibilities and powers, the powers defined by how much discretion the unit has in making use of the firm's resources. These departments perform functions such as purchasing, production, marketing, accounting, finance, etc. Each department has its own rules of thumb and preferences about the actions that the firm undertakes. The rules of thumb are the result of an ongoing search for inexpensive but reasonably efficient methods of solving routine problems (what price to quote, how much inventory to hold, etc.).

These departments coordinate their activities through a process of interdepartmental bargaining, and a good deal of emphasis has been given to the possibility that each department's efforts to make use of its bargaining power to attain its own parochial objectives may result in decisions that fail to maximize profits for the firm as a whole. However, we must appreciate that the power relationships among these functional departments and the department-level goals that they pursue are in turn determined by the firm's top management (which at the least has the authority and responsibility to determine these things). Top management also controls the reporting requirements, the record-keeping and appraisal procedures that motivate middle-level employees to act in ways as fully as possible consistent with the objectives of top management. If the power relationships between departments are such that, say, the production department usually gets its way over the marketing department, a fully competent top management should have considered whether or not power relationships having this result are in accord with the firm's long-term objectives. A profit-maximizing top management obviously cannot induce every employee of the firm to act moment by moment so as to generate maximum profits. The costs of information and supervision, the difficulty of working out employment contracts that align the efforts of employees to the goals of the firm – these and other constraints limit the firm's pursuit of its ultimate goals, so that "optimal imperfection" is the best the firm can achieve. Notice that these limits on the internal coordination of the firm's resources echo the market failures cited in Chapter 1 as the basis for the MNE. Markets and bureaucracies both have their limitations, and one can hope for nothing more than the best attainable compromise among them.

An extension of this organizational description of the firm brings us to the foreign-investment decision. Bower (1970) argued that the firm's investment projects are not planned by top management and often do not even originate at top management's initiative. Rather, projects get proposed and defined "down the line" in some functional department that devises them as a solution to some problem or as an opportunity to use some asset or competence that the department has in hand. Once proposed, such projects must gather sufficient supporters along the organizational hierarchy to bring them with enthusiastic backing to top managers, who cannot exercise a fully informed appraisal of the details of each proposal. A project moving toward approval depends heavily, Bower argued, on *impetus:* A person or persons in the hierarchy decide that the proposal is good enough to warrant putting their reputations on the line to back it. The appraisal and reward structure developed by top management, of course, should influence who undertakes to supply impetus to what projects.

Evidence on the process

Aharoni's (1966) description of the foreign-investment decision process in American business firms presents a pattern closely attuned to that preceding (also see Brooke and Remmers, 1970, Chapter 4). Many companies appear uninterested in exploring foreign-investment opportunities. They may be small or may possess good investment projects for continued expansion in their base industry or diversification in domestic product markets; no one puts any impetus behind a foreign-investment decision. When a company's first foreign-investment project does come to the fore, it may result from some outside proposal (especially from somebody known to the company) or some problem perceived within the firm. The exact precipitating factors are somewhat random (Michalet and Delapierre, 1976, pp. 27–9): An export market may be threatened; a competitor may have gone abroad. An opportunity is then sought to use the firm's available skills or intangibles.[1]

The process by which the firm investigates the foreign-investment option shows certain important properties (Aharoni, 1966, Chapters 4 and 5). Information and search costs are quite high for foreign investment as compared with other investment decisions, what with overseas site visits, the cost of acquiring the necessary approvals from foreign governments, and the like.[2] These high fixed costs of decision making constitute an important reason for expecting that foreign investment will be mainly an activity of large firms able to contemplate making a large capital commitment abroad. Closely related to these fixed costs of search is Aharoni's finding that the perceived risk of foreign investment is quite high. The more costly is information, the less of it one acquires, and the more risky is the outcome perceived to be. At least one survey of MNEs' experience confirms that firms' foreign subsidiaries perform better when they initially choose sites with low information costs and gather infor-

---

[1] It is worth noting that the process of disinvesting in unsuccessful subsidiaries seems rather similar to that of launching new ones. It depends not just on the subsidiary's performance but also on other events affecting the parent company and changes in its strategic posture (Tourneden, 1975).

[2] Aharoni (1966, Chapter 5) suggested that the commitment to invest abroad often comes not from a conscious strategic decision but from a series of investigative steps (investigation and market development) that bring the incremental cost of foreign investment down to a level that finally seems attractive.

mation roundabout by first exporting or licensing independent foreign producers than when they proceed "cold turkey" with the foreign-investment decision (Newbould et al., 1978, Chapters 4 and 6).[3] Because the firm's previous stock of knowledge holds little value for the foreign-investment process itself, an incremental investigation of foreign markets clearly is likely to be an efficient procedure (Johanson and Vahlne, 1978).

The pattern described here can be traced through many historical and case studies. Indeed, the early process of expansion of firms to national-market status in the nineteenth-century U.S. economy was apparently quite similar to their evolution to multinational status more recently (Kindleberger, 1969, pp. 33–5). We have evidence on the behavior of early MNEs such as Singer Sewing Machine Co. (Wilkins, 1970, Chapters 3 and 4). They became foreign investors through a process of incremental problem solving, such as dealing with the unsatisfactory performance of foreign licensees or sales agents. The historical case studies also show that the evolution of the decentralized multiplant and multinational firm depended on nineteenth-century innovations in communications (telegraph and telephone) that allowed the firm to achieve economies of integration.[4]

The historical evidence also confirms the incremental approach that companies have taken to the countries they have chosen for foreign investments. Wilkins (1970, Chapters 6 and 7) stressed that the initial investments undertaken in Canada and Mexico during the 1890–1914 period represented cheap, natural extensions of domestic activities for many U.S. companies. The preference for close-to-home locations among contemporary MNEs was noted in Section 2.4. Dubin (1976, Chapter 5) accordingly found that the smaller the firm and the less diversified its portfolio of overseas assets, the more

---

[3] Some economists have tried to explain these behavior patterns in terms of single-minded decision-making properties such as a "spatial preference" for staying close to home (Richardson, 1971*b*). However, the combination of organizational factors and information costs seems decidedly more satisfying.

[4] Vernon (1977, Chapter 1) made the same point about the expansion of MNEs after World War II.

likely are its foreign assets to be concentrated in familiar countries. As mentioned in Chapter 2, Davidson (1980) has shown how the distribution of U.S. foreign investments among host countries is affected by the sequences of moves by which MNE empires are extended from more to less familiar countries. And Wells (1983, Chapter 7) has explained how the expansion of MNEs from third-world countries is strongly influenced by the presence of expatriate communities that reduce the incipient MNE's costs of securing reliable information.

We have stressed that the combination of risks and information costs facing the novice MNE strongly affects the process of foreign investment. A corollary holds that the average profits of new foreign subsidiaries should be low, and the failure rate should be high. Again, the data offer strong support. Lupo et al. (1978), have shown that the profit rates of foreign affiliates of U.S. MNEs in 1966 were strongly related to the ages of the subsidiaries, after controlling for the country and industry in which the subsidiary is located.[5] Furthermore, the age-profitability relationship is not just a stand-in for a relationship between size and profitability: Profit rates also increase with size, but not so regularly as with age. The age-profit relationship is largely due to the smaller proportion of new subsidiaries running losses, but profit rates increase somewhat with age, even when the figures are averaged only over those earning positive profits.[6]

Another corollary holds that the method of overseas expansion – green-field investment, acquisition of a going concern, joint venture – may be chosen with regard to risks and information costs. The rather extensive evidence on this will be reviewed in Section 3.3.

[5] The study also determined that the profit-age relationship does not result merely from inflation, which it could because the capital of the older subsidiaries is entered onto their books at historical cost. Also see Newbould, et al. (1978, Chapter 8) and Reddaway (1968, pp. 225–31).

[6] No exactly comparable data are available on U.S. domestic companies to tell us if the riskiness of new domestic ventures is less or the age-profit slope is any flatter. Therefore, these data should not by themselves be taken to assert that foreign investment is more risky than domestic expansion. But it *is* risky, and firms clearly behave in ways responsive to the perceived risks.

3.2. **Organizational structure**

Once a firm undertakes its first foreign investment, it must devise ways to integrate that activity with its overall decision-making structure. The devices used build on the organizational structures that have evolved in large enterprises of all types. These organizational devices are economically significant for several reasons. Their design depends on the structures of the markets in which the firm operates, and they influence the way firms behave in the market; therefore, a knowledge of organizational structures helps us to understand the behavior of MNEs as economic actors. Also, certain organizational devices are innovations that have spread outward from the United States, and the changing relative positions of U.S.-based and foreign MNEs depend partly on the diffusion of innovations. Finally, the ease with which MNEs adapt to certain policies imposed by governments depends on their organizational structures.

Organizational forms and foreign subsidiaries

Once an enterprise grows large enough to have a formal hierarchical organization, two principal forms are available to it. The *functional (F) organization* consists of a group of functionally specialized departments reporting to a chief executive. The *multidivisional (MD) organization* takes two or more *F* organizations and places them under the supervision of a single top executive. The *F* organization attains the virtues of specialization: Members of each department concentrate on their own tasks without any redundant communication with other departments. The *F* organization is very good at doing one thing as efficiently as possible. The *MD* form evolved when business enterprises found that they could profitably undertake diverse activities (diversify in products or geographically) so that it was no longer efficient to place all production activities, say, under a single production department. A major strength of the *MD* firm lies in its ability to make each of its divisions a "profit center," responsible for turning a profit on its own designated activities. Also, top management can use this profit performance as its means of supervising its divisions, so that chief executives are freed from detailed supervision of the firm's activities and can concentrate on longer-run strategic matters – anticipating changes, allocating capital among divisions, devising methods for the best use of the firm's resources. Naturally enough, the more diversified a firm's activities, the more likely that it employs *MD* organization. The *MD* form, incidentally, evolved in the United States around 1920 and subsequently diffused throughout the United States and to other countries.

Stopford and Wells (1972, Chapter 2) found that U.S. companies usually are organized in the *F* form at the time they acquire their first foreign subsidiaries. The first foreign venture often is tied to the parent by loose organizational links because of the risk and uncertainty surrounding it, and because nobody knows what performance level to expect from it. Also, it simply does not pay at this stage to establish an elaborate apparatus to administer foreign subsidiaries: Steuer et al. (1973, Chapter 7) found that they are more loosely supervised the smaller their parents (also see Baglini, 1976). As foreign operations mature, the enterprise establishes an international division to coordinate certain functions such as transfer pricing, finance, and the distribution of exports among production units. That event often is related to or is subsequent to the evolution of the parent's overall organization from *F* to *MD*. Adoption of the *MD* form provides the enterprise with a flexibility for entering and coordinating new areas of business that makes the proliferation of foreign subsidiaries more likely. That does not, however, mean that coordinating foreign operations through an international division is a cinch for the *MD* enterprise. Its domestic divisions usually are organized by product, whereas its international division is concerned with overseas production of these same products. Domestic product managers have no direct incentive to hand over assets helpful to foreign units of the international division producing the same line, a problem of "suboptimization" for the MNE. Firms therefore cast about for other organizational structures to evade this problem. One solution is organize the whole company into worldwide product divisions, but that runs into a different problem of suboptimization: Common problems of overseas operations are handled in separate divisions. A solution running in a different direction is to break down an international division into area divisions, each responsible for all operations in some overseas area. This solution is popular when the foreign subsidiaries supply one another with components or intermediate products, requiring close coordination.

It is clear from the preceding that the choice of an organizational structure represents a balancing of advantages among imperfect alternatives, just as did the boundary between intracorporate (MNE) and market transactions considered in Chapter 1. Consider the choice between global product divisions and international or area divisions. The economic principle behind this choice is to place within a division those activities that require extensive communications or coordination with each other and to keep separate those activities not needing continuous or regular communications channels. The more diversified are the outputs that a firm produces abroad, and the more international are the markets for its inputs and outputs, the more likely it is to choose global product divisions. Without them, too much interchange over product-specific problems must pass across divisional boundaries. Similarly, an international division or area divisions for a highly diversified company would get tangled up trying to keep track of internally heterogeneous product lines. A single international division is seldom the structure used if the firm makes 40 percent or more of its sales abroad, because the power structure of claimants for the top executive's ear then gets out of balance. Davis (1976) noted the prevalence of a global product division in firms with heavy research spending, demanding close global management of their product-specific intangible assets. International area organizations flourish where mature product lines are supplied to common end-user markets, so that the MNE's chief coordination problem lies in its regional marketing organization.

Getting its organizational structure properly matched to its pattern of activities is important for a firm's efficiency and profitability. A firm with *MD* organization and diversified operations abroad that are supervised by an international division probably suffers a mismatch. Stopford and Wells (1972, pp. 79–82) found that the mismatched

MNEs they studied were, on average, less profitable than those they deemed properly matched. They also concluded that the *F* form of organization for a MNE is typically less effective than *MD*.

Brooke and Remmers (1970, Chapter 3) took a somewhat different approach to explaining MNEs' organizational structures, but one whose conclusions are consistent with those of Stopford and Wells. They classified management systems in MNEs as "close" or "open," depending on the intensity of the parent's supervision of the subsidiaries and the density of communications and information links between them. The close structures occur in vertical MNEs, where the product flow through one affiliate affects the operations of others in the short run. They also occur in horizontal MNEs that share common technology extensively or that distribute an identically branded good in many different regions, so that malfunction of one affiliate in its local market adversely affects the profitability of other affiliates as well. Another condition for close control is that differences between national markets do not impel local adaptation of the product (Alsegg, 1971, pp. 120–1, 175). Similarly, de Bodinat (1975) related the closeness of control to several traits of the enterprise's technology, strategy, and market environment. Supervision is more centralized where the plant sizes and activities of parent and subsidiaries have greater similarity, where technology is more complex, where greater transactional interdependence binds parent and subsidiaries, and where the market environment (specifically, level of demand) is more predictable. These degrees of centralization pertain to major decisions of the subsidiaries and to decisions on standards and procedures; day-to-day management is not always decentralized, but its variations show no systematic patterns.

The basic organizational structures open to firms are discrete types that cannot be freely mixed within the firm. A dilemma therefore confronts the MNE that needs the types of coordination supplied by both international divisions and global product divisions. Should it live with an impure but imperfect form? Should it attempt the formal synthesis offered by the novel matrix organization? Or should it muddle through with various coordinating devices to patch up the cracks that appear in a traditional organization? Recent surveys (Business International, 1981) have suggested a drift toward global product divisions, but with copious use of patchwork devices.

Economizing on internal coordination

What matters economically for these relationships between the MNE's market environment and its internal organization is not so much the substantive details (which can be left to business practitioners) as the general type of economizing process that takes place. MNEs lavish extensive resources on internal coordination when close coordination pays, as when the profits of different affiliates are strongly interdependent and inconsistent policies would be very costly. Fewer resources are devoted to control when it is costly (for a subsidiary in a remote location) or when the affiliate's local environment is unstable or highly distinctive (making coordination ineffectual) (Alsegg, 1971, pp. 9–11). Fewer resources are used on coordination with a small subsidiary than with a large one, or one in a large and potentially lucrative market.[7]

That a firm adapts its internal control systems to maximize the value of its general strategic posture is a proposition that also applies to the particular types of controls placed on subsidiaries. Surveys of foreign subsidiaries frequently inquire what decisions can be made by the subsidiary's management and which ones must be checked with MNE headquarters. Just as frequently they conclude that firms' practices are highly diverse. Although all MNEs seem to control the financial function centrally (uniform financial reporting, budgeting, accounting, and forecasting for subsidiaries), they are highly diverse in all other matters. This diversity hardly comes as a surprise to an economist, who expects a firm to centralize control over only those decisions of affiliates that affect the profitability of the whole enterprise in an interdependent way. Financial decisions necessarily have this character, because they are central to the firm's global profit maximization, and a dollar expended by one arm of the firm is then not available for expenditure by another. What other decisions will

---

[7] See Alsegg (1971, pp. 209–10) on the effects of formation of the European Community.

have such "externalities" or interdependent effects surely depends on the nature of the MNE's business. Unfortunately, the existing literature does little to form hypotheses about this theoretically predicted pattern of dependence and test them empirically.[8]

We mentioned that organizational choices may vary among MNEs based in different nations. The reasons involve both differences in national cultures and the gradual diffusion of organizational innovations that originated in the United States. Franko (1976, Chapter 8) (also see Jedel and Kujawa, 1976, pp. 60–2) found that European MNEs have made extensive use of informal supervision of subsidiaries through nothing more than a personal reporting relationship between the presidents of the subsidiary and parent. As late as 1971 more than a third of European MNEs surveyed by Franko retained a "mother-daughter" system, whereas the rest used organizational patterns similar to those of American MNEs (global product divisions, international divisions). The mother-daughter system, not dissimilar to the control techniques that American MNEs had used in their earliest stages, represented not so much a lack of control as a personalized and irregular form of it, and the relationship seemed to reflect balkanized and noncompetitive markets in which both parents and subsidiaries were accustomed to operate. Similarly, Chandler (1980) found that U.K. firms went multinational later than their U.S. counterparts because family control survived longer among U.K. firms. The rate at which the family firm can expand without slipping from its owners' control is limited by the family's thrift and fecundity, and the absolute scale of investment in and management of international expansion presses hard on the family's capacities. It was found that U.K. family firms also eschewed expansion by merger for the same reasons.

The leaders among European MNEs in the movement away from mother-daughter relationships were the firms with the largest subsid-

---

[8] It does at least reveal some unexpected coordination mechanisms. Edstrom and Galbraith (1977) described the use of international transfers of personnel in order to create informal networks of communication among employees acquainted with one another; these can usefully supplement the formal channels that may not always carry the full message between the MNE's international units. Also see Brandt and Hulbert (1976).

iaries in the United States; the example of American organizational practice was at hand, and the scale and competitive pace of the U.S. market were unkind to personalized, unsystematic communications. Another market factor encouraging modernized organization was the increased competitiveness of the European markets themselves in the 1960s because of the activities of American MNEs and the tariff reductions involved in the formation of the European Community.[9] Although differences have existed historically between American and European multinationals, a good deal of casual evidence suggests that they may be transitory, reflecting the diffusion of organizational innovations more than intrinsic cultural differences. Furthermore, where subsidiaries of MNEs with diverse national origins operate in similar environments, they often seem subject to control arrangements that show no obvious imprint of the national differences (e.g., Safarian, 1966, pp. 85–6).

The organizational structures of Japanese MNEs hold particular interest because they allow a test of the influence of purely cultural factors on the most efficient choice of organization. Those influences are indeed present. Japanese managerial practice depends heavily on intensive personal communication and therefore tends to work badly over long distance. Japanese foreign subsidiaries often originated (as did those of other countries' MNEs) from threats to export markets. Hence, the subsidiaries often were left under the supervision of the company's export department, gaining less autonomy than comparable subsidiaries of other countries' MNEs (Yoshino, 1976, Chapter 5).

In summary, the evolving organizational patterns of MNEs reflect a quest for efficient organization undertaken in context of the structural environment of the firms' markets, their strategic choices for the use of their distinctive assets and competences, and national cul-

---

[9] As further evidence of this diffusion process, Franko (1976, pp. 204–5) noted that American MNEs generally moved to the *MD* form domestically before they adapted this structure to their international operations. European MNEs, however, tended to modernize their international and domestic organizations at the same time. This is because they were imitating the best practice elsewhere and because their overseas markets often were more competitive than their home markets.

tural factors that influence styles of personal interaction and hence effective forms of business organization.

3.3. Effects of organization: new venture or acquisition?

The relationships developed earlier between the market environment of the MNE and its internal organization hold economic interest because they involve the efficient (or inefficient) use of society's scarce resources. But they do not directly engage the issues of public policy that motivate most economic analysis. Therefore, we show in this section and the following section that some business policy decisions flowing from MNE organizational structures are significant for public policy. Public opinion often takes offense when a national enterprise is acquired by a MNE domiciled in a foreign land. The public may be stirred simply by the nationalistic urges that motivate so much policy toward MNEs, or there may be a more rational concern for competitive effects: Green-field entry by the MNE adds a new enterprise unit to the national market, whereas entry by acquisition does not.

The organizational costs and patterns of MNEs suggest a series of hypotheses about circumstances in which MNEs are relatively more likely to enter a market by acquisition. Some other influences on MNEs' acquisition rates (i.e., the proportions of their foreign subsidiaries begun through acquisition), rooted in the market for control of business units, must also be taken into account.

Risk, size, and experience

Evidence presented earlier has established that foreign subsidiaries are relatively risky ventures. They also entail high fixed and variable costs of administrative coordination, and MNEs incur these only where the expected payout warrants it. The choice between acquisition and green-field entry is related to these considerations because they differ both in expected riskiness and in the importance of various coordination costs. To start a subsidiary by acquisition, the potential MNE goes into the "market for corporate control" and buys up equity shares in a going business. To gain control of an established business, one must compete with equity shareholders (persons and institutions) in general, and that rivalry forces the MNE to pay a price for the acquired business such that an ordinary investor would then earn only a normal or competitive rate of return on the investment. The MNE might earn more than another buyer, of course, if it reaps some economies in the use of its special assets (see Chapter 1) following the acquisition, or if it enjoys a lower cost of capital. In any case, the MNE starting a new venture avoids paying the going-concern value for an established enterprise, which it may not value highly if it wants to install its own management practices from the start (a strong preference of Japanese MNEs, according to Tsurumi, 1976, pp. 194–5).[10] Clearly, no general presumption points to either method of entry, and outside factors may prove quite important; when the stock market is depressed, for example, it may be cheaper to pick up physical assets by buying companies than by building plants.

If entry through a new business has this virtual advantage of avoiding the capitalization of rents by the stock market, it also has the disadvantage of greater riskiness. The going concern is a working coalition. From the viewpoint of the foreign MNE, it possesses an operating local management who "know the ropes" in the national market environment. The MNE that buys the local firm also buys access to a stock of valuable information. These factors surely reduce the uncertainty about how well the new subsidiary will do. Therefore, in general, to choose acquisition rather than a new venture is to choose a lower but less uncertain expected rate of return.

That conclusion can now be linked to the evidence about MNEs' organizational structures. The firm that first goes abroad faces an especially high level of uncertainty and is therefore likely to crave

---

[10] Michalet and Delapierre (1976, pp. 33–4) suggested that acquisition is more likely in sectors where the advantages of MNEs rest in general organizational ability and not technology or other specific assets. One might expect that the survival rate of subsidiaries founded by acquisition would exceed that of newly founded subsidiaries, because of the risk difference. However, the data of the Harvard Multinational Enterprise Project show the opposite: Subsidiaries subsequently exiting (not through merger) seem to account for a larger proportion of those founded by merger than of those founded as new ventures (Curhan et al., 1977, pp. 21, 168).

the information stock and lower riskiness obtainable by entering foreign markets via an acqustion. Of course, the firm launching into MNE status with a real innovation might not locate a going concern suitable for its purposes. But if a suitable partner is available, the new MNE is more likely to go that route. This hypothesis has been confirmed by Dubin (1976, Chapter 5) and Stopford (1976). The MNE past its first steps abroad may have a large portfolio of foreign subsidiaries or only a few. The larger its portfolio, the less does it balk at the uncertainty associated with a new foreign venture. Accordingly, Dubin found that large MNEs are more likely to add new subsidiaries through new ventures than are small ones, especially in recent years.[11] Finally, the MNE's rate of growth may affect its preferred method of expansion overseas. The evidence suggests that the novice MNE's stock of information increases with the time it has been in the business. If age brings wisdom, the fast-growing MNE holds a smaller stock of experience than the equal-size MNE that has reached its current state more slowly. The fast grower will therefore pay more for the information stock in the hands of a going firm and will tend to add a larger proportion of its subsidiaries through acquisition. The work of Dubin (1976, Chapter 6) seems to confirm this hypothesis.[12]

Diversity and other influences on acquisition of subsidiaries
These same propositions can be directed to the role of diversity in the MNE's expansion process. First, consider the geographical diversity already achieved by a MNE. This factor, like size and experience generally, increases the MNE's information stock

[11] Two points of qualification: First, Dubin examined his hypotheses about acquisition behavior one at a time, and so his finding that x and y are related could always be because z is not controlled. Second, there has been a clear trend in the aggregate for more subsidiaries to be added through acquisition (Wilson, 1980), and this trend could color conclusions reached by comparing MNEs that have started their subsidiaries at different points in time.

[12] Similarly, in a fast-growing national market, the entering MNE is reluctant to sacrifice profits because of the longer delay associated with building a subsidiary from scratch. Dubin (1976, Chapter 9) reported higher acquisition rates in faster-growing foreign markets.

and reduces the premium it will pay for the security of acquiring a going firm rather than building anew. Therefore, Dubin (1976, Chapter 5) unsurprisingly found that MNEs already highly diversified among overseas regions are less likely to add new subsidiaries through acquisition. Diversity also enters in the degree to which the product line of a new subsidiary differs from the MNE's established activities. The more remote the new activity, the greater its uncertainty, and the more likely is the MNE to pay for the greater security of entry by acquisition (Dubin, 1976, Chapter 6). Wilson (1980), as well as Dubin, found that the more diversified is the MNE overall, the more likely is it to have acquired its subsidiaries through buying going firms. There is some evidence that widely diversified companies often set up a process of expanding via acquisition, whether in their national home markets or abroad, and there may be administrative scale economies in that process itself.

We can mention some influences on the MNE's method of expansion that come directly from the market for corporate control. The net advantage of buying a going concern depends on the price one must pay. If potential sellers are few, the MNE may find itself in a small-numbers bargaining situation in which the seller can capture some of the revenue-productivity gain that the MNE anticipates by operating the acquired facilities. The more going concerns that are available to be bought, the better market price the acquiring MNE can get. These considerations suggest less frequent use of the acquisition method in less-developed countries, where few suitable firms can be found (Wilson, 1980), and in small economies generally (Dubin, 1976, Chapter 9). This result is particularly striking, because the smaller the market, the more does the firm entering with efficient-scale new facilities stir up competitive rivalry. This force apparently fails to outweigh the influence on MNEs' acquisition rates of the availability of more companies for purchase in the larger market.

The market for corporate control also shows up in the traits of the local firms selected by MNEs for acquisition. Little (1981) found U.S. acquirees to be a bit less profitable than other firms in their industries and notably heavy on long-term debt. That pattern suggests that they were constrained for supplies of capital, a situation that a MNE (or other large company) could remedy. Other financial traits of the acquirees vary from sector to sector in a way consistent with the assets that the acquiring MNE should be able to provide to its new subsidiary. Other studies have indicated trends in the same direction. Erland (1980) found that Swedish firms with foreign participation started out below average for their industries in technology intensity, but the majority showed increases after their takeovers. Stubenitsky (1970, pp. 73–7) investigated the motives of Dutch entrepreneurs selling control of their firms to MNEs; they included the sellers' specific needs for the assets brought by the MNEs (technology, capital) as well as the general reasons that corporate control changes hands (the owner retires, or the firm needs more able management). Reuber and Roseman (1972) stressed the illiquidity of Canadian firms, which would tend to depress their market values, as a cause of international mergers.

3.4. Effects of organization: joint ventures and control of subsidiaries

The logic of MNE organization also influences the willingness of MNEs to hold less than 100 percent control of the equity of their subsidiaries. When control is incomplete, the other owners can be either portfolio holders owning the equities as financial investments or an entrepreneur holding a substantial block of equity and taking an active role in the company. The latter organization is referred to as a joint venture. MNEs' tolerance for joint ventures and minority shareholders is entwined with an issue of public policy. Governments in countries hosting MNEs often respond to public hostility toward foreign control by creating incentives for the MNE to take on local partners or sell equity to local portfolio holders. The organizational and strategic traits of MNEs strongly influence their willingness to comply.

Joint ventures

We emphasize the tolerance of MNEs for joint ventures both because of their popularity with host governments and because of the amount of evidence on them. Economists have studied both the extent to which MNEs participate in joint ventures and the extent to which MNEs have extricated themselves from joint-venture arrangements previously in force. Either approach should serve to test the economic behavior involved, presuming, of course, that we take account of the pressures applied by host-country governments.

The transactional model of MNEs immediately suggests factors that will discourage sharing control of a foreign subsidiary. The parent possesses an intangible asset, the sort associated with its research and marketing activities, that has propelled it into MNE status. The MNE route to maximizing the rents on these assets is chosen in part because of the difficulties of working out arm's-length contracts for sharing them with other firms. The same objection holds to sharing them through joint control of the subsidiary. If the intangibles take the form of secrets, they unavoidably fall into the partner's hands. Even if diffusion of the intangible asset can be avoided, problems still arise with joint control. The partner not supplying the intangible has every incentive to try to appropriate the rents that it yields, but not to invest resources in its maintenance or improvement (the free-rider problem). Hence, we expect joint ventures to be resisted by MNEs in industries where intangible assets are the main basis for foreign investment. Franko (1971, Chapter 2) indeed found that the reversion of joint ventures to single control is positively associated with perceived importance to the parent in marketing policy of internationally standardized product quality, design, and style. MNEs whose strategies depend on standardization fear that selling a poor-quality product under their brand in one country will impair their goodwill asset elsewhere, a circumstance likely to bring conflict with a local joint-venture partner who has only a local stake in the asset.[13] Franko did not find that R&D activity is a predictor that joint ventures will be abandoned, however, because the research results often are exactly what one partner provides as its resource contribution to the joint venture, taking a share of equity in return. This arrangement can work well if there is no problem of the technology

[13] Also see Stopford and Wells (1972, pp. 109–10), Tomlinson (1970, Chapter 2), and Deane (1970, pp. 75–8).

escaping from its owner's control. Nevertheless, Stopford and Wells (1972, pp. 119–23) found a negative relationship between the MNE's rate of R&D spending and the proportion of its subsidiaries organized as joint ventures, a conclusion that supports our original intangible-assets hypothesis.

Franko also found at least some evidence of intolerance to joint ventures in the MNE that faces some problems of rationalizing its subsidiaries' operations. If either its subsidiary *A* or its subsidiary *B* can serve market *X*, the MNE parent will pick the lower-cost supplier (call it *A*). But if *B* is a joint venture and can earn a positive profit from serving *X* (but a smaller profit than can *A*), a conflict arises between the MNE and its local *B* partner, who will want *B* to get the assignment. Similarly, if the MNE's subsidiaries supply components to each other, joint-venture status exacerbates the problem of pricing these intracorporate transactions. On the other hand, joint ventures are less objectionable for nontraded goods or products made behind prohibitive tariff walls.[14]

Tolerance of joint ventures is also related to the organizational structure of the MNE parent. Franko (1971, Chapter 3) noted that a MNE organizing its subsidiaries into geographical area divisions no longer treats each subsidiary as a local profit center and correspondingly finds joint ventures inconvenient (Stopford and Wells, 1972, pp. 114–17). On the other hand, the MNE with worldwide product divisions and a high degree of product diversification may welcome joint ventures to develop certain products or markets that the parent counts as peripheral, thereby letting it economize on managerial and other contributions to the venture.

[14] However, Franko (1971, Chapter 2) could not confirm this statistically. The data of the Harvard Multinational Enterprise Project seem to confirm the pattern. Of subsidiaries wholly owned by their parents in 1975, 12.1% were heavy exporters; the share is 9.4% for majority-owned subsidiaries, 8.2% for joint ventures, and 8.3% for minority-owned subsidiaries. Subsidiaries making heavy sales to other MNE affiliates are about equally numerous among wholly owned subsidiaries (10.5%) and joint ventures (10.4%), but less among majority-owned subsidiaries (8.2%) and minority-owned subsidiaries (7.2%). If the population is confined to subsidiaries based in manufacturing, the predicted patterns concerning joint ventures become clearer still (calculated from Curhan et al., 1977, pp. 386, 394).

Let us turn to the positive factors that cause firms to seek out joint ventures. They are especially evident in the extractive industries where the project is risky or involves a large minimum efficient scale of operation or both. Partnership among several vertical MNEs interested in acquiring the project's output lets them spread the risk and the financial burden and limit the output they receive from the venture to the needs of their downstream facilities. (Such firms often wish to draw vital inputs from several sources to minimize the risks of being cut off from a single supplier.)[15]

Another positive reason for seeking a joint venture is the MNE's lack of some capacity or competence needed to make the investment succeed – a straightforward incentive for a joint venture in light of our transactional model. The most obvious case is the MNE that is diversifying in product as well as geographical space and thus is doubly lacking in managerial know-how for competing in the new market. MNEs based in extractive sectors therefore may seek partners when they start foreign subsidiaries to process their output, because the parents lack the needed marketing skills (Stopford and Wells, 1972, pp. 132–3). Stopford and Wells (1972, Chapter 9) found that joint ventures are particularly likely when the subsidiary's output is diversified from the parent's and the parent has a high rate of R&D expenditures. For such firms, R&D activity occasionally casts up new products suited for markets quite different from the firm's existing ones, and joint ventures annex the marketing knowledge of another firm already present in these markets. The preceding findings for U.S. MNEs have been largely confirmed for British MNEs by Stopford and Haberich (1978). They found (Table 4), for example, that only 28 percent of diversified foreign affiliates are un-

---

[15] Stopford and Wells (1972, pp. 117–19). Stuckey (1981, Chapter 4) presented an intensive investigation of joint ventures in the international aluminum industry. He found considerable support for the scale-economies argument, the rapidly proliferating joint ventures in aluminum being concentrated in bauxite refining, where both scale economies and risk are greatest. He also pointed out that joint ventures provide a simple method of sharing the company-specific intangible technological knowledge common in this sort of industry. He did not find much support for competing hypotheses, such as that joint ventures serve to foster collusion.

der absolute control of their U.K. parents, whereas two-thirds of all other subsidiaries are fully controlled. They also determined (Table 6) that the larger the subsidiary, the more likely it is that the parent has majority control (a fact suggesting that the joint ventures are in small, sideline activities).

Another positive reason lies in the MNE's occasional need for specific resources possessed by local joint-venture partners. These include knowledge about local marketing or other environmental conditions, as well as general assistance in risk bearing (e.g., Tomlinson, 1970, Chapter 2). Joint ventures economize on the information requirements of foreign investment and are thus likely to appeal where these are more onerous. Besides their prevalence in subsidiaries producing diversified products (described earlier), joint ventures are resorted to more often by small MNEs, who presumably need both the information and companionship in sharing risk.[16] Joint ventures also seem to be more prevalent as MNEs proceed toward more unfamiliar host countries. For example, the less "global" U.K. MNEs increase their use of joint ventures once outside the Commonwealth countries (Stopford and Haberich, 1978, Table 7). Joint ventures are uncommon in culturally familiar LDC settings, such as British firms in Malaysia (Saham, 1980, pp. 150–1).

The joint-venture participation of MNEs varies with their national origin. British MNEs take part in proportionally more joint ventures than American MNEs (Stopford and Haberich, 1978, Table 1), and, in general, American MNEs are considered less tolerant of them than MNEs based abroad (Vernon, 1977, pp. 33–6). It seems at least possible that this difference reflects a difference in activities undertaken rather than one due to nationality, but the question has not been examined. It is clear that Japanese MNEs are much more prone to joint ventures than are other MNEs; for one 50-company sample, fully 82 percent of the foreign subsidiaries are joint ventures (Yoshino, 1976, Chapter 5). One explanation is that the great cul-

[16] Stopford and Wells (1972, pp. 138–41); Tomlinson (1970, pp. 74–86); Yoshihara (1978, pp. 39–40). However, in their study of foreign investment by smaller U.K. MNEs, Newbould et al. (1978, Chapter 5) found that subsidiaries 75% or more controlled by their parents were significantly more profitable than those under diluted control.

tural distance between Japan and foreign markets induces Japanese firms to seek expertise on local conditions (Tsurumi, 1976, pp. 204–6). Other explanations are more economic: Many of the subsidiaries engage in extracting raw materials; Japanese firms have been expanding rapidly and are thin on resources (capital and local management talent); Japanese foreign investment runs heavily to countries that require local partners.[17] Echoing Franko (1971), Tsurumi (1976, pp. 206–12) found a tendency for Japanese MNEs' subsidiaries to revert to full control once established.

The propensity of host governments to require that MNEs enter through joint ventures has obviously increased, and some observers, such as Friedmann and Beguin (1971, Chapter 1), see the accommodation by MNEs as a happy response to governments' desires to control their national economies. However, one can voice two reservations. First, imposing joint-venture status on a reluctant MNE curbs its contribution to the resulting company and thereby reduces the venture's productivity. Reuber et al. (1973, p. 86) found that joint ventures have narrowed product lines, smaller scales, and less input of investors' technology. Second, the public policy itself seems dubious if the government's actual goal is public control, because it is not obvious that a profit-seeking native will more eagerly seek to do the government's bidding than will a profit-seeking foreign entrepreneur nervous about his alien status. The joint-venture preference makes more sense as a means to transfer rents to nationals of the host country.

Minority portfolio ownership

Although developing countries often impose joint ventures on would-be foreign investors, industrial countries sometimes simply provide an incentive for admitting some local minority ownership. In general, the same hypotheses should apply to factors favoring and discouraging local participation as to those involved with joint ventures. The matter has not been much researched, however, and the studies available are quite inconclusive. For example, Mich-

---

[17] Most studies of U.S. and U.K. multinationals have omitted subsidiaries in countries requiring joint ventures, in order to control for this factor.

alet and Delapierre (1976, pp. 35–6) observed that the French MNEs' proportions of ownership in their subsidiaries increase with the host country's level of development and with the importance in the industry of commercial marketing factors. Fifty years ago, Southard (1931, pp. 136–7) noted the affinity of companies with proprietary technology for full control, and Dunning and Pearce (1977, p. 13) found that subsidiaries under less than 100 percent parental control accounted for a majority of all equity in subsidiaries in low-technology British industries, but only 11 percent in the high-technology industries. Steuer et al. (1973, Chapter 7) apparently made an ambitious attempt to explain the difference among subsidiaries in the United Kingdom in the proportion of control retained by their parents. These authors came up empty-handed, a reminder that we should not overestimate our ability to explain patterns of business organization and their consequences for the organization of markets.

Assuming that the host government aims to maximize the income of its nationals, why it should promote minority shareholdings rather than joint ventures is unclear. The competitive stock market lets the MNE capitalize any rents its subsidiary enjoys when equity shares in the subsidiary are sold to local investors, who therefore can expect to earn only a normal rate of return. When the host government forces a joint venture on the MNE, the division of rents is not determinate, but the local partner, after being chosen, has a better chance in a one-on-one bargaining situation. The MNE has an interest in stirring up competition among local candidates for the privilege of being the joint-venture partner, and the government has an interest in stifling this competition.

3.5. Summary

The transactional model of the MNE that emerged from Chapter 1 implies that the firm is a contractual coalition of heterogeneous assets – long-term employees, physical capital, intangibles. Although transactional ownership links avert market failures in transactions in these intangible or heterogeneous assets, the internal organization of the MNE itself incurs costs and "organizational failures" that color its market behavior and affect important issues of public policy. Evidence on growth processes in MNEs affirms this characterization. In most companies the decision first to enter MNE activities apparently starts not from a top-level executive decision for strategic change but from the casual seizure of some opportunity perceived down the bureaucratic line. Because of the firm's lack of information and experience, the intrinsically risky first venture usually is into a relatively familiar, low-risk foreign environment.

Organizationally the foreign subsidiary is first held aloof, but then must be integrated into the parent's administrative structure – often a functional organization when the first foreign venture occurs, but likely to gravitate into a multidivisional one. Overseas activities may be integrated either through international or foreign area divisions or through product divisions that span both domestic and foreign markets. The MNE's choice tends to devolve from the principle that activities that share the same problems and need the most communication should be closeted within the same division. How large an investment the MNE makes in administrative apparatus to coordinate its members depends on whether or not its activities yield a high return to close integration (subsidiaries in unfamiliar or unstable environments tend to be left on their own). MNEs vary greatly in regard to what decisions are centralized in the parent; finance is always centralized because it provides the nerve system for the parent's efforts to maximize global profits, and it appears that other decisions are centralized to whatever degree is warranted by the technical and market structure of the firm's activities. National differences have existed in MNEs' organizational structures, reflecting the diffusion of organizational innovations from the United States and the varying persistence of family control and loose organization in noncompetitive markets.

Whether the MNE enters a foreign market by acquiring a local firm or by starting a new business depends on these organizational traits. Making an acquisition gains the entrant MNE a going local management and represents a low-risk strategy for quick entry, but the market for corporate control capitalizes any rents already accruing to the business. Green-field entry preserves these rents but is slower and riskier. We expect and find that novice MNEs or those diversifying into unfamiliar product lines tend to make acquisitions, whereas those with extensive experience abroad in their base activities prefer to start their own businesses. Among host countries the available supply of local firms makes a difference.

Some MNEs choose to operate foreign subsidiaries as joint ventures with another partner or partners, and host governments with increasing frequency require MNEs to take on local partners. MNEs vary greatly in their tolerance for joint ventures. These may prove welcome where minimum efficient scale is large, risk is considerable, or the MNE lacks some vital ingredient (such as knowledge of the local ropes). Joint ventures are shunned by the MNE that cherishes a secret intangible asset or extensively transfers components among its subsidiaries. Where a joint venture is forced on an unwilling MNE, the firm is likely to adapt by cutting back on the resources it commits to the business. An alternative to the joint venture is for the MNE to issue minority shareholdings in a subsidiary on the host country's securities market; our research unfortunately has given few clues to when and why this choice is made. If the host government's policy impels local participation in order to capture some rents from the MNE, it stands a better chance with joint ventures than with local portfolio shareholdings.

4

Patterns of market competition

Among areas of popular concern with the MNE, not the least confusion arises over its relationship to monopoly and problems of competition policy. The MNE often is a large company holding a large share in at least some of the markets where it operates. However, properly analyzed, the normative issues raised by monopoly, large size (or diversification), and international ownership links are quite different. In this chapter we shall investigate the extent and character of the relationships between the MNE and market competition.

4.1. Foreign investment and oligopoly

Entry barriers and bases for foreign investment

The transactional analysis of MNEs set forth in Chapter 1 implies their prevalence in industries with concentrated sellers (Caves, 1971). This is because the influences giving rise to multinational companies are identical with the bases of several barriers to entry into industries, and entry barriers cause high seller concentration. The theory of entry barriers has been controversial at a normative level (Is it socially undesirable that X should put new entrants at a disadvantage?), but there is fairly general agreement about the behavioral incidence of entry barriers (Does X put new entrants at a disadvantage?), our concern here. Consider the following:

1. *Advertising outlays* are associated with an entry barrier in cer-

tain types of industries where advertising dominates the information sought by buyers and its dissemination is subject to scale economies.[1] Advertising is also a good indicator of the prevalence of intangible assets likely to support foreign investment, as we saw in Chapter 1.

2. *Capital-cost barriers* arise where very large outlays are required to enter an industry at an efficient scale of production. Capital markets do not make large sums available for a project unless its promoter puts up substantial equity of his own – insurance that he will seek to maximize profits and not impair the project's capital through opportunistic behavior. Therefore, only an established firm with a large cash flow of internally generated funds can contemplate entry into such industries, and what entries occur are by firms established in other markets. Whether capital-cost barriers are a *sufficient* basis for foreign investment is neither clear nor important. What does matter is that a large firm with the requisite cash flow and *some* dowry of intangibles and management can readily find horizontal or vertical investment abroad the most attractive use for its funds.

3. *Scale economies* in production, the third classic source of entry barriers, have the least affinity for foreign investment because they induce firms to centralize production and export to foreign markets rather than to decentralize production and acquire MNE status (Section 2.2). There are some instances, however, in which scale-economy barriers favor multinational operations. Consider an assembled product such as automobiles, for which scale economies may be modest in the final assembly process but large (relative to the national market) in the production of certain components. If there is no satisfactory international arm's-length market for the components, the MNE can gain an advantage against single-nation entrants by producing these components at a single location and assembling them in individual national markets.

4. *Research and development* should be identified as a source of

---

[1] Without the scale economies, the entrant would be at no disadvantage. Without the dominant role of advertising as an information source, the entrant could use other marketing tactics (lower price, salespersons, etc.).

entry barriers because in some settings research activities involve scale economies and because they provide first-mover advantages to successful innovators.[2] The advantage to the MNE for overcoming such barriers lies in the possibility of centralizing R&D activities worldwide, just as in the production of components subject to scale economies in production. But the centralization of R&D has a further advantage in that shipping intangible research results around the world is less costly than shipping physical components.[3]

In short, each source of barriers to entry bears at least some relationship (a close relationship for some industrial sectors) to the reasons why MNEs exist in the first place. And MNEs have some advantage over newly organized firms, or over single-nation firms, in getting over these barriers to entry (a point to be considered later). Therefore, the height of entry barriers and the extent of foreign-investment activity should be highly correlated. And because entry barriers mostly determine an industry's level of seller concentration, we expect foreign investment and seller concentration to be closely associated.

The empirical evidence clearly supports this conjecture. Dunning (1958, pp. 155–7) found that two-thirds of the U.K.-based foreign subsidiaries covered in his survey operated in highly concentrated markets. Steuer et al. (1973, p. 94) (also see Dunning, 1973*b*) also observed a significant correlation between seller concentration and foreign subsidiaries' shares of U.K. industries' sales; industries with high concentration and substantial subsidiaries' shares usually contained not just one or two foreign subsidiaries among the leading firms but three or more. Fishwick (1981) reported high correlations between seller concentration and foreign investment in the United Kingdom for later years as well as for France and West Germany, and the pattern also appears for Guatemala (Willmore, 1976), Australia (Parry, 1978), New Zealand (Deane, 1970, pp. 300–3), and

---

[2] Like advertising, R&D is not associated with appreciable entry barriers in every setting. See Mueller and Tilton (1969) and Grabowski and Mueller (1978).

[3] See Teece (1977) and the discussion in Chapter 7.

Canada.[4] Pugel (1978, p. 68) found a close relationship for U.S. manufacturing industries between seller concentration and the share of activity carried out abroad. United States MNEs' affiliates in Brazil and Mexico themselves hold market shares high enough (47 percent of the affiliates in Mexico and 60 percent of Brazilian affiliates individually hold at least 25 percent shares of their respective markets) to imply that concentration in their markets must be high.[5]

Several investigators have tried to probe into the bases for this well-established correlation. Fishwick (1981) and Globerman (1979b) suggested that little or no correlation between concentration and foreign investment in the United Kingdom remains once other determinants of concentration are controlled. Rosenbluth (1970) showed that the prevalance of foreign subsidiaries in concentrated Canadian industries could be explained by the facts that subsidiaries tend to be big firms and the leading firms in concentrated industries are large. In the same vein, Steuer et al. (1973) and Fishwick (1981) noted that foreign investment is never prominent in unconcentrated industries, whereas it may or may not be in concentrated ones. (Concentrated industries lack foreign investment when concentration rests on scale economies in production that national firms have attained.)

Effects of concentration on foreign investment

Even if oligopoly and foreign investment share common structural causes, either one may still wield some direct causal influence on the other. But we must tread cautiously when specifying the causal mechanisms and testing them so as to control for their common causes. We should not casually label as "monopolistic advan-

---

[4] Caves et al. (1980, p. 87); Baumann (1975). The exceptions to this generalization hold some interest. Baba (1975) found no correlation for Japan and suggested that the reason might be the government's solicitous protection of concentrated domestic sellers.

[5] Newfarmer and Mueller (1975). Connor (1977, Table 3.19) gave a distribution of estimated minimum four-firm concentration ratios in the industries where these subsidiaries operate. In Brazil, 83% are in industries whose concentration exceeds 50%, 58% in industries where it exceeds 90%. For Mexico, the corresponding figures are 84% and 21%.

tages" (see Lall, 1980) the hypotheses that associate foreign investment with elements of market structure.

What causal links, then, can be established theoretically and empirically? Take first the effect of concentration on foreign investment. Knickerbocker (1973), in a well-known study, argued that the extent of foreign investment depends on the form that oligopolistic interdependence takes in certain U.S. manufacturing industries. If an oligopoly is "tight-knit," its members will share their plans and allocate resources within the industry approximately as will a single monopolist; no more investment will take place abroad than will maximize the monopoly profits available to the industry (the oligopoly group as a whole). In a loose-knit oligopoly, by contrast, firms recognize their interdependence with their rivals but lack sufficient mutual understanding to coordinate their activities. They are therefore likely to adopt simple patterns of imitative behavior: The price leader raises his price, and others follow; someone expands capacity, and the rivals imitate, lest they be left in a disadvantageous position in some ensuing price war. Knickerbocker argued that just this imitative behavior can occur in foreign investment. Rival *A* establishes a subsidiary in France. Rivals *B* and *C* reflect that this investment is likely to knock out their export business in France and give *A* a first-mover advantage if the investment should prove highly successful. Furthermore, *A* might discover some competitive asset in France that it could repatriate to the United States to torment *B* and *C* on their native soil. These considerations dispose *B* and *C* to imitate *A* and found their own subsidiaries in France. Following promptly, of course, is likely to cause excess capacity for a time in the French market – a deterrent. On the other hand, if this or other adversities should make the investments turn out badly for all parties, they do share *some* oligopolistic understanding and hence some excess profits (worldwide) that will make the losses bearable.

This pattern had been noted in surveys and descriptive studies (Hellmann, 1970, p. 244; Hu, 1973, pp. 105, 137–8), but Knickerbocker was the first to devise a way to test it statistically. Using data on subsidiaries founded by U.S. MNEs in 23 countries over 1948–67, he calculated "entry concentration indexes" indicating the extent to which the MNEs in a particular manufacturing industry bunched their investments in particular host countries and periods of time. Of course, some concentration of entry could have occurred simply because all potential investors noticed the same favorable development in France, and some bunching would have occurred just on a chance basis. However, such factors cannot account for the significant relationships that Knickerbocker found between the extent of entry concentration and seller concentration in the U.S. parent industries. Specifically, entry concentration increased with seller concentration up to a point (eight-firm concentration around 60–70 percent), then declined. This is just what his oligopolistic-reaction model predicts: Imitative behavior should occur in moderately concentrated industries, not unconcentrated ones (no interdependence recognized) or highly concentrated ones (tight-knit oligopoly). Bunching is also more evident in industries whose U.S. parent firms went abroad for the first time after World War II. Stable patterns of mutually dependent behavior are less likely to have matured in such industries. Less bunching occurs in industries whose firms are somewhat protected from the cut and thrust of oligopolistic rivalry, because they undertake heavy advertising (which insulates the individual firm's market position) or because they are diversified in product lines (insurance against adverse developments in any one line). Finally, some evidence[6] suggests that imitative behavior is discouraged in industries where scale economies in production are important; imitation then entails either too much excess capacity in the newly entered foreign market or facilities that are too inefficiently small.

Other studies have lent some statistical support for Knickerbocker's main hypothesis. For example, Caves et al. (1980, pp. 86–7) found that the extent of foreign investment in Canadian manufacturing industries (where U.S. companies account for about four-fifths of all foreign investment) is more closely associated with seller concentration in the corresponding U.S. industries than with concentration in the Canadian industries themselves; also, the relationship has the shape predicted and found by Knickerbocker – rising to a

---

[6] Rather weak statistically; see Knickerbocker (1973, Chapter 6).

maximum at concentration levels that correspond to loose-knit oligopoly. Similarly, Caves and Pugel (1980) found that in U.S. manufacturing industries the middle-size firms are more likely to be foreign investors in the more concentrated industries. It should also be noted that Knickerbocker's relationship resembles others that have been uncovered in research on industrial organization. Loose-knit imitative oligopoly also appears to inflate other forms of nonprice competition: Advertising–sales ratios, for example, are higher in moderately concentrated industries than in unconcentrated or highly concentrated ones. Jarrett (1979, Chapter 3), however, did not confirm Knickerbocker's hypothesis in his analysis of the factors determining foreign investment by various U.S. manufacturing industries, perhaps because of multicollinearity among his explanatory variables. And Flowers's (1976) study of foreign MNEs found simply that entry concentration rises with seller concentration in the home industry at a rate that differs from one source country to another.

Effects of foreign investment on concentration

The expected effect of multinational companies on concentration arises from the common bases of foreign investment and barriers to entry into a market, as observed earlier. If significant barriers to entry surround a market, the firms best qualified to overcome them may be MNEs based in the same sector in another country. These considerations imply that the entry of multinational companies into an industry might be unrelated to the height of entry barriers, whereas the entry of newly founded firms is negatively related to the height of barriers – a hypothesis confirmed for Canadian manufacturing industries by Gorecki (1976).[7] They also imply that

---

[7] We expect MNE entry and the height of barriers to be unrelated, because two opposing forces are in fact present and are likely to offset one another. On the one hand, even the MNE faces some entry barriers. On the other hand, as the least disadvantaged entrant, it is positively attracted by the excess profits that lurk behind entry barriers high enough to repel non-MNE entrants. Jarrett (1979, Chapter 3) indeed found a positive relationship between an industry's capital-cost entry barriers and foreign investment by firms in U.S. manufacturing industries.

changes in concentration should be negatively related to the rate of entry of MNEs. This prediction is not so obvious as it may seem, because the gross entry of firms into an industry can be offset by the exit of other firms; those impressed with the competitive clout of MNEs have voiced the fear (to be discussed later) that they will drive other firms from the market and raise concentration. Knickerbocker (1976, pp. 77–8) found a significant negative correlation between the number of entries into the U.S. market by non-U.S. MNEs and the change in concentration in U.S. manufacturing industries in the 1960s. The same pattern held for industries in Italy, France, West Germany, and Canada.[8] Also, some studies (Steuer et al., 1973, p. 97; Fishwick, 1981, Chapter 2) have actually found a negative relationship (significant for Fishwick) between the level of foreign investment and change in concentration for Britain. The absence of a positive relationship is comforting, but a positive relationship to the *level* (not the change) of concentration persists for some countries (see Lall, 1979, on Malaysia) even after other determinants of concentration are controlled.

Knickerbocker (1976, pp. 38–59) and Vernon (1977, pp. 73–8) showed that the total number of MNEs has increased greatly in the past half century, a growing population of both actual competitors in particular national industries and potential entrants to those industries. Knickerbocker (1976, pp. 64–74) also pointed out that the increasing extent of product-line diversification among MNEs' foreign subsidiaries implies that the potential MNE entrants into an industry are not restricted to overseas firms in that same industry. However, the industries that are low on diversifying MNE entrants are, as expected, those with high entry barriers due to product differentiation, research, or high capital costs and extensive scale economies. In short, Knickerbocker's evidence establishes that MNEs are important potential and actual entrants who tend to reduce seller concentration by their entry decisions, but barriers to entry still have some repellent force against even the best-qualified MNE.

---

[8] See Rosenbluth (1970) for the evidence on Canada. The available case studies generally lead to the same conclusion. See Dunning (1974*b*) on various British industries.

The method of the MNE's entry (green-field entry or the acquisition of an existing national firm) poses an important qualification to these findings about entry and concentration. By definition, green-field entry adds another seller to the market in question, whereas acquisition initially leaves concentration unchanged. Entry by acquisition can have a pro-competitive significance if the MNE picks up and revives a failing business or uses its nonproduction assets to make the acquired company more effective (see Chapter 3). Still, the competitive significance of green-field entries should be greater. We do know that acquisition has become an increasingly popular method of entry into foreign markets (Dubin, 1976, Chapter 2). However, some factors affecting the method of entry lend a bit of comfort regarding the MNE's role as a spoiler of high concentration. Green-field entry is more common when the industry the MNE enters abroad is the same industry in which it is based at home (whereupon it should, in any case, be a more effective competitor). Weak evidence, at least, suggests that green-field entry is more common into concentrated industries and into industries where plant-level scale economies are higher and production is more capital-intensive (Dubin, 1976, Chapters 6–8). And entry occurs more often by acquisition when MNEs are hastening to match their oligopolistic rivals' foreign investments (Dubin, 1976, Chapter 10–12): Rates of entry through acquisition rose during the episodes of bunched entry into foreign investment that Knickerbocker (1973) uncovered. Thus, the recognition that MNEs sometimes enter via merger does not qualify out of existence the concentration-reducing effect of MNE entry.

Overall, we have reached the following conclusions: The substantial overlap between the sources of entry barriers and the sources of foreign investment implies that the two should be highly correlated across industrial markets, as indeed they are. These correlations do not themselves prove that any direct causal relationships exist between foreign investment and concentration. Such direct relationships have been found, however. Rivalrous behavior in loose-knit oligopolies tends to promote foreign investment. And the occurrence of new entry by MNEs tends to reduce the level of concentration, even considering that entry now is often effected by acquiring a local firm. Thus, neither of these causal relations works simply to amplify the positive correlation between concentration and foreign investment that derives from their underlying common causes.

4.2. **Market behavior with MNEs present**

The conclusions of Section 4.1 leave us some distance to go with the relation between foreign investment and imperfect competition. The MNE's affiliate is a rival in an ongoing national market. The MNEs that compete in one national market may face each other in many markets and therefore recognize their mutual dependence more fully. If the *new* subsidiary tends to reduce seller concentration, the established subsidiary may build up entry barriers. This section is concerned with such issues of ongoing behavior: Does the presence of MNEs increase, decrease, or simply alter patterns of oligopolistic interdependence in the world market? The question is difficult to answer, not just because of a scarcity of hard empirical evidence but also because the answer depends on what alternative we have in mind. Would markets be less oligopolistic if all transnational ownership links existing among national companies were severed? The answer is almost an automatic yes, because many more companies would populate the world market than before. Would markets be less oligopolistic if no MNE had ever founded or expanded a foreign subsidiary? The answer depends on how many non-MNE companies would have arisen in the absence of competitive pressures from MNEs – no easy matter to determine. Cutting across these issues is the problem of the geographical scope of "the market" in which oligopoly elements may or may not exist. We often tend to think of the nation as the best single approximation to the geographical market – not a bad practice considering how tariffs, transportation costs, and the effects of shared legal and cultural systems make economic communication easier within nations than between them. Still, some products are clearly sold in international market, others in national markets, and still others (fresh fish) in localized markets within nations. We shall thread our way through these difficulties as best we can.

Mutual dependence among MNEs

Associations of the MNE with international oligopoly are taken for granted in left-leaning writings on the MNE (e.g., Barnet and Müller, 1974, pp. 213–14), and a substantial amount of evidence supporting this proposition can be found in historical instances of the 1900–40 period. Let us consider some of the types of collusive agreements, checks, and counterchecks that have been uncovered.

For firms based in different national markets to recognize their oligopolistic interdependence, they must have encountered each other as specific and significant market rivals. Conceivably this rivalry could be only potential: *A* sells only in Australia, *B* only in Belgium, but each appreciates that enlightened self-interest might drive the other to export or invest in his market, or license intangible assets to his local rival. In practice, however, the potential-rivalry case is surely less important than the case of rivalry that has become to some degree actual. In our example, if potential rivals *A* and *B* agree never to compete, neither becomes a MNE, and the outside observer can hardly blame the allocative consequences on the "monopolistic tendencies of multinational enterprises."[9] What we expect to find in the historical record, therefore, is evidence that oligopolistic understandings have emerged between firms that initially came into contested rivalry through foreign investment or some other international competitive move. At the extreme, markets can wind up less competitive after the peace treaty is signed than they were before the initial aggressive move. An example of this adverse development was the British tobacco market after the entry of American Tobacco in 1901. Induced by the British tariff structure, American purchased a leading British producer. That event caused 13 dismayed British rivals to merge into Imperial Tobacco. After a year of duopolistic rivalry, a peace treaty gave Imperial a monopoly of the British and Irish markets, and American got a guarantee that Imperial would not sell in the United States or its dependencies. British-American To-

---

[9] Vernon (1974*a*, pp. 276–7) argued that international cartel agreements not to compete can explain the almost complete lack in the interwar period of foreign investments by certain U.S. industries.

bacco was organized as a joint venture to handle business in the rest of the world.[10]

In most instances, however, no clear conclusion emerges about whether or not the ensuing oligopolistic rapprochement is sufficient to offset the pro-competitive thrust of the initial move. Sometimes, rivalry among foreign investors or exporters has led to agreements not to compete with foreign rivals, often cemented by licensing agreements or other devices to neutralize competition among established subsidiaries.[11] Some agreements have been forged by means of joint-venture subsidiaries or fractional shareholdings exchanged among the parent companies themselves.[12] International cartels have been worked out to mitigate competition among established MNEs during recessions.[13] In the aluminum industry, an American parent firm, aware that it could not legally collude with foreign rivals under U.S. antitrust laws, organized and employed its Canadian subsidiary to maintain such contacts.[14]

International collusive arrangements among MNEs or potential MNEs evidently prevailed at some time before 1940 in a majority of industries where MNEs were active. But the record since World War II offers no such chronicle of successful collusive arrangements. Why? We cannot rule out, of course, that the arrangements exist but have been concealed more successfully.[15] There are, however, several reasons for believing that the extent of effective international collusion has decreased markedly. During 1945–55 many U.S. MNEs were successfully prosecuted under the antitrust laws for their earlier collusive behavior, an experience they found sobering (Wil-

---

[10] Dunning (1958, pp. 30–1); Wilkins (1970, pp. 91–3). The explosives market during 1896–1914 provides a similar example (Wilkins, 1970, pp. 89–91), the metal-container industry a more recent one (Wagner, 1980). Also see Hu (1973, pp. 163–5) on the automobile industry.

[11] Wilkins (1974, pp. 79, 80, 82, 86–8, 151); Wilkins (1970, p. 87). See Dunning (1958, pp. 158–60) for more recent experience.

[12] Wilkins (1974, pp. 68, 78–9, 292–4); Franko (1976, Chapter 4).

[13] Wilkins (1974, pp. 173, 175).

[14] Wilkins (1970, pp. 87–9).

[15] Examples do still turn up. Kudrle (1975, Chapter 10) documented parallel action of the farm-equipment MNEs to price-discriminate against the North American market for farm tractors. Also see Newfarmer (1980, Chapter 4).

kins, 1974, Chapter 12). Other countries passed antitrust laws after World War II, and if these varied in toughness and degree of enforcement, they were still tougher than nothing at all. Partly in response to these legal changes, partly seizing the opportunity opened by the wartime destruction of their European competitors, U.S. MNEs shifted from cooperative behavior to aggressive behavior during 1955–65 and rapidly expanded the number of standardized product lines (i.e., not intensive in R&D) produced in Europe; by contrast, the growth rate of these lines produced in Europe during the next decade (1965–75) was no more rapid than in the rest of the world.[16] With the successful recovery of Europe and Japan, there are simply far more "significant" companies (actual and potential MNEs) worldwide in most industries than there were 50 years ago, and levels of seller concentration measured at the *world* level probably have declined in many of the more concentrated industries (Vernon, 1977, p. 81). Finally, the mix of important industries probably has shifted from those producing homogeneous primary materials (wherein collusion is always a strong temptation to the producers) toward those producing differentiated or heterogeneous goods (in which the differentiation supplies natural insulation to the individual seller at the same time that it greatly complicates the maintenance of collusion).[17]

Whichever explanation is correct, the recent evidence suggests not so much successful collusion among MNEs as the sort of imitative rivalry that Knickerbocker (1973) associated with loose-knit oligopoly among American multinationals. This behavior results in the formation of subsidiaries to preempt a rival or to punish one for an aggressive move undertaken elsewhere. Although examples of such behavior go back many years,[18] it has been systematically documented only by Graham (1978) for the years 1950–70. He hypoth-

---

[16] Vernon (1977, pp. 63–5); data from Harvard Multinational Enterprise Project.

[17] Evidence from the United States and the United Kingdom rather strongly associates price fixing and market-division agreements among domestic producers with the traits of product homogeneity. See Hay and Kelley (1974) and Swann et al. (1974, Chapter 4), as well as Vernon (1974*b*).

[18] Wilkins (1970, pp. 89–90); Wilkins (1974, pp. 78, 83); Franko (1976, Chapter 4). Arthur D. Little (1976, p. 103) discussed some other reasons for this type of behavior.

esized that a large company in MNE-prone industries, finding its domestic market invaded by a new subsidiary of a foreign MNE, is likely to retaliate by invading the foreigner's home turf. The affronted firm is likely to have the assets necessary to make a go of the subsidiary, including an incentive to shift its investment from its newly more competitive home market to *some* market abroad. And a subsidiary on the invader's turf establishes both a means of retaliation and a hostage that can be staked out in any subsequent understanding between the two parents. In a group of manufacturing industries, Graham determined the dates when European MNEs established subsidiaries in the United States and tested whether or not they were bunched in ways that significantly suggested a response to a previous bunching of American investments in Europe. He found such associations for a number of industries, and the lagged response seemed to be more clearly evident in those industries with higher levels of seller concentration, high R&D outlays, and extensive product differentiation.

Franko (1976, Chapter 6) reached conclusions similar to Graham's in his attempt to explain the rapid proliferation of subsidiaries of European MNEs in other European countries after World War II.[19] This was a period when tariffs were being eliminated within the European Community, a move that by itself should have promoted the concentration of production at the most efficient sites. However, it was also a time when the "negotiated environment" of soft competition under complaisant government supervision was giving way to more aggressive rivalry among European firms – both those based in the same and in different national markets. Of course, some of these proliferating subsidiaries may have served as hostages to the parent's cooperative behavior, vulnerable to a crushing counter-strike if the parent should commit an aggressive move.[20]

Another issue in the interdependence of MNEs should be mentioned, although it is a nonissue now largely laid to rest. In the 1960s

---

[19] Also see Tsurumi (1976, pp. 64–7, 121–3) on the experience of Japanese MNEs.

[20] Franko (1976, pp. 149–50) reported circumstantial evidence that a network of joint ventures in the plastics industry serves to give hostages against price cutting.

the fate of (actual or would-be) European MNEs often was be-
moaned because, however successful in their home markets, they
were much smaller than the leading U.S. companies and so could
not compete with them in the international market. By the late 1970s
the shoe had shifted to the other foot, but the analytical issue remains. Research indicates that in domestic industries one usually
finds a range of large and small firms in competition with one another. Furthermore, this size distribution typically is quite stable
over time, which suggests that no size class has an insuperable advantage over its rivals. Although theoretical models can be devised
in which it pays a larger company to invest in the predatory destruction of a smaller competitor, the necessary conditions are stringent
enough to make the event fairly unlikely even before we count in the
resistance of public policy. Therefore, neither theoretical nor empirical evidence indicates that foreign MNEs will desist from vigorous
competition with their U.S. rivals for fear of being devoured whole.
Rowthorn's (1971) statistical analysis of the growth of large U.S.
and non-U.S. companies indicated that the larger of the giants had
definitely not been growing faster; if anything, the small were catch-
ing up with the large. Also, when firms' growth rates were related
to their national origins, he found that the faster-growing companies
were those based in the faster-growing national economies, a role
that the United States had ceded to Japan and several European nations.[21]

MNEs and other market rivals

The concept of *strategic groups* helps us to understand the
competitive role of MNEs and their subsidiaries. Active rivals in a
market, the concept suggests, may not be identical as peas. They
may differ in their participation in other markets: Some are vertically
integrated or diversified, others not. They may differ in how they
compete in the market at hand: Some produce a full product line,
whereas others specialize; some advertise heavily, whereas others do
not. Research on industrial organization has shown that, other things

---

[21] Also see Franko (1976, Chapter 1) and Buckley et al. (1978).

being equal, the more complex an industry's strategic-group structure, the more competitive is the market (Newman, 1978). This is because strategically similar firms readily recognize their interdependence with one another, pursue similar proximate goals, and react alike to disturbances. Members of different groups lack these natural harmonies.

The strategic-group concept immediately suggests the hypothesis that MNEs may take part in different strategic groups than their national competitors, or that MNEs domiciled in one source country may constitute one strategic group, whereas those from another parent country constitute a different group.[22] At least a few industry studies seem to confirm this hypothesis. Sciberras (1977), for example, divided the U.K. semiconductor industry into two groups that are largely congruent with MNEs and national firms. And statistical evidence has supported the hypothesis in several ways. Studies of both Canadian and Spanish manufacturing industries have found that the structural forces determining the profitability of national enterprises and MNEs' subsidiaries are quite different, the latter being much less fully explained by conditions in the local market.[23] The same two countries have also supplied evidence that the profits of domestic companies are lower the larger is the MNE group with which they compete.[24]

A good deal of anecdotal evidence supports this systematic evidence on MNEs' distinctiveness as competitors. A MNE new to a national market likely proves a disturbing competitive force. Any entrant is likely to disturb an imperfectly competitive industry, but the MNE, lacking familiarity with local folkways, is less likely to fall in with any prevailing pattern of cooperative, mutually dependent behavior, a prediction documented by the loud complaints of its national rivals (Behrman, 1970, pp. 43–52, has provided examples). On the other hand, as the subsidiary ages and "goes native," its competitive manners improve as its market conduct be-

---

[22] These possibilities are discussed in more detail elsewhere (Caves, 1974c).

[23] Caves et al. (1980, Chapter 9); Donsimoni and Leoz-Arguelles (1980).

[24] Caves (1974a); Donsimoni and Leoz-Arguelles (1980).

comes less distinguishable from that of domestically controlled enterprises.

The particular evidence on MNEs and oligopoly interdependence, stressed in this section, should not obscure a larger and more general point about MNEs and competitive processes. As Vernon (1974*b*, 1977, Chapters 3–5) has argued extensively, the ways in which MNEs behave in the market are of a piece with the forces that make these companies multinational in the first place. Those oriented toward research and technology tend to compete heavily in innovation. Even with the shrinkage of the U.S. lead in research, European-based MNEs still have felt pressed to match the absolute sizes of the research outlays that U.S.-based MNEs can manage. Vertically integrated MNEs selling relatively homogeneous products often enjoy some protection from scale-economy entry barriers, but their relatively undifferentiated products and high fixed costs interest them strongly in defensive arrangements to avert the risks of competition. MNEs stranded in industries where they no longer enjoy any special advantages have tended to decline in importance relative to national companies or to hang on only by plying accumulated skills and experience that are not a serious barrier to new entrants.

Market performance

Our concern for the effective performance of markets motivates our curiosity about the competitive effects of MNEs, and some statistical evidence bears on market performance. Hypotheses about market power ("monopoly") as an influence on the performance of domestic industrial markets usually are tested by examining the influences determining industries' profitabilities. Several studies of the profitabilities of MNEs have been conceived and executed along these same lines; their results hold considerable interest, but their interpretation demands a good deal of care. Connor (1977, Chapter 5) based his study on subsidiaries of U.S.-based MNEs operating in Brazilian and Mexican manufacturing industries. Their profits, he hypothesized, depend on how concentrated are their industries (concentration measured over all the sellers), how high is a subsidiary's own market share, how extensive are its local investments and intangible assets (advertising, R&D), and assorted other variables. The variables listed resemble those used in conventional investigations of domestic industries' profits – measures of market dominance and entry barriers. Connor's findings are statistically erratic and differ somewhat between Mexico and Brazil, but they do yield a few generalizations. For Brazil, at least, a subsidiary's profits increase with its own market share and with the concentration of sellers (foreign subsidiaries and domestic companies) with which it competes. The latter relationship is conventional and has been reported for overall industry profits in many other studies. The former relationship (the influence of the subsidiary's own share) is the one requiring subtle interpretation. A firm that possesses a particularly valuable patent or intangible asset, a particularly adroit marketing skill, or some other asset clearly superior to those of its rivals is apt to gain a larger market share than its rivals and to earn rents on the asset that turn up in its accounting profits. This relationship is part and parcel with one we noticed in Chapter 2: The larger firms in an industry are more likely to be multinational. The lion's-share profit of a dominant firm can also flow from its lordship over the oligopoly bargain. However, Connor did not perform the statistical test needed to distinguish between the "rent" and "market-power" interpretations.[25] A few of Connor's other results deserve comment. He did not find a relationship between a subsidiary's profits and its own advertising or R&D – not unnaturally, because much of its dowry of intangible assets surely comes from its parent and not from its own outlays. He found no relation between the subsidiary's profit rate and its parent's total size (worldwide assets), whereas a positive relation may exist if MNE parents dip into their war chests to "buy" their subsidiaries market positions that are insulated from competition.

Another study of profits and foreign investments has been provided by Bergsten et al. (1978, Chapter 7), who were concerned with the effects of foreign investments by U.S. companies on the

---

[25] The problem of disentangling industrywide monopoly rents from firm-specific rents to differential luck or ability was considered by Gale (1972). Gale's test was to determine if the relationship of the firm's profit to its own market share was stronger in concentrated industries than in unconcentrated industries.

profitabilities of their domestic operations. These investors presumably expect that any resources placed abroad will *at the margin* earn as much as if they were placed in the United States. The *average* profitability of these companies may nonetheless be augmented through their foreign investments, in three ways quite different in their normative implications. First, intangible assets discovered or developed in the firm's initial domestic success may yield rents when used abroad. The fixed costs of these assets, spread over more business, yield higher profits.[26] This gain runs into no obvious normative objection. Second, the MNE's diversification allows it to undertake riskier activities than firms with fewer options for pooling their risks, and therefore earn higher average worldwide profits than national firms, because riskier activities, on average, command a higher profit rate. Of course, with *enough* MNEs around, these rents will be competed away. Third, and less desirable, assets picked up in its overseas activities may allow the American MNE to blockade entry, intimidate rivals, or otherwise make the American market less competitive than otherwise.[27] Bergsten et al. found that the domestic profits of U.S. industries increase significantly with the extent of their overseas activities, as well as with their research and sales-promotion outlays. However, a company's absolute size (including overseas assets) is not a determinant of its profits. Bergsten et al. asserted that this statistical result points to the third link between MNE activity and profits, but in our judgment their study does not succeed in distinguishing the third from the first and second.

This discussion must conclude with the agnosticism that began the chapter. MNEs are large firms that often operate in concentrated industries. However, there is no decisive evidence that multinational status feeds back to make industries still more concentrated or less competitive. Nor is there evidence that rules out the possibility of these adverse effects.

---

[26] Severn and Laurence (1974) concluded that the profits of U.S. MNEs were augmented by their ability to amortize the cost of their research activities over worldwide markets.

[27] Their foreign fruits may make them top bananas at home, as Thomas Horst once put it. Also see Horst (1974*a*, Chapter 5).

4.3. **Competition policy and national welfare**

The MNE's competitive behavior raises issues of public policy, because transnational ownership links affect the competitiveness of markets even if the effects are not unambiguously for better or worse. Every industrial country has some form of competition policy on its statute books – enforced with some degree of vigor, and pursuing objectives that usually, but not always, are pro-competitive. Welfare economics affirms that competition policy can help to avert some market failures. The details are complex, and dilemmas definitely arise in which more competitive markets bring society closer to one normative goal while taking it further from another. Nonetheless, the case for the normative superiority of competitive versus noncompetitive markets is broad enough that we assume more competitive markets to be desirable for purposes of the following discussion.

In competition policy we encounter for the first time, but not the last time, the dilemma of national objectives in policy toward the MNE. Welfare economics usually assumes that the proper and expected goal of national economic policy is to maximize the national income – expected because the government is elected by those who receive the national income, proper because a maximized income can *potentially* be distributed so as to make everyone better off. If each nation acts to maximize its own national income, however, that does not mean world income is maximized, because many policies can potentially raise one country's income while lowering that of another. Such redistributions naturally require some transmission belt that links market conditions in the two countries, and we shall see that the MNE can provide that transmission belt in many circumstances. National welfare maximization is thus a basis for conflict among nations, because a redistribution toward *A* is, of course, an exaction from *B*. Furthermore, the policies that will maximize national incomes taken separately are not identical with those that will maximize world income.

In competition policy, the form of that dilemma is quite clear. Within the national economy, optimal competition policy calls for competitive markets. Maximizing national income in international transactions, however, demands that the nation's citizens extract the maximum monopoly rents from foreigners – that is, charge the monopolist's profit-maximizing price on everything they sell and pay only the monopsonist's profit-maximizing price for anything they buy. The MNEs, along with the exporters and importers, are citizens whose activities invite interference in pursuit of these objectives. Of course, just as each nation rationally seeks to gain monopolistic advantage over others, it also faces the problem of repelling their efforts to wrest the same types of rents from its own citizens. MNEs, especially because legally their incorporated subsidiaries are citizens of their countries of residence, are inevitably caught in the conflict. We shall now sketch a few theoretical points concerning competition policy with MNEs present, then briefly explore the encounters that have taken place between MNEs and U.S. antitrust policy.

MNEs and the theory of competition policy

The normative criteria that welfare economics provides for competition policy in the open economy are a simple translation of those it provides for tariff policy. Domestic markets should be competitive, with the social marginal value (generally equal to market price) in each market set equal to social marginal cost. On foreign sales, however, the social marginal cost should be equated to the nation's marginal revenue. On purchases from foreigners, social marginal value should be equated to the extra revenue expended on the last unit bought. In the context of tariff policy, and with all markets assumed to be competitive, these prescriptions call for a series of taxes on imports and exports calculated so as to exploit any monopoly or monopsony power that the nation possesses. An alternative, equivalent under some circumstances, is simply to allow and encourage the nation's international sellers and buyers to do the monopolizing themselves. The only general difference between the two policies is that the revenues gained turn up in the public treasury in one instance and in private hands in the other. This prescription of monopoly/monopsony applies to MNEs as well. If the nation possesses MNEs that produce and sell abroad, they should be encouraged not to compete with one another if their outputs are distinctive and lack perfect substitutes abroad. Similarly, national MNEs acquiring goods abroad for domestic sale should be discouraged from competing as buyers.

The plot thickens if the rival firms that invest and sell (or buy) abroad also do business in the domestic market. Conceivably the government can allow them to behave as monopolists abroad but sternly admonish them to behave competitively at home. Indeed, most countries attempt just this strategy with their exporters by allowing them to collude on their foreign transactions in ways that would be illegal if done in the home market (Organization for Economic Cooperation and Development, 1974). As a matter of market behavior, however, this solution has its problems: How can rival firms huddle to collude on the foreign price while competing vigorously to set the domestic price? Auquier and Caves (1979) showed what compromise competition policy should choose if it must accept the same degree of monopoly[28] in international and domestic transactions. The more international an industry's business, the higher the degree of monopoly that should be allowed by competition policy. Indeed, under some assumptions, the degree of monopoly should be set equal to the fraction of sales made abroad. These conclusions were developed for exporting industries, but the logic extends directly to imports and to multinational companies making either sales or purchases abroad.

The nation that buys goods from a foreign monopolist, whether MNE or not, can wield policies to improve its national welfare. If the monopolist profitably supplies the country's market through imports, imposing a tariff can improve the home country's welfare. The welfare gain does not depend on the monopolist producing under increasing cost, as it does when the foreign industry is competitive. Even if the monopolist produces abroad under constant average and marginal cost, the tariff reduces his profit-maximizing price net of the tariff and thus increases welfare by saving the country part of the

---

[28] The monopolist marks up his price above his marginal cost to a degree determined by the elasticity of the demand he faces. The "degree of monopoly" is defined as a fraction of this markup.

excess-profit component of its cost of imports (Corden, 1967; Katrak, 1977). But that optimal tariff may induce the monopolist to switch over to serving the home market through a local subsidiary. Svedberg (1977, Chapter 3, 1979) showed that this switch can leave the home country better off because it can then tax the subsidiary's profits. But the home welfare level associated with a taxed subsidiary can fall short of that attained when a tariff captures part of the monopolist's profits from selling imports. If so, the home country should ban the foreign investment.

Competition policy as well as tariffs may help to deal with monopolistic foreign sellers – a role that becomes analytically interesting if we assume that industries are neither purely monopolistic nor purely competitive and that their populations of firms in general include both nationals and foreign-controlled firms. Poor market performance in this setting of oligopoly stems from collusive or parallel conduct among the incumbent firms. Competition-policy authorities coming to the rescue neither can nor should distinguish between native and foreign firms. Any monopoly that oligopolists possess is a shared private (but not social) asset. This market power cannot be seized from the foreigners without relieving the natives of it as well. Of course, if the competition-policy budget precludes fixing all offending market situations, those perpetrated by foreign subsidiaries get first priority. These monopolistic distortions cost the country a transfer of real income from domestic buyers to foreign profit recipients as well as a deadweight loss. Nonetheless, eliminating monopolies due to foreign firms has only a priority over attacking those enjoyed by domestic sellers. Ultimately, both should go.

This analysis of the MNE and competition policy changes somewhat if the social loss from monopoly consists wholly or partly of productive inefficiency. The monopolist (or collusive group) may take its gains partly in profits garnered by raising prices above costs, partly in the joys of sloth that results in costs elevated above the minimum attainable. When costs have been inflated, making production inefficient, the top priority for competition-policy authorities shifts from foreign-controlled monopolists to domestic monopolists. That is because part of the real cost of foreign-controlled monopoly comes from the pockets of foreign shareholders, whereas the domestic monopolist is squandering domestic real income.[29]

Suppose that competition-policy authorities eschew these nationalistic policies and turn a blind eye to the parentage of firms in the national market. MNEs still raise problems for optimal competition policy. One national MNE acquires a company selling the same product line in another country. If the two nations' officials detect monopolistic tendencies by watching the concentration of domestic *producers*, the usual practice, neither authority sees anything amiss. That is because producer concentration remains unchanged (at least initially). But the merger leaves one less independent firm in the world market, and so international *seller* concentration has necessarily increased. And higher seller concentration results in one or both of the countries if either of the now-combined firms formerly exported to the other nation. The world's interest in competitive markets is therefore not automatically tended by national authorities, even if they forswear taking monopolistic advantage of each other. Having each national competition-policy authority promote effective competition among whatever firms operate in its own national market is a good policy. But it does not attain the maximum of effective competition. International coordination of competition policy is generally necessary for best results.[30]

U.S. antitrust policy

A thorough survey of national competition policy toward MNEs is beyond the scope of this volume, but a brief sketch will illustrate the relationship between theory and policy.[31] Perhaps be-

---

[29] See Caves et al. (1980, Chapter 14). As we shall see in Chapter 8, the nation's corporation income tax also affects these welfare distributions.

[30] Suppose that multinational firms based in countries A and B agree to form an international joint venture to monopolize C's market. C's competition-policy authority may lack any policy instruments to prevent this result, but A's and B's authorities could stop it.

[31] Brewster (1958) provided the major study of international aspects of U.S. antitrust policy; Wilkins (1974, pp. 291–300) offered a convenient summary of the major cases and some of their consequences. Organization for Economic Cooperation and Development (1977, pp. 17–34) summarizes recent cases in other countries.

cause of its large and relatively closed economy, the United States has traditionally applied antitrust policy more vigorously than the other industrial nations, whose economies are smaller and more open. United States policy has allowed domestic producers less freedom to collude when selling abroad, on the hunch that foreign-market collusion is likely to spill onto the domestic market. American antitrust policy generally has leaned toward world welfare, not just domestic interest. International mergers have come under fire several times because the foreign firm acquired by a U.S. enterprise was a significant potential (if not actual) competitor in the U.S. market. Some antitrust actions have seemed to aim only at improving world welfare, as when the probably anticompetitive effect lay partly or even wholly outside the United States. A series of cases after World War II attacked joint ventures that U.S. MNEs had formed with their overseas competitors. Some of these deals simply implemented agreements to divide markets and exclude foreign competitors from the United States, in which case domestic economic welfare was the main issue. Other joint ventures, however, had bolstered U.S. MNEs' ability to extract rents from foreign markets. The courts specifically rejected the contention that laws allowing U.S. producers to collude on export sales justified joint or collusive behavior in establishing subsidiaries overseas. In short, U.S. antitrust policy has taken appreciable chances of losing rents from foreign markets in order to promote competition in the domestic economy.

4.4. Competitive processes with vertically integrated MNEs

Our treatment of competitive processes surrounding vertically integrated MNEs will be brief, not because the subject is trivial (quite the contrary) but because the analysis quickly becomes entangled with national policy interests and governmental behavior. However important the efforts of exporting nations to seize the maximum rents from their natural resources and the efforts of importing countries to fight off these monopolistic exactions, they bear only a limited relationship to the microeconomic behavior of multinational firms. And economists' fancy line of models of the vertically integrated enterprise (see Chapter 1) unfortunately has been little tested on the competitive behavior of vertical MNEs.

Rents and the extractive MNE

Consider a competitively organized series of production processes – one extracting a nonrenewable natural resource, then selling it to the first refining or processing stage, which then passes it along to the next. With each of these stages competitively organized, the equilibrium price paid by the final buyer yields only a normal rate of return to each of the processing stages. At the initial extractive stage, however, the owners of the natural resource may collect scarcity rents over and above the costs of inputs to the extractive process. These rents result from the recognition by all market participants that the ultimate physical scarcity of the resource will cause its net price to be bid up over time. The owners therefore do not extract any unit of the resource under their control if they think that its current discounted value will be increased if it is left in the ground and extracted at a later time. This is individually rational action on their part; no collusion among resource owners is involved. In addition to these scarcity rents, some resource owners earn differential or "Ricardian" rents because their resources are of better quality, are cheaper to extract, or are more conveniently located than other deposits in use.

Now let one or more of these vertically related stages become monopolized. Under certain assumptions, one maximum lump of monopoly profits can be extracted from the whole set of vertically related processes. A monopolist operating at any stage can claim it. If a monopolistic tourniquet has been tightened at one stage, the emergence of monopoly at another stage in the chain cannot generate any larger lump of total monopoly profits. The two (or more) monopolized stages can, however, misallocate resources in a worse manner than does a monopoly at just one stage – whether the monopolists are adjacent in the production stages and bargain with each other or are at nonadjacent stages. Although the single-stage monopolist can grab the maximum profit lump at any stage, the natural-resource owners are in a peculiar position for monopolizing the resource. This is because they hold a stock of the resource, rather than dealing in a flow of output. If they raise price today and reduce demand, units of the resource must sell at a lower price in some future time period. In theory, a monopolistic owner of a fixed-stock natural resource might plan the same profile of output over time as a competitive industry. That the monopolist might choose a slower extraction rate is quite possible, but it depends on complex factors of time horizons and the shape of the demand curve (its elasticity at various prices). Clearly, though, a resource owner like the Organization of Petroleum Exporting Countries (OPEC) can wallow in short-run monopoly rents when it surprises its customers with an unexpected price rise, and their short-run elasticity of demand is lower than in the long run, when they can substitute other materials for the monopolized resource.[32]

Vertically integrated MNEs enter into this tale of vertically related markets at two points. First, they interact with the ultimate owners of the natural resources. In most countries, legal rights to subsurface natural resources are vested in the government rather than in owners of the land's surface, so that the "market behavior" here consists of striking bargains with national governments in the host countries. Second, vertical MNEs compete with each other in small-numbers situations. They may be rivals for rights to extract particular natural resources, a factor that should affect the bargain struck with the resource owners. And they may also affect the behavior of markets at other stages in the sequence.

LDCs, MNEs, and the division of resource rents

Vertical MNEs strike a bargain with the host government over the shares of rents attributable to natural resources, and that bargain has changed dramatically over time. Most of the story is decidedly "political economy," because the MNEs usually are citizens of the nation consuming the resource-based products rather than

---

[32] See Scherer (1980, Chapter 10) for a textbook treatment of vertical integration and Pindyck (1978) for an account of recent work on the monopolization of stock resources.

the nation in which the raw materials are located. Natural-resource rents are, of course, a component of the national income of the resource-owning country, whose government therefore naturally tries to minimize the rents captured by any foreign extractive enterprise. But the vertical MNE may also be used by its home-base government as a policy instrument to assure supplies of an "essential" material and insurance against being held up for ransom by foreign suppliers.

The story traverses much of the history of colonialism and political interference by the metropolitan countries with the independence of undeveloped areas. An issue quite central to the vast, ideologically charged debate over the nature and purpose of colonial expansion is whether or not economic objectives related to resource rents were central in the pursuit of colonies. The economic behavior of multinational companies, however, becomes an important issue only in the postcolonial years, when these companies found themselves bargaining with sovereign host governments concerned with the maximum welfare of their own citizens. Surveys of this experience (Vernon, 1971, Chapter 2; Smith and Wells, 1975, Chapter 2; Bergsten et al., 1978, Chapter 5) have revealed the changing outcomes of these bargains. The changes affect both the deal struck when the MNE enters and its revision once the resource development is under way.

Deals on initial investments have changed with the growing independence and sophistication of LDC governments and, in many markets, the increased numbers of MNEs clamoring for resource projects. At one time, MNEs got long-term contracts giving them extensive rights in return for fixed and modest royalty payments. The royalty payment is an inefficient device, however, because it raises the MNE's marginal cost and restricts output. Royalties gave way (roughly in the 1950s) to taxation arrangements for sharing the rents, which removed that problem and also shifted some risk to the host government (Sebenius, 1980, pp. 195–215, has provided a theoretical analysis). The hosts also sharply raised their shares of the rents, often taking their gains partly in the form of policy commitments to development objectives (local processing of materials, training nationals, etc.). Host governments increasingly demand an equity share in the project, which is really no different from taxing the MNE's profits and may actually leave the host government with less of the rents (Smith and Wells, 1975, Chapter 2; Garnaut and Clunies Ross, 1975; Gillis et al., 1980).

Another change has occurred in the relationship between the original deal struck by MNE and government and the terms subsequently imposed. When the first investment to develop an LDC's resources is contemplated, great uncertainty surrounds the future economic returns to the investment. Heavy fixed costs, themselves uncertain, must be incurred by the MNE at the start – not only to develop the extractive plant itself but also to build the transportation facilities and other infrastructure needed if the project lies in a remote location. Because the investment is uncertain and irreversible, the MNE holds out for a high expected rate of return before making a commitment. The LDC host government at the outset may lack information on the project's probable returns and may be eager for projects that will create jobs and tax revenues. Therefore, the terms of the initial agreement by which the foreign firm enters the country may allow the MNE to appropriate an appreciable share of the natural-resource rents.

If the project equals or exceeds the MNE's expectations, the MNE earns economic profits, and the host country loses income to the claimants to the MNE's profit stream. In that event, the host nation is likely to grow dissatisfied with its terms. Kindleberger (1969) observed that the public is particularly sensitive to seeing a foreigner carry off the wealth of the soil: "There is a little bit of the peasant in all of us." Even if the government that signed the original agreement stands by it, the process of political competition (whether electoral or revolutionary) brings onto the scene government officials who demand renegotiation of an agreement seen to yield "excessive" profits to the foreigner. In the 1950s and 1960s this pressure usually led to the expropriation of the subsidiary by the host government, with the MNE paid off at negotiated terms. The payoff often was at book value, which would let the MNE recoup its investment but not capitalize the stream of rents that it has been enjoying. Surveys have indicated that extractive MNEs were far more concerned about the hazard of expropriation than were other MNEs (Barlow and Wender, 1955, p. 128). And Williams's data (1975) (also see Truitt, 1974, and Sigmund, 1980) on the extent of nationalization of foreign investments by LDCs showed the heaviest incidences in agriculture and mining and smelting, along with public utilities.

As host-country governments gained sophistication, they came to realize that nationalization did not necessarily maximize host-country benefits from MNEs' extractive projects. Expropriation, a highly aggressive action, may provoke the victimized MNE to bring its own government to its aid. Perhaps the host government cannot run the operation as effectively as did the MNE, so that the rent stream shrivels appreciably. And the expropriating government may need the downstream refining and marketing arms of the MNE to process and distribute the output of the nationalized plant.[33] Taxation is a less obtrusive and possibly more effective method for the host government to seize the rents. Therefore, the conflicts with MNEs have shifted from expropriation to the "obsolescing bargain." The MNE enters under agreed terms for the tax and royalty payments it makes to the host government. If the project yields excess profits, the government simply demands higher payments in some form. The host government, extending its palm, must consider whether the investment project is complete or whether more investment funds are to come from the MNE. The company commits no more funds if encroachments on its cash flow leave less than a normal rate of return. However, if the project is built, the host government need allow the MNE only the minimum cash flow to cover its variable costs. The

---

[33] Williams's (1975) data provide some evidence on this point in the differences among sectors in the extent to which the expropriated companies were compensated for the book value of their investments. Presumably a government that has undertaken to nationalize will compensate the victim only to the extent necessary to maintain some goodwill. The strongest case for compensation comes when the government expects that it will indeed need to maintain future transactions with the victim. Therefore, the highest proportion of nationalized assets compensated should be in the vertically integrated sectors. Indeed, Williams (1975, Table 6) found the highest proportions in oil production and refining and in mining and smelting; however, the proportion in agriculture was very low.

host country then appropriates not just any rents obtained by the MNE but its quasi rents as well – the "normal" profit and depreciation flows from its investment in facilities. Clearly, the host country can gain more by taxation than by expropriation, at least if nationalization is compensated at book value.[34]

The obsolescing bargain as described is a process of bilateral monopoly between the company as "buyer" of a natural resource and the government as owner or agent for citizens holding title to it. Obsolescence is unrelated to competitive processes and depends only on the individual firm's sunk costs.[35] In the aluminum industry, the aggressiveness of various host countries with bauxite deposits has varied with the rents and quasi rents potentially available to them. Countries located short distances from the major consuming countries have levied higher charges than those some distance away, to collect Ricardian rents due to lower costs of transport to consuming countries. Also, countries with recently developed deposits, where the MNE may be willing to consider additional investments, do exercise more restraint (Mikesell, 1975).

McKern (1976, pp. 189–93) attempted a comparative analysis of the bargaining outcomes in Australian extractive sectors by calculating approximate ratios of their rates of return to foreign-supplied and domestic capital. The calculation did not impute a rent to the resource itself. He found Australia's profit share lower in sectors that are highly technology-intensive at their downstream processing stages, so that barriers to entry protect the foreign investor from competing bidders. Australia's share increased with the size (relative to world reserves) and quality of the Australian resources, confirming the nation's ultimate access to the rents.

A corollary of the obsolescing bargain is that MNE investments should shift away from the developing countries. Radetzki (1980) suggested that the share of foreign direct investment in the minerals

---

[34] These taxation practices will be considered further in Chapter 8.

[35] Of course, if the MNE had few rivals when it negotiated its initial contract with the host government, it presumably won more surplus that could "obsolesce" once its fixed capital had been given over as hostage; Diaz Alejandro (1979) has surveyed some of the evidence. The effect of MNE competition on the initial bargain will be discussed later.

sector allocated to LDCs did indeed drop substantially by 1966, although it has been fairly stable since then. This decline occurred just as the industrial countries' mineral outputs were faltering because of exhausted deposits and environmental controls, which should have pushed activity toward the LDCs. Yet the LDCs' apparent share of mineral production has continued to rise. Clearly, other organizational forms have replaced the MNE in these sectors.

Rivalry among vertical MNEs

How does the prevalence of vertically integrated firms (MNEs) affect competition in an industry? Economic theory gives no short, clean answers. Nor is any systematic cross-sectional evidence at hand. But the descriptive literature on individual sectors is rich, and so we shall analyze some strategic features and events in the petroleum and aluminum industries.

The market dominance of the Seven Sisters (the largest vertically integrated petroleum refiners) has become a matter of folklore, and, indeed, that was an accurate description of the industry between World War I and World War II. These companies varied in terms of rates and patterns of expansion into the international industry, and one can observe repeated strategic moves by each company designed to keep its capacity at the crude and refining stages in balance (Wilkins, 1974). It is clear that the companies believed their positions highly risky and sought to limit that risk by maintaining an administratively controlled series of production stages reaching from crude extraction to retail distribution.[36] But the profit earned by these vertically integrated networks was highly vulnerable to competition because of the large specialized investments and high fixed costs. These conditions fostered a strong demand for collusion and stability among the companies that was amply met by agreements to stabilize shares of markets and limit rivalry for crude supplies.

One particular focus of cooperative efforts was joint ventures, notably the large-scale joint ventures in crude production in the Middle

---

[36] The reasons for vertical integration in petroleum have been discussed by Penrose (1968, pp. 46–50, 253–9), Greening (1976), and Teece (1976), among others.

East countries. These ventures had many positive aspects. They allowed the companies to spread risks by giving each participant access to crude oil from a number of fields around the world, and they permitted effective use of specialized assets and capacities that could not have been utilized effectively otherwise (Wilkins, 1974, pp. 211–18). But they also helped the companies to coordinate output decisions for that portion of their crude output entering into international trade. Adelman (1972, pp. 82–9) pointed out that a joint venture may have no significance for its partners' coordination of their total outputs if the venture simply supplies its owners whatever quantities they desire at long-run marginal cost. On the other hand, if they take fixed shares of output and the joint venture is an important component of their total crude supplies, then the process of planning the joint venture's output becomes necessarily a vehicle for communicating total output plans between the partners. Adelman argued that most of the important crude-producing joint ventures fell into the latter category.[37]

A vitally important development after World War II was the entry of new firms into the multinational oil industry and the decline in seller concentration. Four-firm concentration in the production of crude for shipment into the world market fell from 82.6 percent in 1950 to 55.8 percent in 1969, and the shares of the largest firms became more nearly equal (Adelman, 1972, p. 81). Although the industry is still concentrated, the process of entry of new firms – usually single-nation companies from the United States or new "national champions" from Europe – had a profound effect on the terms of bargaining for concessions with the oil-producing countries. The triumphant monopolization of the industry by OPEC was clearly started on its course by the success of certain countries in wringing better terms from crude-short companies newly entering into the international market, and with nothing to lose from any renegotiation of contracts signed in the past. OPEC's first major across-the-board

[37] Adelman (1972, pp. 94–7) (also see Greening, 1976, Chapter 2) also stressed the role of forward integration into distribution in stabilizing market shares and maintaining points of contact among the majors for evaluating each others' plans. Litvak and Maule (1977) discussed this pattern in another industry.

increase in 1973 can clearly be traced to the effects of competition for concessions in certain North African countries in the 1960s (Vernon, 1976*a*, pp. 159–78). Even before that, the majors had been willing to go along with tax increases by the producing countries because these taxes were calculated in a way that made them a deterrent to price cutting by the companies in their sales of petroleum (Penrose, 1968, pp. 200–10).

The characteristics of the international aluminum industry rather closely match those of the petroleum industry. There has been a slight downward trend in the extent of vertical integration of the leading companies over 1955–77, but newcomers still proceed toward full vertical integration as expeditiously as possible. Stuckey (1981, Chapter 2) voiced some surprise at this trend because the industry's total output has grown faster than the efficient scale of facilities in refining, so that one might expect less integration as well as more competition in the emerging structure. However, he found that many factors preserve vertical integration. In the bauxite-alumina-aluminum sequence, alumina refining is specialized to the raw-material inputs used, and this and transport costs create tight vertical links between pairs of alumina and bauxite facilities. Such factors fragment the potential worldwide market into a series of long-term bilateral market relationships for which the participants have only imperfect alternatives. As with petroleum, facilities are long-lived and specific and entail high fixed costs. The pursuit of integration has also appeared in the aluminum fabricating industry in the United States during recent years, where primary producers lacking fabricating capacity have acquired many independent fabricators, and certain important fabricators have integrated backward into primary production.[38]

International joint ventures in aluminum have grown explosively in the last two decades, so that by 1977 they accounted for 36.2 percent of bauxite production, 44.7 percent of alumina, and 38.0

---

[38] Stuckey (1981, Chapter 5). A particularly interesting actor is Alcan, Alcoa's former Canadian affiliate, which lost its guaranteed U.S. market after its antitrust divorce from Alcoa. After the period of excess demand for aluminum ingot in the 1950s ended, Alcan scurried to acquire substantial fabricating capacity in the United States.

percent of primary aluminum. Stuckey (1981, Chapter 4) advanced a series of pertinent explanations. Joint ventures permit companies to invest in facilities such as bauxite mines where minimum efficient scales are very large relative to the additional bauxite that a single company might wish to take; a joint venture transferring its output to several parents can solve this problem. Joint ventures provide a way around imperfections in the markets for intangible assets; for example, a MNE with skills in production and technology can unite with a national company knowing all about conditions in the country where the venture is located. Finally, joint ventures can help to restrain competition. After World War II, many new entrants came into the aluminum industry, including Japanese firms and public enterprises in countries that were not traditional aluminum refiners. Not only did their entry make the industry more competitive per se, but also their "strangeness" fragmented it with a strategic-group structure, rendering mutual understandings difficult. Stuckey suggested that the established firms welcomed the newcomers into joint ventures partly to socialize them and to ease communication within the industry.[39]

4.5. Summary

Our underlying transactional model of the MNE predicts that it will generally not be found in purely competitive markets. The same features of a market's structure that explain the coming of MNEs also can give rise to barriers to the entry of new firms. Because of these common causes, we expect, and find, an appreciable correlation between industries' levels of seller concentration and the prevalence of MNEs. Correlation is not causation, however, and the question of causal relationships between MNEs and concentration is a rather intricate one. Knickerbocker (1973) showed that foreign investment in some moderately concentrated industries behaves like other forms of nonprice competition: It is inflated in oligopolies,

---

[39] By a contrary policy of freezing them out of joint ventures, the established firms might have weakened them or deterred their entry. Stuckey suggested that this strategy was not used because entry barriers were in any case no longer sufficient to keep out certain major potential entrants (large copper and oil companies).

where leading firms recognize their rivalry but imitate each other defensively rather than cooperating. As a result, an industry's foreign-investment decisions become bunched. The possible effects of MNEs on seller concentration are various, but one clearly demonstrated is the MNE's role as a favored potential entrant. When high entry barriers surround a national market, MNEs elsewhere in the world often are the least disadvantaged entrants. This pro-competitive role is weakened by MNEs' blossoming taste for entering markets by acquiring established local firms.

Of course, the rivalrous effect of the MNE as an actual or potential market entrant need not persist once the entry has occurred. Many observers have voiced concern that MNEs readily collude among themselves, or that they drive single-nation rivals to merge or retreat, and thus leave the market less competitive than before the MNEs' arrival. The evidence supports a stern indictment of the MNE for anticompetitive behavior prior to World War II. Since the war, however, the situation seems to have turned around substantially: Many more MNEs populate most industries than before, and more countries are serious about competition policy. MNEs make the strategic-group structures of markets more complex, a pro-competitive development. Statistical analyses of MNEs' profits do not effectively test their competitive behavior, because those profits include rents to the MNEs' transactional advantage as well as any monopoly profits.

MNEs pose a dilemma for competition policy insofar as national policy seeks to maximize national welfare, not that of the trading world as a whole. Maximum national welfare calls for competition in home markets but seizure of any opportunity for the nation's MNEs (and other citizens) to dip into foreign pockets for any available monopoly rents. In domestic markets there is no general case for competition-policy authorities to discriminate against foreign monopolists unless policy resources are insufficient to go around, and then only if the problem is monopoly pricing and not monopoly sloth. United States antitrust policy has, for whatever reason, been rather sensitive to international linkages and foreign national welfare in cases dealing with MNEs.

Important special issues of competitive behavior arise with vertically integrated MNEs. One concerns their competition for nonrenewable natural resources, a process that brings them into acrimonious bargaining with host-country governments naturally bent on maximizing the contributions of resource rents to their national incomes. This encounter led to heavy waves of nationalization earlier in the post-World-War-II period. More recently, taxation has provided a less obtrusive but sharper scalpel for relieving the MNEs of resource rents via the obsolescing bargain. The presence in markets like oil and aluminum of parallel vertically integrated MNEs has strongly affected competition in those markets.

5

Income distribution and labor relations

The MNE's relationship to wages and income distribution raises questions at two levels of analysis. In general equilibrium, the MNE reallocates capital between nations. That transfer may (or may not) alter the income distribution within the source and host countries. In the individual industry (partial-equilibrium analysis) the MNE affects the labor-management bargain just as it does the process of competition in the product market (Chapter 4). We shall take up these two levels of analysis in turn; the concluding section will suggest some propositions about the relationship between them.

5.1. Income distribution in general equilibrium

In the early 1970s the U.S. labor movement campaigned strenuously to restrict foreign investment by U.S. corporations, in the name of saving American jobs. Economic analysis does not buy the proposition that foreign investment permanently changes the level of unemployment, but it does affirm that short-run increases in unemployment and permanent declines in real wages can result. Neither prediction is categorical, and both depend sensitively on what we assume about the nature of direct investment and the structure of the economy. We shall start with the long-run effects on income distribution and wages, then treat employment effects as their short-run counterparts.

Theoretical models

International-trade theory contains several models that relate international factor movements to the distribution of income. They abstract from a great deal, as do all tractable general-equilibrium models, but they offer an irreplaceable starting point for the analysis. Suppose we have two countries, Home and Foreign, each with a fixed factor endowment of (homogeneous) capital and labor. Each country produces a single good, and no commodity trade takes place between them. Suppose that (initially) the real return to capital is higher abroad, inducing some domestic capital to migrate to Foreign. In Home, each worker now is assisted by less capital in the production process; the marginal product of capital therefore rises, and that of labor falls. If all markets are competitive, including markets for factors of production, the wage falls. Home's national income rises because the capital that went abroad earns more for its owners than before. The returns to all units of Home's capital rise. Factor rewards go the opposite way in Foreign; the inflow of capital bids up the real wage and erodes the return to Foreign's native capital. Thus, self-interested labor opposes the emigration of domestic capital abroad but welcomes an influx of foreign MNEs.

This theoretical conclusion persists after we allow for commodity trade, so long as each country produces but a single commodity for domestic consumption and export, or all the commodities that each produces utilize capital and labor in the same proportions at any given set of factor prices.

The analysis does change substantially, however, if each nation produces more than one good, and the production functions differ in their factor intensities (proportions of capital to labor used at any given factor-price ratio). Then we are into the rich framework of the Heckscher-Ohlin model, described in Chapter 2.[1] The structure of the nation's trade does part of the adjusting to any international fac-

---

[1] We now make the assumptions, necessary for most propositions deduced in that model, that all product and factor markets are purely competitive, that labor is completely immobile internationally, but that capital moves internationally so long as any differential exists in capital rentals.

tor movements – an important new element in the model. Suppose that Home possesses more capital per worker than does Foreign, so that Home is well suited to produce capital-intensive goods. It tends to export capital-intensive goods, therefore, and import labor-intensive commodities; unless Home's citizens' tastes lean disproportionally toward capital-intensive goods, these will be cheap in Home in the absence of trade. Now suppose once again that some Home capital migrates to Foreign, leaving Home with a lowered level of capital per worker and Foreign with more than before. This shift in their factor endowments cuts into the international comparative advantage of Home and Foreign and generally predicts a reduced level of international trade between them.[2] Within each country the change in factor endowments induces a shift of the factor stock away from the exportables industry and into import-competing activities.

But that shift itself mitigates the negative effect of capital's emigration on the wage of Home's labor. That is because in *neither* Home's exporting industry nor its import-competing industry is the decline in the capital–labor ratio as large as it is for the country as a whole. That seeming impossibility results because the transfer of factors from Home's export-competing industry releases a lot of capital, and only a little labor, relative to the proportions called for in Home's import-competing industry. The interindustry shift of factors of production thereby does part of the job of adjusting to the economy's overall lower capital–labor ratio. Because the capital–labor ratio in each sector falls less, the wage falls less than it otherwise would.

In the extreme, the adjustment of Home's output pattern and international trade could account for the system's whole response to an outflow of capital, so that wages (and returns to capital) at Home

[2] See Section 2.3. In alternative versions of this model, trade and international factors movements are complementary rather than substitutes. Purvis (1972) showed that a flow of capital from Home to Foreign can expand the trade between them if production functions differ in the two countries so that Foreign's import-competing industry has a relative productivity advantage (even though it has been "disadvantaged" by Foreign's small endowment of capital). Also see the discussion in Section 7.3.

would be unaffected by the capital outflow. This outcome is possible if Home is a small country whose exportable and import goods' prices are set competitively in a larger international market. Home's terms of trade then cannot be affected by the capital outflow. True, the outflow tends to cheapen Home labor and raise the return to Home capital, as before. But any such tendency generates profits for Home's import-competing industry (which uses relatively much labor) and makes Home's exportables industry (using more costly capital) run losses. Factors are shunted to the import-competing industry, as before. Indeed, because the terms of trade are given, this factor reallocation must go until the capital-labor proportions in all industries are back to their levels before the disturbing capital outflow. Then the old wage and capital-rental levels are consistent once more with equilibrium: Home's markets for labor and capital are cleared, and each of Home's commodity sectors earns normal profits.[3] This adjustment through the shifting of factors between industrial sectors will break down, of course, if Home's exportable industry is actually wiped out before the *ex ante* factor rewards are restored. Should that occur, Home would be back in the situation of the one-commodity model described earlier, and the direct connection between the economy's capital-labor endowment and the returns to its factors of production would again operate.

The preceding paragraph shows that real wages and capital rentals can be left quite undisturbed by exogenous international movements of capital or by other "quantity" disturbances such as shifts of demand between products. What the factor rewards in a country then depend on is the terms of trade, the price of the exported good rela-

[3] Chipman (1971) generalized this situation to the world economy. He provided conditions under which, with labor immobile but capital freely mobile internationally, the terms of trade in the world economy are unaffected by shifts in demand among products. Capital rentals are also unaffected, as is the distribution of income. The transformation curve for the world economy as a whole (transformation curves for individual countries were represented in Figures 2.2 to 2.4 in Chapter 2) must have a "flat spot" on it – meaning that various quantities of food and clothing can be obtained from the world's factor endowment at given terms of trade. However, shifts in world demand from one of these combinations to another may require the reallocation of capital between countries, as described in the text.

tive to that of the good produced in competition with imports. International factor movements or demand shifts that leave the equilibrium terms of trade unchanged also leave relative factor rewards unchanged. But if Home's terms of trade should improve, for example, the rise in the price of its capital-intensive export good is associated with a rise in the rentals to capital and a fall in the real wage. This proposition is known as the Stolper-Samuelson theorem.

An important corollary of the Heckscher-Ohlin model is that a country's tariff policy affects international capital movements (Mundell, 1957). Suppose that Foreign wishes to adopt a policy that will provide higher rentals to its domestic capitalists. Aware of the Stolper-Samuelson theorem, it imposes a tariff on imports of capital-intensive goods, raising their domestic price and therefore tending to raise capital rentals. But suppose also that capital remains indifferent as to the country in which it "works." If Foreign is a small country, its tariff and the resulting rise in capital rentals set off unlimited capital inflows from abroad, which persist so long as the local reward to capital lies above the world level. The favor that Foreign's tariff does for its capitalists' income is therefore transitory, because the capital inflows from the rest of the world continue until its return is pushed back down to the world level. Foreign winds up with a larger capital stock in residence, but no permanent change in either capital rentals or wages.

In Chapter 2 we developed a variant on the basic Heckscher-Ohlin model by assuming that capital is perfectly mobile between countries but not between industries. Then "food capital" earns the same rental everywhere in the world, as does "clothing capital," but the two rentals need not equal one another. The qualitative implications of that model for income distribution and real wages differ only in some respects from those of the simpler Heckscher-Ohlin model developed here. An outflow of either type of capital from Home will lower Home's real wage, unless factor rewards are locked in to the terms of trade in the way described earlier. Assume an exogenous rise in the price of Home's import-competing good (i.e., a deterioration in Home's terms of trade). This terms-of-trade change affects the real wage in this specific-capital model in a different way than in the basic Heckscher-Ohlin model. Capital rentals rise in Home's labor-intensive clothing sector (clothing is assumed the labor-intensive good, as in Chapter 2), and they fall in Home's export-oriented food sector. But now we cannot tell whether Home's real wage will rise or fall.[4] Somewhat in the same spirit is Hartman's (1980) model, in which MNE capital and Foreign's capital are complements in foreign-subsidiary production. Expansion of MNE capital in Foreign then raises the demand for Foreign capital and could lower Foreign wages.

Empirical evidence

The only empirical estimates of the effect of foreign investment on U.S. income and its distribution have used a simple model that makes no allowance for the important role of international trade in curbing the redistributive effects of international capital movements – the one-commodity model described earlier. Musgrave (1975, Chapter 9) simulated the consequences of repatriating to the United States the stock of direct investments that it held abroad in 1968. Her results depend on the measure of capital used and the assumption made about the elasticity of substitution between capital and labor in U.S. production (the lower it is, the more does the repatriated capital drive down capital's share and raise labor's). But the basic story is simple: Although the repatriation does not change U.S. total income much,[5] it substantially increases labor's income (and share) and lowers the income flowing to capital. A study by Thurow (1976), using a similar model, came to the same qualitative conclusion. It is unfortunate that these studies neglected the influence of international trade on income distribution, because, as we have seen, their conclusions could be greatly altered if the Heckscher-Ohlin relationship between the terms of trade and the distribution of income holds empirically (Bergsten et al., 1978, p. 104–10).

Frank and Freeman (1978, Chapter 8) rested their estimates on a somewhat more ambitious model, although their efforts were ad-

---

[4] The marginal product of Home's labor falls in terms of food but rises in terms of clothing. Whether or not labor is better off in real terms therefore depends on workers' preferences for food relative to clothing.

[5] The repatriation is actually estimated to increase the nation's total income, but that is because of taxation features discussed in Chapter 8.

dressed to taking account of saving behavior rather than international trade. In their model, Home is a single-product economy using labor and capital, but Foreign contains two sectors – one using only imported (MNE) capital, the other using only domestic capital, both employing domestic labor. Productivity may differ between Home's economy and Foreign's MNE sector: The higher is Foreign's relative productivity, the greater the incentive for Home's capital to go abroad. Similarly, MNE capital in Foreign may enjoy a capital-specific productivity advantage over domestic capital. At this stage the model yields the same conclusion as that of Musgrave and Thurow: Repatriating all of Home's exported capital will raise the real wage in Home, lowering the return to capital.[6] Home's saving rate is next made endogenous in the Frank-Freeman model. This change affects the results strongly. The chance to place capital abroad in high-productivity activities now increases Home's rate of saving. Conversely, requiring the repatriation of Home's MNE capital restricts saving in Home and cuts the capital stock, rather than providing more capital to work with Home's labor. Therefore, the action lowers Home's wages and national income. Thus, Frank and Freeman identified a second significant theoretical omission from those stimulations that confidently predict that MNEs' exports of capital lower the domestic wage: the adaptive adjustment of saving, as well as of international trade (also see Koizumi and Kopecky, 1980). The distributional consequences of foreign investment in the long run remain a strictly unsettled issue.

5.2. **Employment and wages: short run and long run**

The late 1960s and early 1970s saw extensive controversies in the United States over whether or not foreign investments by U.S. MNEs were reducing employment in America and worsening the balance of payments. These two short-run effects are related to each other as well as to the long-run analysis just set forth. Here we continue to focus the analysis on income distribution and employment, leaving the balance-of-payments question for Chapter 6.

---

[6] As in Musgrave's analysis, Home's national income actually expands when all foreign investment is repatriated, because of the effect of the corporation income tax.

Under certain assumptions, the effect of foreign investment on employment is the short-run counterpart of its ultimate effect on real wages. If foreign investment reduces Home's real wage in the long run, then in the short run Home's export of capital brings labor into excess supply – increases unemployment – at the going wage rate. Some interesting analyses, however, deal with the short run directly, rather than borrowing from the long-run context. They lack standard names in the literature, but we shall call them the *investment-substitution* and *export-substitution* questions.

1. When a unit of capital is transferred from Home to Foreign, does it really add an extra unit to Foreign's capital stock and subtract one from Home's? This is the investment-substitution question.
2. When a unit of capital has been transferred from Home to Foreign *and* changed the two countries' capital stocks unit for unit, does it actually reduce the scope for commodity trade as the Heckscher-Ohlin model predicts? This is the export-substitution question.

Both questions turn on the behavior of variables other than employment and real wages. However, they certainly do affect those variables, and so they can usefully be considered here. Although both are concerned with aggregative economic adjustments, they draw on the microeconomic analysis of the MNE built up in the preceding chapters.

Investment substitution

What makes these short-run models differ from the long-run analysis of Section 5.1 is their recognition of a direct administrative link between international capital movements and commodity-output decisions. This link, the essence of the MNE, is missing from the long-run general-equilibrium model. The long-run model is at least internally consistent, because in perfectly competitive markets the manufacturing firm plays no essential role as an owner or exporter of capital; capital exports affect firms' production decisions only by altering the prices of their factor inputs. If a competitive firm also runs a foreign subsidiary, it will see no connection between its decisions to place capital abroad and its decisions about what goods to produce at home or abroad; each decision depends solely on market prices.

The investment-substitution question arises from two properties of the firm as a microeconomic organization. First, MNEs and other firms compete directly in particular product markets. If a MNE spots an investment opportunity, it transfers a substantial sum of capital[7] and establishes a new subsidiary. This action preempts the investment opportunity for any local firms or other MNEs that have had their eyes on it, and they adjust their investment plans accordingly. Of course, in a neoclassical competitive model we expect the addition of some capital to a nation's stock to drive down capital's marginal product; the investment-substitution problem arises because large, lumpy investments may be involved, and the adversary relationship appears in particular product markets. The second property concerns the firm's ability to finance projects. The competitive model assumes that each firm can borrow (or lend) unlimited amounts of funds at "the" market rate of interest – a property preserved in sophisticated modern models of competitive capital markets. However, there are also good reasons why capital markets may be imperfect in the sense that the individual firm faces a rising marginal cost of borrowed funds; the more it borrows, the higher rate of interest it must pay. This constraint puts alternative uses of the firm's funds in competition with one another in a way not recognized in the purely competitive model. Internally generated funds (i.e., retained earnings) may be adequate to support an investment in a foreign subsidiary or an expansion of domestic capacity, but not both. If the less profitable opportunity cannot be justified at the higher interest rate demanded for funds borrowed on the capital market, another firm may grab the project.

The investment-substitution problem concerns the possibility that a dollar of capital transferred from Home to Foreign may not correspond to the change that actually occurs in the two countries' capital stocks. Hufbauer and Adler (1968), who explored the alternatives, described as *classical* the assumption that the amount of capital moved internationally corresponds to the change in each country's capital stock. The first alternative that they posed, the *reverse-clas-*

---

[7] We neglect for now the possibility that the firm borrows an appreciable proportion of its investment in the country where the project is installed.

sical assumption, rests on product-market competition between the MNE and other firms. The MNE invests one dollar in Foreign. It preempts an investment opportunity that would otherwise have been taken by a domestic firm, which now cancels its investment plans. As a result, total investment in Foreign does not increase. When our MNE invests abroad, we can imagine that it strains its investment capacity so that it must withdraw from some investment project in Home. But this abandoned project leaves an opening for some other Home firm, and as a result total investment in Home does not fall. The reverse-classical case leaves the world's capital stock unchanged, as does the classical case; unlike the classical case, it also leaves each country's capital stock unchanged.

To provide microeconomic underpinning for Hufbauer and Adler's third assumption, suppose that our MNE produces distinctive goods with no close substitutes either at home or abroad. It makes a foreign investment, but without reducing its capital expenditure in Home. No other firm in Foreign finds its market shriveled, and so no offsetting decline in expenditure occurs there. And no other Home firm perceives an investment opportunity left untended, and so Home's capital formation is not further affected. In this, the *anticlassical* case, Foreign's capital stock is expanded, but Home's remains unchanged.

These three alternative assumptions about international investments and capital stocks rest on conflicting views about the market context of foreign-investment decisions. Each is logical under some assumptions, and each can be spun into a consistent story about general-equilibrium adjustments in the economy.[8] They have quite dif-

---

[8] The chief problem concerns the behavior of saving, if saving and investment decisions are to be in equilibrium. The reverse-classical case requires that supplies of saving in each country be highly elastic in response to expected rates of return. Otherwise, when Home's MNE borrows to invest abroad *and* its rival borrows to finance the domestic investment that the MNE passes up, the rate of return in Home's capital market will be driven up, and one or another firm will be discouraged from its plans. Similarly, the depressed profit expectations in Foreign must reduce saving there, or otherwise the rate of return will fall and tempt *some* Foreign firm to make an investment. The anticlassical case requires the same assumption about an elastic supply of saving in Home, but in Foreign either the available investment opportunities (the marginal

ferent implications for employment in the short run and real wages in the long run. The reverse-classical version involves no change in nations' capital stocks, only in their ownership. Therefore, a capital transfer does not affect real wages. The classical assumption about transfers implies the real-wage effects outlined in Section 5.1. The anticlassical version entails an increase in Foreign's capital stock but no reduction in Home's; it cannot be analyzed simply, but its implications for real wages are likely to lie between those of the classical and reverse-classical cases.

Export substitution

The export-substitution question stands forth most clearly if we make the classical assumption about capital transfers: Home's capital stock falls and Foreign's rises by the amount of the transfer. What happens to Home's equilibrium level of exports?[9] What does the effect on exports in turn imply for real wages and employment? In the long-run Heckscher-Ohlin model of Section 5.1, capital transfers, on certain assumptions, substitute for exports, reducing Home's equilibrium level of international trade (exports and imports) overall. The capital transfer also lowers Home's real wage under most assumptions. However, the shriveling of trade and the reduction of real wages are not inevitably connected, and indeed a capital transfer can lower wages without affecting trade, or vice versa.

Most discussion of export substitution, however, has taken place in a more microeconomic and political context: Are American MNEs "running away" from American labor to serve their foreign markets through plants abroad rather than by exports from the United States? The Heckscher-Ohlin model shows that this emotive charge could be theoretically well grounded. However, as with the

efficiency of investment) must be quite elastic or the supply of saving must be inelastic.

[9] The qualification for "equilibrium level" puts aside a problem of short-run adjustment associated with the capital transfer itself. When Home transfers capital to Foreign, the financial consequence is an increase of total spending in Foreign and a decrease in Home. That change by itself raises Foreign's imports and reduces Home's. But the change in trade is merely transitional, and it dies away once the capital transfer ceases. This "transfer process" is discussed in Section 6.4.

investment-substitution question, the simple case ignores the MNE as an organization and the product-market setting in which it operates. One response to the runaway charge is that capital transfers from the United States are purely defensive, intended to preserve the U.S. company's stake in a market that it can no longer serve profitably via U.S. exports. This case is essentially Hufbauer and Adler's reverse-classical assumption: Somebody puts capital in place abroad to serve the foreign market and oust U.S. exports, and the only question is whether that export-displacing plant is owned by a U.S. MNE or by somebody else. This counter to the runaway charge, once again, can be made logically tight with a friendly set of assumptions. Give the U.S. exporter and potential MNE a goodwill asset resting on its past exporting and sales-promotion activities in the foreign market, but an asset that will crumble if product-market rivals increase their local capacity to supply competing goods. Impose some disturbance that shifts absolute advantage so as to favor serving the foreign market from a plant abroad. It then follows that the foreign market is lost to U.S. exports in any case, and the only question is whether or not the U.S. firm invests abroad – goes multinational – in order to defend the cash flow from its goodwill asset.

Another response to the runaway charge focuses not on whether or not exports fall without the foreign investment but rather on whether or not they rise subsequent to the foreign investment. In the extreme, exports and foreign investments may be complementary rather than substitutes – an outcome defensible from our findings in Chapter 1 about the bases for MNEs. Suppose that high costs of information about foreign markets can be greatly reduced if the MNE has a plant in the foreign market. Suppose that the plant's presence increases the firm's credibility as a reliable source of supply and reduces the cost of selling locally its full line of goods, including exports from the home base. Then the foreign investment might initially displace some of the firm's exports to a market, but ultimately these transactional factors could bring its exports to a higher equilibrium level than before the subsidiary was founded. The transactional approach to the MNE (Chapter 1) shows that this outcome is possible, and some empirical evidence on the mixture of vertical and horizontal relationships lends it some plausibility.[10] However, the fact that it is possible does not make it inevitable for the individual firm.[11] Furthermore, the ultimately complementary relationship between exports and foreign investments runs into some trouble in general equilibrium. Firm *A* may profitably lay hands on the capital required both to found a plant abroad and to expand its export capacity at home. But the country's capital stock is ultimately limited by its savers' responsiveness to higher expected rates of return. Therefore, not every firm can tread the primrose path of export complementarity without the game being spoiled by overall resource constraints. Once again, the issue joins onto the investment-substitution question: Export complementarity has a close affinity for Hufbauer and Adler's anticlassical assumption that foreign investment actually raises the capital stock abroad without reducing it at home.[12]

In summary, we have suggested that the short-run and partial-equilibrium approaches to the effects of MNEs on real wages and income distribution lead into a messy array of considerations that can be grouped around the questions of investment substitution and export substitution. These questions substantially overlap each other and lead to the adduction of a series of models that one by one sound

[10] This discussion has followed the literature in assuming that the MNE under study is horizontal, producing the same line of goods abroad as at home. Other types give different results. Forward vertical integration in the foreign investment can prove complementary with exports if the subsidiary secures inputs from its parent for further processing. On the other hand, a backward integration to secure an input from abroad can expand imports and reduce the demand for labor at home. Finally, a diversified foreign investment is unlikely to affect the investing firm's trade activities directly.

[11] Not even all transactional considerations point toward complementarity. For instance, the subsidiary goes through a learning process in its production activities such that it grows able to self-supply more and more components, rather than importing them from the parent. This import-displacing effect was noted by Safarian (1966, p. 158) and Brash (1966, p. 206).

[12] Detailed literature references are not provided on the export-substitution question because much of the discussion has been diffuse and casual, and the more cogent contributions have also been concerned with empirical evidence and therefore will be mentioned later. For critical surveys, see Bergsten et al. (1978, Chapter 3 and 4) and Frank and Freeman (1978, Chapter 2).

partial and arbitrary, but together provide some feeling for the array of possible outcomes. And they show how the transactional under-pinnings of the MNE can be related to general-equilibrium models that emphasize the constraints on the economy's overall stock of resources and its influence on resource allocation and factor rewards.

Empirical evidence

Empirical evidence relevant to these models takes several forms. One is simulated calculations that illustrate the consequences of these various models but do not help us to determine which is more nearly correct. Other approaches employ either case studies or statistical analysis to test the predictions directly.

One simulation that received much attention in the United States was prepared by the U.S. Tariff Commission under a Congressional charge. Concentrating on export substitution, it sought to determine the short-run effects of U.S. investments abroad on jobs provided by U.S. industry under various assumptions about export substitution or complementarity. The U.S. Tariff Commission (1973, pp. 651–72) concluded that all foreign investments that had occurred through 1970 had cost the United States 1.3 million jobs, on the assumption that all foreign production by MNEs (whether U.S.-based or foreign) could instead have been replaced by production at the MNE's national base – full export substitution. However, this large loss can be turned into a slight gain by shifting to the following assumption: If foreign production by U.S. MNEs were eliminated, U.S. exports would hang onto only that proportion of the displaced subsidiaries' market equal to the share that U.S. exports to that market held of all goods exported to that market. Also, an allowance was made for the increased jobs provided in the United States by investments from abroad associated with the gain that had occurred in foreign coun-tries' share of world exports. This case can be described either as limited export substitution or as a partial embrace of the reverse-classical assumption about investment substitution. Frank and Free-man (1978) attempted to get somewhat further, estimating what share of foreign markets would be lost if U.S. companies had to serve them from higher-cost domestic production facilities (1978,

Chapter 3), and they also pursued domestic job losses due to foreign investment by means of the input-output structure of the economy (1978, Chapter 5). Useful though they are, these calculations still pursue the implications of their own assumptions, rather than discriminating among the competing models.

That brings us to the case studies and statistical analyses. The case studies, in the nature of things, are of limited value because they represent small and nonrandom samples. In a collection of nine cases, Stobaugh et al. (1976) concluded that foreign investment by U.S. MNEs is not generally hostile to jobs in the United States. Some foreign investments had little to do with American exports or imports; others allowed the investing firm to avoid losing its foreign market entirely. The only foreign investments deemed to displace U.S. exports served markets that would have grown noncompetitive for U.S. exports anyhow. Critics have not been won over by Stobaugh's cases. Some of them can be read to yield different conclusions. Case studies from other sources support no clear-cut conclusions.[13]

Statistical approaches have also been rather diverse in their results, but together they do leave a fairly clear set of conclusions. They have, one way or another, sought to determine whether exports and foreign investments of the United States are substitutes for one another or complements. Several studies, such as that of the U.S. Tariff Commission (1973, pp. 334–41), noted that exports and imports undertaken by U.S. MNEs were growing faster than other U.S. trade or that U.S. domestic output and employment were growing faster in industries with more foreign investment. But neither finding really bears on the question of what would happen to exports or employment if the industries making foreign investments made fewer of them. Several cross-sectional statistical studies described in Chapter 2 concluded that tariffs raised around a national market promote an inflow of foreign investment and can be presumed to reduce imports. That result suggests that exports and foreign investments are substitutes, but it does not preclude the possibility that the for-

[13] For critical surveys, see Bergsten et al. (1978, pp. 59–65) and Frank and Freeman (1978, Chapter 2).

eign subsidiaries, having taken root, can *later* draw in enough complementary imports to offset the initial substitution.[14]

The most revealing statistical analyses are those that examine the net relationship between exports of U.S. companies and the sales of their foreign subsidiaries after controlling for as many as possible of the variables that should affect both (such as the advertising and research activities of the U.S. industry, scale economies in production, and various other factors relating to U.S. comparative advantage in international trade). Bergsten et al. (1978, pp. 73–96) concluded that investment abroad is complementary with U.S. exports up to a point: U.S. exports increase with net local sales of U.S. subsidiaries until the latter reach a certain level, but the further overseas capacity starts to displace exports.[15] This conclusion accords well with the organizational model of the MNE that has emerged in previous chapters: Foreign subsidiaries' role in promoting exports should depend on the subsidiaries' existence, but not especially on their size.

Lipsey and Weiss (1981) undertook an analysis similar to that of Bergsten et al. and reached similar conclusions about the general complementarity between U.S. exports and the net sales of overseas affiliates. But some additional findings also turned up: The complementarity relationship holds for most major commodity groups, and it holds for both developed-country markets and LDCs. The sales of U.S. subsidiaries abroad prove to be substitutes for exports to their local markets coming from industrial countries other than the United States. There is also weak evidence that the subsidiaries of foreign MNEs are hostile to the performance of U.S. exports (Glejser, 1976). The Lipsey-Weiss study thus suggests that the complementary export and subsidiary sales by U.S. MNEs are both in a com-

---

[14] Adler and Stevens (1974) tried to estimate cross-elasticities of demand between American exports and the output of foreign subsidiaries that would directly reveal complementarity or substitution by their signs, but no significant results emerged pointing in either direction.

[15] This conclusion holds both for exports of U.S. multinationals to their own foreign affiliates (where the complementary relationship is especially likely) and for the total exports of U.S. manufacturing industries, whether sold to affiliates or sold at arm's length. Also see Swedenborg (1979, Chapter 7) on Sweden and Reddaway (1968, pp. 282–97) on the United Kingdom.

petitive relationship with sales by other exporting countries and their MNEs.

Neither of these statistical inquiries into export substitution addressed the general-equilibrium problem, and thus they cannot be generalized to the overall effect of foreign investment on real wages. For example, if foreign investments and exports are complementary up to a point, that could merely mean that the U.S. capital stock is diverted toward industries that undertake foreign investments (which place it partly at home, partly abroad) and away from those uninvolved in foreign investment. Whether real wages rise or fall will then depend in part on the relative capital intensities of the two sectors, a question with no obvious empirical answer. Furthermore, we should recall that the investment-substitution issue has been left unenlightened by empirical evidence. Some macroeconomic studies (Lubitz, 1971*a*; Van Loo, 1977) have supported the classical assumption, finding that capital formation in Canada expands by at least one dollar when a dollar inflow of foreign investment is received. But the experiences of other countries have not been studied.

5.3. **Labor-management relations and collective bargaining**

Beyond its effects on overall wages and income distribution, the MNE may change the welfare of workers through its employment policies and its stance in collective bargaining. Recent research (Pugel, 1980*a*) has confirmed that trade unions capture some fraction of the monopoly rents available to employers, and thus firms' multinational status may affect the wage bargain by placing rents imputed to the MNE within the union's reach. Or the MNE may curb wage demands by means of bargaining tactics not available to single-market rivals. The MNE's influence on the labor bargain may devolve simply from its large size or the size of its plants, not its international operations. For example, recent research suggests that workers' pay and their discontent with the job both increase with the size of the plant that employs them.

Study of this subject is complicated by the diversity of objectives that trade unions may pursue and differences among countries in collective-bargaining practices. For example, in West Germany, labor possesses important statutory rights of codetermination – to be represented in decisions concerning the enterprise. American unions, although they may try to block some decisions of MNE managers, persist in the tradition of confrontational relationships between labor and management and show interest in codetermination only in special situations.

Organization of labor relations within the MNE

How far the MNE decentralizes its labor-relations activities provides useful background evidence to the analysis. The large differences between countries in terms of the legal and cultural environment of labor relations predict that MNEs will choose a substantial degree of decentralization. So do the patterns of organization typically found in MNEs, described in Chapter 3. Because labor markets are, at most, national in scope, and because the firm's labor-market decisions are largely, if not entirely, tactical and short-run decisions, most decision-making responsibility should devolve to the national subsidiary or even to the plant. The empirical evidence clearly supports this prediction. A Conference Board survey (Hershfield, 1975) of both U.S. MNEs and foreign companies operating in the United States found that subsidiary managers in nearly three-fourths of the companies could conclude formal labor agreements without seeking parental approval.[16] The independence increases with the physical and cultural distance of the subsidiary from its parent: Only the labor relations of U.S. MNEs' Canadian subsidiaries are closely integrated with those of their nearby parents. Most large British MNEs similarly stay out of actual collective bargaining by their subsidiaries (Roberts and May, 1974). The more countries in which the MNE operates, the more likely is a hands-off policy. But 63 percent of the U.K. firms occasionally advise subsidiaries on labor-relations matters and four-fifths are at least sometimes involved with subsidiaries' changes in pensions and other investment-type decisions.[17]

[16] Jedel and Kujawa (1976, pp. 32–41) reported similar conclusions for foreign subsidiaries in the United States. For a description of the decentralized system of a major U.S. MNE, see Kujawa (1975, Chapter 6).
[17] Apparently, there is not much evidence on why some companies decentralize more than do others (see Roberts, 1972). Kassalow (1978) pointed out a key trade-off at issue: the company can sustain the commu-

This evidence of decentralization need not imply that the MNE's labor relations are indistinguishable from those of a neighboring national enterprise. Rather, the pattern simply accords with the evidence that labor markets are nationally distinctive and independent of one another, so that MNEs typically see little advantage in the transnational coordination of their collective-bargaining activities. But bargainers on labor's side may nonetheless find it useful to recognize and exploit the MNE's international affiliations. Furthermore, labor relations are a "latently transnational" issue (Kujawa, 1975, Chapter 7), because they may involve investment-type commitments that significantly affect the expected future cash flow of the subsidiary and thereby trespass on the MNE's centralized financial functions.

Hypotheses about MNEs

The descriptive literature on MNEs' labor relations suggests a number of hypotheses about how a company's MNE status might affect the outcome of collective bargaining. The following are representative:

1. The successful MNE generally holds some firm-specific rent-yielding assets. The more closely does the cash flow approximate a pure rent, the more attractive a target it is for trade-union bargaining efforts. To the extent that national wage-setting processes permit bargaining at the level of the firm (rather than industrywide or economywide), employee-compensation levels should be elevated where such rents can be appropriated.

2. Multinational status may carry a variety of advantages in the bargaining process that counter the MNE's attractiveness as a target. Transfer pricing can serve to obscure the appropriable cash flow of any one subsidiary and thus frustrate the appropriation effort. The MNE enjoys bargaining ploys that national firms lack. If the MNE maintains capacity to produce the same goods in different national markets, output curtailed by a strike in one market can be replaced from another subsidiary's plant. The cash flows of corporate affiliates permit a given subsidiary greater discretion in taking a strike.

nications costs of a centralized system or the employee costs of staffing the subsidiaries with high-quality labor-relations personnel.

The MNE can credibly threaten to close down a given plant, or shelve any expansion plans there, and choose another national market for any additions to output. These ploys can be used either to forestall assaults on the MNE's rent stream or to take bargaining advantage of any inelasticity in the labor supply that it faces.

3.   Apart from the substance of the labor bargain, the MNE's presence as bargainer may wield qualitative effects on labor relations and productivity. These effects also run in various directions. The MNE's management comes equipped with an inventory of labor-relations practices that, at least initially, reflect conditions in its national base and harmonize poorly with those in the host nation. Even without foreign gaucherie, long lines of bureaucratic communication may impair the MNE's responsiveness to local labor problems (to the extent that the delegation of authority to subsidiaries is incomplete). And the universal suspicion of foreigners can afflict any of the MNE's transactions in the host economy. Counter to these disadvantages, the MNE may arbitrage successful practices and innovations from one labor market to another.

These hypotheses lead to diverse predictions about the wage levels that MNEs will pay, the harmony of their labor relations, and the plant productivity that they will attain. One can only turn to the empirical evidence to let the data sort out these diverse possibilities.

Evidence on labor relations

The available studies of MNEs' wages and working conditions have controlled for far too few extraneous influences to shed much light on these hypotheses, but they are worth a brief review.[18] United States affiliates of foreign companies pay compensation per employee 7 percent higher than that for all U.S. companies. However, nearly all the difference can be explained by differences in the industrial and regional distributions of the subsidiaries; with these controlled, no clear difference remains.[19] Outside the United States,

[18] The numerous fragmentary studies of wages have been summarized by the International Labour Organization (1976*b*).
[19] Whichard (1978) showed that the subsidiaries tend to be located in higher-wage industries but lower-wage regions than is all U.S. business. The analysis-of-variance method that he used does not drop out a pure residual imputable to foreign ownership per se.

the only systematic study of other industrial countries has been that of the U.S. Tariff Commission (1973, Chapter 7), which provides data on the wages of U.S. MNEs and national enterprises in the United States and in six other countries. The data come from diverse sources and may not be comparable. Overall, the MNEs' wages exceed those of indigenous firms in the United States and Canada, are about the same in Belgium-Luxembourg, France, and West Germany, and are a little lower in the United Kingdom. These comparisons did not control for industry mix, region, or other variables. Dunning and Morgan (1980) added controls for differences in the industry mix between MNEs and indigenous firms – a desirable step, because high technology and product differentiation as bases for foreign investment bias the MNEs' distribution toward high-wage industries. They found that control for industry mix halves the excess of MNE parents' wages in the United States but still leaves them significantly above national firms; the same holds for Canada. In the European countries, however, control for industry mix pushes the U.S. MNEs' wages significantly below those of national firms. Company size differences may explain the pattern. United States MNEs are the largest firms (and often operate the largest plants) in the United States and Canada, whereas on average they are smaller than the leading national firms in the European countries. Considerable evidence suggests that wages tend to increase with size of plant and company within national labor markets. Unfortunately, no studies have controlled for both industry mix and company (or plant) size (not to mention region), and so we do not know the size or sign of any residual difference that could be attributed to MNE status per se.[20]

Casual evidence that MNEs pay higher wages than national firms is fairly abundant for LDCs. The pattern held for Mexico in the U.S. Tariff Commission study, for example, and Reuber et al. (1973, pp. 175–6) found quite a strong effect on wages of skilled and semi-skilled labor. This difference in the setting of LDC labor markets

[20] Dunning and Morgan (1980) employed a crude test of association between the wages paid by U.S. multinationals and their profitability. A positive association would confirm the hypothesis that unions intercept some of the rents accruing to MNEs. No association was found – which may mean either there is no association or the data are inadequate.

suggests another feature that often is not controlled in comparisons between MNEs and other firms. One reason suggested why large plants and companies pay higher wages is to secure "better" workers, meaning those more congenial to accepting responsibility or direction and thus cooperating harmoniously in a large and complex organization. In LDC labor markets there is probably great variance in individual experience with the discipline of a complex organization. This would increase the differential advantageously paid by large companies, especially those with alien management, to buy improved supervision at the plant level. Taira and Standing (1973) tested this hypothesis by inquiring whether or not the wage differentials paid by MNEs are proportionally greater in LDCs where quality differentials in the worker population (as defined earlier) are greater – indicated by low literacy rates and average income per capita. The hypothesis was confirmed.

Overall, the evidence on wages paid by MNEs does not affirm any pervasive differences due strictly to their transnational status, once we take account of their industry mix, size, and so forth. Most of the case studies (comparisons made within one industry or a single country) have shown no appreciable difference (International Labour Organization, 1976*b*, pp. 4–18). Nonetheless, the organizational models of the MNE do lead us to expect some differences in other aspects of the MNEs' labor relations. One promising avenue is the incidence of labor disputes. This performance dimension has been studied particularly in the United Kingdom, where the issue is frequently to the fore. Steuer and Gennard (1971) investigated differences in the frequencies of strikes affecting foreign subsidiaries and their industrial competitors in Britain. For two years in the 1960s they found the MNEs to experience fewer strikes. The distribution of strikes by duration indicated that the MNEs in particular incur fewer of the short, unpredictable strikes that seem so costly to industrial productivity in Britain. However, Forsyth (1972, Chapter 7, 1973) examined the pattern for U.S. MNEs in Scotland over the 1960s decade and failed to confirm the overall pattern found by Steuer and Gennard. The difference may be due to different size distributions of foreign-controlled and domestic plants, or to the particular traits of a somewhat backward industrial region. Creigh and Makeham (1978) employed a statistical procedure that allowed them to control for at least two relevant variables – the labor intensity of the industry and the average size of its plants. Both should be positively related to the incidence of strikes, and in fact they are. With these variables controlled, no relationship exists between strike-proneness and foreign ownership among British manufacturing industries.

A certain amount of anecdotal evidence supports the proposition that MNEs make some innovations in labor relations as one aspect of the international arbitrage of skills and intangible assets.[21] An important example is the introduction into British labor relations of productivity bargaining – negotiations to remove work rules that drain productivity in exchange for higher wages. Gunter (1975, pp. 150–1) noted that MNEs' innovations sometimes have far-reaching effects on the organization of labor relations. In Europe, the presence of MNEs accelerates a trend toward more labor bargaining at the plant level rather than at industry and national levels. This occurs partly at the urging of MNE managers and partly because of the opportunity MNEs offer for trade unions to gain a share of higher productivity levels (alternatively, to evade the downward pull on industry-determined wages of marginal producers' ability to pay). In LDCs, the foreign subsidiaries sometimes prove more adept at dealing with trade unions than do inexperienced domestic companies (Kassalow, 1978). Another effect of the MNE is to complicate the legal arrangements for worker participation in management that prevail in a number of European countries, because the centralization in the parent of certain important decisions on finance, investment, and employment puts them outside the reach of workers' representatives in the subsidiary. Still, the overall judgment holds that MNEs have not worked any transforming effects on national systems of labor relations (Banks and Stieber, 1977, pp. 6–9, 120–34).

[21] For evidence, see Steuer and Gennard (1971), Gunter (1975), and International Labour Organization (1976*b*, especially p. 50). Foreign subsidiaries in the United States seem at least to have integrated themselves successfully into the American labor-relations system (Jedel and Kujawa, 1976, pp. 49–56).

Multinational union activity

We noticed that MNEs often enjoy rents to their specialized assets – rents that present an attractive target to trade unions or others whose bargaining power might give access to a slice. Yet there is no broad-based evidence that MNEs pay above-market wages in the industrial countries where trade unions' bargaining power is most likely to count. Unions' efforts may not have been crowned with success, but have efforts been made at all? Hostility toward the MNE has been in good supply among industrial-country trade unions. In this section we shall explore their bargaining relationship to the MNEs, emphasizing the effort to coalesce labor's bargaining power across national boundaries. The view taken of trade unions here is a narrowly economic one that assumes the exertion of monopoly power in the labor market to be one of their functions. Would labor gain from extending the bargaining process across national boundaries? If so, are transnational union coalitions an actuality or a likely prospect?

First, some analytical points. In the case of the horizontal MNE – actual or potential – a monopolistic seller of labor clearly gains from a bargaining coalition across national boundaries. If the firm can (actually or potentially) serve a given market from plants in several countries, its demand for labor is more elastic in any one country than in the whole set, and so monopolizing its labor supply internationally should yield larger rents than would monopolizing it country by country. But the gains to unions from international bargaining with MNEs should not be oversold. The monopoly power of internationally coordinated labor actually does not depend on transnational ownership links among companies. Unions that coalesce to force up widget-industry wages in both Home and Foreign will find themselves facing a less elastic derived demand for labor whatever the organization of the industry. Also, the short-run situation with established horizontal MNEs differs from that in an industry of non-MNE national producers only if the MNEs can juggle their market supply patterns in the short run but independent firms cannot work out equivalent arm's-length transactions among themselves.

Nonetheless, let us put aside these doubts and assume that MNEs do in fact increase the rents unions can expect from transnational bargaining. How likely, then, are the necessary coalitions of unions across national boundaries? The theoretical models set forth in Section 5.1 make the point that sellers of labor in different countries face the same plight as any potentially colluding sellers: Although they benefit from acting jointly, each has an incentive to cheat on the coalition and free-ride on the price increases exacted by the others. In the general-equilibrium model, capital transfers from Home to Foreign lower Home's real wage (under some conditions) and raise that in Foreign. The same proposition holds for the single industry: If Home's union demands a higher wage but Foreign's does not, the MNE shifts to Foreign and increases the demand for labor there. In short, the international solidarity of union bargaining has the same built-in tendency to self-destruct as does any collusive arrangement.

Discussions of transnational bargaining in the field of labor economics stress not this theoretical stumbling block but rather the national labor markets' differing institutions and legal systems. National unions differ in their goals. Some are concerned with the paycheck and immediate working conditions, others with broader social and political goals. Bargaining takes place at different points in the market – the individual plant or company, across a whole industry, or indeed for the whole national labor force. There is obviously little room for international cooperation in bargaining when labor's claims are targeted to an industry that contains assorted MNEs and also a roster of national firms. Labor-relations systems differ on the issues bargained over. Fringe benefits central to one country's bargaining arena may be mandated by legislation in another, and thus removed from contention. These points are merely examples, but they serve to establish the general point that differences among countries in general and specific objectives, labor-market structures, and legal frameworks are formidable deterrents to the international coordination of labor's bargaining power.[22]

---

[22] Among the many authors discussing this issue have been Kujawa (1971), Roberts (1973), Curtin (1973), Flanagan and Weber (1974), Gunter (1975), Banks and Stieber (1977, Introduction), Bergsten et al. (1978, pp. 110–18), Kujawa (1979), and Northrup and Rowan (1979, pp. 535–44). All reached essentially the same conclusion.

With the dice loaded against transnational coordination of labor's demands, how far has the process actually gone? These coordination efforts cost real resources for the unions involved. Like other rational economic actors, unions can be expected to make only modest investments in games that are unlikely to be worth the effort. That simple prediction seems well supported. American unions have been active in a general way in encouraging labor organization in other countries, but not with specific coordination in mind. They have urged their counterparts abroad to demand U.S.-level wages and working conditions in the overseas plants of U.S. MNEs, but in light of the generally higher levels of real productivity prevailing in the United States, that posture is surely intended more to deter foreign investment than to maximize labor's income internationally once the foreign investment is in place. American labor has also tried to use the machinery regulating labor-management relations to wield some influence on companies' decisions to invest abroad (Kujawa, 1973, pp. 253–8). This strategy joins with complaints over the centralization in MNEs of authority for decisions that affect jobs and the employment bargain in local labor markets. However, neutral observers have concluded that the issue in the United States is strictly the substance of the decisions, not a desire for codetermination.

What international coordination does take place adds up to much less than internationally coordinated bargaining. There may be exchanges of information designed, say, to determine the joint profitability of a MNE's various arms and the effects of a strike in one country on its operations in another. There may be gestures of sympathy in one country over a labor dispute taking place in another. There may be efforts to get a MNE's labor contracts to expire at the same time in several countries, to pave the way for parallel international wage demands. But actual successes in bringing about international collective bargaining with a single MNE seem essentially nonexistent.[23]

---

[23] For descriptions of coordination efforts in the labor movement, see Blake (1972), Roberts (1973), Curtin (1973), Kujawa (1975, Chapter 5, 1979), Weinberg (1978, especially Chapter 3), and the exhaustive investigation of Northrup and Rowan (1979).

These generalizations have been confirmed by survey evidence for the United States (Hershfield, 1975) and the United Kingdom (Roberts and May, 1974). The U.S. survey determined that 10 percent of U.S.-based MNEs had been contacted by unions on a transnational basis. These contacts had not actually led to transnational bargaining, only to union representations on transnational issues. Another 10 percent of companies knew of union efforts to undertake international coordination but had not yet been confronted with the results. Of non-U.S. MNEs contacted in the U.S. survey, somewhat larger proportions had encountered international union activity – one-fifth being contacted about transnational issues, another one-quarter aware of coordination efforts. In the survey of British MNEs, 10 percent indicated some international coordinating mechanism in place among their unions, and another 10 percent expected to face this prospect in a few years.

These surveys also provided some evidence that transnational efforts at labor coordination take place where the expected rewards are highest. Hershfield (1975, pp. 10–11) found that target companies tend to be larger and more involved internationally, which would increase the return expected of unions' investment in coordination efforts. Target companies also are much more centralized in their labor-relations policies, so that unions might find it easier to hammer out coordinated demands with some hope of their acceptance. Those areas of the industrial nations where international unionism has made some headway also match one's economic predictions. They are the United States and Canada, with similar language, culture, and productivity levels (Crispo, 1967), and the European Community, with its rapid expansion of international business (Gunter, 1975, pp. 151–7).

Despite the modest headway made in transnational union activity, the general expectation seems to be that it will increase. This prospect points to some scope for research on whether or not MNEs have in fact tended to make movements of money wages – as the outcome of the labor bargain – behave more similarly among countries. Dunning and Morgan (1980) found no evidence in a crude test, but more remains to be done.

5.4. **Summary**

The effects of MNEs on real wages and income distribution can be examined in both general equilibrium and the partial-equilibrium context of the individual industry. In the simplest version of general equilibrium, capital export by MNEs reduces the real wage, and capital import increases it. In the Heckscher-Ohlin model, however, international trade does part of the adjusting to an international capital flow, and, in the limit, it can do all the adjusting and eliminate any effect of capital flows on real rewards to factors of production. Simulation studies that have neglected this trade-adjustment effect have shown, not surprisingly, that repatriation of the stock of capital invested abroad by U.S. MNEs will redistribute income substantially toward labor.

These general-equilibrium models can be given a short-run content by supposing simply that any change that lowers real wages in the long run lowers employment in the short run. However, empirical controversies over the effects of foreign investment on employment and the balance of payments have flushed out some additional theoretical considerations. The investment-substitution question addresses the possibility that a transfer of capital does not actually lower the sending country's stock or raise the recipient's by the full amount. If it does not reduce the domestic capital stock, then the adverse effect on wages should not arise. The export-substitution question asks whether or not, in the MNE's own sourcing decisions, its foreign investment necessarily substitutes for export sales. The nature of the MNE's activities suggests that a complementary relationship might prevail – up to a point, and in some settings. The statistical evidence gives appreciable support to the complementary relationship (with its "up to a point" qualification attached), and that mitigates the theoretical likelihood that investing abroad will be adverse to real wages in the home country.

The effect of MNEs on wages can also be analyzed in the partial-equilibrium context of the MNE's bargaining with its own employees. MNEs' access to alternative overseas production sites may make their demand for labor more elastic than other companies' and thus more resistant to unions' wage demands. Or the MNE's rents may themselves be subject to capture by labor. As background evidence, it is useful to note that MNEs decentralize their wage and employee-relations decisions because labor markets are local and highly institutional. Studies of wages paid by MNEs have suggested that they are generally neither above nor below those of comparable local firms, once other factors are controlled, except that in LDCs the MNE is likely to pay higher wages to acquire better "quality" labor. MNEs' foreignness is a disadvantage and might be expected to render MNEs' employee relations less tranquil than those of local firms; on the other hand, they may also be able to arbitrage innovations in labor relations across national boundaries. Empirically, the MNEs seem to suffer no serious disadvantage in handling labor relations. They are responsible for some innovations, but their presence has not transformed national labor-relations systems. Potentially, trade unions can gain from international coalitions to bargain with MNEs, and they have made some efforts along this line, but there are strong reasons why such coalitions are unlikely to succeed.

6

Investment behavior and financial flows

The MNE's financial behavior raises questions that by now are familiar: What difference does the MNE's presence make to the operation and allocative outcome of markets? And how is national policy making affected? Previous chapters investigated why MNEs invest resources in overseas facilities at all. The focus now shifts to why they undertake overseas capital expenditures at the rates they do, and what explains their choice of methods of financing these expenditures. Their financial behavior raises broad questions about international capital markets. In the long run, does the MNE integrate national capital markets that would otherwise be balkanized by national boundaries? In the short run, do its money-management decisions affect countries' exchange rates and short-term credit conditions?

The firm's balance-sheet identity and its changes over time provide a helpful framework for the analysis that follows (Stevens, 1972). A growing foreign subsidiary may choose to expand its assets – fixed (plant and equipment) or liquid (receivables, working capital). This expansion must be financed from some increase in its liabilities: retained earnings from its previous profits, new equity or loans from its parent, and borrowing from external sources (call it local borrowing). Similarly, the subsidiary's parent can expand its fixed or liquid assets in its home base, but also its investment in or claims on its subsidiaries. This expansion of the parent's assets can be financed by retained earnings (either its own earnings or those of its subsidiaries) or by securing new debt or equity funds outside the firm. These balance-sheet identities highlight several issues that recur through the following discussion. In empirical research, a good deal of emphasis has been placed on explaining subsidiaries' acquisitions of fixed assets and parents' investments in increased net worth of their subsidiaries. The latter – the increase in foreign direct investment – is an increase in the subsidiary's liabilities and is not necessarily identical with the subsidiary's increase in fixed (or even total) assets. That is because local borrowing can also change. When the subsidiary expands its plant and equipment, or when the parent raises its investment in the subsidiary, some increase generally occurs in the liabilities on one or both balance sheets. How closely tied are these changes? Does the firm make its investment decision simply by comparing its expected yield to some uniform opportunity cost of capital? Or do the changes in fixed-asset holdings depend on the firm's particular structure of liabilities? They could, because existing liabilities influence the firm's ability to raise new funds. Finally, does the balance sheet of the subsidiary have a life of its own? Does anyone care about the relationship between its various assets and liabilities? Or does only the parent's fully consolidated balance sheet matter, with lenders and other onlookers watching the global structure of its assets and liabilities but attaching no importance to whether or not given assets and liabilities are lodged in a particular subsidiary or country?

In the first section of this chapter we shall summarize some empirical research on subsidiaries' fixed investments and parents' changing financial interests in their subsidiaries. Then we shall proceed to the deeper theoretical and empirical questions raised by the MNE's liability structure in relation to the market for financial assets. The chapter then continues with an analysis of the MNE's management of short-term financial assets and certain public-policy issues that surround its international financial transactions.

6.1. Capital formation and foreign direct investment flows

The interesting questions about MNEs' capital-formation decisions arise from macroeconomics and the concern of public policy with how the major components of gross national product behave. Given the presence of MNEs, what explains the year-to-year changes in their subsidiaries' capital-formation rates, or their net international transfers of funds to the subsidiaries? Although these questions grow from macroeconomic policy, their answers demand an understanding of the MNE's microeconomic behavior.

We expect the MNE, like any other business, to plan its investment outlays by selecting from the stock of projects open to it those whose expected internal rates of return exceed the firm's cost of capital. This rule applies to the MNE that maximizes global profits; although other hypotheses about the firm's motives clamor for attention, profit maximization seems to explain most of the action.[1] Although we assume that the MNE maximizes its long-run profits (specifically, its stock-market value to its ultimate owners), we shall bump into the hypothesis that the MNE also avoids risk when making its investment decisions. It might shun risk either on behalf of its owners or to maximize utility for its managers.

Determinants of foreign investment and overseas capital formation

The assumption that profit guides MNEs' investment decisions merely tells one how the MNE reckons, using its information about capital costs and investment projects' expected net cash flows. We still must decide what variables that we can observe are correlated with those governing the firm's expectations. Several general models of investment behavior have been applied to flows of direct investments or capital-formation rates by overseas subsidiaries.[2] One approach has been Jorgenson's (1963) neoclassical model, which identifies investment as adjustment to or toward the capital stock that will be optimal for a competitive firm or industry. That stock depends on the desired or expected output level, the capital-output relation, and the price of output relative to the user cost of capital (interest and depreciation rates).

[1] Horst (1974b) reviewed the candidates in the context of multinational activity. He pointed out that the alternatives do supply some specific and potentially testable predictions about MNEs' investment behavior.
[2] For surveys and discussion, see Richardson (1971a) and Stevens (1974).

Although the neoclassical model has proved popular in statistical studies of MNEs' investment decisions, its origins in the competitive model have aroused some doubts. It does not apply to discrete projects – the foreign-investment opportunity in which the MNE finds itself facing a downward-sloping demand curve for the output of a novel project. The firm has in mind some expected profit-maximizing output from that project, but the outsider cannot predict it, say, from current output data. But then what model can replace the neoclassical model's formal structure? Investigators have simply cast about for general economic indicators of the unobserved specific market data that might form the MNE's conjectures about future cash flows. They dredge up such coarse indicators as the level of GNP or sectoral output in the foreign country (or whatever market is intended), or some measure of the growth rate of output formulated in the spirit of the "accelerator" relation.[3]

A number of time-series statistical investigations have proceeded along this line, usually aiming to explain flows of foreign direct investments by U.S. MNEs or plant and equipment spending by their subsidiaries. They test various predictors, although usually not in a directly comparative way; they differ in the technical methods employed to deal with the lag between a firm's decision to make an outlay and when it is actually undertaken. Stevens (1969) analyzed the investment behavior of 71 individual well-established foreign subsidiaries, using a modified version of Jorgenson's model. He found (pp. 174–6) a significant effect of the subsidiary's sales, as an indicator of its desired capital stock; investment outlays also increased with the subsidiary's profits (indicating the marginal profit of additional investment) and its depreciation allowances (indicating the erosion of its existing capital stock). Kwack (1972) examined aggregate data for changes in overseas assets of U.S. companies. He also found support for a Jorgenson-type formulation, using a weighted average of the gross national products of principal host countries of U.S. MNEs to proxy the movements of the subsidiaries' desired output levels.

---

[3] The demand for additional capacity depends, in the accelerator model, not on the size of the intended market but on changes in its size.

Stevens (1972) similarly addressed the aggregate data on plant and equipment expenditures of U.S. MNEs' overseas affiliates, getting somewhat unsatisfactory results for the Jorgenson model and better ones for a simple flexible accelerator (investment depends on past sales, their rate of growth, and past capital stock). Lunn's (1980) methods and results resemble those of Stevens. Severn (1972), working with data on individual firms, found overseas gross fixed capital formation to be related to the lagged change in overseas sales – the accelerator relation, again. Rather weak evidence emerged to support two other indicators of investment opportunities – the firm's overseas income and the price of the parent's equity shares (a high price at a given time will indicate that the stock market sees it enjoying opportunities to raise its future profits, presumably by investment either at home or abroad). Boatwright and Renton (1975) analyzed changes in the stock of MNE capital moving both into and out of the United Kingdom. For both inflows and outflows a neoclassical formulation of the desired capital stock proved statistically significant. However, the lag structure of the relationships was not estimated accurately, and at an intermediate step in the analysis the authors had to resort to assuming an implausibly high elasticity of substitution in production between capital and labor.

Goldsbrough (1979) took up a different aspect of the MNE's investment demand – one congenial to the microeconomic model of the MNE developed in the preceding chapters. He included not only measures of activity in foreign markets but also international shifts in unit labor costs as affected by exchange-rate changes. He confirmed that the MNEs' allocations of funds among four major industrial countries have been attuned to placing production facilities in the lowest-cost location.[4]

Consistent with this evidence is the finding of several studies (Rowthorn and Hymer, 1971; Buckley et al., 1978) that the growth rates of large MNEs are correlated with the growth rates of their

---

[4] In this context we can recall the studies described in Chapter 2 that associate shifts in MNEs' investment decisions with major changes in tariffs, such as the formation of the European Community. See Hufbauer (1975, pp. 278–80).

home national economies and their chief industrial bases within those economies. For large firms this is hardly a surprise. Buckley et al. (1978) found that their firms' growth during 1962–72 was at least weakly correlated with the extent of their multinational operations in 1972. Again no surprise, because increasing overseas assets is one way for the firm to grow.

Finance and capital costs

So far, we have emphasized only those variables dealing directly with the demand-side influences on the MNE's desired capital stock. Most of these statistical studies also made some investigation of how the MNE's investments are financed. The model of Boatwright and Renton incorporates international capital arbitrage by the MNE, making the adjustment of overseas capital stocks depend on international differences in interest rates (long-term government bonds). The statistical significance of this term is somewhat erratic. Kwack (1972) allowed the adjustment of overseas assets of U.S. companies to depend on their retained earnings and depreciation allowances in the recent past – a source of liquid funds – and this influence was confirmed statistically. Reuber and Roseman (1972), analyzing takeovers of Canadian companies by foreign enterprises, found this financial-investment decision to depend on corporate liquidity. Low liquidity in Canada puts more enterprise units on the market and also reduces the bid tendered for them by other Canadian firms, thus increasing foreign takeovers. They also offered indirect evidence that U.S. liquidity is positively related to these takeovers. Reuber et al. (1973, Chapter 4) reported that MNEs' internal cash flows strongly affect their investments in ongoing subsidiaries, but the parent's liquidity has little influence on the decision to start a subsidiary.

Stevens (1969, 1972) and Severn (1972) both treated the MNE's overseas capital-formation outlays as determined jointly with its domestic capital-formation and global-financing decisions. Severn supposed that the firm's internal funds (depreciation allowances and retained earnings) represent a preferred form of financing and that its access to borrowed funds deteriorates as it becomes more highly leveraged (i.e., as its debt–equity ratio increases). Accordingly, he expected the MNE's rate of capital formation abroad to be retarded by a high debt–equity ratio of the parent (confirmed statistically) and its capital formation at home to increase with the income it has earned abroad in the recent past (also confirmed). Severn's results are roughly consistent with the assumption that the MNE makes its investment decisions around the globe as a package, taking into account the funds it has generated in all of its current operations. Stevens (1969) explicitly tested the hypotheses that plant and equipment outlays of subsidiaries are decreased by the parent's global alternative investments and increased by its global supply of liquidity, and both hypotheses were, in general, confirmed. Ladenson (1972), starting from the flow-of-funds identity for the firm, built a model that reveals a good deal of interdependence among financial flows and changes in assets in the form of systematic processes of lagged adjustment of one variable to another. And McClain (1974, Chapter 7) found that changes in British MNEs' assets are related positively to the subsidiaries' cash flows but negatively to investment opportunities in British domestic manufacturing; domestic (U.K.) cash flows do not wield a significant influence. Symmetrically, McClain found that capital stock in U.K. manufacturing is expanded less rapidly the better are the investment opportunities of U.K. MNEs' subsidiaries in the United States.

Stevens (1972) was concerned with the hypothesis that MNEs are averse to the risk of changes in foreign-exchange rates. They scale their borrowing abroad to the assets and earnings of subsidiaries that are exposed to depreciation of the host country's exchange rate. When the depreciation cuts the home-currency value of these assets, it also shrivels the burden of any liabilities denominated in the host country's currency. Stevens found quite a stable relationship between changes in assets overseas and changes in foreign borrowing, but the relationship is not dollar-for-dollar at the margin, and his test does not seem finely honed to support this particular hypothesis about foreign-exchange risk. Goldsbrough (1979) launched a more frontal attack on this question, deriving a formal model that shows how the proportion of a MNE's borrowing done abroad will depend on international interest-rate differentials, the distribution of its capital investments between countries, and the covariation of cash flows from those investments with exchange-rate changes. Goldsbrough's model is consistent with a constant proportional relation between assets and liabilities denominated in foreign currency. Gilman (1981), similarly concerned with foreign-exchange risk and the liability structures of subsidiaries' balance sheets, found that foreign-currency financing is more closely related to changes in subsidiaries' total assets than to their current assets, implying that all assets abroad are viewed as subject to the risk of exchange-rate changes.

Stevens's results (1972) and other results are inconsistent with one hypothesis about MNEs' financing of their subsidiaries that has appeared in the literature. Barlow and Wender (1955, pp. 164–7) proposed a rule of thumb for investing in highly uncertain foreign activities: Inject an initial sum, but no more; plow back all earnings, and hope for a big win. Perhaps this "gambler's earnings" hypothesis should be expected to apply, if at all, only to the financing of new subsidiaries.[5] In any case, it is inconsistent with most statistical evidence. Stevens (1969, pp. 168–9) noted the continuing infusions of funds to established subsidiaries by their MNE parents, and both Stevens (1972) and Severn (1972) found evidence that expansions of subsidiaries' assets are normally financed by borrowing from some combination of corporate affiliates and independent parties.

A preliminary assessment of this statistical research on MNEs' investment and financing suggests the following conclusions: Subsidiaries' plant and equipment outlays depend on expected cash flows, as extrapolated from both general market trends and indirect indicators of future profitability (earnings, exchange-rate changes, etc.). However, there has been little effort by researchers to sort out exactly what variables are the best predictors. Contrary to the pure neoclassical approach to investment by the firm, the MNE's global capital-formation decisions are influenced by its global capacity to generate internal funds for reinvestment. It appears, consistent with

---

[5] Robbins and Stobaugh (1973, Chapters 3 and 4) did argue from survey evidence that the hypothesis holds for new subsidiaries. Also see Brooke and Remmers (1970, p. 203).

evidence presented in Chapter 3, that the MNE coordinates its long-run capacity decisions centrally; subsidiaries do not function as separate investment-decision centers, as has sometimes been suggested, even if subsidiaries' financial transactions with their parents on average are quite a small part of the subsidiaries' overall finance (U.S. Tariff Commission, 1973, p. 424).

6.2. Long-term financing decisions and financial-asset markets

Although this evidence marks the MNE as a global coordinator of its financing activities, it does not identify the practices that the MNE is expected to follow or their consequences for the world's capital markets. The capital-arbitrage hypothesis (Chapter 2) implied that the firm would simply borrow in the world's cheapest capital market, without regard to the location of its own physical assets. The hypothesis that the MNE avoids risks, including those of exchange-rate changes, implies that the currency of denomination of its liabilities is closely aligned to the location of its physical assets. We could investigate these hypotheses directly. It turns out, however, that they float atop some more fundamental models and hypotheses about how capital markets work – within nations, and perhaps between them. We must establish some theoretical properties of markets for financial assets in order to determine the options open to the MNE in making its global financing decisions.

Theory of international capital markets

The financial behavior of the MNE is clearly the context for closer examination of the capital-arbitrage hypothesis. But this question quickly takes us into deeper waters – the modern theory of financial-asset pricing, a major development in economics during the past quarter century. The model's core is a description of how financial assets – the liabilities of MNEs and other companies – will be priced by perfectly competitive but risk-averse capital markets. Conclusions about the cost of capital and the financing decisions of non-financial companies then follow. Although the analysis seems incompletely developed at this time, this model of perfect capital markets provides an invaluable vantage point for thinking about the MNE's financial role in international capital markets that may be far from perfect.

The capital-asset pricing model (CAPM) explains how risk-averse financial investors behaving as pure competitors set prices in the market for financial assets that convey claims to uncertain streams of future income. The asset holders seek to compose diversified portfolios in order to avoid risk as well as to maximize their wealth. In adding an asset to the portfolio, they are therefore concerned with its incremental effect on the riskiness of the portfolio as a whole. The security's effect depends not on its own riskiness but on how closely its expected ups and downs (in the face of various possible future conditions in the economy) coincide with the expected ups and downs of other securities in the portfolio. This analysis leads to the conclusion that the financial rate of return set by the capital market on any given security – that is, on the uncertain stream of income to which its ownership conveys title – is equal to the risk-free rate of return (e.g., on short-term government securities or some such risk-less asset) plus a risk premium. The risk premium depends on the correlation or covariance between the asset at hand and the "market portfolio," which can be thought of as an aggregate of all other se-curities in the portfolio. When we say that the market sets a high risk premium on a given security, that is to say that it sets a low market price on the expected income stream to be yielded by the security. How well a given security comes off in the riskiness ratings thus depends not just on how uncertain is its own income stream but also on how closely its uncertainties coincide with those of other finan-cial-asset income streams in the economy generally. Suppose that securities *A* and *B* are both expected to yield average income streams of one dollar per year and that security *A*'s random yield fluctuates in perfect harmony with the economy in general, whereas *B*'s ex-pected earnings bounce around in an unrelated way. Security *A* is no help to the portfolio holder for reducing the "systematic risk" inher-ent in all risky assets in the economy; it commands a higher risk premium than security *B*, which helps the asset holder to make his portfolio less risky than otherwise.

The CAPM emphasizes the behavior of financial-asset holders in the market for outstanding securities, not that of the nonfinancial companies that issue new assets. When a company issues securities in order to carry out an investment project (e.g., to start a new foreign subsidiary), the perfectly informed capital market simply looks through the skein of the firm's existing assets and activities to the expected return and risk from the project itself and prices the asset accordingly. The model has many striking corollaries for the borrowing firm's behavior. The value-maximizing firm does not please its shareholders by acting in a risk-averse fashion, because they can themselves diversify away any nonsystematic risk to which the firm is exposed. If the projects open to the firm offer a choice between those expected to prove profitable but risky and the less profitable but safe projects, it should choose so that the marginal trade-off between risk and return is the same as the price that the financial-asset market places on risk. Another corollary (the Modigliani-Miller theorem) holds that the firm's leverage (ratio of debt to equity in its liabilities) should have no effect on its overall cost of capital. Given the risk/return properties of the income stream flowing from the firm's real assets, the capital market can diversify around the riskiness (or safeness) the firm builds into whatever bonds and equity shares it chooses to issue. The sum of market values of all financial liabilities that the firm issues will remain the same no matter what diverse risk structures the firm builds into the individual securities.

CAPM has enjoyed more success in explaining the behavior of securities markets than nonfinancial companies' financing decisions. The reasons for this difference are clear. Among CAPM's neglects are the differing tax status of the firm's interest-bearing debt, not subject to the corporation income tax, and its equity securities giving claim to its taxable corporate income. Another neglect is the transaction cost of reorganizing its legal and financial structure or of dispersing its assets should the firm go bankrupt. The desire to avoid bankruptcy costs induces the firm to restrict its issuance of debt instruments bearing fixed-interest obligations. The tax-free status of interest payments, on the other hand, tempts the firm to issue as much debt and as little equity as possible. The two forces operating together probably create an optimal leverage for the firm, contrary to the Modigliani-Miller theorem. Finally, transaction and information costs for individual investors limit their ability to diversify their portfolios freely and may leave them willing to pay a premium for a prediversified income stream such as that generated by a MNE.

This background now brings us to two questions crucial for the financial behavior of the MNE itself. Can CAPM be related to the fissures that apparently exist between national capital markets – exchange-rate risks, extra transaction and information costs, and so forth? How do we expect the MNE to behave if national capital markets are segregated from one another, so that CAPM does not hold internationally? If international capital markets are segregated, to what degree does the MNE integrate them?

Several theoretical models have sought to extend CAPM to the international capital market, taking these fissures into account. Their interest lies in what they must assume away in order to transplant some of the CAPM conclusions to the international economy.[6] Where information and securities transactions are costly, portfolio holders obviously cannot attain optimal diversification. These costs are always present, but they appear much higher for international than for national securities trading. Government restrictions on international movements of securities spoil the game. Taxes will also do the job. A more subtle question arises because exchange rates can change. Any given change is likely to shake up the rates of return on foreign securities in one's portfolio. But what does the variability of the exchange rate do to those correlations among expected yields that dominate CAPM's workings? Assume that investors may own Home and/or Foreign securities, and the exchange rate between the dollar (Home's currency) and the zit (Foreign's) is subject to random market fluctuations. The dollar value of the zit earnings of Foreign securities can stay unchanged, when the zit's price falls, only if the fall reflects a rise abroad in all zit-denominated prices, and thus in the security's zit earnings stream. This indepen-

[6] See Solnik (1974), Grauer et al. (1976), and Senbet (1979). Adler and Dumas (1977), have provided a useful survey. For empirical evidence of unexploited gains from international portfolio diversification, see Grubel (1968), Levy and Sarnat (1970), Severn (1974), and Biger (1979).

dence is conceivable only if exchange-rate changes are simply *assumed* to be independent of changes in zit earnings even though real disturbances and changes in relative prices may lie behind exchange-rate changes. Neither assumption is persuasive. Suppose that a security represents a claim on the profits of Foreign's coffee-exporting industry and that coffee profits and the value of the zit both take a dive whenever consumers' tastes shift (randomly) away from drinking coffee. The example suggests that real factors can readily affect exchange rates and that exchange rates are related to changes in returns to securities. These kinds of assumptions, however, seem necessary to preserve the conclusion that portfolio holders can optimize their portfolios and set market values on securities in international capital markets according to the CAPM model.[7]

MNEs' financial decisions

Where does all this leave the MNE? If the world were one securities market in perfect CAPM equilibrium, the MNE treasurer's office would be a quiet place. It would not matter to the company's profitability or the world's welfare where the MNE borrowed funds, in what currency it denominated its debts, what risk structure it gave those securities, and so forth. But when CAPM does not hold internationally, all these decisions matter, and the MNE operating in internationally segmented capital markets can both enrich itself and improve the markets' operations by seizing the arbitrage possibilities at hand (Naumann-Etienne, 1974). One of these is plain old capital arbitrage by borrowing in cheaper locations. Plasschaert (1974) described some of these arbitrage processes in practice. More subtly, average costs of capital may not differ between countries, but lenders can still find themselves incompletely diversified against fluctuations in exchange rates. In that case the MNE has reason to consider whether or not the dollar returns from its own investment in Foreign are hedged against fluctuations in the exchange rate of the zit. The MNE may find that the market will pay more for its securities if the

---

[7] Another formal problem also arises – identifying what might be meant by "the risk-free asset" in an international capital market with exchange rates variable. CAPM requires such an asset to allow holders to adjust the riskiness of their portfolios through a suitable admixture of risky assets and the risk-free security.

real assets bound up in its Foreign subsidiary are hedged by borrowing some of its funds in zits. If lenders are perfectly diversified, they will pay no more for the firm's securities once this hedge is accomplished.[8] Hartman (1979) developed a model to show how a MNE serving risk-averse home-country investors determines its optimal foreign borrowing (given its foreign assets, and assuming foreign and domestic interest rates are the same). The best amount to borrow depends on how the home-currency rate of return on foreign assets varies with the exchange rate. If it is unaffected by exchange-rate changes, no borrowing need be done abroad. If it changes proportionally with the exchange rate, foreign borrowing should finance all foreign assets. Shapiro (1975a) considered somewhat similar issues, basing his model of the imperfectly competitive MNE on that of Horst (1971).

Even if MNEs may be rational in some circumstances to tie local borrowing by their subsidiaries to the stock of assets at risk in a given currency, that does not mean each subsidiary should do its own financing. Value maximization still requires that the MNE co-ordinate its financing activities worldwide (Adler, 1974; Shapiro, 1978).[9] The capital market is expected to heed the risk exposure of the MNE's assets and fixed liabilities worldwide. Both in making its financing decisions and in determining its cost of capital (to guide its

[8] If the constraint on international diversification is the transaction cost for the diversifying party, the question then becomes whether asset holders can diversify more economically by themselves or by buying securities of MNEs that have done the job for them. Soenen (1979) explored the MNE's trade-off between exchange risk and hedging costs. Adler and Dumas (1975) distinguished between imperfections in the international money market (avoidable by an efficient forward-exchange market) and imperfections in international securities markets (due to more intractable forces). Gilman (1981) argued at length that the MNE fails to maximize global profits by treating its home currency as safe and foreign-currency net assets as risk-exposed; however, if shareholders' portfolios are undiversified internationally and their consumption streams are heavily weighted by domestic nontraded goods, that policy represents optimizing behavior by the MNE on behalf of its owners.

[9] Adler (1974) presented a model in which financial decisions can be decentralized efficiently to the MNE's subsidiaries, but it requires that the MNE be able continuously to adjust its ownership shares in the foreign subsidiaries, including taking short positions. This practice is hardly consistent with the MNE's central role as an administrative coordinating device.

capital-formation decisions), the MNE should make best use of all specific capital markets available to it. This advantage-taking is influenced by the corporation income taxes to which its earnings are exposed. Suppose that Foreign's tax rate is less than Home's and that the MNE's taxes paid to Foreign give rise to a credit against the MNE's tax liability to Home's government.[10] Then the MNE gains a capital-cost advantage from retaining the earnings of its subsidiary abroad, because the plowed-back earnings retained after Foreign's low tax then face a "topping up" tax bite from Home's government only when they are disentangled and repatriated to Home. The MNE should rationally take that low opportunity cost of foreign retentions into account in assessing its cost of capital and making its investment decisions.

A further implication is that the capital structure of the MNE's (wholly owned) subsidiary has no automatic significance of itself. The MNE should issue debt capital in Foreign to the extent that borrowing-cost advantages there assist in minimizing its global cost of capital. The amount to borrow in Foreign has no necessary relationship to the amount of capital the MNE plans to invest in Foreign (unless there is some specific need, as explained earlier, to hedge risks associated with fluctuations in the zit exchange rate). The capital structure on the subsidiary's books (how much equity and debt consist of liabilities to its parent, how much of local borrowing) has no logical life of its own. This argument assumes, it should be noted, that the MNE guarantees the debt of its subsidiaries, so that a subsidiary cannot go bankrupt independent of the MNE as a worldwide legal entity. Although such a guarantee is not a legal necessity of the MNE's operation, empirical research has suggested that it is close to universal practice.[11]

Insofar as the subsidiary's funds come from its parent and not other lenders, should they be called equity in the subsidiary or debt of the subsidiary? The logic of the relationship implies that these

---

[10] See Chapter 8. This arrangement has prevailed in the United States and other important home-base countries for MNEs.

[11] Stobaugh (1970) reported that not one of 20 medium-size and large U.S. MNEs would let a subsidiary default on its debt (even if it were not formally guaranteed), and only one of 17 small MNEs would contemplate this event.

two statuses are not economically distinguishable, and the choice will have no effect on the capital market's evaluation of the parent's securities. Shapiro (1978) pointed out that what one calls the subsidiary's liabilities to its parent will depend largely on legal and tax criteria. Calling the liability debt may allow the company to siphon foreign profits out of the reach of a voracious foreign tax collector (and into the gunsights of a less demanding domestic one). The liability structure affects the nominal profit rate that the subsidiary appears to earn – perhaps with some effect on public policy in the host nation. But, these factors aside, the form of the subsidiary's liabilities to its parent has no life of its own.

If the MNE does not come upon already perfect international capital markets, its arbitrage activities should tend to integrate them. Lee and Sachdeva (1977) supposed that financial-asset markets are segmented so that Home's investors can diversify into Foreign-based assets either by buying Foreign securities or by buying the liabilities of Home MNEs operating in Foreign. But Foreign investors are not permitted to buy Home securities, and no MNEs claim Foreign as their home base. Home's capital market by itself, like Foreign's capital market in isolation, displays the perfection described in the CAPM model. Lee and Sachdeva showed that if Home's MNEs compete among each other (as perfect competitors) to buy up control in Foreign's local firms, the effect of the acquisitions is the same as if Home's investors themselves freely diversify among Home and Foreign securities. However, if Home's MNEs recognize their mutual dependence in driving up the price of equity control in Foreign's market for companies, they make insufficient acquisitions to bring full diversification gains to Home's investors. But Foreign's investors lose from these acquisitions made by Home's MNEs. The reason is obvious: The rate of return on Foreign securities is bid down, lowering the returns to Foreign's investors, but their riskiness is unchanged.

Empirical evidence

This theoretical material on international capital markets raises questions about the MNE's financial behavior that reach beyond the evidence surveyed in Section 6.1. There we found that the

MNE seems to coordinate its financing decisions globally. What it borrows in a given national capital market depends on international interest-rate differentials but also on the extent of its own commercial operations and (theoretically, at least) the interaction of commercial risks to its investments with risks of changes in foreign-exchange rates. We saw evidence that MNEs tend to finance a stable proportion of their overseas plant and equipment outlays abroad, but no explanation why the percentage should be what it is.

The first question raised in the preceding section is the MNE's role in supplying diversification gains to the holders of its liabilities and thereby integrating international capital markets. Holding shares in an internationally diversified MNE may for the shareholder be an alternative to holding an internationally diversified portfolio of national securities.[12] We have at least indirect empirical evidence of this gain to shareholders in a study by Agmon and Lessard (1977) (also see Hughes et al., 1975; Aggarwal, 1980*a*, 1980*b*). The diversification value that a company's shares offer to investors in its national capital market depends, according to CAPM, on the covariance of its returns with the market factor – the general, undiversifiable risk attached to all income streams originating within that nation. The shares of a MNE, to an extent that increases with the fraction of its assets placed abroad, should exhibit a lower covariance with the domestic market factor. By the same token, its income stream should exhibit some covariance with the market factors of the foreign nations in which it operates. Agmon and Lessard confirmed this hypothesis statistically, their results implying that MNEs' securities do offer a special diversification value to shareholders.

Another question left without satisfactory answer is why MNEs seem to borrow in local capital markets a stable proportion of the assets placed there. The survey evidence underlines the avoidance of exchange-rate fluctuations, without indeed giving much attention

---

[12] We may note Aliber's (1970) argument in a very different vein that MNEs arise not to supply international diversification but because investors in the securities of their nation's MNEs myopically fail to notice the exchange-rate risks to which their overseas assets are exposed – risks they would not welcome should they add foreign securities to their personal portfolios.

to the effect of the policy on the MNE's total debt-servicing costs. Behrman (in Mikesell, 1962, pp. 95–8) found the vast majority of the U.S. MNEs interviewed to minimize the dollar equity invested abroad, and many sought to borrow as much as possible in the host country. This motive and decision rule also appear in the survey evidence of Brooke and Remmers (1970, pp. 182, 195) and Robbins and Stobaugh (1973, Chapter 4). Finally, there is some suggestion that MNEs have used local borrowing as a form of off-balance-sheet financing, to make the parent's leverage look less than a full enumeration of its worldwide debt would indicate – a procedure that may be deceptive if the parent does in fact guarantee the local-currency debt of its subsidiaries. Robbins and Stobaugh (p. 127) noted that subsidiaries show higher aggregate ratios of current liabilities to current assets than do their parents' domestic operations, consistent with a risk-induced reliance on local-currency financing.

The preceding analysis indicates that how the wholly owned subsidiary's borrowing from its corporate affiliates gets split between debt and equity is economically arbitrary. Tax and regulatory factors govern the choice. Where the host country's rate of corporate tax is higher than that in the source country, the MNE should denominate the maximum proportion of its subsidiary's liabilities to the parent as debt in order to siphon revenues as tax-deductible interest past the foreign tax collector. Also, should the host country tighten its regulations on payments made abroad by residents, interest payable abroad by subsidiaries may claim a higher priority than profit remittance. Although these motives will not apply to every set of bilateral relationships between host and source country, data on U.S. MNEs suggest that they do prevail in the aggregate (Brooke and Remmers, 1970, pp. 194–9). The leverage of all majority-owned foreign affiliates of U.S. MNEs in 1966, measured by the ratio of assets to net worth, was 2.15, versus 1.69 for their U.S. parents. In 1970 these figures for a smaller sample of respondents were 2.41 and 1.88 (Leftwich, 1974).

Subsidiaries' practices in remitting dividends to their parents (versus retaining the funds locally) also call for scrutiny. One influence, minimizing the company's global tax bill, will be considered in

Chapter 8. Other influences reflect the general interdependence of MNEs' financial decisions, discussed earlier. For example, subsidiaries remit less of their earnings if their desired capital stocks are growing rapidly (Kopits, 1972) or high rates of profits are earned (Mauer and Scaperlanda, 1972). Zenoff's (1966) survey of 30 large U.S. MNEs confirmed the influence of taxes and reinvestment opportunities but also flagged some factors not consistent with profit maximization. For example, parent MNEs that traditionally pay out a fixed proportion of net earnings as dividends tend to require subsidiaries to remit a comparable percentage. The findings of Brooke and Remmers (1970, Chapter 6) are similar. Because the U.S. tax system penalizes the payment of dividends by corporate parents, economists wonder why dividends are paid at all,[13] and that goes for a decision rule imposing the same practice on subsidiaries. A MNE not consolidating its subsidiaries' finances fully into the parent's financial statements may vary dividend remittances so as to "dress up" the financial position that the parent reports to the public, Zenoff suggested. This practice leaves the public partly in the dark about the MNE's global activities and implies some advantage to the company from painting a picture less than completely truthful. Overall, Zenoff distinguished between mature companies with extensive networks of subsidiaries that manage dividend remittance through rules of thumb and MNEs with less experience or less far-flung empires that attune their remittance practices to the needs of the hour. One cannot say whether or not a statistically significant distinction exists between worried novices scrambling to get things right and mature players coasting on satisfactory rules of thumb.

6.3. **Foreign-exchange rates and short-term transactions**

The preceding sections have shown how the MNE and financial markets respond to the greater risks of international transactions. These include the political risks of being unable to deter the

---

[13] Dividends paid are subject to taxation as personal income for the shareholder. If they are plowed back into the enterprise, they become capital gains on the shareholder's equities, taxed only when the shares are sold and then at the lower rate pertaining to capital gains.

hostile action of an alien government, the economic risks implicit in the higher costs of information about foreign environments (one buys less than complete information, and so faces greater risks), and the economic risk of changes in exchange rates. In this section we shall consider how MNEs react to exchange-rate variability in handling their short-term transactions. We shall also review the MNE's problem of evaluating the effects of exchange-rate changes on its profitability and reporting them to the world at large. This latter problem, "translation" of the changing values of assets and liabilities denominated in foreign exchange into the parent's native currency, gets surprisingly dominant emphasis in the business literature. One might suspect that businesses fret less over how to deal with future exchange-rate changes than over what to tell the public about those just past.

Responses to expected exchange-rate changes

To isolate the behavior at issue, suppose that the MNE's decisions about committing resources can be divided cleanly into two groups: Long-run commitments cannot be soon reversed, but short-run commitments can be altered within periods for which the MNE can reasonably hope to forecast actual exchange-rate movements. Long-run decisions by the risk-averse firm may rest on an expectation about how variations in the price of foreign exchange will be correlated with variations in the subsidiary's foreign-currency earnings, but by assumption the MNE cannot predict the specific ups and downs. However, exchange rates three months hence may be fair game for a sporting bet. Various sources have described the many strategies open to MNEs to obtain gains or avoid losses from exchange-rate changes.[14] Some maneuvers involve transactions between branches of the MNE and other parties. The transactional opportunities here are, in general, the same for the MNE as for any other agent; the qualification "in general" allows for the MNE's advantage in holding information acquired in other dealings that may

[14] Rutenberg (1970); Robbins and Stobaugh (1973, Chapters 1, 4, and 5); Jilling (1978, Chapters 2 and 3). Itagaki's model (1981) develops several aspects of the MNE's reaction to exchange-market conditions.

help it to take expeditious action in the foreign-exchange market. Other transactions are internal to the MNE and take place between its various national branches. In internal transactions, the MNE has a clear-cut advantage. Consider a major type of intracorporate transaction – speeding up payments due in a currency expected to appreciate and delaying payments denominated in a currency expected to depreciate. In transactions between independent parties, the payment is affected by a precontracted due date and other terms, and it may be difficult to rearrange the deal on short notice to let the parties take mutual advantage of an expected change in exchange rates (Jilling, 1978, pp. 150–2).

Company surveys have provided revealing information on companies' practices for dealing with fluctuations in the foreign-exchange rate.[15] Rodriguez (1980, Chapter 2) found the exploitation of leads and lags in interaffiliate payments the method most commonly used. Of course, this requires no external transaction for the MNE. Next came money-market transactions: Borrow in a currency expected to depreciate; lend in one expected to appreciate. There was the classic maneuver of covering long or short positions in a foreign currency by a sale or purchase in the forward-exchange market. Finally, the MNE may change the currency in which its payables or receivables are denominated. Shifting the terms of an arm's-length transactions in order to snatch a short-term gain is unlikely to go over well with a trading partner, and so this instrument is an unwieldy one. Jilling's results (1978, pp. 146–57) generally agree with the priorities found by Rodriguez, as do the findings of Robbins and Stobaugh (1973, Chapter 7).

If the MNE actively pursues expected profits by all these routes, it will, of course, be setting itself up as a financial speculator – a role often charged to it by harassed governments and just as often denied by the companies. A good deal of commentary has suggested

---

[15] Jilling's survey, taken in 1975, found that the management of foreign-exchange risk, like other financial functions, was highly centralized for most MNEs. Resources committed to the task had been increasing, in reflection of the increasing variability of exchange rates during the early 1970s. This expertise is subject to scale economies and so increases significantly with size of company. See Jilling (1978, pp. 89–90, 95–6, 113, 314).

that the nonfinancial company is keener to avoid losses in the foreign-exchange markets than to pursue speculative profits. The majority of Jilling's respondents preferred to make neither gains nor losses; many emphasized minimizing losses, and this attitude was more prevalent among smaller U.S. companies outside the largest 500 (Jilling, 1978, pp. 144, 274, 327). Similarly, Rodriguez (1980, Chapter 2) devised an interview strategy to reveal whether or not managers held asymmetrical attitudes toward foreign-exchange gains and losses; they displayed a strong allergy to losses. Defensive postures can extend to taking an open position in the short-term forward-exchange market so as to hedge a long-term fixed investment exposed to exchange risk, but this hedge is not self-liquidating and leads to reported short-term gains or losses (Jilling, 1978, p. 64).

That MNEs and other nonfinancial companies should limit their exchange-market activities to defensive maneuvers seems a bit puzzling. If a company is to form the administrative apparatus needed to deal defensively in the foreign-exchange market, why not deal aggressively? The answer probably lies in economies of specializing in the activity of foreign-exchange speculation as well as in nonfinancial companies' attitudes toward risk (Aliber, 1978, Chapter 11). There is yet another reason why MNEs may avoid committing resources to activities in the foreign-exchange market – a reason that harks back to the analysis of Section 6.2. If the MNE finds that the forward market for foreign exchange is already populated by competitive, well-informed speculators, then it cannot hope to "beat the market" with any regularity by speculating outright or entering the forward market only selectively to hedge its exposed foreign-exchange assets and liabilities.[16] True, it can choose to hedge its exposed positions regularly, up to whatever future maturities are of-

---

[16] Economists have devoted a great deal of effort, probably fruitlessly, to testing the efficiency of forward markets. After the event, it often turns out that a speculator could have made profits over a period of time by applying some simple decision rule to forward-exchange transactions (see, e.g., Rodriguez, 1980, Chapter 3). But hindsight beats foresight, and there is no way to show whether or not market participants efficiently used all information and opportunities available to them before the event.

fered in the foreign-exchange market. But the transactions costs cut into its long-run expected profits as the price of its risk aversion. Therefore, the risk-neutral company will avoid hedging if it thinks that the market is efficient (although it will arrange transactions in hope of exchange profits when it thinks it can beat the market).

Rodriguez (1980, Chapter 4) analyzed data on the foreign-currency positions of 36 companies to test hypotheses about their motives and practices in the foreign-exchange market. Nearly all of them experienced substantial changes in exposure to exchange risks; so they could not have followed the "risk-paranoid" pattern of avoiding open positions at all cost. Rodriguez also ruled out the possibility that companies think that markets are efficient and can never be beaten. The most consistent position, she found, is that companies sometimes think they can beat the market; in fact, during 1967–74 they moved funds toward strong currencies and away from weak ones.[17] The statistical pattern suggests that they acted as if they had noticed that the foward-exchange markets were systematically underpredicting the movements of those currencies. She also found specific evidence of more actions to counter foreign-exchange exposures that might lead to losses than to enlarge those showing promise of gains.[18]

Researchers have focused particular attention on the behavior of MNEs at times of major changes in exchange rates, such as the devaluations of the U.S. dollar in 1971 and 1973. As was mentioned earlier, these incidents hold interest because of scholarly concern over whether or not MNEs can anticipate such events so as to protect themselves and because of political concern with whether or not they thereby complicate the task of governments trying to ward off the

---

[17] These patterns of intermittent, successful speculation emerged in Rodriguez's data only after she separated the operating accounts from the financial accounts of her companies. The operating accounts reflect marketing considerations, and their foreign-exchange components cannot easily be manipulated in the short run. The financial accounts reflect the firm's opportunities to manage its own liquid assets. Evans and Folks (1979, pp. 19–20) similarly found a strong preference for managing foreign-exchange risk through financial rather than operating transactions.

[18] Batra and Hadar (1979) provided a theoretical model that seems interestingly consistent with Rodriguez's empirical results.

changes. Rodriguez's data (1980, Chapter 5) suggest a strong tendency in both the 1971 and 1973 crises for companies to move internally generated funds toward strong currencies, but little evidence of borrowing in weak currencies and lending in strong ones. Klein (1974) and a U.S. Senate study (1975), based on different sets of data, agree in general. Both of these inquiries found that the outflows of foreign direct investment itself were abnormally high during the crisis periods, indicating that U.S. MNEs chose those times to acquire additional long-term foreign assets. And the U.S. Senate study (1975) found that the foreign subsidiaries of U.S. companies increased the share of their payments to third parties denominated in dollars, thereby reducing their dollar balances. Klein (1974) concluded that the MNEs' aggregate contribution to the speculative outflow of funds was proportionally not very large in either 1971 or 1973, but it does appear that MNEs were active in anticipating the exchange-rate changes.[19]

Reporting effects of exchange-rate changes

We noted earlier that however successful or unsuccessful its bets on changes in exchange rate, the MNE faces the problem of translation – reporting to its shareholders and to the world at large how exchange-rate changes have affected its balance sheet. This question holds some economic interest for two reasons. First, observers have noted an appreciable if diminishing tendency for business to confuse translation and transactions aspects of the foreign-exchange problem, undertaking purposive actions on foreign-exchange exposure to improve the nominal results that they report, rather than truly to maximize the firm's value (Rodriguez, 1980, Chapter 2). Second, what asset and liability values are affected by exchange-rate changes is itself essentially an economic question (Shapiro, 1975*b*).

Suppose that Home's MNE has a subsidiary operating in Foreign,

---

[19] Similar evidence has appeared for other currency crises. Brooke and Remmers (1970, pp. 189–90, 199–203) noted that U.S. subsidiaries in Britain, anticipating a devaluation of sterling, in 1964–6 undertook heavy borrowing in sterling and remitted larger-than-average dividends to their parents.

and the price of Foreign's currency (the zit) declines. The subsidiary's balance sheet includes both long- and short-run assets and liabilities denominated in zits. How should the MNE report the depreciation's effect on the dollar profits of the whole enterprise? Suppose that exchange-rate changes in general are not thought to involve changes in countries' long-run terms of trade. That assumption implies that the zit's depreciation probably entails no permanent change in the dollar-denominated profits that the subsidiary's plant and equipment in Foreign can produce. By implication, the zit's depreciation will then correspond to an increase in Foreign's zit-denominated price level relative to Home's dollar-denominated price level. Then the depreciation will not be the occasion for saying that the MNE's owners have taken a loss on their long-run Foreign assets. But what about the subsidiary's accounts receivable for past zit-denominated transactions? Or what about the subsidiary's short-term borrowing from Foreign banks, now repayable in depreciated zits? The MNE's Home shareholders would seem to have taken a capital loss on the subsidiary's zit balances and its explicit contracts to receive zit payments, but scored a gain on the subsidiary's obligations to pay in zits. These current, monetary assets and liabilities, however, are the only clear case. What about the subsidiary's inventories, whose future sale value or replacement cost may be affected in diverse ways by the devaluation? What about long-term debts payable in zits, which may undergo many further fluctuations in value before ultimately being paid off?

MNEs' accounting practices in treating exchange-rate changes have varied among countries as well as over time. Common practices have included the following (Prindl, 1976, Chapter 2; Evans and Folks, 1979):

1. *Closing-rate method.* All the subsidiary's balance-sheet items are simply converted at the end-of-period exchange rate. If the zit has depreciated and all the subsidiary's assets and intercorporate liabilities are zit-denominated, then Home's shareholders are told they have taken a capital loss on their equity in proportion to the depreciation.

2. *Current/noncurrent method* (also called working-capital method). All the subsidiary's short-term (under one year) assets and

liabilities are translated at the end-of-period exchange rate, long-term items at whatever historical exchange rate obtained when they originally went on the books. When the zit depreciates, Home's shareholders are told they have taken a loss if the subsidiary's current zit assets (cash, current receivables, inventories) exceed its current zit liabilities (accounts payable, short-term bank loans).

3. *Monetary/nonmonetary method.* All the subsidiary's monetary assets and liabilities (of whatever maturity) are translated at the end-of-period exchange rate, everything else at the historical rate. The shareholders are notified of a capital loss if the subsidiary's monetary zit assets (cash, current and long-term receivables) exceed its zit liabilities (accounts payable, all zit-denominated loans).

The closing rate method has been popular among U.K. and European MNEs. The practices of U.S. MNEs have been more varied. A 1975 survey (see Evans and Folks, 1979, p. 6) found 35 percent using the current/noncurrent method and 6 percent using a variant on it, 14 percent using the monetary/nonmonetary method and 26 percent using a variant (inventories translated at the current rate). In 1975 the Financial Accounting Standards Board imposed as standardized practice (FAS 8) what was called the temporal method: Items valued on the subsidiary's balance sheet at historical cost should be translated at historical exchange rates; those valued at current or future cost or value should be translated at current exchange rates. This logical-sounding procedure came close to imposing the monetary/nonmonetary method. For most firms it means that inventory, a current but nonmonetary asset, will be translated at historical exchange rates.

The other important feature of FAS 8 was to forbid MNEs to establish valuation reserves that could be used to segregate unrealized foreign-exchange gains and losses from current operating profits. Previously, unrealized exchange losses could be recognized by a deduction from current income, and a reserve could be created for later use to absorb unrecognized gains. This smoothing of the reporting of unrealized foreign-exchange gains and losses was precluded by FAS 8. Some 37 percent of firms sampled in 1975 had been indulging in some deferral.

FAS 8 proved highly controversial. That was because, with exchange rates fluctuating widely and rapidly, the bulk of year-to-year changes in MNEs' reported overseas profits could be due to exchange-rate changes, not changes in local-currency operating profits. Should the zit be appreciating relative to the dollar while the subsidiary holds an advantageous long-term loan in zits, the shareholders must be told each period that they are suffering a capital loss, although the interest the MNE is paying is less than otherwise. Should the zit depreciate, the MNE must indicate a translation loss on its subsidiary's inventories, even though the price level in its market is expected to rise in proportion to the depreciation, giving the subsidiary a zit-denominated capital gain on the inventories. As Burns (1976) noted, the very diversity of firms' practices before FAS 8 suggests that different translation methods may have given the least distorted views of firms' performances in different market settings, so that standardization was achieved at the expense of each firm giving the public, on average, a noisier set of accounting signals than before.[20]

Economists' ruminations on these problems of accounting practice have indicated that no simple way exists to translate an economic evaluation of the effects of exchange-rate changes into accounting rule (see Aliber, 1978, Chapter 8). The economic evaluation depends on forecasts of the future courses of exchange rates and other prices. In the absence of comprehensive futures markets (or a reliable oracle), those forecasts never command more than a modest amount of confidence. Economists can impose some strong forecasts by making certain assumptions about markets' operations: The purchasing-power-parity hypothesis holds that a country's price level rises in proportion to its currency's depreciation; if true, the real assets of the subsidiary in that country are free of exchange risk. The Fisher "open" hypothesis holds that nominal interest rates adapt to any changes in price levels and exchange rates to maintain a constant real rate of interest; if true, the exchange losses on any monetary assets held by the subsidiary are offset by rises in the zit interest

---

[20] A little over 80% of the managers contacted by Evans and Folks (1979, p. 8) had to modify their translation practices to come into conformity with FAS 8.

rates they earn. But these hypotheses are just hypotheses. Shapiro (1975*a*) pointed out that the ultimate effect of an exchange-rate change depends on the market structure surrounding the company, supporting Burns's argument for diversity.

If the public understands perfectly the effects of all economic changes on firms' prospects, it will not matter what the accounting numbers say. If they depend on accounting information, then accounting practices affect their perceptions, and business managers have an incentive to maneuver the accounts in order to induce the most favorable perceptions. Therefore, we expect that firms will change some of their real economic decisions when a change in accounting practice, such as FAS 8, alters the signals.[21] Evans and Folks (1979, p. 15) reported evidence that firms that had to modify their reporting practices spent more on foreign-exchange risk management for self-protection and that they decreased significantly their long exposures in certain currencies.[22] Shank et al. (1979, Chapter 4) suggested that the majority of MNEs had at times incurred real costs in order to avoid reporting translation losses.

If FAS 8 caused MNEs to reveal new information to the public and to incur new economic costs, we might expect the stock market's valuation of these firms to be affected. A number of studies (e.g., Shank et al., 1979; Dukes, 1980) have inquired whether or not after 1975 the market shifted its valuation of MNEs forced to change their accounting practices by FAS 8. No significant valuation shifts have been found, whether the control group has been domestic companies

---

[21] Also, Dietermann (1980) pointed out that accounting practices affect companies' internal appraisals of their personnel and policies, so that the efficiency with which they operate depends both on what set of accounting rules they follow and on how much maneuvering they do to modify the rules' effect on reported financial results.

[22] It is not clear that Evans and Folks always distinguished responses to FAS 8 from responses to the general increase in the variability of exchange rates in the 1970s. However, they did find that increased use of forward-exchange markets to hedge exposure was more common among firms that formerly smoothed out their reporting of unrealized exchange gains and losses than among those that always recognized exchange adjustments immediately. And confirming evidence has appeared in Shank et al. (1979, Chapter 4) and in the business press (*Business Week*, July 21, 1980, p. 167).

or MNEs whose accounting practices have required no change to conform to FAS 8.

The grumbles in the business community over FAS 8 finally brought a major overhaul in late 1981 (FAS 52). The key change from FAS 8 brings practice closer to the closing-rate method described earlier, in that a company's gains and losses from currency translation are distinguished from its operating profits and are shown as a direct gain or loss in the owners' equity. The practice invites the public to distinguish between how well the MNE's foreign subsidiaries do in their real economic transactions abroad and what happens to the fruits of their labors as a result of exchange-rate changes. Although the wealth-maximizing enterprise should consider exchange-rate prospects in making its operating decisions, it seems wise to separate the two kinds of forces in appraising the outcome.

6.4. **MNE finance and public policy**

In this section we shall briefly note some public-policy issues that have risen around the MNE's financial decisions. We shall argue more generally in Chapter 10 that clashes between MNEs and national governments often arise because governments are unwilling either to accept market allocations of resources as they come or to impose unambiguous rules (taxes, rationing devices, and the like) to change them. The resulting compromise is a rolling set of informal or limited pressures on economic agents to "do the right thing." The MNE may, for various reasons, not be an easy mark for this "moral suasion," and so it gets denounced as a traitor to the national cause. But our concern here is not with the political economy of policy but with the substantive issues that abut on the MNE's financial decisions.

Balance of payments

Governments' concern with the balance of payments probably has been the chief policy issue to bear on MNEs' financial behavior, particularly in the 1960s, when almost all the industrial countries chose to maintain fixed exchange rates. To fix an exchange rate at an officially declared value is to kill off the price of foreign exchange as an adjustment device. There is no reason why Home's aggregate demand for purchases from Foreign will equal the aggregate value of Foreign's purchases from Home in the short run. Although many prices other than the exchange rate can respond to such imbalances, the inability of the exchange rate to adjust means that governments see themselves frequently facing imbalances – deficits or surpluses – in their balances of international payments. In the short run, deficits are harder to manage than surpluses, and therefore governments with fixed exchange rates have often found themselves bending every policy instrument to ward off payments deficits. To borrow a term from economic planning, they have behaved as if the "shadow price" of foreign exchange were higher than the official exchange rate.

With the shadow price divorced from the actual exchange rate and the market signals it supplied, a government facing a payments deficit then found itself picking and choosing among the private sector's international transactions, imposing this control or that voluntary restraint in order to keep the country's external purchases and sales in line. MNEs were promptly fingered for their international capital transfers, and direct investment outflows were restricted by the United States.[23] Much of the surrounding policy discussion was of abysmal cogency, but through the murk two pieces of economic analysis proved helpful:

1. *The transfer process.* In the short run, when a MNE transfers one dollar from Home to Foreign, real spending is likely to expand in Foreign and fall in Home. Extra real spending in Foreign falls on all goods consumed, including those imported from Home, and so Home's exports rise. The reduced spending in Home comes partly out of imports, and so Home's imports fall. Home's balance of trade improves, and indeed could improve enough to "requite" the capital outflow so that it involves no short-run deterioration of Home's overall balance of payments. The analysis of the transfer process devel-

---

[23] We note the various statistical investigations seeking to confirm that U.S. restrictions on foreign-investment outflows did indeed succeed in curbing them. Kwack (1972), Herring and Willett (1972), Boatwright and Renton (1975), Mantel (1975), and Goldsbrough (1979) have all investigated the question.

oped by Hufbauer and Adler (1968) was summarized in Section 5.2. The net effects of capital transfers on the balance of payments are determined by factors slightly different from those that determine their effects on employment, but the analyses largely coincide.

2. *The payback period.* Just as one dollar of foreign investment is expected to earn a flow of profits for the MNE, it is expected to bring a reflux of foreign-exchange earnings into the nation's balance of payments. If the government believes that the shadow price of foreign exchange is above the market level, it reasonably examines investment-type outflows to see how soon the return flows will offset the resulting drain. Economists have accordingly measured payback periods for foreign investments (see criticism of the payback concept by Lindert, 1970). The relationships analyzed resemble the questions of investment substitution and export substitution discussed in Section 5.2. For instance, an investment outflow may either support or replace Home's exports – the former effect favoring, the latter harming, Home's balance of payments. And if exports are replaced, their loss may have been inevitable because of the investment-substitution problem. In addition to these effects, payback calculations consider the remittance of dividends by the MNE and perhaps an ultimate repatriation of capital.

Hufbauer and Adler (1968, Chapter 5) sought to estimate these payback periods for U.S. direct investments, as did Reddaway (1967) for the United Kingdom. In some instances the outflows were broken down by individual foreign investing sectors for closer scrutiny (e.g., Makinen, 1970). These measurements by themselves do not prove much about MNEs' behavior. There is no connection between the payback period and the profitability of foreign investment, because the proceeds of a profitable investment may be plowed back, leaving an increasingly valuable but unrepatriated foreign asset; or an unprofitable investment may be promptly dismantled and the surviving funds brought home. However, some investigations of payback patterns have seized on a "life cycle" of foreign investment. Penrose (1956) considered balance-of-payments effects of foreign investments in the context of subsidiaries' tendencies to expand into new activities as they mature. Prachowny and Richardson (1975) attempted a statistical test of life-cycle effects of foreign investments on the balance of payments, finding that as they mature, subsidiaries rely increasingly on internal funds to finance expansion, earn increasing profits, and generate increasing royalty payments (although these eventually fall off). These results predict something about the time-shape of the payback flow from foreign investment – little at first, but then large as the subsidiary matures.

Investment stability and allocation

The other policy issue surging about the MNE's financial decisions concerns the rate of capital formation in the national economy. Governments pursue stable full employment or otherwise adopt macroeconomic goals that touch on gross capital formation and its financing. Two seemingly contradictory hypotheses about MNEs' effects on this effort are common in the literature. The first, pressed by Barnet and Müller (1974), among others, holds that freedom from competitive pressures allows MNEs to delay in adapting their international investment decisions to changed economic conditions (see the discussion by Bergsten et al., 1978, pp. 283–8). The second holds that their access to international financial markets makes them more responsive to investment incentives than are other firms, because they are not constrained by credit conditions in the national market where the investment inducement pops up (e.g., Dunning, 1973*a*).

These hypotheses are not so contradictory as they may seem, either with each other or with the analysis of preceding chapters. Even if the MNE is no more slothful than any other company, it will make tardier investment decisions than will other firms in an important class of cases. Suppose that the seller of product *A* faces a downward-sloping demand curve in each of its markets. Cost conditions have shifted so as to call for a shift in production from Home to Foreign. However, the shift is not so great that the MNE's costs in a new plant in Foreign will be below its variable costs in the old Home plant. The MNE charges the profit-maximizing price for its product (wherever it sells). The MNE does not (yet) invest in a new plant in Foreign. However, an independent firm, influenced by the

MNE's present price and its expected reaction to an entrant, may well make the investment in Foreign sooner.

If product-market considerations and sunk costs potentially make the MNE a laggard in adjusting its investment plans, its role in integrating capital markets (outlined earlier) obviously cuts the other way. Therefore, we have no a priori answer to the following question: Do MNEs with market power adapt their investments to changing market conditions slower or faster than single-nation firms?

Therefore, one proceeds to the empirical evidence without much prior theoretical guidance. Stonehill (1965, Chapter 7) concluded that foreign-controlled companies in Norway were not a source of macroeconomic destabilization, relative to domestic enterprises. Hawkins and Macaluso (1977) found some evidence that subsidiaries can substitute retained earnings and external funds from overseas affiliates for local funds when a credit crunch is on. Of course, governments will not always take the same normative view of the MNE's ability to arbitrage funds between national markets. If the credit crunch represents a policy choice, the MNE's access to credit on terms not controlled by the government may be resented. But at times when more investment is desired by the government, the verdict will go the other way.

6.5. **Summary**

The MNE's financial behavior raises questions about both the macroeconomic and microeconomic environments in which it manages its assets and liabilities. Studies of flows of new investments from parents to subsidiaries and capital-expenditure rates of subsidiaries have sought to find good macroeconomic predictors of these flows. These predictors are nothing more than macroeconomic variables that should be correlated with the events that influence the MNE's assessments of the cash flows it can expect from its new investments. Appreciable support turns up for the neoclassical model of capital formation. However, several statistical investigations of MNEs' financial decisions have supported the unneoclassical conclusion that internally generated funds hold a lower opportunity cost for the MNE than do funds borrowed externally. In any case, the evidence confirms that the MNE makes its investment and financial decisions on a global basis, so that its rate of capital expenditure in one country will tend to fall when its expected returns rise for investment somewhere else.

The capital-arbitrage hypothesis suggests that the MNE borrows wherever in the world funds are cheapest and invests them wherever expected returns are highest. A more subtle view of the MNE's financial decisions must take account of risk and of the degree to which international capital markets are already fully integrated, prior to any arbitraging done by MNEs. Modern finance theory shows that if this perfection were to be achieved, where the MNE would borrow and how it would structure the riskiness of its liabilities could be matters of indifference. But there are general grounds for thinking that exchange-rate movements as well as government restrictions and transactions costs may leave arbitrage possibilities open to the MNE. And the MNE will then rationally relate the scale of its borrowing in each country to the extent of its capital assets placed there, as well as relative borrowing costs and expected behavior of exchange rates. Furthermore, this optimization needs the parent's centralized attention; it cannot be decentralized, nor can the debt-equity structure of financial relations between parent and subsidiary take on any "market" significance of its own (it depends only on tax considerations). The empirical evidence on these questions suggests that MNEs do enjoy opportunities for international arbitrage of funds and that investors recognize the value of the international diversification built into the MNE's liabilities. The relationship between local borrowing and investment by the subsidiary, its practices in remitting dividends, and similar financial decisions are generally consistent with the conclusion that the MNE is a present-value maximizer operating in imperfect international capital markets. However, there is also some evidence of behavior that serves only to placate myopic shareholders.

The MNE also makes short-run decisions about where to hold its liquid assets in light of expected exchange-rate changes. Although all agents are expected to seek profits or avoid losses from exchange-rate changes, the MNE enjoys advantages in this regard from cheaper access to information and greater flexibility in manipulating transactions that are internal to it but that would be at arm's length for national companies. The survey evidence confirms that MNEs' hedging efforts center on these internal transactions. It also suggests that corporate risk aversion influences the extent and character of the MNE's exchange-market transactions and that MNEs generally do not embrace a purely speculative role. But they also do not assume that they can never "beat the market" in anticipating exchange-rate changes.

Exchange-rate variations confront the MNE with problems not only of market behavior but also of their information systems – how to assess and report changes in their asset values when exchange rates change. This issue has greatly bothered corporate accountants for the good reason that the right answer depends on forecasting what today's change in exchange rates portends for future exchange rates as well as for future local-currency prices abroad.

MNEs' financial decisions frequently bring them into conflict with public policy, the conflicts often arising because governments hope to promote economic behavior that is *not* what rational economic actors will undertake based on the signals of current market prices. This form of conflict has appeared most clearly when governments have sought to defend fixed but disequilibrium exchange rates. At times of "exchange crises," MNEs have been found to take self-interested actions, although in company with plenty of single-nation agents. These conflicts also raise the issue of how the MNE's long-term international transactions affect the balance of payments. The transfer process, outlined in Chapter 5, helps us to investigate the immediate consequences of direct investment for the balance of payments. The concept of payback periods assists us to think about the longer-run consequences. MNEs' financial behavior also may collide with government policies toward capital-formation rates and monetary conditions. MNEs' ability to arbitrage capital internationally can make them unpopular with governments seeking to enforce a "shadow interest rate" that diverges from the cost of capital internationally.

7

Technology and productivity

The MNE's rationale, according to the transactional model of Chapter 1, lies in its prowess at evading the failures of certain arm's-length markets, especially those for intangible assets. Premier among those assets is the knowledge that represents new products, processes, proprietary technology, and the like. Therefore, the MNE takes the central role in the production and dissemination of new productive knowledge. In this chapter we shall examine how the MNE performs these functions. Although arm's-length markets for technology are failure-prone, they do exist. Many companies that produce new knowledge are not multinational, and much knowledge is sold or rented between unrelated parties. Persons hostile to MNEs often have proposed that the arm's-length market be expanded and the scope of activities of MNEs cut back. Therefore, an important function of this chapter is to explore this trade-off. Indeed, arm's-length transfer of technology is an alternative to the MNE, somewhat parallel to exports from the firm's home base (discussed in Chapter 2).

This chapter starts with a positive analysis of how the MNE makes its decisions about producing and disseminating technology. It proceeds to a treatment of the consequences of this activity for economic change and economic policy. The policy issues are particularly urgent in this case. Not only does the market for knowledge bristle with potential failings, but also international trade in technical

195

knowledge runs into the familiar conflict between the interests of source and host countries.

7.1. The MNE as producer of technical knowledge

Research on the production and distribution of industrial knowledge customarily distinguishes three phases of the process. *Invention* covers the generation of a new idea and its development to the point where the inventor can show that "it works." *Innovation* takes the invention to the point of being placed on the market; this phase includes building and proving out any needed production facilities as well as testing and refining the invention itself. *Diffusion* is the process by which all potential users of the innovation actually come to make efficient decisions to adopt it.[1] In relating the MNE to these stages of technological development, we shall largely collapse the invention and innovation phases. The process of diffusion, however, is closely connected to the MNE's distinctive activities and requires close attention.

Foreign investment and R&D outlays

The affinities between R&D and the MNE are extensive. We know from Chapter 1 that the extent of R&D spending is an excellent predictor of MNE activity in an industry. Most formal R&D is undertaken by firms of at least moderate size; similarly, scale-economy considerations allot foreign investments to the larger firms. Hence, in those industries where most R&D takes place, both the R&D and the foreign investments are likely to be concentrated among the larger firms. Just as R&D promotes foreign investment, it is possible that foreign investment promotes R&D. The established MNE has in hand the knowledge needed to predict the payout to innovations in diverse national markets, not just the home market. If the MNE's information network indeed yields an advantage for this purpose, it enjoys both a higher and more certain mean expected return from investments in innovation than a similarly placed single-

---

[1] See Mansfield (1974) for a summary oriented toward MNE issues involving the state of our knowledge about R&D.

nation company. Therefore, the causation should run both ways between MNE activity and R&D spending.[2]

Only one study has closely investigated the effects of overseas sales opportunities on R&D – Mansfield, Romeo, and Wagner (1979). They found that the large U.S. companies included in their two samples expect to draw 29 to 34 percent of the returns from their R&D projects from overseas markets via all marketing channels – foreign subsidiaries, licensing, and export of innovative goods.[3] The more research-intensive the company, the larger the share of its R&D returns that comes from outside the United States. The overseas share is greater for research projects, in pursuit of basic discoveries, than for development projects, which tend to adapt innovations to a particular market's needs. These authors also asked the respondent firms how much they would cut back on R&D if they could collect no rents from overseas. The reductions would be 12 to 15 percent if research results could not be exploited through the firms' foreign subsidiaries, 16 to 26 percent if all overseas rents were cut off. The larger the share of the firm's global sales derived from its foreign subsidiaries, the larger the cut. The more extensive is the firm's overseas activity (both exports and foreign subsidiaries), the higher is the rate of return it expects from R&D activities and the more does its R&D tend toward basic research and long-run projects.

Although one wishes more evidence were available, the study by Mansfield, Romeo, and Wagner leaves little doubt that large firms carrying on research base their R&D investments on the revenues they expect to earn worldwide. This global orientation of research activities is seen in mirror image in the patents taken out in countries that are not themselves major research centers; most such patents are registered by foreign nationals seeking global protection from imitation of their inventions. This positive effect of overseas opportu-

---

[2] Similarly, product-market diversification has been held to favor R&D, and the statistical evidence shows a positive association with causation running both ways (e.g., Caves et al., 1980, Chapters 7 and 8).

[3] The firms included in their sample were not necessarily all MNEs, although the MNE percentage must have been quite high. The statistical results of Severn and Laurence (1974) are consistent with the importance of global profitability to the R&D decisions of MNEs.

nities on R&D should also be related to the conclusion stressed in Chapter 1 that R&D activities themselves predict the rise of MNEs. Research outlays and MNE status reinforce each other: Anything that expands research expenditures tends to enlarge a firm's (or industry's) multinational activity, and anything (other than research) that expands multinational activity tends to increase R&D spending (Hirschey, 1981).

If foreign investment functions partly to garner rents to the parent's R&D assets, it also serves as a method of acquiring knowledge assets abroad (Alsegg, 1971, pp. 218–20). Tsurumi (1976, pp. 116–17) pointed out that Japanese companies expanded their foreign investments in research-intensive countries such as the United States and West Germany in order to improve their access to technology flows after companies in those nations, conscious of burgeoning Japanese competition, grew more reluctant to license.

Overseas R&D spending by MNEs

If MNEs take account of worldwide revenue potentials when setting their R&D budgets at home, they also increasingly decentralize R&D activities around the world. Part of the spread is due to government policies, for many governments aim to promote R&D activity on their own soil (Behrman and Fischer, 1980, Chapter 6). However, economic processes once again are at work within the firm. The MNE must determine not only how much R&D to undertake worldwide but also where to put it. This process sheds light not just on the economics of R&D activity itself but also on the transferability of technical knowledge across national boundaries.

In Chapter 2 we reviewed theory and evidence suggesting that the MNE allocates its production facilities around the globe so as to maximize the net revenue it earns from serving any given market. If its intangible R&D output could be transferred costlessly among its various plants, the R&D laboratory would simply be put down in the world's most nearly ideal cost-minimizing location. However, important forces keep all R&D from settling in at some technological Shangri-la. Effective execution of R&D requires a continuous interchange of information with the manufacturing facilities of the company, for research to be directed to significant economic problems and for the R&D solutions to prove operational. Because of the strategic role of R&D, a similarly close interface with top corporate management is also important. These requirements for close communication and interchange, along with any scale economies in the R&D function itself, seem to dominate the decision where to situate R&D activities. They call for centralization at company headquarters, but qualified by the centrifugal pull of manufacturing facilities dispersed to serve far-flung markets.

Both statistical evidence and survey evidence[4] on the experience of U.S. MNEs confirm this framework. First, the agglomerative tendencies for research to remain at the corporate headquarters remain strong, and not much over 10 percent of U.S. MNEs' research is carried on outside the United States. However, that percentage has been growing rapidly in the past two decades; so there is little doubt that MNE managers do think about the optimal locations for their research labs. Another revealing fact is that overseas R&D is oriented rather more toward development and less toward basic research than is R&D done in the United States.[5] The pattern confirms the expectation that research aimed at adapting economic activity to local market conditions often is undertaken in that market. However, there are exceptions: Basic research is more footloose than is applied research, and some of it goes abroad to seek out particular scientific specialists.

Statistical studies have found that the MNE's R&D outlays are more dispersed abroad the larger the percentage of its global sales made by subsidiaries and the less the firm relies on exports to serve

[4] Statistical studies have included Mansfield, Teece, and Romeo (1979), Lall (1979*b*), Parry and Watson (1979), Hewitt (1980), and Hirschey and Caves (1981). Survey data and case studies have been provided by Safarian (1966, Chapter 6), Creamer (1976), Ronstadt (1977), Germidis (1977), and Behrman and Fischer (1980).

[5] Creamer (1976, Chart 4.2) provided the following data on the functional distribution of domestic and overseas R&D by a large sample of U.S. MNEs. In 1972 the overseas affiliates spent 69.0% for development, 29.9% for applied research, and 1.1% for basic research. The corresponding figures for their U.S. parents were 59.8%, 33.9%, and 7.3%. Parry and Watson (1979) found that in Australia, 42% of subsidiaries' R&D is spent modifying technology from abroad.

foreign markets. Scale economies also wield a clear-cut influence: The more important are scale economies in research, the less is it decentralized overseas; however, the more a firm's overseas production is concentrated in a few subsidiaries (where R&D scale economies can be realized), the more does it decentralize its R&D.[6] With these influences controlled, MNEs also show some sensitivity to variations in the costs of R&D inputs from country to country. Decentralization was speeded up in the 1960s, when U.S. R&D personnel were substantially more expensive than their counterparts abroad, and this process apparently has slowed lately as that differential has disappeared (Mansfield, Teece, and Romeo, 1979, Table 3).

7.2. **International transfer of technology**

We now come to the international transfer of technology and the MNE's role in the process. After describing the arm's-length market for industrial technology, we shall turn to the transfer of technology by MNEs, which leads into the product life cycle and overall patterns in the flow of technology and innovations among countries.

Arm's-length markets for technology

The market for technology entails transfers between firms of technical information (designs, descriptions, plans, etc.), including the right to use or infringe on patents, and frequently the services of the licensor's personnel to install and debug the technology or train the licensee's personnel. Agreements may be one-shot, transferring a discrete technology, but often they join the parties in a continuous and long-lasting relationship.[7] The agreement includes a

---

[6] See also Hood and Young (1976). Mansfield, Teece, and Romeo (1979) presented direct estimates of the minimum efficient scale (MES) of overseas R&D facilities. These estimates vary a great deal, suggesting that MES depends on the exact type of work done by the lab. Quality control and "customer engineering" have small minimum scales relative to the development of new products or components (see also Ronstadt, 1977, Chapter 9). Parry and Watson (1979) reported small scales for most industries, but with some exceptions.

[7] Contractor (1980); Herskovic (1976, p. 24); Rosenblatt and Stanley (1978).

royalty rate, frequently some round-number percentage of the licensee's sales revenue or factory costs, perhaps with a minimum payment. The agreement also often contains ancillary restraints: The licensee will grant back to the licensor any improvements made in the process or product; the licensee will not export to certain markets or will otherwise refrain from competing in the licensor's product markets. Licensing is more common the less physically complex are the goods and hence the more easily can technical information be conveyed. It is discouraged in more complex products, such as durable goods, for which much research may involve reconfiguring the product for competitive reasons; the resulting discoveries have little value for licensing to other firms (Wilson, 1977).

The terms of licensing agreements reflect competitive conditions in important ways. First, although the evidence is limited, it appears that much licensing of technology takes place across national boundaries rather than between firms in the same country (Taylor and Silberston, 1973, Chapter 7). To license one's technology to another firm is usually to strengthen another maker of the same product; the rival in a geographically separated market can be licensed without threatening one's own product-market profits. The more international the industry and the less are markets separated by tariffs and other transactions costs, the less licensing we expect to occur. No evidence bears on this hypothesis directly, but Peck (1976, pp. 535–58) observed that the rising royalty rates on international licenses in the late 1960s – just as more sellers of technology were coming on the scene – may have reflected licensors' heightened awareness that licensed technology was strengthening their potential, if not actual, international rivals.

The terms of licensing agreements reflect both the infirmities of the market for information and competitive conditions in that market. Licensors impose various restrictions (how the technology is used, where its output is marketed, what tied purchases must be made from the licensor) in order to make the transfer technically effective in the first place, or to assure themselves an economic advantage from the licensing agreement (Teece, 1981). But restrictions imposed by the licensor also have some negative effects on licensees' willingness to pay. A licensor who restricts his licensee from exporting is forgoing potential license revenue for protection from competition (for empirical evidence, see Herskovic, 1976, pp. 40–7). Licensors of established technology tend to make that sacrifice, but not licensors of novel technology that is likely to become obsolete before the licensee's competition starts to hurt. Similarly, companies are more likely to license their peripheral technologies than technologies used in the firm's core business activity, and licenses of core technologies are more likely to contain market restrictions on the licensee.[8]

Licensees in the technology market behave in ways consonant with the analysis of corporate strategy presented in Chapter 3. Licensing has its risks for them, but it pays where the alternative of doing one's own R&D is poor – for example, where the efficient scale of R&D is large relative to the efficient scale of production (Herskovic, 1976, p. 20). Licensing also pays the firm that is well fixed for using but not producing the technology. A licensee will take on licenses that require a costly and specific physical investment when the technology lies close to the firm's established competence, but it will avoid large investments in specialized facilities when the licensed technology involves diversifying into unfamiliar territory.[9]

The means used by licensors to extract rents through their licenses are important for reasons indicated in the theory of patents. Society grants the inventor a monopoly over his discovery, that theory suggests, because otherwise the intangible knowledge that his discovery represents could be freely copied by others. The inventor would lack any profit incentive to invest in finding new discoveries. The worth of the inventor's monopoly depends not just on his securing and preserving a legal monopoly but also on exploiting it skillfully. Here the market for licenses comes in: Use of a licensed technology yields the licensee a certain revenue, and every dollar of it the licensor

---

[8] These conclusions have been supported by unpublished research by Harold Crookell on the licensing policies of 22 large companies. Also see Behrman's contribution to Mikesell (1962) and Casson (1979, pp. 20–2).

[9] Unpublished research by Peter Killing has documented these and other aspects of rational behavior by licensees. Also see Taylor and Silberston (1973, Chapter 7) and Herskovic (1976).

extracts as royalties brings him closer to maximizing rents from his innovation. A profit-maximizing licensor, fully informed, will write license terms that leave the licensee with just a normal profit. Of course, not every licensed technology is monopolized, and competition drives down each licensor's return. Once the licensor has incurred the fixed costs of developing and proving the technology, the cost of transferring it dwindles to the variable cost of getting it up and running in the licensee's plant.[10] Any competition among licensors tends to drive their returns down to this variable cost.

We have only a little information on where in this range fall the returns actually earned by licensors. One source has claimed that U.S. licensors typically shoot for a royalty rate that will relieve an efficient licensee of one-third of his profits – which is not to extract the full potential rent (Baranson, 1978a, p. 64). Contractor (1980) found that large U.S. licensors typically face competition from other suppliers of technology,[11] but his statistical analysis only weakly confirmed the negative effect of competition on the total (lifetime) returns to a licensing agreement. He did find that they increase significantly with the size of the licensee's plant, which presumably is correlated with the rents that the licensee can earn from the licensed technology.[12] Taylor and Silberston (1973, Chapter 7) also found that the royalty rate decreases as the volume of sales under royalty grows, confirming a fixed component in the charges. They also found that royalty rates are positively related to the amount of knowhow supplied and the cost of supplying it and that royalties are higher for products subject to price-inelastic demands.

---

[10] Plus any premium added to allow for the licensor's expected decrease in future profits due to strengthened competition from the licensee.

[11] Two to 5 rivals in 34% of the cases in Contractor's sample, 5 to 10 rivals in 10%, 11 or more rivals in 29%. The licensor monopolizes in only 27%.

[12] Contractor (1980) tested a number of hypotheses, usually getting the expected sign but not a statistically significant coefficient. In this sense he found that the returns tend to be higher when the licensee is permitted to export (and thus presumably will pay a higher royalty rate) and when the licensor's patent has a long time to run; they are lower when the technology is old. The gross returns to the licensor increase with the direct costs he incurs implementing the agreement or adapting the technology for the licensee.

Licensing versus foreign investment

For our purposes, however, the chief importance of the licensor's market position lies in the (potential) MNE's choice between starting a subsidiary and licensing an established firm in an arm's-length transaction in order to serve a given foreign market. Our transactional model indicated that the horizontal MNE arises because of shortcomings in arm's-length markets for intangible assets, and the statistical evidence established that high-R&D industries with ample technology assets are very prominent among the foreign investors. We therefore expect the relative advantages and disadvantages of licensing and foreign investment to determine where one stops and the other starts. And the empirical evidence on their prevalence ought to confirm these advantages and disadvantages. Put a bit more formally (Davies, 1977; Buckley and Davies, 1979), an efficient local firm will see greater present value in a given project than will a foreign entrepreneur, other things being equal, because of the latter's unfamiliarity with the territory. If the foreign firm holding licensable intangible assets could negotiate licensing terms to extract the local firm's entire rent, it would always license and never choose direct investment. But the choice tilts toward foreign investment when the foreigner cannot collect the full rent or when suitable local firms are not to be found (e.g., in LDCs).

Several empirical studies (especially Baranson, 1978*a*, and Telesio, 1979) have exposed the factors that govern this choice between licensing and foreign investment. They suggest, first off, that companies do contemplate foreign investment and licensing as direct alternatives, preferring foreign investment for its greater rent-extracting potential, turning to licensing only if that potential cannot be realized (Telesio, 1979, p. 37). The following determining forces emerge:

1. Licensing is encouraged where entry barriers deter the firm from foreign investment. Barriers presumably operate when the firm decides that the market is too small, meaning that entry at minimum efficient scale is not warranted given the market's size (Telesio, 1979, pp. 19–20, 38). Telesio (pp. 21–2) also argued that market competition disposes the asset holder toward licensing rather than

entering. However, this hypothesis also must rest on barriers to entry by the foreign investor, because otherwise competition would also shrivel the rents that a potential licensee would be willing to pay.

2.   Licensing is encouraged when the licensor lacks some assets needed for foreign investment. These might include a stock of accumulated knowledge and experience with foreign markets,[13] managerial skills, or capital (meaning that the firm's shadow price of funds is high because of good competing uses). These considerations help to explain why the smaller the firm and the more valuable its internal uses of its resources, the more likely it is to resort to licensing rather than foreign investment (Telesio, 1979, pp. 78–80).

3.   Licensing is discouraged where arm's-length licenses are costly to arrange because of haggling over complex terms, enforcing the agreement, preventing quality deterioration by the licensee when a trademark product is involved, and preventing leakage of a technology from a licensee's hands into those of unlicensed competitors.

4.   The lead time required to license an established producer usually is less than that required to start a subsidiary from scratch. If so, licensing is encouraged where the rents to the intangible asset are short-lived, say, because the industry's technology is changing rapidly (Michalet and Delapierre, 1976, pp. 16–17, 24). This consideration probably explains why Telesio (1979, Chapters 5 and 6) found that the proportional reliance on licensing (relative to foreign investment) actually increases with the importance of R&D for a firm: Foreign investment increases with R&D, but licensing increases even more.

5.   Risk considerations affect the choice between licensing and foreign investment in diverse ways. The licensor exposes no substantial bundle of fixed assets in the foreign market and so avoids a downside risk (e.g., when expropriation is a possibility) that might deter foreign investment. On the other hand, the risk of leakage of a technology into the hands of competitors deters a firm from licens-

---

[13] Telesio (1979, pp. 84–6) provided evidence from interviews. He also claimed that experienced firms place proportionally greater reliance on licensing (Chapter 5). However, his proxy for experience was itself the extent of foreign investment, and that builds in a statistical bias toward acceptance of the hypothesis.

ing its core technology. This consideration probably explains why firms diversified in product markets are more disposed to license.[14]

6.   Licensing is discouraged if the opportunity cost of capital is higher in the recipient country than in the country of the potential licensor, because the licensee then will value the expected stream of rents to the technology less than will the owner of the technology (Jones, 1979, p. 264). This implication of the capital-arbitrage model of foreign investment (Chapter 2) has not been tested on national aggregates, but it has been confirmed by case evidence on how the opportunity cost of funds affects companies' choices between licensing and foreign investment.

7.   Licensing is encouraged by possibilities for reciprocity: If you license a technology to another enterprise, some day it may in return license one that you require. Telesio (1979, Chapter 4) found this practice quite common in certain industries, where it supplies a motive for licensing independent of those listed earlier. The evidence marks reciprocal licensing as one form of mutual understanding among oligopolistic rivals in certain markets, a policy not without its negative implications for competition and market performance. The process seems fairly innocent when firms thereby assist each other in filling out their product lines. It becomes less innocent when going firms cross-license each other without royalty payments but decline to license to newcomers, thereby creating a barrier to entry (Telesio, 1979, pp. 62–4).

8.   Finally, licensing is discouraged in settings where the relevant knowledge is subject to much lower transfer costs within the MNE than between independent firms. As Teece (1981) put it, codified knowledge may be subject to relatively modest transfer costs either way, whereas uncodified knowledge that rests on learned skills or team experience is both more expensive to transfer any way and *relatively* more costly (or difficult) to transfer at arm's length.

Some additional light is shed on the trade-off between licensing and foreign investment by Davies's (1977) study of British MNEs'

---

[14] Telesio (1979, pp. 76–7) suggested that diversification may also be associated with shortages of complementary assets needed to start foreign subsidiaries for the purpose of exploiting peripheral technologies.

operations in India, where government regulations forced them to choose between licensing and joint ventures with Indian firms. The MNEs were clearly willing to hand over more extensive packages of technologies, provide more extensive auxiliary information, and take the trouble to adapt the technology to Indian conditions when an equity share was retained through a joint venture. Although joint ventures have their own limitations (see Section 3.4), they apparently also avert some of the disincentives to trade in intangible assets through arm's-length agreements.

Finally, Teece (1977) provided unique data on the costs of internal and external transfers of technology. He upset the familiar assumption that information once developed costs nothing to transfer. In the average project that he surveyed, the costs of transferring a production process amounted to 19 percent of the total costs of the project receiving it, with the range (for 26 projects) running from 2 to 59 percent. Teece found that these transfer costs vary from case to case in predictable ways: They tend to be higher the first time the technology is transferred, and higher for newer technologies. They are lower the more prevalent are similar technologies among other companies, and the more experienced in manufacturing is the recipient unit.[15]

MNEs, technology transfer, and the product cycle

A well-known effort has been made by Vernon (1966) and many followers to build a model of the international diffusion of technology under the rubric of the "product cycle." Although primarily concerned with explaining international shifts in production and trade, this model does relate foreign investment and the transfer of technology by the MNE to the diffusion of innovations. The product-cycle model was recently laid to rest by its progenitor (Ver-

---

[15] Surveys and case studies generally have supported Teece's findings. Tsurumi (1976, pp. 189–92) found that the expatriate personnel needed to transfer a technology increase with its complexity, independent of the scale of the recipient facility. And Sekiguchi (1979, pp. 65–7) noted that the effectiveness of transfers of Japanese textile technology has been impaired where recipient countries have restricted the presence of foreign personnel.

non, 1979), although with no surrender of claims for its empirical explanatory power for two to three decades following World War II.

The model's interest for our purposes lies in the link it forges between the diffusion of an innovation and the location decisions of MNEs, a link quite consistent with the transactional model of the MNE that emerged in Chapters 1 and 3.[16] The model starts with the incentive to innovate. Most innovations, we assume, are labor-saving. Process innovations substitute capital for labor, or reduce input requirements for labor more than they do for capital. Product innovations such as household durable goods often substitute capital for labor in the production of utility within the household. The pay-out to such innovations is therefore greatest in those countries where wages and therefore the value of people's time are highest relative to the user cost of capital. Invention is an economic search process bestirred (in part) by the inventor's perception of a need to be filled and a profit to be made; given the random nature of the inventor's search, his eye most probably falls on nearby opportunities. Therefore, inventions and innovations are concentrated in high-income countries. Not only invention but also early-stage production is tied closely to the high-income goegraphical market where the innovation has the best prospects. Methods of producing it are fluid and small-scale in the early stages. Uncertainty about optimal production methods and configurations of the innovation discourages either the development of large-scale production or world-wide search for the most efficient production location. They are also deterred by low price-elasticities of demand, small market sizes, and the low levels of competition likely to prevail for a new product. Therefore, production as well as consumption of the innovation initially sticks to the high-income market.

Eventually, use of the new technology spreads to other countries as their rising real wages (and values of household labor time) make capital saving more profitable and as the real price of the innovation falls. This demand is at first served by exports from high-income areas, a prediction that accords with the high R&D intensity of the

[16] Johnson (1968) probably did the most to bring out the analytical under-pinnings of the product cycle, and his account is followed here.

export industries of the United States. However, as the innovation's technology and production method settle down, a search intensifies for low-cost production locations, and this search tends to carry production outside the highest-wage countries. Increasing price-elasticities of demand, as users grow more familiar with the innovation, and sharper competition in the product market pull in the same direction. Exports from the high-income innovating countries are displaced by expanding production in other industrial countries. Finally the shifting pattern of production and use, as the innovation matures, may carry production toward the LDCs, and the industrial countries may lose their comparative advantage entirely. Of course, the "mature" innovation may get displaced by its successor before this final stage is reached.

Most systematic empirical research on the product cycle has concentrated on patterns of production and trade rather than on the activity of the MNE (Wells, 1972). Yet the prevalence of MNEs in high-R&D industries (shown in Chapter 1) and the disabilities of the arm's-length market for technology transfer both imply that the MNE functions prominently in the international dissemination of innovations. The model explains why the United States was a fertile source of innovations and a prolific source of MNEs and why U.S. foreign investments have been concentrated in innovative industries both early (Vernon, 1971, p. 85) and late (Gruber et al., 1967) in the twentieth century. As an epicycle on the product cycle, the European countries' shortages of native raw materials bred an incentive to innovate in materials-saving technologies, a pattern reflected in the industry composition of Europe-based MNEs (Franko, 1976, Chapter 2; Tsurumi, 1976, pp. 174–6).

Still, not much research on the product cycle has focused specifically on the question of how much difference the MNE's presence makes to the speed and direction of the diffusion process. Tilton's (1971) study of the semiconductor industry emphasized the importance of newly founded foreign subsidiaries in transplanting U.S. innovations to the European countries. Older foreign subsidiaries, however, tended to behave rather like any incumbent firm: An established company will rationally innovate later than a new firm if the innovation makes its facilities obsolete but is not so good that it pays to scrap the existing capacity immediately. Globerman (1975) found no statistical evidence that foreign subsidiaries in the Canadian tool-and-die industry adopted numerically controlled machine tools faster than did domestic firms. Stobaugh's (1972) investigation of petrochemicals and Hufbauer's (1966) investigation of synthetic materials both suggest that scale economies in production and marketing retard diffusion. The firm that introduces the innovation gains a sustained first-mover advantage and delays taking production outside the country. When diffusion does occur, scale economies point foreign investment toward large host markets. Leroy (1976, Chapter 6) found that overseas transfers of a majority of sampled products followed Vernon's export-then-produce-abroad sequence; in a minority, however, production started in the MNE's host country and then stayed lodged there.

Apparently the only statistical investigation of the speed of diffusion and its relationship to MNEs has been that of Lake (1979), who was concerned with the relationship between market structures and the international diffusion of technology among MNEs. His data on the semiconductor industry in the United States and the United Kingdom weakly affirm the conclusion from many single-nation studies that diffusion is faster the more competitive is the industry in which it occurs. He also found diffusion to be faster when it takes place among firms with previous experience in the process, a result consistent with Vernon and Davidson's (1979) finding that diffusion processes are accelerating over time. Lake also claimed to find that U.S. MNEs' subsidiaries have outperformed domestic competitors in the diffusion of innovations in U.K. industry, but his methodology is somewhat suspect.

The most comprehensive data on the MNE's role in the diffusion of innovation have recently been assembled by Vernon and Davidson (1979). They covered the overseas spread through subsidiaries and licensees of 406 innovations introduced since 1945 by 57 U.S. MNEs. Their results tend to confirm the hypothesis that the MNE's information network and ready apparatus for making technology transfers do affect the diffusion process. The higher the MNE's initial proportion of sales made abroad (through both exports and subsidiary sales), the quicker are innovations transferred for production abroad. Transfer comes quicker when the innovation lies in the firm's principal product line and when the firm has had previous experience with transfers in this product line. Similarly, the more previous experience with transfers to a given country, the faster is the next innovation transferred to that country. The MNE with a high ratio of R&D to sales (either relative to its base industry or relative to other MNEs) transfers technology abroad more rapidly.

The Vernon-Davidson data also provide some information on the use of subsidiaries relative to licensees in the diffusion process. For a sample of 32 firms, transfers to licensees were 28.5 percent of all transfers over 1945–75, the share declining slightly from 1945–55 to 1966–75 (perhaps because the firms' networks of subsidiaries were growing more extensive). Subsidiaries were predominant in the first couple of years of the diffusion of an innovation, but then licensees started to catch up. Licensees play more of a role for true innovations than for new products that imitate other firms' innovations; presumably the imitations are attuned largely to oligopolistic rivalry among firms and hence have little value for licensing (see Wilson, 1977). Firms are more likely to resort to arm's-length licenses when they have had substantial past experience with transfers of technologies of all types, and when the technology lies outside their base industry (Davidson and McFetridge, 1981).

The Vernon-Davidson results and others bearing on MNEs in the product cycle do not lead us to clear-cut formal conclusions – certainly not about the product-cycle model itself. However, they are broadly consistent with the preceding analysis of international transfers of technology and, indeed, the explanations of MNEs' activities developed in earlier chapters. They are consistent with intracorporate transfers of technology having some advantages over the arm's-length market for licenses. They are consistent with international transfers of technology being deterred by transfer costs, but with firms' alacrity to incur them increasing with the gross returns expected from the transfer.

Indeed, the consistency of the evidence with rational behavior by well-informed MNEs makes one slightly suspicious of parts of the original product-cycle formulation, which invoked myopia and uncertainty in the introductory stage of an innovation to explain why diffusion beyond the innovating country is delayed (see Leroy, 1976, Chapter 1). Vernon's recent (1979) revision of his views allows that the global information network of the established MNE may sever the link between the site where the invention is first proved and the markets where the commercial innovation takes root – possible, though expensive, according to Teece's (1977) data on costs of technology transfers. He also pointed out that the United States is reft of its predominant role as a probable site of innovation because of the convergence of wage levels and per-capita incomes among the industrial countries.

7.3. **General-equilibrium and welfare aspects**
The international licensing market and the MNE's development and transfer of technology have been studied at the microeconomic level. We shall now consider their implications for resource allocation in the overall economy and for economic welfare.

Theoretical contributions
Economists pursuing technology transfer into the realm of general equilibrium have had a difficult time of it. Such models are traditionally static and do not easily make room for imperfectly marketed assets like proprietary knowledge. Even if one gets around the market for intangible assets, the effects of technical change on production functions can be complex to model. The relevant contributions are complicated, and so the following summary is selective (see Pugel, 1981, for a more complete account).

Krugman (1979) presented a model that does not explicitly capture the MNE as a capital arbitrager but does develop the general-equilibrium implications of technology transfers. Krugman's starting point is the product cycle (Vernon, 1966). Suppose that new technology consists of a continuing stream of product innovations and that these all emerge initially in one country (Home). With a random lag, each new good's technology becomes known in the other country (Foreign). New goods are those whose technology is still known only in Home; old goods are those producible in Foreign. Labor is the only factor of production, immobile between Home and Foreign. Under these assumptions, Home's labor may share the rents from the extra value that consumers everywhere place on new goods. Depending on how highly consumers value new goods relative to old ones, Home may specialize completely in new goods, in which case Home workers earn a higher wage. However, if in equilibrium Home also produces some old goods, its labor earns no premium over Foreign's. Product innovations make both Home and Foreign better off – Home by improving the terms of trade, Foreign by making more kinds of goods available for consumption so that a higher level of utility can be enjoyed. The transfer of technology, when a new good becomes an old good, also increases the world's real income (because it is then produced by cheaper Foreign labor rather than dearer Home labor). Foreign clearly gains from the technology transfer. Home, however, can either gain or lose: As consumers, Home citizens find that the relative price of the "newly old" good has fallen, but as workers they find that their wage has fallen slightly in terms of all other goods.[17]

Homogeneous, internationally mobile capital can be added to Krugman's model, with its rate of return the same in equilibrium in Home as in Foreign. Innovation tends to raise the marginal product of capital in Home and pull capital in from abroad; the transfer of technology pushes capital abroad to Foreign. Capital movements in Krugman's model are a consequence of transfers of technology, not a cause. There is also a sense in which they substitute for technology transfers in making world production as efficient as possible. That is, technology transfers shift the world's production-possibilities frontier outward because they permit producing the existing quantity of the new good at a lower resource cost. From such an equilibrium,

---

[17] In a somewhat similar model, McCulloch and Yellen (1976) showed that Home can gain if Foreign turns out to have such a comparative advantage in an innovative good that production of the newly old good shifts entirely to Foreign. Krugman's model does not allow for comparative-advantage differences among old goods. The McCulloch-Yellen paper will be discussed later.

with Foreign constrained to be completely specialized in old goods, it will also be possible in some cases to attain efficiency in world production by letting enough of Foreign's capital migrate to Home to produce new goods. McCulloch and Yellen (1976) developed this proposition as well as the implications of technology transfers for labor's real income. For example, with capital immobile internationally, Home labor benefits from transfer of Home's technology advantage to Foreign if the advantage is in the capital-intensive good. Then, after the transfer, Home's capital stock must be reallocated toward the labor-intensive industry, raising the marginal product of Home's labor in terms of both new and old goods.[18]

For an effort to show the formal consequences of MNEs as transferors of technology, we turn to Findlay (1978) (also see Koizumi and Kopecky, 1977). In his model, Foreign suffers a systematic technology gap. Being backward offers a sort of advantage: The further behind the leader you are, the more easily can you pick up the leader's innovations and narrow the gap. Findlay argued, however, that this property of relative backwardness really implies not a complete catch-up but an equilibrium lag behind the frontier. He assigned the capital that Home's MNEs invest in Foreign the role of a generalized promoter of technological improvement: The more chances do Foreign's native factors have to observe Home's advanced technology used by Home's foreign subsidiaries, the faster does Foreign's technology level grow. Thus, Foreign's general rate of technical progress is higher the larger is Foreign's stock of Home-originated MNE capital relative to domestic capital, and the lower is Foreign's technology level relative to Home's. The model contains a complex mechanism that adjusts the stocks of domestic capital and MNE capital in Foreign in relation to the levels of technology in Home and Foreign. When Home's MNEs employ relatively advanced technology in Foreign, they earn high profits, which are taxed by Foreign's government. This tax revenue is channeled to

---

[18] McCulloch and Yellen also developed the consequences of technology transfers for employment in a Brecher-type model in which the real wage is fixed in terms of the old good. Home's transfer of technology to Foreign can then either raise or lower Home's employment.

finance expansion of the share of Foreign's domestic capital, cutting down the rate at which the MNE capital promotes the advance of Foreign's technology frontier. Also, Foreign's wage level is assumed to rise with the expansion of that technology frontier, and wage inflation thereupon cuts into the profits of the MNE sector and slows its investment rate. The upshot is that the stocks of MNE capital and domestic capital in Foreign possess long-run equilibrium values that are determined jointly with the technological gap.

The assumption that MNE capital has a "positive contagion" in spreading technological improvement has striking implications that appear in some of the model's comparative-statics properties. Foreign's increase in the tax rate on resident MNE capital raises the relative stock of domestic capital and lowers dependence on imported capital, but it also enlarges the long-run equilibrium technology gap; so does an increase in the rate of domestic saving in Foreign. Whether or not the positive-contagion hypothesis has any empirical validity is, of course, a separate question; the point of Findlay's model is that if technology transfer takes this form it has quite surprising implications for economic policy.

Other approaches to technology transfer have emphasized its relationship to the commodity terms of trade, as did Krugman (1979), but have employed a different strategy in building the model. Jones (1979, Chapter 16) allowed Home's superior technology to be embodied in capital goods invested abroad by one of Home's industrial sectors.[19] The capital export is likely to expand world output of the affected commodity, even though risks to Home's foreign investors inhibit the superior technology from driving Foreign's inferior technique totally from Foreign's market. Home may lose from this export of technology (and capital) if the transferred technology pertains to Home's export good, lowering its relative price and worsening Home's terms of trade. Home will then maximize its welfare by

---

[19] In an earlier report, Jones (1970) showed in the context of the Heckscher-Ohlin model how technology differences (and thus technology transfers) between countries may affect their equilibrium relative commodity prices in the absence of trade. This model allows for both differential effects between industries and differential biases in the proportional reduction of input requirements for each factor of production.

taxing the export of technology. However, if the exported technology expands the output of Home's imported good, Home will gain by subsidizing technology exports.

Kojima (1975) was similarly concerned with technology transfer in the context of sector-specific technology and capital, so that technology transfers affect a particular sector and thus the terms of trade. His analysis stems from his empirical observation that Japan's foreign investment in manufacturing has emanated from the country's import-competing sector. When it raises technology levels in the recipient countries (in Southeast Asia, say), it is their export industries that are benefiting, and so international trade tends to expand. On the other hand, he argued that foreign investment by Western countries typically proceeds from their export industries to their counterparts that are import-competing industries abroad; capital movements then tend to reduce and substitute for trade (as in the Heckscher-Ohlin model discussed in Section 2.3). Kojima was not so successful formally in developing either a mechanism to induce this transfer of technology or a normative framework for evaluating its effects,[20] but he did usefully suggest that sectorally biased transfers of technology may have empirical importance.

The studies summarized so far have generally been concerned with the effects of free dissemination of Home's technology to Foreign and the optimal policy for Home to follow given that no proprietary owner collects rents on the exported knowledge.[21] Rodriguez (1975) concentrated on the policy alternatives available to Home's government for maximizing the contribution of the nation's

[20] He suggested that technology transfers should be judged favorable to welfare if they expand trade, unfavorable if they contract it. As Jones (1979, Chapter 16) has shown, that conclusion may pertain to the welfare of the transferor country in a two-country world, but not to world welfare.

[21] McCulloch and Yellen (1976) did show that free dissemination is never optimal for Home if trade is free of tariffs and Home's resources are fully employed; with unemployment due to a fixed minimum wage, the optimal royalty rate may be anything from zero to prohibitive. Jones (1979, Chapter 16) emphasized the relationship between Home's optimal tax on technology embodied in sector-specific capital goods and Home's commodity terms of trade.

proprietary technology to its own welfare. In a general-equilibrium model he showed that under certain assumptions (notably, constant opportunity costs: the slope of a country's transformation curve does not change as factors are reallocated between sectors) Home's problem of maximizing rents from its technology is identical with the problem of maximizing monopoly rents on its trade with the rest of the world. Suppose that Home produces soft drinks and controls the secret formula for producing their flavoring. Foreign's consumers are assumed to be better off consuming some soft drinks than if they consume only the other goods that Foreign can produce without access to Home's exports or technology. Then Home achieves the same welfare level (and also leaves Foreign in the same welfare position) whichever of the following policies Home's government adopts: (1) an optimum tariff on Home's trade with Foreign; (2) a tax on soft-drink technology licenses that maximizes Home's monopoly profits; (3) authorization of a multinational subsidiary in Foreign to monopolize the soft-drink business in Foreign's market and maximize its profits.[22] Rodriguez's model becomes somewhat more complex if his countries' transformation curves are not flat, indicating constant opportunity costs, but rather bowed out to reflect increasing costs (as in Figure 2.2); then Home needs to impose both a charge for technology licenses and a tax on trade in order to maximize its real income.

The preceding theoretical studies have suffered from treating Home's stock of technology as exogenous. They have thus neglected the basic dilemma stemming from failures in the market for proprietary knowledge: One cannot simultaneously distribute the existing stock around the world efficiently and reward inventors so as to induce investments in new knowledge. Pugel (1980*b*, 1981) investigated how induced R&D investments change the consequences of

---

[22] The license fee is assumed to take the form of a royalty per bottle of soft drink. If, instead, Home holds out for a lump-sum royalty payment, it is, in effect, making an all-or-nothing offer that can potentially relieve Foreign's consumers of all the surplus they enjoy from soft drinks – not just the part that a simple monopolist would get. Then the technology license becomes superior to the other policies from Home's viewpoint.

Foreign's natural bent to free-ride on imported technology or tax away any rents collected in Foreign's markets on Home's behalf. Clearly, the globally optimal royalty payment for the use of technology becomes positive, and Foreign may even improve its own welfare by coughing up royalty payments so as to induce a continuing flow of cost-reducing research. Foreign's taxes on royalty payments for Home's technology then have negative externalities for Home, because in cutting R&D investments by Home's producers, they render Home's own (future) unit costs of production higher than they would otherwise be. In the same vein, Koizumi and Kopecky (1980) associated the production of technology with learning-by-doing in the use of the firm's capital stock. The more rents the firm can gather by transferring cost-reducing improvement abroad, the larger capital stock it then chooses to maintain at home in order to generate such experience-based improvements. In this model, transfers of technology abroad can have an adverse short-run effect on the wages of Home's labor for the usual reasons, but a positive long-run effect because of the extra capital formation induced to capture overseas rents from the technology improvements.

Empirical evidence

The preceding models together suggest that international transfers of technology may weigh importantly in the welfare economics of foreign investment. If the MNE is a significant agent in transferring technology, the positive effect on world welfare can be large. Therefore, it is important to consider empirical evidence bearing on the MNE's role as a transfer agent. However, ideally the evidence will also shed light on the adversary interest of transferor and transferee countries in capturing the associated economic rents. These rents, we have seen, raise problems for policymakers. What they should do depends on whether or not private-property rights attach to the knowledge. Other vital influences are the incidental effects of the transfer on the terms of trade. Most of the empirical evidence bears on two questions: To what extent does seller competition erode the rents potentially accruing to MNEs' technology? Just how superior is the technology used by MNEs, on the average, and how much of it leaks out to competing domestic factors of production?

There is some evidence to indicate how market competition affects the rent streams accruing from international sales of technology and how national governments seek to divert these streams. How nearly like monopolists are the commercial firms controlling Home's technology when they sell in Foreign's markets? Is rivalry among them eroding Home's total monopoly rents and transferring them to Foreign's consumers? The evidence from industry studies cannot be called hard evidence, but they have shown a tendency for firms unsuccessful or inactive in foreign investment to license their technology abroad, thereby competing with the foreign-subsidiary sales or exports of other national companies.[23]

Indirect evidence on competition and technology licensing comes from the behavior of governments in this area. If sellers of technology competed as Cournot price rivals, rents on technologies would tend to yield only a normal rate of return on the resources used in the transfer (not the production) of knowledge. Transferee governments could not gain from intervening in the market for technology transfers so as to force terms of trade more favorable to their citizens. However, if transferors retain appreciable monopoly power, a government may usefully intervene to override the bargains struck by its own citizen-licensees and force a cost-minimizing all-or-nothing offer on the foreign owner of the technology. The gains from government intervention should be greater where its citizens bid competitively for the license. Peck (1976) concluded that the Japanese government has appreciably raised national welfare by intervening in its licensees' negotiations and stifling competition among them. Davies (1977) similarly claimed that the Indian government managed to halve average royalty rates and cut the duration of agreements. The apparent success of these interventions does suggest that licensors otherwise command appreciable monopoly power in arm's-length transactions. And, of course, the discrimination in patent pol-

---

[23] See Tilton (1971, pp. 118–19) on AT&T's licensing policy in semiconductors and Baranson (1978a) on competition among U.S. manufacturers of light aircraft and its consequences for licensing a Brazilian producer.

icy against foreign applicants, employed by many LDCs and some developed countries, operates to the same end (Penrose, 1973; McQueen, 1975).

Much more evidence bears on our other empirical question: To what degree do technologies and related proprietary assets transferred abroad escape from their owners' control? Given the stock of knowledge, such leakage probably increases the recipient country's welfare and world welfare, while reducing the welfare of the country that invested to produce the knowledge. But in the long run, reduced appropriability causes underinvestment in such knowledge assets and hence potentially reduces world welfare. For the policymaker in the country generating the technology, there is another question: Do its citizens who use or license technology abroad correctly value the risk to the national welfare of the knowledge thereby escaping from proprietary control? For example, Baranson (1978*b*) and others have voiced concern that U.S. MNEs do indeed "give away the store" by licensing their latest and best technologies abroad to dubious customers who are all too likely to make off with the nation's intellectual treasure.[24]

A number of general studies have shed light on the leakage of MNEs' intangible assets, but only Mansfield and Romeo (1980) have focused closely on measuring and evaluating the leakage of specific technologies. From a sample of technology exports by U.S.-based firms, they determined the average time elapsed between a technology's introduction by one of the firms and its transfer abroad. The mean lag was 6 years for transfer to the firm's subsidiaries in developed countries, 10 years for transfer to subsidiaries in LDCs, and 13 years for transfer to joint ventures or transfer through arm's-length licenses. In most cases, use of the technology abroad was not thought to speed its imitation by a foreign competitor. However, in

---

[24] Baranson's (1978*b*) case studies yielded little direct support for his normative conclusions because they failed to consider the royalties received from technology licenses by the U.S. licensors and the extent of competition from non-U.S. technology suppliers. Case studies by other investigators (Hayden, 1976) have given a more favorable assessment of the bargaining sagacity of U.S. MNEs, even in the difficult situations stressed by Baranson where foreign investment is a poor alternative and foreign-government involvement is high.

about one-third of the cases the appearance of a competing product or process was speeded up by at least 2.5 years.[25] Mansfield and Romeo also secured from domestic firms in the United Kingdom estimates of how often their innovative efforts had been speeded up by technology transfers from U.S. MNEs to their competing subsidiaries in the United Kingdom. Over half believed that at least some of their products and processes had been introduced (or introduced sooner) because of the competitive effects of these transfers.

Beyond Mansfield and Romeo, a number of studies have touched on the productivity growth and level of MNEs in relation to competing domestic firms (especially in host countries). They have sought to address issues that range beyond those of technology transfer, such as the question whether or not MNEs are "more efficient" than other companies. Some studies have examined productivity in foreign subsidiaries and competing domestic enterprises in Australian and Canadian markets. If the two types of firms coexist, and superior technology or productivity imported by the subsidiaries progressively spills over to their domestic rivals, the subsidiaries' superiority should appear as a differential-rent component of their value added. And if domestic firms follow more closely the more they are exposed to the subsidiaries, the domestic firms' relative productivity should increase with the subsidiaries' share of the market. Caves (1974a) and Globerman (1979a) both found reasonably strong evidence to support the hypothesis. Neither study rested on data that would permit measuring efficiency within the context of fully estimated production functions for the foreign and aomestic firms, but both attempted to control for the shortcoming so far as their data would permit.

The pursuit of technological (or other) advantages of MNEs through data on productivity is risky. As Hufbauer (1975, pp. 268–71) has shown, under some assumptions a MNE's productivity ad-

---

[25] The acceleration was greater for process technologies. A product innovation usually is imitated by "reverse engineering": Buy the innovation, take it apart, and figure out how it works. This does not depend on propinquity to the factor. Process innovations, however, can be imitated only by observing them, contacting suppliers, hiring away employees, or other methods for which distance matters.

vantage will enlarge its market share without yielding any differential in productivity. Therefore, some interest attaches to studies that have investigated company size along with productivity differentials. Parry (1974*b*) seemed to find that subsidiaries' sizes relative to their domestic competitors in Australia are greater in research-intensive industries. Caves (1980*b*) treated relative size and relative productivity as being jointly determined and also filtered out some influences (scale economies in production, marketing assets of MNEs) that affect revenue productivity but are unrelated to technology. At least for a few countries – and research has concentrated on the most likely cases – MNEs have appeared in statistical studies to play some role in the international transfer of technology. Case studies for these same countries have provided confirming evidence (Brash, 1966, pp. 194–202) with regard to MNEs' suppliers and customers as well as competitors (Dunning, 1958, pp. 224–5; Forsyth, 1972, pp. 145–50).

This conclusion requires delicate treatment, however, because of the complexity of the question and the incompleteness of the statistical studies. It has not been shown, for example, that the presence of MNEs reduces productivity gaps after one has controlled for other avenues of technology transfer. Also, other hypotheses suggested by the technology-transfer process have fared only moderately well in their statistical tests. If the MNE is a uniquely vital link in transfers of technology, then industrial productivity for countries that are mainly technology importers should be relatively higher in industries congenial to MNEs' operations. This hypothesis has been tested on Canada relative to the United States with mixed results (Caves et al., 1980, Chapter 10; Saunders, 1978) and on the United Kingdom relative to the United States with negative results.[26] It is worth recalling that locational and policy-related variables (e.g., transportation costs and tariffs) can lure foreign subsidiaries into markets where they may operate inefficiently, say, at suboptimal scales, but yet be profitable because of the dowry of intangible assets supplied by their parents

---

[26] Caves (1980*a*, pp. 153–4, 170–1); also see Dunning and Pearce (1977, pp. 69–72) and Solomon and Ingham (1977). Katz (1969, Chapter 7) provided positive evidence from Argentina's experience.

(e.g., Parry, 1974*a*). These influences are adverse to the productivity of MNEs and of the industries in which they operate.

Similarly, studies of the relative productivity or profitability of MNEs and their domestic competitors demand careful interpretation. These will not be considered in detail, but their general thrust has been to find that MNEs are more profitable or display higher productivity than selected single-nation rivals.[27] These researchers have imputed these results to various of the MNE's possible advantages that can raise profitability or productivity, including marketing and managerial skills,[28] product differentiation, and many factors other than technology. In light of the preceding chapters, this whole line of inquiry leaves one fairly unsatisfied. Companies do not become multinational unless they are good at something. To find that the profit rates or productivity levels of MNEs exceed those for single-nation rival companies is unsurprising, on the one hand, and fails to identify the exact source of the rent, on the other. Therefore, the most revealing study of this type has been Vendrell-Alda's (1978) exhaustive analysis of establishment-level data for Argentina. After controlling for a large number of industrial and strategic factors affecting foreign- and domestic-controlled plants in his sample, he found no significant residual productivity differential for the foreign manager per se. His result suggests that any technology or productivity advantages possessed by MNEs are endogenous to the market-structure environments in which they emerge and have no pure residual component.

7.4. Summary

This chapter first examined the microeconomic behavior of the MNE in developing and transferring technology, alongside the arm's-length international market for technology licensing, and then moved to the general-equilibrium significance of these institutions.

---

[27] See, for example, Dunning (1970, Chapter 9), Dunning and Pearce (1977, pp. 69–72), Brash (1966, Chapter 7 and 10), and Forsyth (1972, pp. 64–90).

[28] United States MNEs apparently have served as vehicles for transferring innovations in management and organization as well as technical innovations. See Section 3.2 and Brash (1966, Chapter 5).

MNEs tend to be found in research-intensive sectors, and there is evidence that they consciously allocate their R&D activities around the world to best advantage. R&D is pulled toward the parent's headquarters by the need for efficient supervision and scale economies in the R&D process itself; it is dispersed toward the subsidiaries by the advantages of doing developmental research close to the served market (and sometimes by the goal of minimizing costs). Empirical evidence confirms that U.S. MNEs will undertake less research in the United States if they cannot expect to garner rents on it from foreign markets.

The marketing of technological knowledge is failure-prone for the same general reasons as any market in knowledge assets. Nonetheless, such a market exists in which licensor and licensee strike agreements. Empirical evidence tells something about the kinds of firms that gain from both licensor and licensee activities, and it also identifies the resource costs of technology transfers that make technical knowledge something less than the "public good" assumed in most economic analysis. Technical knowledge may be transferred either within the MNE or between independent firms, the division depending on the MNE's assorted advantages and disadvantages. Arm's-length licensing is encouraged by risks to foreign investors and barriers to entry of subsidiaries, by short economic life of the knowledge asset, by simplicity of the technology, by high capital costs for the potential foreign investor, and by certain types of product-market competition that favor reciprocal licensing.

The microeconomic evidence on licensing and foreign investment can be fitted into Vernon's product-cycle model, which employs a number of mechanisms to suggest that as a product's technology matures, its production becomes more footloose and disseminates toward countries less active in producing new technical knowledge. The MNE seems to influence the rate of diffusion at certain stages of the cycle; by implication, the cycle runs its course more rapidly with MNEs active than if technology is diffused only through arm's-length licensing and other channels.

International economists have recently provided a number of models helpful for understanding technology transfer in general equilibrium and its implications for nations' welfare. If Home, the innovating country, cannot collect rents on its technology that disseminates to Foreign, the dissemination generally makes Foreign and the world as a whole better off but leaves Home worse off. But Home may gain from the dissemination if its terms of commodity trade improve enough (e.g., Foreign is very efficient at making the innovation and begins to supply it as a cheap import to Home). If technology disseminates through its attachment to the MNE's international movement of capital, Foreign can benefit from encouraging capital inflows. If technology transfers and capital movements are independent, however, they can be substitutes for one another: Maximum world output can be attained by moving the technology to the capital or the capital to the technology. Home, of course, maximizes its own welfare by charging a monopoly rental for its superior technology; this rental may be an alternative to taxing exports of the innovative good, or Home may need to use both instruments to maximize its income.

Empirical evidence relevant to these theoretical welfare considerations has shown that competition among suppliers of technical knowledge serves to beat down the rents they collect. It also indicates something about the leakage of proprietary knowledge from the control of MNEs: Some leakage occurs, but there is no presumption that the MNEs themselves undervalue the risk when licensing or placing their technology abroad. Limited aggregative evidence suggests that the presence of MNEs is associated with more rapid diffusion of technical knowledge, at least in industrial-country markets. Empirical research in this area must make some delicate discriminations, however, because successful MNEs at any given moment should be earning rents not accruing to their national competitors. Not all the rent-yielding assets are technological, and each of them is subject to a variety of depreciation and dissemination processes.

8

Taxation, MNEs' behavior, and economic welfare

Beside the great issues of progress, sovereignty, and economic justice that swirl around the MNE, taxation sounds like a matter for petty minds that warm to accountancy. That instinct is squarely wrong, because it turns out that arrangements for taxing corporate net incomes constitute the dominant factor in the division of spoils between source and host countries. In this chapter we shall consider the normative effect of corporation income taxes imposed on MNEs – first on global welfare, then on the welfare of source and host countries separately. We shall take up some empirical aspects of the MNE's responses to taxation, emphasizing how prices on intracorporate transactions can be manipulated so that reported profits surface in tax-minimizing locations.

8.1. Corporation income taxes, market distortions, and world welfare

All countries levy taxes on the net incomes of corporations at marginal rates typically between 40 and 50 percent (Kyrouz, 1975). Textbooks traditionally have identified the profits tax as a levy on a pure economic rent or surplus that has no effect on saving or output decisions. But in real life the tax falls on profits in the popular sense – the sum of the opportunity cost of equity capital plus any rents or windfalls accruing to suppliers of equity capital. Therefore, the corporation income tax drives a wedge between the net return received by savers and the gross earnings of their savings when invested by companies. We expect it to depress the amount of saving and capital formation, even though a pure tax on monopoly rents will leave the monopolist grumpy but with no incentive to change his price or output. How much the tax falls on savers and how much on final buyers of the goods and services provided by capital depends on various elasticities. As always with tax incidence, the inelastic curve takes the drubbing; if the supply of equity capital were perfectly elastic (because people could save in nontaxed forms, or simply consume more of their incomes, if a tax reduced the net return to equity capital), the incidence of the tax would fall entirely on the users of capital's services.

The plot thickens when foreign investment occurs, so that Home's savers can place their capital either in domestic industry or abroad, and Foreign's users of capital services can draw funds from either local or imported sources.[1] Two concepts of tax neutrality serve to identify the effects of taxes on these allocations. Capital-export neutrality refers to the choice that Home's MNEs make between investing their funds in domestic activities and investing overseas. All relevant taxes taken together are neutral if domestic and overseas investments that earn the same pretax rates of return also yield the MNE the same returns after taxes.[2] Capital-import neutrality addresses the competition between Foreign's domestic savers and MNEs to supply the capital that helps to produce goods for Foreign's final buyers. The tax system is neutral if equal before-tax returns at the margin to the competing suppliers of capital translate into equal after-tax earnings. Neutral tax systems have virtue both because they seem fair and because they promote efficient use of resources. Import neutrality places competing domestic companies and foreign subsidiaries on equal footing in that Foreign's tendency to buy capital services from the cheapest source is not distorted by taxes.

Neutrality depends on who pays what tax, not which government

---

[1] The basic analysis in this section stems from Richman (1963), Krause and Dam (1964, Chapter 4), and Musgrave (1969).

[2] Neutrality (or its absence) can also be inferred by evaluating the *immediate* effect on after-tax returns to capital of imposing some new tax or taxes on an initial equilibrium situation. A nonneutral tax will then leave after-tax returns unequal. Of course, this is not an equilibrium situation, and capital stocks will then tend to adjust until after-tax returns are again equal in all uses and pretax returns accordingly unequal.

collects it. Now we shall consider the implications of various priority arrangements between the Home and Foreign tax collectors. Suppose that Home (the source country) imposes no corporation income tax, but that Foreign (the host country) levies a 40 percent tax on all resident capital, whether of domestic or MNE origin. Capital-import neutrality prevails in Foreign, but capital-export neutrality is violated as Home's MNEs divert their funds toward untaxed domestic investment projects rather than pay Foreign's 40 percent tax. Suppose, instead, that Foreign imposes no tax but Home levies 50 percent on all profits earned by Home's citizens, whether their capital is placed at home or abroad. Capital-export neutrality obviously prevails, but not capital-import neutrality (Foreign's capital use is diverted toward the activities carried on by untaxed local capital).

With both taxes in force, the net effect depends on which tax collector gets first crack at the profits accruing to MNE capital, and what heed the second one takes of this first exaction. Under the arrangement that prevails almost universally, the host country takes the first bite. Home can then choose among the following three policies:

1. *Exemption*. Home can exempt from further taxation any income of MNE capital that has been taxed abroad. Foreign's tax rate then governs the allocation of MNE capital. Where Home's and Foreign's tax rates differ, as in the example given earlier, capital-import neutrality will prevail, but export neutrality will be violated.

2. *Tax credit*. Home can tax MNEs' foreign profits at the same rate as Home's domestic capital but give a credit for taxes paid abroad. If Foreign's tax collector relieves the MNE of 40 cents of each profit dollar earned by its Foreign subsidiary, Home's tax collector gives a credit of 40 cents against the 50 cents that the MNE owes to Home, so that the MNE must then cough up an additional 10 cents. The effective tax rate is therefore Home's, and export neutrality prevails. The same will be true if, instead, Foreign's rate is 50 percent and Home's rate is 40 percent, so long as Home rebates to the MNE the 10 percent excess of its tax credit over its domestic tax liability. In practice, however, source countries limit tax credits to the company's domestic tax liability on the same income; so the MNE pays the foreign or domestic tax rate, whichever is higher.

Accordingly, either capital-import neutrality or capital-export neutrality prevails, depending on which tax is higher. Both import neutrality and export neutrality can exist only if both countries levy the same corporate tax rates and Home gives a full credit for the tax paid to Foreign. With equal tax rates, the same neutrality will prevail if Home lays the first claim on the MNE's taxable income and Foreign gives the tax credit.

3. *Tax deduction*. Home can allow taxes paid by MNE capital to Foreign only as a deduction from income taxable by Home, so that the MNE's capital placed abroad is subject to double taxation. The overall tax rate on MNE capital is then $t = t_H(1 - t_F) + t_F$ where t_F and t_H are, respectively, the Foreign and Home tax rates. If Foreign's tax is 40 percent and Home's tax is 50 percent, $t = 70$ percent. Obviously, neither export nor import neutrality will be served in this case. The deduction treatment has little use in international tax practice. Nonetheless, we shall see that source countries have reason to prefer it.

With capital-import neutrality and capital-export neutrality both prevailing, taxes do not distort the foreign-investment decision. Governments raise the revenue they need at minimum cost of resource misallocation. But what arrangement for taxing MNEs makes for the least distortion if Home and Foreign choose to levy their general corporation income taxes at different rates? Musgrave (1969, Chapter 7) and Horst (1980) have addressed this issue. If taxes on capital's income fail to depress saving in either Home or Foreign, the tax on MNE profits (whoever levies it) should be the same as Home's general profits tax, so that capital-export neutrality prevails. If the demand for capital services is completely inelastic in both countries, Foreign's tax rate should apply to MNEs, and import neutrality should prevail. If taxation depresses supplies of domestic capital to the same degree in both countries, then the optimal tax on MNE capital should lie between the overall domestic rates levied by Home and Foreign.

8.2. Tax conventions and national welfare

World welfare has thus far guided our evaluation of the different ways to tax MNEs' corporate incomes. But these taxes on

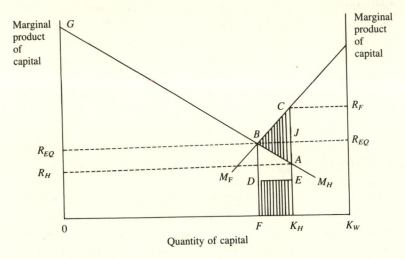

Figure 8.1

MNEs can be collected by either Home's treasury or Foreign's treasury, or some combination of the two. Yet the country's tax revenue
is part of its national income, so that both Home and Foreign have
national interests in grabbing the tax revenue. More generally, the
tax system that maximizes Home's or Foreign's national welfare is
not consistent with maximum world welfare. Macdougall (1960)
pointed out that in a world of competitive industries, and with no
externalities, the host country's primary benefit from foreign investment lies in its first crack at the profits accruing to the capital committed locally by the MNE. And that same effect can make Home a
loser from foreign investment. Assume that Home allows credit for
taxes paid to Foreign's tax collector, up to the limit of the MNE's tax
liability to Home on this same income. We have seen that if Foreign's tax rate is no higher than Home's, then capital-export neutrality prevails. But Home is, at the margin, clearly not making the best
use of its capital.

Figure 8.1 illustrates the argument. Assume that the world's capital endowment is K_W, measured along the base of the diagram. K_H
of this belongs to Home, the rest to Foreign. For each country, a

function shows the marginal product of capital, diminishing with increases in the endowment of capital applied to the rest of the nation's factor endowment (call it labor). Home's schedule is M_H. Foreign's schedule, M_F, is measured from right to left using K_W as the origin. Initially, suppose that no foreign investment has occurred. In Home, the marginal product of capital is $0R_H$, before-tax income of capital is $0R_HAK_H$, income of labor is R_HGA, and Home's national income is $0GAK_H$. Similarly, the marginal product of capital in Foreign is R_FK_W. Suppose now that capital is made mobile internationally and that each country's corporation income tax rate is 50 percent. When Home's (new) MNEs have shifted the equilibrium amount of capital abroad, FK_H, the pretax return to (and marginal product of) capital becomes FB (or $0R_{EQ}$) in each country, and FD of it $(FD = 1/2FB)$ is the tax payment. With the first crack going to Foreign's tax collector and Home giving a tax credit, Foreign's tax revenue from Home's MNEs is $FDEK_H$. Now the gain in world income from the foreign investment is the triangle ABC, the excess of the increase in Foreign's gross domestic product over the decrease in Home's. But Foreign's increase in national income is BCJ, a gain to Foreign's labor, plus $FDEK_H$, Foreign's MNE tax revenue. And Home loses by $FDEK_H$ minus BJA, even though Home's MNEs enjoy more after-tax profits. The Home profit rate after taxes rises from $1/2K_H A$ to $1/2FB$.

Clearly, this outcome does not maximize Home's national income. From Home's viewpoint, its capital should be allocated so that the profit earned on the last unit placed abroad after paying Foreign's taxes equals the pretax return on the last unit placed at home. But the MNEs on their own will place capital to equalize after-tax profits in the two countries. The deduction method described earlier maximizes Home's national welfare, as Musgrave (1969) and others have pointed out.

Foreign, the importer of direct investment, has a symmetrical interest under the prevailing tax convention in luring MNEs for the national-income gain that results when Foreign's treasury captures their tax payments. With the tax-credit system, the MNE pays whichever is higher, the source or host tax rate, and so Foreign only gives up revenue by setting a rate below those of the leading source countries. A rate higher than theirs might be optimal, depending on the distribution of pretax profit opportunities that MNEs perceive on Foreign's soil. Foreign may devise policy instruments that inflate MNEs' profit opportunities and thereby increase the tax rate that can be imposed without deterring them. Corden (1967) pointed out that raising Foreign's tariffs does the trick when it induces the MNE to shift from exporting to direct investment in Foreign. The tariff is second best, however, because it distorts consumption patterns.[3]

Taxing for monopoly gain

The simple account of national and international interests in taxing MNEs' net incomes has recently been extended in a number of important ways – by some authors in general and theoretical terms, by others in terms of the interests of particular countries. One general point originally made by Macdougall (1960) and subsequently developed by others concerns any effect that the quantity of foreign investment may have on its earnings. Assume that neither Home nor Foreign imposes a tax on corporation income, so as to put aside the first-crack problem of tax credits already discussed. Whatever the structure of Foreign's markets in which Home's MNEs compete, assume that additions to their capital invested in Foreign drive down the average rate of profit that they earn there, as in Figure 8.1. If the MNEs in fact compete with each other and do not monopolize their individual market activities in Foreign, no one of Home's

---

[3] Horst (1971) provided a more elaborate treatment of the effect of Foreign's tax on the MNE that can serve Foreign's market through local production, exports from Home, or some combination of the two. He found that the leverage Foreign has on promoting local production through manipulating its tax rate depends not only on the level of the tariff but also on whether or not the MNE's product pricing is constrained by arbitrage. That is, given its costs and the demand elasticities in Home and Foreign, some pair of product prices will maximize the MNE's profits in Home and Foreign, but the differential between these profit-maximizing prices must not be so large that independent parties can profitably buy in the cheaper location and resell in the dearer. Horst showed that Foreign's tax rate may have considerable effect on the location of production when this arbitrage constraint is binding, but (under certain circumstances) not when the MNE's pricing is unconstrained. Also see Itagaki (1979).

MNEs will take into account that its expanded foreign investment drives down the earnings of the others – a negative externality from Home's viewpoint. Home's potential monopoly power over its foreign investment goes unexploited, and Home's government will maximize national welfare by imposing a tax on the earnings of foreign capital that will effectively exploit this monopoly power. Home's motive for discriminating against foreign investment so as to maximize national monopoly profits is, it should be stressed, quite independent of the motive to discriminate to avoid the first-crack problem. The quest for monopoly gains may afflict the country receiving foreign investment as well as the source. Suppose that MNE capital is supplied competitively from abroad, but its supply price increases with the amount entering Foreign's economy (a conventional upward-sloping supply curve). Foreign raises its national welfare with a tax that exploits this monopsony power in foreign borrowing, reducing capital imports and driving down the supply price.[4]

Recent contributions have brought both the first-crack problem and the monopoly issue to bear on Home's optimal tax strategy and have also taken account of the rivalrous relationship between Home's and Foreign's tax collectors. Hartman (1980) provided a useful reference point. His general-equilibrium model assigns to Home and Foreign each an endowment of capital and labor able to produce either of two commodities. However, his is not quite the Heckscher-Ohlin model that has done service for many other researchers (see Chapters 2, 5, and 7). Foreign investment is induced not by general differences in the returns to capital in Home and Foreign but by a specific productivity advantage enjoyed by Home's MNEs when they go abroad and hire some of Foreign's labor force. The MNEs may operate in either Home's export industry or its import-competing industry. Which sector is chosen makes a lot of difference, because investment abroad in Foreign's import-competing sector expands world production of the good that Home exports,

---

[4] We noted in Section 4.3 (Katrak, 1977) that this maneuver will pay for Foreign even when dealing with a monopolistic MNE that operates with constant marginal costs.

driving down its price and thus worsening Home's terms of trade; Home's income-maximizing tax on foreign investment is always higher when the MNEs operate in Home's exportable-goods sector. Another significant feature of Hartman's model is that MNEs ship abroad only part of the capital they need in Foreign. They borrow a given fraction locally, perhaps because of the risk-bearing considerations discussed in Chapter 6. Each country imposes a general proportional tax on corporation incomes. When a tax change occurs, this model allows not just for the change induced in foreign investment but also for the reallocation of capital and labor within each country and the adjustment of flows of international trade.

Hartman's conclusions stem from simulating the effect on national income of Home's choice from among the policies of exemption, credit for taxes paid abroad, and deductability of taxes paid abroad. In general, Hartman's results confirm that a deduction policy comes closest to maximizing Home's welfare, and Home's optimal tax on foreign investment can run even higher than that. The simulations allow Home's export (and MNE) industry to be either capital-intensive or labor-intensive. Home's welfare gain in moving from exemption to whatever tax on foreign investment is optimal is about the same in either case, but a much lower tax is optimal when the export good is capital-intensive. The optimal tax is higher the more of its funds does the MNE borrow abroad. Hartman also investigated the effects of these tax policies on income distribution. When Home's exportable good that the MNEs produce abroad is labor-intensive, Home's labor naturally gains as higher taxes discourage foreign investment. However, unlike some models discussed in Section 5.1, Hartman's model implies that labor does best with a policy that stops short of forcing the repatriation of all of Home's foreign investment. (The tax strategy that maximizes labor's real wage also maximizes the national income.) If the exportable sector in which foreign investment takes place is capital-intensive, tougher taxation of foreign investment is not clearly in the interest of Home's labor. Thus, whether the taxation of foreign investment aims to raise national welfare or to redistribute income toward labor, the deduction policy may or may not be the best one – the results depending sensitively on which good MNEs produce abroad, how much capital they borrow locally, and also how large their cost advantage over native firms.

Nor did Hartman (1980) exhaust the factors complicating the simple conclusion that Home gains most from applying a deduction policy when taxing foreign investment. Beenstock (1977) pointed to the implications of two-way movements of direct investment for the nation's use of its monopoly power in taxing foreign capital. Home's government raises its tax on its MNEs' overseas profits, looking on with approval as they reduce their investment in Foreign and thus drive up their profit rate. But the general return to capital also rises in Foreign, causing Foreign's own MNEs to repatriate some capital they had exported to Home. Because Home gets first crack at the profits of the overseas subsidiaries of Foreign's MNEs, the induced repatriation cuts Home's tax revenue, a loss that partly offsets Home's monopoly gains from driving its MNEs' foreign profits. Home's tax can garner no monopoly profits at all by contracting its foreign investment if Home MNE capital repatriated from Foreign is matched dollar for dollar by Foreign MNE capital repatriated from Home.

Another complication surfaces in models of the Heckscher-Ohlin variety that allow for international movement of capital. These models emphasize the relationship between the factor endowment (capital and labor) of the country and its comparative advantage in international trade, implying that a change in the factor endowment when capital moves abroad induces a compensating adjustment in its international trade. Jones (1967) (also see Kemp, 1966) has shown that this connection affects the process by which a country loads a welfare-maximizing tax onto international capital transactions. In this model, a flow of capital from Home to Foreign simply increases Foreign's overall stock of capital – MNE capital is not specific to a particular sector, nor does it have any productivity advantage. Thus, when Home changes its tax on international capital movements, it changes the overall equilibrium return to capital in Foreign. That shift in factor prices changes commodity outputs there, and the relative prices of commodities (Home's terms of trade) if Foreign is incompletely specialized and produces both of the commodities in the model. Jones showed not only that Home must set its optimal tariff on commodity trade and its optimal tax on international capital jointly, in this case, but also that either the optimal tariff or the optimal tax may be negative. That is, Home may gain by subsidizing its capital exports rather than by taxing them monopolistically if a capital subsidy works a sufficiently favorable change on the structure of product prices. If Foreign produces only its export good (completely specialized, in this two-good model), Home's optimal tariff and capital tax will be independent of each other, and both will be positive (zero in the limit).

Batra and Ramachandran (1980) explored some effects of taxes in the specific-factors version of the Heckscher-Ohlin model (capital is mobile internationally but not between sectors). They were uninterested in sectoral differences and terms-of-trade issues, but they did allow MNE capital (originating in Home) to be distinguished from Foreign's local capital. Foreign's tax on the income of its own capital, assumed in fixed supply, has no allocative effect. But Foreign's tax on MNE capital sends some of it packing back to Home. Raising this tax raises Foreign's welfare, up to a point (Home does not tax corporate income), and reduces Home's welfare.

Strategic behavior

The contributions discussed thus far have treated the optimal taxation of international capital as a problem for the single country. The rest of the world passively puts up with the choice and makes the indicated economic adaptations. Recently, Feldstein and Hartman (1979) (see also Hamada, 1966) have considered the strategic aspects of capital taxation, in which Home must make some conjecture about how Foreign will react to Home's policy change. In their model, Home is a large country, in that its MNEs place enough capital abroad to affect wage rates in the receiving countries. Foreign can be thought of as a composite of small host economies, all identical, and each setting its corporation income tax on the assumption that Home's tax can be taken as given. Home's officials understand this reaction function and set Home's own corporate income tax so as to maximize Home's welfare, with Foreign's reaction taken into account. Home's government also employs another policy instrument – the rate at which MNEs can take a credit against taxes paid to Foreign. The remaining structure of their model is identical with that of Hartman (1980), described earlier. Their basic-case conclusions are already familiar from research summarized earlier: Home should give only a deduction for taxes its MNEs pay to Foreign, and if the MNEs' investments are large enough to drive up wages abroad, Home should discriminate even more against its capital exporters. How do Foreign's tax authorities react to an increase in Home's tax on overseas capital? Feldstein and Hartman showed that under standard assumptions about production technology, a rise in Home's tax reduces Foreign's welfare-maximizing tax. That property of Foreign's reaction function makes Home's optimal tax on overseas capital even higher than in the model's basic case. The Feldstein-Hartman analysis only began to explore the question of international strategic reactions in capital taxation. It did, however, dramatize the problem of national and international welfare that is involved. Even without anticipating foreign reactions, capital-exporting countries will restrict capital flows below the levels optimal for world welfare. With strategic behavior allowed for, the tendency to overrestriction apparently becomes greater still. The dilemma echoes those already identified over competition policy (Chapter 4) and technology rents (Chapter 7).

8.3. National tax policies: empirical patterns

Empirical research on national tax policies toward MNEs' incomes has focused on two questions: Are tax laws set so that they systematically violate the criteria of neutrality and distort the allocation of MNE capital? How do actual laws relate to the divergent goals of maximizing national and global welfare and to the division of gains from foreign investment between source and host countries?

Corporation income taxes and MNE location decisions

The effects of tax provisions on MNEs' location decisions can be examined in two ways – by measuring the sensitivity of foreign direct investment to tax incentives and by simply evaluating the neutrality of actual tax systems. A good deal of descriptive evidence bears on the latter; the scarcer evidence of the former type will be considered in Section 8.4. Descriptions of countries' taxes on MNE income have suggested that capital-export neutrality and capital-import neutrality are not too seriously violated. The major industrial countries levy the same tax rates on foreign subsidiaries operating within their borders as on domestic companies. They do frequently discriminate against foreign investors and violate capital-import neutrality by imposing withholding taxes on dividends and similar payments remitted to foreigners (often around 15 percent). However, there is a series of bilateral tax treaties that commit host countries to nondiscrimination and result in reductions in or exemptions from these withholding taxes.[5]

Most commonly, a source-country government gives its MNEs a credit for taxes paid to host-country governments, up to the tax that the source-country government would collect on this income. This arrangement produces capital-export neutrality if source-country tax rates are no lower than those of host countries. But in the United States and other countries, an additional important provision called deferral violates neutrality and encourages foreign investment. Foreign subsidiaries (but not branch plants) may postpone paying taxes on profits earned abroad until they are repatriated; then the foreign tax is added back onto the remitted dividends, source-country tax liability is calculated on the pretax profits, and the credit is taken against the foreign tax already paid. If the host's tax rate is lower than the source's rate, deferral lets the MNE retain earnings and plow them back into the subsidiary, paying the higher source's tax rate only when profits are ultimately repatriated. Thus, deferral violates capital-export neutrality when the host's rate lies below the source's rate. It encourages too much foreign investment.

[5] See Musgrave (1969, 1975), Sato and Bird (1975), Kyrouz (1975), Ness (1975), Snoy (1975, Part IV), Kopits (1976*a*), Bergsten et al. (1978, Chapter 6), and Adams and Whalley (1977). The effect of withholding taxes on capital-import neutrality also depends on how the host taxes dividend income received by its own citizens (see Sato and Bird, 1975; Lent, 1977).

We pointed out earlier that both export neutrality and import neutrality prevail only if all countries have the same corporation tax rates; where the rates differ, we can have one form of neutrality but not both. Therefore, a general assessment of the system's neutrality turns on how tightly clustered are the corporation income tax rates of the major source and host countries. Tabulations have shown a rather tight scatter in the high-40s percentage range. Only 19 of 54 countries Ness (1975) examined had corporate rates above that of the United States; their withholding taxes brought another 15 countries above the U.S. level. The pro-foreign-investment bias of deferral and the anti-foreign-investment bias of withholding could together induce either too much or too little foreign investment for a global optimum. But the resulting allocation does not seem wildly off the mark.

National policies and national interests

Tax arrangements that maximize individual countries' welfare do not, we have seen, generally maximize world welfare. One source of divergence, the first-crack issue, affects all countries: they need not be big enough to influence MNEs' worldwide returns. The second source, monopoly power in foreign investment, applies only to large countries. But MNEs' affinity for imperfectly competitive markets (see Chapters 1 and 4) implies that even a small nation's MNEs can face downward-sloping demand curves in their external markets, giving it an incentive to act "large."

Host countries enjoy substantial gains from the prevailing tax-credit system, as a few appraisals have indicated. Jenkins (1979) estimated the gains for Canada, a major recipient. Of the various refinements built into his estimates, one holds particular interest. What happens to native Canadian capital when foreign investment enters Canada, driving down the rate of return that would otherwise accrue to native capitalists? To make the worst case, Jenkins assumed that this depressant effect of inbound MNEs induces all the foreign investment flowing outward from Canada; so the sums Canada loses to foreign tax collectors partially offset the gains from taxing foreign subsidiaries in Canada. Canada's gains from taxing foreign subsidiaries amount to no less than 2.5 percent of gross national product without this offset, 1.5 percent even with the offset. Similarly, Grubel (1974) (also see Rugman, 1980*b*, Chapter 6) evaluated the net social rate of return to the United States from its foreign direct investments in a number of industrial countries. He found that the average net rate of return was negative for the period 1960–9, – 5.9 percent annually. It remains negative even if royalties and fees remitted by subsidiaries to their U.S. parents are assumed to add a pure "rent" component to the parents' profits. Grubel noted that including gross fees and royalties as profits is inappropriate if the marginal costs of transferring intangibles abroad are substantial, as Teece (1977) has shown them to be.

The gains that host countries enjoy from taxing foreign investments have been sorely neglected in debates over MNEs (see Chapter 10). The various benefits and costs most commonly proclaimed either defy our best measuring instruments or are entirely conjectural; the substantial gains generated by the tax system often go unnoticed. The point is particularly pregnant for LDCs which have sometimes accorded MNEs substantial tax concessions in order to lure foreign investment. As Musgrave (1969, p. 75) pointed out, they may thereby give up their biggest benefit from the inflow.[6]

In principal source countries, such as the United States and the United Kingdom, concern about the effects of foreign investment first arose in connection with the countries' balance-of-payments positions (see Section 6.4). But tax issues soon surfaced in the ensuing scrutiny of MNEs' economic effects. In the United States it was recognized that the foreign tax credit and deferral were not sufficiently restrictive of foreign investment to maximize national welfare. Similarly leaning toward global rather than national welfare

---

[6] Musgrave (1969, p. 94) noted that developing countries often combine a low corporation income tax with a high withholding rate on remitted dividends, so as to encourage MNEs to invest heavily and make maximum use of their deferral opportunities. Also, the tax giveaway is mitigated by the shakedown losses that leave a foreign subsidiary with slender taxable profits in its early years (see Hughes and You, 1969, pp. 158–60, 183–6).

were certain policies affecting taxation of dividends remitted by subsidiaries in developing countries[7] and depressing MNEs' charges to their subsidiaries for R&D services (thus inflating their profits taxable overseas) (Bergsten et al., 1978, pp. 206–7).

Horst (1977) (also see Bergsten et al., 1978, Chapter 6 and Appendix B) has undertaken the most ambitious investigation of the resulting welfare effects, a model of the profit-maximizing MNE facing all the essential features of the U.S. tax system. The company can manipulate financial instruments such as the subsidiary's rate of dividend payout, transfers of new funds to the subsidiary, and the MNE's rate of capital formation at home and abroad. The model displays, for example, the incentive that deferral provides the MNE to favor foreign over domestic investment and to slant its intracompany financing of the subsidiary toward equity rather than debt. Horst's simulations indicated the effect of repealing the deferral provision so that U.S. MNEs would be liable for U.S. taxes on their foreign profits as earned. Investments in the subsidiaries would fall by 8.5 percent, whereas the parents' investments at home would rise by 3.9 percent; a sharp drop in transfers of funds to the subsidiaries indicates that they would rely more on funds borrowed abroad. Domestic and foreign taxes paid by U.S. manufacturers would rise by 9.1 percent. Repealing both deferral and the tax-credit provision, so that foreign taxes would be only a deduction from income taxable in the United States, would raise the U.S. tax take by 50 percent while cutting the MNEs' capital formation abroad by 56.2 percent and raising it in the United States by one-fourth. These data suggest that switching from a tax system that (roughly) maximizes global welfare to one that (roughly) maximizes U.S. domestic welfare would produce substantial changes in both the volume of foreign investment and the government's tax take. The calculation did not include all

[7] For subsidiaries in qualifying countries, remitted dividends are not grossed up, and the U.S. tax is calculated on the lower actual dividend flow. The effective tax rate t then becomes not the U.S. tax rate t_{US} (given that the U.S. rate exceeds the foreign rate, t_F), but $(1 - t_{US})(t_{US} - t_F) + t_F$. Ness (1975) pointed out that the minimum total tax liability for the MNE occurs under this arrangement when $t_F = 1/2t_{US}$.

possible adjustments of either the MNEs (they might reincorporate outside the United States) or foreign governments (which might change their own tax rates).[8]

8.4. Effects of taxation on MNEs' behavior

The normative analysis of Section 8.3 simply assumed that the MNE arranges its affairs so as to minimize its tax burden, but it did not address the actual evidence on the ensuing maneuvers. Negative commentary on MNEs often raises the charge that they seize available opportunities to dodge paying taxes. That motive hardly distinguishes them from other economic agents, but they may enjoy opportunities not open to single-nation enterprises. In this section we shall first review evidence on how taxation influences the resource allocations made by MNEs. Then we shall turn to transfer pricing, their key opportunity to minimize total taxes by making their reported profits surface in low-tax jurisdictions.

Tax effects on transactions

The evidence reviewed in Chapter 6 indicated that MNEs generally manage their financial flows so as to maximize expected posttax global profits. That they should be sensitive to tax factors is hardly an exotic hypothesis.[9] Surveys and interview studies of corporate motives usually have rated tax factors less important than key

---

[8] Hartman (1977) pointed to a strategic consequence of ending the deferral provision. Because of deferral, foreign countries now have an incentive to hold their corporation tax rates on subsidiaries of U.S. MNEs below the U.S. rate in order to attract taxable U.S. investment. With deferral ended, however, the tax-credit provision would immediately siphon the subsidiary's tax benefit into the U.S. Treasury. The host country would therefore have no reason to keep its corporation tax below the U.S. level.

[9] That higher taxes on foreign income will repel foreign investment is a proposition not without its exceptions. When the government taxes foreign-source profits, it annexes part of the profits but also part of the risk to which the MNE is exposed. Suppose, with Hartman (1979), that at the margin foreign investment is financed entirely from tax-deductible debt and that domestic debt is risk-free to borrowers. Then increased taxation of its foreign profits on equity causes the MNE to increase its borrowing and capital formation overseas.

nontax factors governing pretax rates of return. As Snoy's review (1975, Chapter 28) suggested, the surveys that have given the most attention to tax variables have ranked them below quantifiable costs and political stability in importance but ahead of some other influences. That tax factors do not contribute more to explaining key foreign-investment decisions indicates only that they vary less among countries than the factors that govern pretax rates of return.

Some statistical investigations have explored the influence of taxes on new foreign investment and other MNE financial flows. Snoy (1975, Chapters 26 and 27) examined investment flows over the years 1966–9 from several leading source countries to a number of host-country destinations. His explanatory variables included source–host tax differentials bearing on either retained earnings or remitted dividends of foreign subsidiaries, as well as other controls such as national growth-rate differentials. The tax variables are not very robust in their statistical significance, but their coefficients always take the predicted signs, and their magnitudes imply that tax changes would have large effects. For example, unifying the European host countries' tax rates would change the growth rate of U.S. foreign direct investment in the various individual countries by one-third or more. And Root and Ahmed (1978) included corporation tax rates among the factors they employed to explain foreign-investment flows into 41 developing countries, finding a significant negative effect.

A few other statistical studies have analyzed the effects of taxes on dividend remittance or retention of earnings by subsidiaries. Kopits (1972) found that the dividend flows from U.S. MNEs' foreign subsidiaries depended, as expected, on their after-tax profits, interacted with a factor indicating the host country's differential tax rates on retained and distributed earnings. Ness (summarized in Kopits, 1976a, pp. 647–8) similarly found that the retention of earnings in various host countries depended on a measure of the opportunity cost of funds with tax incentives appropriately embedded. Ladenson (1972) detected no influence of tax-rate differentials on dividends, but aggregation of statutory tax rates across regions may have caused this. And Hartman (1981) offered some tentative evidence that retentions abroad of profits earned by U.S. MNEs are sensitive to taxes because of the deferral provision.

In summary, the direct statistical tests of the effects of taxes on MNEs' financial decisions have been quite limited, but they have offered no reason to doubt that companies react the same way to a one-dollar tax-induced change in after-tax expected returns as to a one-dollar change due to some other economic disturbance.

Transfer pricing

A great deal of attention has been given to the possibility that MNEs avoid taxes and accomplish other unsavory deeds by manipulating the prices assigned to intracorporate transactions. Casson (1979) urged that transfer-pricing maneuvers, undertaken solely to divert tax revenues away from governments, cause an overextension of foreign investment. And Vaitsos (1974) stated that MNEs siphon unduly large flows of purchasing power out of the developing countries through transfer-pricing practices (also see Lall, 1973).

We shall be concerned at first only with the theoretical effects of transfer prices on the global tax bill, not any information function they may play within the firm. Consider the MNE that exports a Home-produced good to Foreign for resale by its subsidiary. The transfer price set by the MNE affects its total tax bill in two ways. It determines the ad valorem tariff paid to Foreign's customs officer on the imports, and it determines how much of the MNE's profits are taxed as net income originating in Foreign, how much as originating in Home. Horst (1971) (also see Copithorne, 1971, and Booth and Jensen, 1977) showed that the MNE will choose the lowest possible transfer price (its marginal cost of production, say) in order to minimize its tariff payments unless the proportional excess of the tax on Foreign-originated profits over Home-originated profits exceeds the tariff rate.[10] If taxes on Home-originated income are greater, the

---

[10] What matters to the company, of course, is the total tax it pays on profits originating in the two markets, not which tax collector gets them. Other formal analyses of transfer-pricing practices have been provided by Nieckels (1976), Verlage (1975), and Mathewson and Quirin (1979).

MNE's dominant goal is always to minimize its customs duties. Ita-gaki (1979) developed a somewhat similar model in which the MNE produces an intermediate good in Foreign that it may either fabricate there for local sale or import to Home. With the conventional tax-credit arrangement operating, the MNE always sets a transfer price to minimize its customs duties on the import. Even if Foreign's prof-its tax is lower than Home's, the tax-credit arrangement makes Home's tax the operative one (see Eden, 1978).

Apart from complex cases where tax minimization interacts with avoiding tariffs, MNEs should use transfer prices simply to place profits in low-tax jurisdictions. Where Home's tax rate exceeds For-eign's but deferral is allowed, transfer pricing can shift profits to-ward Foreign to the extent that investment opportunities there war-rant. If Foreign's taxes are higher than Home's, or (as in some developing countries) profits are regulated or their remittance is sharply restricted, transfer pricing can favor shunting reported prof-its toward Home. Some countries function as "tax havens" where MNEs can accumulate profits subject to very low taxes, even though they carry on little or no real economic activity there, and transfer pricing can waft profits away from hostile tax jurisdictions to these havens of rest. The appeal of tax havens to the MNE, of course, also depends on deferral being permitted by the source country.[11]

A few statistical studies have assessed the use of transfer-pricing opportunities. Ness (summarized by Kopits, 1976*a*, p. 657) exam-ined the determinants of after-tax rates of return on the book value of U.S. direct investment on the presumption that these reported earnings would reflect both real profitability and transfer-pricing in-centives to move funds toward stable, low-tax countries. His results for the tax-differential variable were statistically insignificant, and the research design ran into the problem of the risk premium inflat-

---

[11] Plasschaert (1979, p. 115) described the mechanism involved. In 1962 the United States changed its tax laws to deny the deferral privilege to MNE income reported in tax-haven countries. Musgrave (1969, pp. 85–8) pointed out that this reform's economic benefit to the United States was in fact dubious, because profits that would anyhow be remitted to the United States then had to be reported in higher-tax foreign jurisdic-tions, transferring real income to foreign countries through the tax-credit mechanism described earlier.

ing real profits required to warrant investment in high-risk environments. Kopits (1976*b*) fastened on intracorporate royalty payments as a likely candidate for transfer pricing, because arm's-length standards for a "reasonable" price are largely lacking. MNEs will seek to conceal remitted profits as royalty payments from foreign countries with higher tax rates on dividends but lower tax rates on royalties than the U.S. corporate tax rate. The substitution of royalties for dividends is significant and seems to be almost dollar for dollar among some industrial countries. Kopits estimated that about one-fourth of royalty payments from industrial countries represent concealed profit remittances, about 13 percent from LDCs. Müller and Morgenstern (1974) attempted a statistical analysis of underpricing of the exports of foreign subsidiaries based in Argentina, but the apparent confirmation probably resulted from a faulty statistical model (the effect of foreign ownership was not tested conditional on the occurrence of interaffiliate trade).

The MNE's scope for transfer-pricing maneuvers depends on the firm's internal flexibility in setting them. Two constraints may be important. First, large firms generally are not in a position to "keep two sets of books," and the transfer prices used to affect profits reported to the tax collector also determine the profits perceived by the firm's division managers to flow from its various activities. The control and internal evaluation of a large, far-flung corporate empire usually depend on treating each subsidiary or division as a "profit center," so that top management assesses its performance not from direct observation but simply by examining its reported profitability. Similarly, transfer prices directly affect decentralized decisions in the large firm – for example, whether some component should be secured from a corporate sibling or bought on the open market. The transfer price serves as a "shadow price" within the company to guide its own resource-allocation decisions.[12] In short, the MNE

---

[12] Companies' quests for efficient transfer prices rather closely resemble the processes by which economists identify efficient shadow prices. An arm's-length price in a competitive market is the ideal choice, but unlikely, in the nature of things, to be available for many intracorporate transactions. Alternatives constructed from the company's internal data have various strengths and weaknesses. See Arpan (1971, Chapter 2) for

hoping to confuse the tax collector runs some danger of confusing itself and demoralizing subsidiaries required to report low profits. The second constraint on transfer pricing is, of course, the tax collector's own enforcement effort. For a government maximizing its tax take, intercepting a dollar of concealed profits may, at the margin, be worth up to 50 cents in enforcement costs.

Some investigators of businesses' transfer-pricing practices have taken account of this interplay of tax and administrative considerations. Arpan's (1971, Chapter 4) survey of foreign MNEs with subsidiaries in the United States revealed a rough distinction between large companies in noncompetitive environments and small ones facing more competition. The former group lack arm's-length bases for setting transfer prices. And they can justify the overhead expense of a complicated cost-based system of transfer pricing capable of compromise among administrative and tax-avoidance objectives. Overall, the companies do heed tax considerations and some other government fiscal incentives, but they clearly also manage transfer prices for internal-control objectives. Minimizing U.S. customs duties is not an important goal, partly because the possible savings are small, partly because costly litigation can result. Burns's (1980) survey of factors considered by U.S. MNEs agreed with Arpan's results in all important respects. Tax factors weigh in substantially, although with less force than does the need to motivate subsidiaries effectively. The distinction again appears between large, noncompetitive MNEs and small, competitive ones in the transfer-pricing method that they use and the extent to which tax rates influence their policies.[13] Tang (1979, Chapter 6) sought from U.S. and Japanese MNEs rankings by importance of the factors influencing their methods of transfer pricing. The primary roles of global profit maximization, minimization of tax and tariff payments, and the need to mo-

a survey. Tang (1979, Chapter 5) provided a comparison of the practices of U.S. and Japanese MNEs (they are quite similar).

[13] Lessard (1979) and Brooke and Remmers (1970, pp. 117–22) also commented from casual survey evidence on the degree to which administrative considerations constrain the unfettered use of transfer pricing to avoid taxes. Greene and Duerr (1970) provided more systematic evidence on the point.

tivate foreign-subsidiary managements were all confirmed. Several other studies have suggested more generally that many companies find the gains from transfer-pricing maneuvers to be small relative to the administrative costs and risks involved (Joachimsson, 1980; Rugman, 1980*b*, Chapter 7; Plasschaert, 1981).

Finally, some authors have considered the effects of transfer pricing on the welfare of the affected nations. Jenkins and Wright (1975) examined the practices in the U.S. petroleum industry, which enjoyed a long-standing special incentive to transfer its profits upstream to crude-petroleum-producing countries, paying as a result almost no corporation income taxes to the United States. Jenkins and Wright sought to measure this profit transfer away from consuming countries other than the United States by assuming that the oil MNEs' investments in those nations should have earned profit rates as high as did the average manufacturing investment of U.S. MNEs in those countries. They concluded that in 1970, transfer pricing cost those consuming countries at least $240 million. Vaitsos (1974) undertook a detailed inquiry into transfer pricing by MNEs operating in four major sectors in South America. Transfer prices on components or intermediate goods imported to Latin American countries were carefully compared with market prices for identical goods elsewhere in the world. Vaitsos's (1974, Chapter 4) comparisons between sectors and between Latin American host countries confirmed a number of expectations about transfer pricing. For Colombia, imports were particularly overpriced in pharmaceuticals – a sector in which firms were subject to a limit on the nominal profits that they could repatriate. Overpricing of transferred merchandise was less in sectors where the MNEs compete appreciably with each other; with competition there should be fewer excess profits for clandestine repatriation through transfer pricing.[14] Vaitsos (1974, pp. 73–4) also made some reference to price controls, suggesting that intermediate imports are overpriced in order to establish a high cost base for de-

[14] Tariffs were also set so as to encourage the overpricing of intermediate pharmaceuticals – low on intermediates, high on competing final goods (Vaitsos, 1974, pp. 90–1). Transfer pricing to conceal excess profits gleaned in the host-country market has been spotted in some industrial countries as well (see Greenhill and Herbolzheimer, 1980).

termining permitted prices. Chile, a country with a high corporate tax rate, experienced proportionally high royalty remittances, and in Colombia royalty remittances were also high in the sectors with strong transfer-pricing incentives (Vaitsos, 1974, pp. 85–6; also see Lall and Streeten, 1977, pp. 146–7). Vaitsos's general discussion flirted with the idea that MNEs systematically transfer wealth away from the developing countries, as if this propensity were somehow built into the decision structure of a MNE. However, his evidence journeyed toward a somewhat different conclusion: MNEs' transfer-pricing maneuvers are due not to their distinctive motives but to a conjunction of motive with market opportunity and incentives based on the LDCs' own policies (also see Vernon, 1977, Chapter 7).[15]

8.5. **Summary**

Corporation income taxes on MNEs' investments abroad can be analyzed for their normative effects on world welfare or on the national welfare of the source and host countries separately. The taxation of foreign-investment income affects world welfare if either of two forms of neutrality is violated. Capital-export neutrality prevails if taxes do not distort the market's incentives for placing capital in domestic or overseas uses. Capital-import neutrality prevails if taxes do not distort the market's incentives for recruiting capital services from domestic or imported sources. Both export neutrality and import neutrality can be achieved only if all countries employ the same tax rate. Conventionally, the host country's tax collector gets first crack at taxing the incomes of foreign subsidiaries. The source country's tax authority can then exempt the same income from further taxation (import neutrality is attained), give a credit against taxes paid abroad (this method prevails in practice and results in either export or import neutrality, but not both), or allow the foreign tax as a deduction from income taxable at home (neither form of neutrality results).

[15] A study by the U.S. Tariff Commission (1973, pp. 434–5), analyzing data for 1966 and 1970, concluded that average ex post tax rates on foreign income of U.S. MNEs exceeded that on income reported in the United States, which would indicate an inducement on average to move profits toward the United States through transfer pricing.

National-welfare effects of taxing foreign income diverge from those on global welfare for two reasons. First, globally efficient taxes can be collected by either country, but each nation cares whether or not its treasury receives the tax revenue. Home wants MNE capital allocated so that the marginal pretax return at home equals the marginal return from foreign investment after foreign taxes are paid. This pattern demands the deduction method of treating foreign taxes. Foreign faces certain incentives to lure in MNE capital so as to garner the tax proceeds. The second divergence between global welfare and national welfare stems from monopoly gains. If Home's MNEs compete among themselves in Foreign's market and drive down their mutual rate of return, Home has an incentive to discriminate in its tax structure against foreign investment. If MNE capital is industry-specific, Home's motive for restricting the outflow is amplified if foreign investment expands world production of Home's exportable good, worsening its terms of trade. Similar conclusions follow from a Heckscher-Ohlin model in which MNE capital loses its sector-specific identity: Home's taxation of capital exports for monopoly gain may be tempered or reversed by any induced change in the structure of Foreign's production that tends to improve Home's commodity terms of trade.

The national interests of Home and Foreign are adversary to one another, in the light of both first-crack and monopoly criteria for taxing foreign capital so as to raise national welfare. Some researchers have investigated strategic reactions between countries, discovering that (if Home is a leader and Foreign a collection of small follower economies) Home may wish to tax foreign-investment income even more heavily than domestic considerations would warrant, because Foreign rationally responds by reducing its own tax.

Actual tax systems of the industrial countries violate global-welfare criteria, but apparently not in massive ways. Import neutrality is impaired by withholding taxes on dividends abroad, but these are frequently waived or reduced under bilateral tax treaties. The prevalent tax-credit arrangement is potentially consistent with export neutrality, although deferral does introduce a bias toward excessive foreign investment. Export neutrality and import neutrality cannot both prevail unless all countries impose the same tax rate; actual rates are unequal, but they are rather bunched for the leading industrial countries. MNEs can react to tax provisions by rearranging their allocative decisions so as to maximize after-tax profits. Then one would expect a one-dollar change in expected profits due to tax changes to have the same effect as a one-dollar change from any other source. The empirical evidence does not contradict this prediction.

MNEs can also manipulate the prices attached to intracorporate transactions so as to move taxable profits into jurisdictions where they pay a lower tax. Transfer prices, therefore, may be set so as to reduce the MNE's global tax bill, as well as for internal needs of control and evaluation of the corporation's performance. The MNE's transfer prices must withstand close scrutiny by governments whose tax revenues are at stake, but room for maneuver surely exists in transfers such as technology payments, where no arm's-length standard is available. Empirical evidence shows that substantial advantage is taken of transfer-pricing opportunities, especially in royalties and related intangibles transactions. Large companies whose internal transfer prices are not readily compared with market prices apparently do maintain complex transfer-pricing systems aimed in part at minimizing taxes. Smaller companies and those in more competitive environments, whose transfer prices the tax collector can readily check against market prices, do not find such maneuvers to their advantage. Although the theory of transfer pricing points to the effects of the declared price on ad valorem customs duties as well as corporate income taxes, the evidence does not assign much empirical importance to this consideration. In situations where government regulations provide strong incentives for manipulative transfer pricing (U.S. petroleum companies, MNEs operating in high-tax jurisdictions with price ceilings and other regulatory constraints), the amount of manipulation that MNEs undertake grows in response.

9

Multinationals in developing countries

MNEs have encountered hostility and resentment in all countries that host substantial foreign investment, but nowhere more than in the LDCs, where they get blamed for the national economy's manifest shortcomings, not to mention the historical sins of colonial domination. Economic analysis has played no great part in resolving disputes between critics and defenders of the MNEs' role in development processes. There is little consensus on what institutions and policies most effectively promote the goal of economic development, and writings on the economic role of MNEs have correspondingly run a high ratio of polemic to documented evidence.

In the face of this high-altitude turbulence, the present chapter will fly at lower elevations. Advocates of diverse policies toward development seem to concur on a diagnosis that key markets are malfunctioning, or important prices are misaligned to their shadow equivalents, so that saving and investment, the foreign-exchange rate, wage rates, returns to human capital, and other such important magnitudes may be far off the mark. Appropriate levels for them may therefore differ greatly from what the market signals to private decision makers. The MNEs' allocative decisions become important as they affect these imbalances and distortions. Does the MNE's presence mean more capital formation or productivity growth than otherwise? Can sticks and carrots be applied to the MNE to produce more desirable allocations? Our discussion will focus on these questions about the instruments of development policy, not its ends or the political and social processes by which they are defined.[1] This approach is not calculated to maximize the difference between LDCs and developed countries; on the contrary, some industrial-country policies toward MNEs rest on these same perceived shadow-price discrepancies.

Another issue of procedure grows out of a problem that plagues much research on the effects of MNEs on LDCs' economies. Conditions in the host LDC affect the prevalence and character of MNEs' activities there. Hence, to test any hypothesis about the MNEs' effects on the performance of the host economy, one must control for this reverse causation. This is almost never done. Therefore, we start with a review of the evidence on what determines MNEs' presence in the developing world.

9.1. **Determinants of MNEs' activities**

Foreign subsidiaries operating in the LDCs tend to divide sharply into three categories. The exporters of natural resources and resource-based products need no explanation: They go where the resources are, if conditions in the sector call for vertical integration. The second class is made up of exporters of manufactured goods or components. The third class comprises producers largely engaged in serving the LDC's domestic market. An important point of fact is the sharpness of the distinction between the second and third groups. The theory of MNEs' locational choices (see Section 2.2) indicates that, given scale economies and the very small domestic markets of most LDCs, a foreign subsidiary will locate there either to serve the market or to export extensively, but it will not serve the domestic market and export "a little" (Horst, 1971, 1973). This pattern is affirmed in the data. The 80 projects analyzed by Reuber et al. (1973) were divided into export-oriented projects (26) and those

---

[1] Those interested in a broader approach may consult the work of Biersteker (1978), who did a heroic job of lining up the "critics" of MNEs and the "neoconventionalists" on these large issues, and the analyses of Evans (1979), Hood and Young (1979, Chapter 8), Vernon (1971, Chapters 2, 5, and 7, 1977, Chapters 7–9), Lall and Streeten (1977, Part 1), and Kumar (1980).

serving the domestic market (54); the average proportion of output exported was 87 percent for the former group and 3 percent for the latter. This pattern is not intrinsic to LDCs but rather to small national markets generally; it also turns up in countries such as Ireland (Andrews, 1972; Buckley, 1974). Accordingly, generalizations that span the export and domestic-market subsidiaries are somewhat suspect.

Export-oriented and local-market manufacturing subsidiaries

The forces explaining MNEs' presence in the domestic markets of LDCs are about the same as those explaining their presence in industrial countries.[2] The novel part of the story therefore concerns MNEs' role in the export sectors. Helleiner (1973) pointed out that these exports fall into four rough categories. Locally produced raw materials can be subjected to further processing, and MNEs sometimes undertake this role either as an economic choice or in response to host-country inducements. Second, some LDCs have become heavy exporters of simple manufactured goods whose production processes are suitable to their factor endowments. MNEs' involvement in these products will be discussed later. Third, labor-intensive processes in manufacturing operations may be carried on in LDC facilities that import unfinished goods and reexport them

---

[2] Nankani (1979) confirmed that foreign investment in LDCs by various industrial source countries depends on the prevalence in the source countries of industries congenial to foreign investment. Morley and Smith (1971) suggested that MNEs respond to LDCs' tariff incentives in industries where intangible assets are important. Juhl (1979) confirmed for West Germany Nankani's finding that foreign investment in LDCs increases with an industry's plant scale and allocation of resources to producing intangible assets, and he did not find physical capital intensity a deterrent to investing in MNEs. Hughes and You (1969, pp. 179–83) pointed out that MNEs often have initial contact with LDC markets as exporters, and so import-substituting foreign investments reflect the comparative-advantage structure of the exporting country. Finally, students of Japanese foreign investment (Yoshihara, 1976, Chapter 4, 1978; Ozawa, 1979a, 1979b; Tsurumi, 1976) all have stressed defensive investment by smaller-scale Japanese enterprises in unlikely industries such as textiles; these investments utilize managerial and capital assets of firms lacking opportunities for domestic growth and/or responding to threats in either their domestic or overseas market.

after additional processing. Evidence summarized in Section 1.2 indicates that MNEs play a significant role in these offshore fabrications, but a good deal of business is also done at arm's length between industrial-country firms and local LDC enterprises (Hone, 1974; Sharpston, 1975; Sprietsma, 1978; Jarrett, 1979). Fourth, in some of the larger and more advanced LDCs, some import-competing manufacturing industries have turned around to become successful exporters, and MNEs have been represented in these transformations.[3]

Scattered information has suggested that MNEs account for a moderate proportion (20–30 percent) of the manufactured exports from the more successful LDC exporters, less from the other LDCs. At least over the short period 1966–74 the MNEs' share apparently was declining a bit, although the reasons for this are unclear (Nayyar, 1978). De la Torre (1972) showed that in several Latin American countries exports of differentiated manufactures encounter marketing barriers to entry in industrial-country markets, and so smaller proportions of these outputs are exported than the proportions of undifferentiated manufactures. But subsidiaries of MNEs enjoy advantages against these barriers, therefore exporting larger proportions of their outputs than local firms and accounting for larger shares of exports of such products. Considerable evidence from other studies supports this conclusion.

The contrast between export-oriented and local-market subsidiaries extends to many facets of their activities. They of course differ in the general types of incentives that affect the MNE's investment decision. The export-oriented investments are footloose and are determined largely from unit labor costs,[4] whereas the local-market

[3] Helleiner (1973, p. 26) noted that MNEs have been firm supporters of regional free-trade arrangements among LDCs because of the resulting opportunity to rationalize small-scale facilities and develop exports.

[4] Of course, low unit labor costs are not the same thing as low wages. Therefore, statistical studies of the relationship between foreign investments in host countries and their wage rates have yielded mixed results. Riedel (1975) found that foreign investment in Taiwan does depend on wage differentials between Taiwan and the investing country. Jarrett (1979, Chapter 8) did find that more offshore procurement tends to occur among low-wage countries. But studies of the intercountry distribution

investments depend on the same factors identified in Chapter 1 as determining horizontal foreign investments in general. This conclusion of Reuber et al. (1973, pp. 115–20) has been confirmed by a number of other statistical studies (e.g., Nankani, 1979) and case studies (e.g., Evans, 1979, Chapter 3). There is not a lot of evidence to determine what parameters of the LDC economy attract or repel MNEs, but a clear positive correlation exists between GNP per capita and the stock of foreign investment per capita (Reuber et al., 1973, pp. 113–14 and Appendix A); obviously its causal significance is uncertain, but it could point to an attraction of MNEs to countries with tastes and factor prices less distant from those of their industrialized home bases. Nankani (1979, Chapter 3) found that aggregate foreign investment in manufacturing shows at least a weak positive relationship to political stability and negative relationships to hostile investment climate (specific threats to foreign investors) and ideological orientation toward socialism, but his data did not distinguish between export-oriented and local-market investments.[5] Another important influence – government inducements – will be discussed later.

Export-oriented and local-market subsidiaries also differ in a few strategic operating characteristics. Reuber et al. (1973, pp. 82–7) found that the MNE parents hold significantly higher fractions of equity in the export-oriented subsidiaries. The difference arises partly from public policy, partly from the MNEs' own preferences. LDC governments frequently demand that MNEs take on local partners in joint ventures. MNE's generally resist this (more in some

of foreign direct investment itself, such as those of Nankani (1979) and Dunning (1980), generally have found no relationship at all or even a positive relationship between foreign investments and host-country wage levels. The positive relationship does not cast doubt on the presumption that minimizing costs is a prime determinant of industrial location decisions. Rather, in cross section, a higher level of development and economic organization raises both productivity and wages; with no control imposed for the attraction of productivity and organization for foreign investment, a positive relationship between foreign investments and wages could emerge even for export-oriented projects.

[5] The evidence of Reuber et al. (1973, p. 95) suggests that these elements of political economy pose less uncertainty for export-oriented projects. Also see Root and Ahmed (1978) and Dunning (1981).

settings than in others, as we saw in Section 3.4), but local entrepreneurs obviously can prove more useful allies when the project aims to serve the local LDC market. Export-oriented MNEs are likely to be especially resistant if the subsidiary produces components or undertakes processing for transfer to the parent or other affiliates. Furthermore, MNEs out to place footloose export-oriented subsidiaries surely enjoy a stronger bargaining position in dealing with potential host governments and so can avoid being bedded down with unwanted local partners. Some other differences appear in the financial flows of the two types of investments. Reuber et al. (1973, pp. 87–97) found that local-market subsidiaries rely more than do export-oriented projects on funds secured in the LDC. The funds supplied by local partners account for part of the difference, but it should also matter that export-oriented subsidiaries have little incentive for local borrowing to hedge assets whose yields ride on the real exchange rate of the local currency (Shapiro, 1975a). Reuber et al. found no robust difference in the average profitabilities of the two investment types. Export-oriented investments show higher nominal profitability (not robust, in their statistical analysis), but local-market subsidiaries remit much larger percentages of earnings as royalties and fees and surely face in greater measure the regulatory incentives for manipulative transfer pricing discussed in Section 8.4.

LDC government incentives

Reuber et al. (1973, pp. 120–32) emphasized the variety and types of incentives that had been offered by host countries to the projects covered by their survey.[6] The incidences of various incentives found by Reuber et al. were as follows: tariff protection, 34 of 76 cases (the mean tariff rate was 68 percent); import-quota protection, 34 of 77; tariff reduction on imported equipment, 43 of 78; tariff reduction on imported components, 29 of 75; tariff reduction on imported raw materials, 26 of 76; tax holiday, 37 of 80 (mean length five years); accelerated depreciation for tax purposes, 20 of 71; public provision of infrastructure investments, 18 of 70. The

---

[6] Indeed, 22 of the 80 projects surveyed were initiated because of requests from the host governments (pp. 77–80).

form of assistance naturally shows some correlation with the type of investment. Export-oriented investments tend to receive the tax holidays and infrastructure investments; domestic-market projects tend to receive the protection from competing imports. Correspondingly, the MNE respondents were prone to declare import protection essential to inducing their local-market investments, and financial incentives as important for inducing export-oriented investments.

Overall, Reuber et al. (1973, pp. 127–32) did not accord these various inducements a vital role in inducing foreign investment, and they noted that previous empirical studies had led to a mixed evaluation.[7] For one thing, companies tend to discount inducements on the presumption that what the government gives with one hand it may well take away with the other. Also, some evidence suggests that government's efficiency and predictability in dealing with MNEs (something on which the government cannot readily bargain) may weigh quite heavily relative to the specific inducements put forth.

In light of the results of Chapter 8, we pause for some normative analysis of these forms of assistance. First, economists have made a start at theoretical analysis of assistance in its most comprehensive form, the duty-free zone. These zones are organized to attract export-oriented projects, prominently including the processing of manufactured components. They are simply a device for bundling together many concessions from the host country's prevailing taxes, tariffs, labor regulations, and the like. The government can thereby relax onerous regulations that it does not wish to repeal outright (Wall, 1976).[8] Hamada (1974) considered this institution in the con-

---

[7] See Reuber et al. (1973, p. 131, note 53) and also Cohen (1975, Chapter 4). Bond (1981) pointed out that tax holidays induce firms to exhaust their capital services by the holiday's expiration, or to liquidate then and sell their secondhand assets to a new firm.

[8] Baerresen (1971) described Mexico's experience, and Fröbel et al. (1980, Part III) provided an extensive international inquiry. In the countries for which data are available, garments, textiles, and electrical goods account for three-fourths of the activity. Fröbel et al. also described the West German garment industry's participation in these foreign investments, indicating a trend toward more and smaller German firms going abroad, and increasingly toward low-wage countries as recipients of these investments. They (pp. 139–41) and Baerresen agree that worker productivity in duty-free-zone activities closely approaches its level in the MNEs' national home bases.

text of the two-sector Heckscher-Ohlin model of international trade. The small, labor-rich LDC exports the labor-intensive commodity and imports the capital-intensive one. The LDC imposes a protective tariff on imports, and this impairs its economic welfare because it is too small to improve its terms of trade thereby. If MNE capital were to flow into the LDC's domestic economy, it would simply shift the output mix toward the import-competing capital-intensive good, leaving the private incomes of domestic factors of production unchanged but the country as a whole worse off because the government would no longer collect customs duties on the displaced imports.[9] If the MNE capital instead enters the duty-free zone, exactly the same thing happens: Now it attracts labor out of the domestic factor endowment instead of adding capital to it, with the same unfavorable effect on welfare. One senses that the Heckscher-Ohlin model, with pure competition and all factors of production fully employed, captures little of the institutional setting of the LDC economy. Hamilton and Svensson (1980) tried to improve things by making capital sector-specific in what is otherwise the same simple two-sector model. An inflow of MNE capital to the LDC's export sector then will improve the LDC's economic welfare, and an inflow to a duty-free zone may do so, but the outcome depends on some hard-to-interpret technical conditions.

The formal analysis cropping up around the duty-free zone really involves special cases of the general issue of the second-best: When one market is distorted from its optimal status (whether by government intervention such as a tariff or by a flaw in the market itself), welfare may not be maximized by letting other markets find their competitive equilibria. Theoretical examples abound in the literature on development. A MNE may not raise the LDC's national welfare when it enters with some productivity or cost-reducing advantage, if

---

[9] Brecher and Diaz Alejandro (1977) pointed out that the welfare impairment caused by a small inflow of MNE capital will be reversed if the inflow proceeds far enough to affect domestic factor prices and offset the welfare-curtailing effect of the LDC's import tariff. Where the LDC's optimal tariff is positive, Svedberg (1977, pp. 43–52, 1979) has shown that it may need to ban foreign investment in order to prevent welfare-reducing foreign investment from being induced by the tariff. Markusen and Melvin (1979) examined these issues in the context of a two-country model.

the MNE enjoys both tariff protection and monopoly power. Even a competitive national firm can reduce welfare by importing a technological improvement when factor markets are distorted (the wage exceeding the shadow price of labor, say) (Berry, 1974; also see Lapan and Bardhan, 1973). One conclusion about second-best models should be kept in mind. Whether the market equilibrium provides too much or too little depends on the particular case. The distortions in LDC economies therefore do not point to any general excess – or deficiency – of foreign investment.

Can one make normative sense of LDCs' inducements to foreign investment under different assumptions about their economies? Or are their favors to MNEs the deadweight loss that critics charge? Two considerations suggest that LDC governments may have valid reasons not recognized in these models. The first concerns employment effects. If the LDC is characterized by underutilized labor, employment given at the going wage yields a rent to the worker and an increment to the national income. This gain depends on the workers employed by the MNE coming from the currently unemployed or underemployed work force, or at least indirectly inducing additional employment. For the largely female work forces often utilized in duty-free zones, the assumption may be reasonable, although in general one does not expect the foreign entrepreneur to be looking for workers "straight from the farm." The other consideration bears on the LDC's gains from taxing foreign capital, discussed in Chapter 8. Although economists have not explored the matter closely, the effects of tax credits and deferral by the principal MNE source countries create rich strategic opportunities for host countries. An import tariff that induces an inflow of foreign capital imposes its own welfare cost, but that may well be small compared with the gains from having first crack at taxing the foreigners' profits.[10] Although a permanent tax give-up by the LDC would obviously be irrational, a short tax holiday could conceivably be efficient. It would allow the

[10] Svedberg (1977) considered this question both theoretically (pp. 52–9) and in the context of statistical evidence on foreign investment in Latin America (Chapter 4). His data suggest that the comparative disadvantage of the import-substituting foreign investments is great enough to make the host country's optimal inducement quite small.

MNE to take maximum advantage of any deferral provision of the source country's tax, plowing back most of the early profits to swell the profit flow later taxable by the LDC. The tax holiday's efficiency depends closely on the time-profile of the subsidiary's profits and detailed features of the source country's tax system.

9.2. Effects on economic development

Against this background we turn to the effects of foreign investment on the LDC host economy. Possible effects run from the narrowly microeconomic to the aggregative (savings, investment, growth of real income) to the political and social systems. We proceed along this array but stop short of the political and social, where neither economic analysis nor the organized stock of informed observation offers much help.

Industrial structure and performance

The effects of MNEs on the structure and performance of LDC industries raise the same questions reviewed in Chapter 4, but their various weights differ to reflect LDC conditions. We shall draw on Lall's (1978a) survey of this diffuse literature. He observed (pp. 226–9) that the correlation between the presence of MNEs and the concentration of sellers in the market, regularly seen in the industrial countries, prevails in the LDCs as well. However, most studies observing that correlation have not grappled with the problem of common causes giving rise to both foreign investment and high concentration, and so the usual conclusion that MNEs cause concentration is not automatically supported. Lall's (1979a) study of Malaysia did attempt this control. In consumer-good industries, the common-cause hypothesis prevails, but in producer-good industries, the presence of MNEs seems to wield a net positive influence on concentration.

The soundest way to determine the effects of MNE entrants on concentration is to follow industries over time. As Lall (1979a) pointed out, the initial effect of reducing concentration can be followed by an ultimate increase, and the normative significance of that increase depends on how it comes about. The best of the time-profile studies[11] have suggested several generalizations. First, in some sectors the entry of MNEs (indeed, of modern industry generally) has brought the demise of artisan and small-scale local producers. This event is basically like any displacement of a less efficient technology by a more efficient one, but of course the negative effects on the welfare of the displaced producers may be a matter of national economic and cultural concern. The effects of MNEs' entry on local industrial competitors are largely consistent with what we found in Chapter 1 about the market shares commanded by MNEs. In industries where MNEs tend to hold decisive advantages, local entrepreneurs may be expelled; in other sectors, MNEs may claim moderate market shares but settle into a market equilibrium along with viable domestic competitors. The MNEs' subsidiaries typically are larger firms than their domestic rivals (Lall, 1978*a*, p. 232), a finding that also holds for the less industrialized and smaller developed countries (such as Canada and Australia). Also, studies of individual markets (Evans on Brazilian pharmaceuticals) have suggested that MNEs and domestic firms often may carry out different arrays of activities when they compete in the same general market.[12] Some evidence suggests that MNEs' shares in LDC markets may, on the average, be rising. However, the world's population of MNEs is also growing, including those originating in LDCs, which will be discussed later; put in that context, a rising trend in their aggregate share does not have any necessary implications for seller concentration in the markets tenanted by MNEs.

One element in LDCs' concerns over the market activities of MNEs is the displacement of domestic entrepreneurs. If natives can

[11] Biersteker (1978, Chapter 6) on Nigeria, Evans (1979, Chapter 3) on Brazil. Also see Newfarmer (1979, 1980).

[12] The question whether or not these differences exist should itself vary predictably from industry to industry. Cohen (1975, Chapter 3), for example, undertook a rather unmotivated comparison between paired foreign-controlled and domestic firms producing 11 narrowly defined commodities in Singapore, Taiwan, and South Korea. The sample leaned toward simple manufactures and toward export-oriented production. It is not surprising that Cohen found in these sectors no obvious differences in terms of share of output exported, wages, employee turnover, thickness of the value-added slice, or other descriptive features. Also see Gershenberg and Ryan (1978) and Riedel (1975).

learn the entrepreneurial ropes in a softer environment without MNE competitors, the argument goes, they can then spread their skills throughout the economy. The argument has sharp limitations,[13] but it does flag certain empirical issues. MNEs have been entering LDC markets more and more frequently by buying out local firms; indeed, this mode of entry is more common the larger the supply of "good" local firms to buy.[14] Concern therefore arises about the fate of native entrepreneurs in "denationalized" enterprises. Evans (1979, Chapter 3) noted a handful of cases in which bought-out entrepreneurs transferred their skills to other industries in which local enterprise suffered less disadvantage or no disadvantage. The evidence does not rule out the possibility that MNEs may have a negative effect on the development of nationals' talents for business management in LDCs, but it does suggest that the conclusion cannot be drawn simply from the fact that foreign subsidiaries often are headed by aliens. Vernon (1976*b*) suggested that since World War II, local LDC enterprises have become more viable competitors by sending managers abroad for business training.

A similar issue arises in connection with R&D done by MNEs and local firms. Although MNEs have shown an increasing tendency to decentralize their R&D to subsidiaries' locations (see Section 7.1), partly in response to host-government pressures, levels of local R&D spending often are perceived as low by host governments. The implicit model of market failure holds that the skills acquired by nationals in undertaking R&D yield greater value for the national economy than their opportunity cost, presumably because not all rents on new knowledge of special local relevance get collected by the R&D proprietors, or because R&D skills somehow yield spillover value for other activities. If national firms undertake R&D at

---

[13] Nationals also learn the ropes by working for MNEs before venturing on their own, one could reply. Also, the fact that nationals may rise to the occasion when put on their own mettle does not contradict the possibility that more can be learned by watching the successes (and mistakes) of foreign managers.

[14] One implication of MNEs' lower opportunity costs of capital is that they will discount the expected future cash flow of a national firm at a lower rate than will its LDC owners and hence will be willing to pay more than their asking price.

all, the evidence from Chapter 7 leads us to expect that their spending rates will be higher than those of local foreign subsidiaries. Evans (1979, Chapter 4) concluded that Brazilian domestic pharmaceutical firms have done reasonably well in developing local products, whereas the foreign subsidiaries have depended on their parents' innovations.

Numerous studies have also addressed differences in productivity and profitability between MNEs and local firms. The various sources of rents to MNEs' activities, identified in preceding chapters, imply that MNEs will generally be more profitable than competing single-nation firms, although that margin will vary from sector to sector. Lall's (1978a) survey concluded that most studies have found a difference in this direction, although in the more careful inquiries it has not always proved statistically significant.[15] Aggregate data for the United States indicate no difference in the profitability of subsidiaries between developed countries and LDCs once the petroleum sector has been omitted (Leftwich, 1974). Although there are reasons for expecting that MNEs' activities may be more profitable in LDCs (risk premia, monopoly positions in small markets), there are also reasons why actual or reported profits in LDCs may be lower (regulations, transfer-pricing incentives). In any case, the evidence on MNEs' profitability in LDC surroundings is consistent with the theoretical expectations and evidence on their profitability generally.

Productivity comparisons raise all sorts of complex issues, some of which will be developed later, but they yield a few generalizations. Among the more advanced LDCs, MNEs seem to enjoy no intrinsic productivity advantage independent of the transactional advantages that make them MNEs in the first place. This has been shown most elaborately for Argentina by Vendrell-Alda (1978). Similarly, Tyler (1978) found no differences within most Brazilian industrial sectors, although MNEs seem to enjoy higher residual productivity when all industries are lumped together. Tyler's results as-

---

[15] Gershenberg and Ryan (1978); Willmore (1976); Lall and Streeten (1977, Chapter 6). Yoshihara (1976) applied no statistical tests to his extensive data on Singapore, but they seem consistent with no significant difference.

sociate the advantage with scale economies enjoyed by the MNE rather than with intrinsic efficiency. Lim (1976) found for Malaysia that large raw differences in capital utilization favoring the MNEs disappear when controls are imposed for various factors including the professionalism of management, which Negandhi (1975) also found to differ between foreign subsidiaries and comparable local firms.

The general line of analysis developed here suggests that LDC entrepreneurs, beyond withstanding MNE competition in some markets, may even go multinational themselves. The information available on MNEs based in developing countries[16] generally accords with the organizational model of the MNE set forth earlier. We might expect a LDC-based MNE to possess the distinct advantage of technology appropriate to the cost conditions of LDCs, and that pattern often appears. LDC-based MNEs are found in industries with mature technologies and small minimum efficient scales of production. They never go abroad to exploit high technology, and seldom for marketing advantages. Investments often are held by individual entrepreneurs rather than corporations (Yoshihara, 1976, Chapter 7), although international business organizations may still be involved. Reducing risk by diversifying abroad is a common goal of LDC-based MNEs. Although this goal has the air of second-best about it, considering LDCs' efforts to keep domestic capital from emigrating, it may also contain an element of efficient risk taking. Lecraw (1977) found that LDC-based MNEs were less sensitive to risks in LDC host countries than MNEs based in developed countries, as well as more amenable to joint-venture arrangements.

Skills, wages, and employment

The next group of issues concerns the wages that MNEs pay, the training that they provide, and the level of employment offered. Although MNEs' affiliates are expected to pay the going local

---

[16] See Lecraw (1977), the chapters by Wells and Diaz Alejandro in Agmon and Kindleberger (1977, Chapters 5 and 6), Yoshihara (1976, Chapter 7), Heenan and Keegan (1979), Kumar and McLeod (1981), and Wells (1983).

wage for labor of given qualifications, the statistical evidence (see Chapter 5) suggests that they pay, on average, higher wages in the LDCs. The survey of Reuber et al. (1973, pp. 175–6) found that the majority of MNE respondents pay the prevailing wage, but an appreciable minority pay more, and national surveys (e.g., Markensten, 1972, pp. 88–93, 102–10) typically have reported higher wages in MNEs. Lim (1977) offered the most careful statistical analysis, finding the MNEs' wages in Malaysia to exceed those of national companies, even with many variables controlled, although the excess comes in fringe benefits rather than the basic wage. The normative significance of the wage differential is an open question. It may involve the transfer of rents to the LDC work force. It may reflect a preference of alien entrepreneurs for better "quality" workers, or those already accustomed to industrial work in local firms (which suggests that the local firms' lower wages may partly reflect training benefits). Neither of these cases involves any transfer of rents to the LDCs except to the extent that foreign investment reduces structural unemployment.

Some sources (e.g., Gordon and Grommers, 1962, Chapter 8) have suggested that MNEs invest considerably in training LDC labor. But training does not appear to be a major or distinctive activity of MNEs, and it conveys no spillover benefits to the host country if employees themselves finance it through apprentice wages. Reuber et al. (1973, pp. 172–4) found no evidence of apprentice wages. Also, they noted appreciable rates of labor turnover in the foreign subsidiaries,[17] which implies that the MNEs cannot capture all the rents of the training that they provide. But Svedberg's (1977, pp. 123–32) analysis of the limited evidence available indicated that the aggregate value of the resulting externality is not likely to be very high. Reuber et al. (1973, pp. 169–72) also provided evidence on the use of native employees in skilled and managerial positions, where any significant training benefits should accrue. Managerial and engineering positions had only a bare majority of nationals when

---

[17] Other investigators (Cohen, 1973) have disagreed, finding low rates of labor turnover among foreign subsidiaries. Diverse patterns are likely, but subsidiaries that pay higher wages should expect thereby to reduce turnover. Host-country gains from rents to labor therefore trade off against any gains from the circulation of trained personnel.

the average project began, but the proportion had risen to 70 percent by the time of the survey. This survey also showed that the skilled proportion of the work force is much lower for export-oriented subsidiaries than for those serving the domestic market.

In industrialized host countries, the main labor-force issue has been the stability of employment. McAleese and Counahan (1979) explored this issue for Ireland. They found ad hoc reasons why employment in foreign subsidiaries might be either more or less stable over a recession period than in domestic companies, but no compelling factor running either way. They found employment to be more stable in larger plants and in firms performing a marketing function locally (and perhaps thereby able to "manage" demand somewhat), but no difference associated with nationality.

Choice of technology

A strong suspicion among LDCs holds that MNEs create too few jobs because they fail to adapt their technologies, designed for industrial-country wages and capital costs, to the factor prices prevailing in LDCs. This issue has been extensively investigated, perhaps because the thought of capital and labor optimally combined can drive economists to ecstasies that other humans find baffling. It involves not just MNEs but also the larger question of whether or not technology developed in the industrial countries gets adapted efficiently by whatever firms implement it in the LDCs. As Lall (1978a) suggested, the issues boil down to (1) whether or not the advanced-country technologies familiar to the MNEs are economically adaptable to the LDCs' conditions of labor abundance, (2) whether or not the MNEs do in fact adapt them, and (3) whether or not they adapt better than local firms.[18]

The first question can receive only a general answer here. The labor intensity of a production process may be quite inflexible: There is only one way to make x, or only one that is efficient over a wide range of factor costs. Alternatively, technologies may be adaptable to LDCs' factor costs, but only with an investment in devising and proving out the technology that will deter the individual firm. Why,

[18] For more complete surveys, see Lall (1978a), Chudson and Wells (1974), and Moxon (1979).

then, does some firm not make the adaptation and license the results profitably throughout the LDC world? The limitations of the market for proprietary technology (see Chapter 7) supply one answer. Also, technology can be specific to many local conditions besides relative factor costs.

Some studies have investigated MNEs' adaptations to LDCs' local cost conditions by surveying them directly. Reuber et al. (1973, Chapter 6) reported that MNEs make rather infrequent adaptations of technologies that they take to LDCs, the process technology being unchanged in 73 percent of their cases, quality-control systems being unchanged in 83 percent. Courtney and Leipziger (1975) employed an interesting statistical research design that compared the technology choices of foreign affiliates of U.S. MNEs located in LDCs with the choices made by their affiliates in other industrial countries. They determined whether or not the two sets of subsidiaries appeared to operate from the same production function and, if they did, whether or not the LDC subsidiaries adopted more labor-intensive technologies appropriate to their surroundings. In most industries, more labor-intensive technologies were chosen in the LDCs; in some cases the underlying production functions seemed to differ, in others only the equilibrium capital–labor ratio chosen along a common function. Yeoman (1976) found the amount of adaptation to vary greatly from industry to industry, which could be due to intrinsic differences in technology. Several results in these surveys suggest that adaptations of technology may be costly, so that only the inexpensive or the necessary ones get made. Yeoman (1976, Chapter 6) suggested that adaptation takes places only in activities where the potential effect on the product's unit cost is substantial. Reuber et al. (1973) found that what adaptation occurred frequently was because of the smaller scale of operation in LDC markets, rather than different factor prices per se. This conclusion has been echoed in other studies, such as those of Morley and Smith (1977*a*) and Hughes and You (1969, pp. 193–4), who found that a lot of adaptation takes place, but mostly because of small scale. Strassmann (1968) reported fairly widespread use of secondhand machinery by MNEs in Mexico and Puerto Rico – a low-cost way to assume that factor intensity of the last generation of industrial-country technology, presumably less capital-intensive than what succeeded it (Mar-kensten, 1972, pp. 97–101). Both MNEs and domestic companies tend to stick with machinery from their own nations (Morley and Smith, 1977b; Lecraw, 1977); one possible reason is the transactions costs of making a worldwide search to investigate other wares. For-syth (1972, pp. 124–7) suggested that the amount of adaptation in-creases with the subsidiary's age and experience.

If the evidence spottily suggests that MNEs do some (but not much) adopting of technology to LDCs' cost conditions, how do their input choices compare with those made by local firms? Our conclusion, in brief, is that numerous studies have found differences between technologies chosen by local firms and foreign subsidiaries, although only a few have controlled for many of the factors that might explain why the differences occur. When there is little or no control for industry mix, for example, a sufficient explanation for greater capital intensity in MNE plants will be their tendency to pop-ulate more capital-intensive industries than native enterprises. Even with reasonably good controls for industry mix (and perhaps other variables), the results are still somewhat divergent. Morley and Smith (1977b) found foreign firms to be more capital-intensive in about half of the industries they analyzed, and size differences were not involved. Mason (1973) examined a small number of matched pairs of MNEs and local companies in Mexico and the Philippines, finding the subsidiaries to be more capital-intensive on both stock and flow measures of capital. Wells (1973) identified specific tech-nologies in his industries, so that the choices made by his Indonesian firms could be unambiguously classified; four-fifths of the foreign firms chose the capital-intensive technology, but only one-tenth of the local firms. Forsyth and Solomon (1977) (also see Solomon and Forsyth, 1977) found a similar difference for Ghana, as did Bier-steker (1978, pp. 123–9) for Nigeria.[19] Most studies not reporting the result, such as Pack (1976), Cohen (1975, Chapter 3), Riedel (1975), and Chung and Lee (1980), have been based on industries not heavily tenanted by MNEs or export sectors in which MNEs are expected to implant labor-intensive processes.

[19] Lecraw (1977) concluded that LDC-based MNEs operating in Thailand make more efficient adaptations than do developed-country MNEs.

These studies have suggested several factors to explain this pattern. MNEs may indeed face different factor prices than domestic firms. The analysis of Chapter 6 showed that the MNE will rationally not be influenced exclusively by local capital costs, and several papers that have found MNEs more capital-intensive have also reported that they pay higher wages (Wells, 1973; Mason, 1973; Forsyth and Solomon, 1977; Biersteker, 1978, pp. 137–42). A frequent suggestion (Strassmann, 1968) is that labor-intensive processes incur increased costs of supervision and coordination that can easily offset their ostensible advantages. Several studies have suggested that a monopoly market position mutes the incentive to adapt efficient technology (Wells, 1973; Yeoman, 1976; White, 1976). Wells (1973) argued that an absence of market pressure allows playroom for "engineering man," who relishes technical sophistication for its own sake. However, monopoly cases blur into those where capital intensity serves to maintain quality control of a product subject to a worldwide trademark (Wells, 1973; Keddie, 1976), and it is not clear that a technical-inefficiency explanation is needed.

Several studies have classified the enterprise population more elaborately than MNE versus local. Forsyth and Solomon (1977) divided national enterprises in Ghana into those owned by natives and those owned by resident expatriates. What factor-intensity differences they found distinguished native-owned firms (less capital-intensive) from all others, suggesting that something other than entrepreneurial residence may be involved. Morley and Smith (1977*b*) made two-way comparisons among U.S., West German, other Western European, and national firms in Brazil. Value added per worker turned out to be greater for U.S. MNEs than for other MNEs, and greater for MNEs than for national firms. They concluded that these differences reflect some unknown combination of factor proportions and outright efficiency.

Linkages

A concept stressed in the literature on development is linkages of input–output relationships extending back from the purchases made by a firm and forward through the inputs that it supplies to other processes and activities. The implicit assumption is that many cells in the input–output table of a developing country are empty because of lack of entrepreneurial efforts or other forces. With the encouragement of a specific demand for an output, or a concrete supply of an input, a viable activity may spring up. MNEs' critics in the developing countries tend to claim that MNEs do not generate enough of these linkages (Singer, 1950). Although this proposition is not itself operational, some factual evidence does appear that can be related to our expectations about MNEs' behavior. Studies of foreign subsidiaries in industrial countries have observed that their purchases of inputs from the host-country market tend to increase proportionally as the subsidiary matures (Safarian, 1966, Chapter 5; Forsyth, 1972, p. 115; McAleese and McDonald, 1978). In LDCs this pattern has not been documented, but LDC governments often take some of the rents they can extract from MNEs in the form of requiring that more inputs be either produced or purchased locally. Activities undertaken by MNEs differ considerably in terms of linkage potential; MNEs doing labor-intensive processing of components for export will be expected to make few local purchases of inputs, and Reuber et al. (1973, Chapter 5) accordingly found that the export-oriented projects in their sample buy locally only half as large a proportion of their inputs as do other projects. Reuber et al. also investigated forward linkages, finding that most of their respondents claim none, but a substantial minority boast (perhaps self-serving) of encouraging an appreciable number of local distributors or sales organizations.

A few studies have investigated these linkages statistically. Biersteker (1978, pp. 89–91) found that MNEs' affiliates in Nigeria purchase a larger proportion of inputs from abroad than do native firms, but the difference stems largely from MNEs' prevalence in newer products, for which strategic inputs may be available only from abroad. Cohen (1973), whose sample restricted his comparisons to closely paired foreign and domestic firms, also found that the foreign subsidiaries import more. Buckley (1974), McAleese and McDonald (1978), and O'Loughlin and O'Farrell (1980) found that foreign subsidiaries in Ireland buy fewer inputs from the Irish economy than do national firms, especially if the subsidiary acquires some of its inputs from an overseas affiliate. Foreign subsidiaries make smaller proportions of their sales into the Irish economy (potential forward linkages) than do domestic firms, but that proportion has been increasing.

The literature on linkages suffers acutely from the problem of "as compared with what?" The fact that a foreign subsidiary may generate fewer linkages than a domestic enterprise has an unambiguous significance only if one assumes that the two enterprises substitute for each other directly. On that assumption, the behavioral traits of foreign investment suggest that the foreign subsidiary will generate fewer linkages (at least in its immature years), and the evidence supports that view. But whether or not the one-for-one substitution assumption corresponds to any actual policy question is another issue.

Capital inflows, saving, and balance of payments

The next issue concerns the net contributions made by MNEs to the capital stocks of developing countries. Closely related is the effect of their financial activities on an LDC's balance of payments. The simple view of foreign investment as capital arbitrage contrasts sharply with the observations that foreign affiliates borrow appreciable amounts of their capital locally, earn high profits, and shortly are removing more capital from the LDCs than they imported at the outset. As we saw in the theoretical analysis of Sections 5.2 and 6.4, drawing conclusions about these questions once again entails a tricky controlled-experiment issue. But larger truths do emerge from our analysis: The MNE is not primarily an arbitrager of capital, and risk-bearing considerations indeed do call for some matching of local-currency assets and liabilities – probably more in LDCs than in industrial host countries.

The qualitative impression that MNEs are unimportant sources of net capital inflows seems to prevail in many studies. The capital stock of the typical nonextractive subsidiary in a developing country is small (Cohen, 1975), and MNEs seem to account for only a small proportion of the capital inflow to some of the more successful LDCs, such as Korea (Westphal et al., 1979).

Whether the capital that MNEs bring to developing countries is "a lot" or "a little" may not itself be a very important question for the welfare of the LDCs. If capital is indeed scarce and commands a high return, that reward tends to pass directly to the foreign investor (excepting what the tax collector intercepts). The arbitrage premium does not raise the LDC's own national income. Indeed, by driving down the return to capital, an influx of MNE capital can lower the rate of return to domestic savers, depressing their rate of saving and hence the growth rate of the LDC's national income. The same proposition can be stated in other ways: The reward to domestic labor may rise and that to domestic capitalists may fall, reducing saving if only the capitalists save; or the MNE may preempt investment opportunities, discouraging local capitalists from saving in order to seize them. A number of studies have investigated this relationship statistically; Areskoug (1976) has provided a recent example. Using data for 21 developing countries, he related aggregate domestic fixed-asset investment to various sources of gross saving available to the economy – foreign private investment (including direct), government borrowing abroad, and domestic GNP (source of domestic saving). If a dollar of capital inflow is associated with less than one dollar of domestic investment, we can suppose that domestic saving was reduced somewhat and consumption increased. Areskoug found that for the typical LDC, both private foreign investment and government borrowing abroad produced a good deal less than a dollar of capital formation per dollar of inflow. This "leakage" appeared to be less in LDCs with more authoritarian governments, where agents in the private sector probably enjoyed less chance to make an economic response to the injection of capital from abroad.

Areskoug's results are generally consistent with those of a number of other studies that will not be reviewed in detail. However, one that holds particular interest is that of Weisskopf (1972). He accepted the familiar "two-gap" model of development planning, which suggests that the LDC's growth rate may be constrained either by the amount of savings available for investment or by the nation's foreign-exchange earnings available to buy development-related imports. Weisskopf identified those countries in which savings appear to be the binding constraint, and for them he estimated that a given net capital inflow from abroad prompts a 23 percent offset in the form of reduced domestic savings.

The two-gap model and the foreign-exchange constraint on development provide the basis for much critical discussion of the MNE because of its repatriation of profits and other payments (such as royalties). MNEs contribute foreign exchange when they first invest in the LDC, of course. The ongoing foreign subsidiary borrows locally, plows back its profits, but eventually remits cumulative earnings that may be large relative to its initial injection of foreign exchange. Its output may replace imports (and save foreign exchange), but its purchases of imports from abroad are a drain on foreign currency. Obviously, no general presumptions arise as to the effects of MNEs in the LDC that places a high shadow price on foreign exchange.[20] As we saw in Section 6.4, we can draw no presumption about the relationship between the real return to foreign investment and its effects on the balance of payments.

Rate of growth

MNEs' effects on the LDC's rate of economic growth might seem to provide the ultimate relationship to be investigated. Unfortunately, it may be a rather ineffective focus for research. All the effects of foreign investment noted earlier can alter the LDC's real growth rate one way or another, and there is a clear-cut case for pursuing the individual strands of influence rather than trying to measure some amalgam of diverse effects, each with its own time-structure of operation. No clear theoretical prediction connects the stock of foreign investment in the LDC to the rate at which its national income grows. Even if foreign investment should have spillover effects that raise the *level* of national income, these need not translate into an ongoing favorable effect on the rate of growth. If foreign investment generates a flow of investible tax revenues for the government, it can increase the growth rate. If it reduces the

---

[20] See Biersteker (1978, pp. 93–7) and Lall and Streeten (1977) for typical analyses. Bos et al. (1974) have developed an ambitious model.

LDC private sector's rate of saving, it can lower the growth rate. Many other hypotheses are possible.

The empirical research on this topic has suffered both from this lack of theoretical guidance and in some cases from a surfeit of special pleading by the researchers. It is generally agreed that the stock of foreign investment per capita is correlated across LDCs with GNP per capita (Reuber et al., 1973), but that fact settles nothing about the causation involved or about the effect of today's stock of foreign capital on tomorrow's rate of national economic growth. An inflow of MNE capital, of course, enlarges the rate of growth as it affects gross domestic investment. Papanek (1973), for example, found that private capital inflows had about the same effect on growth (dollar for dollar) as did domestic saving and foreign short-term borrowing, although foreign aid seemed to have a substantially larger effect. But that direct effect of an inflow of MNE capital leaves open the issue of its indirect effects once in place.

The statistical studies of this issue, however, have flowed largely from scholars who have held firm prior beliefs about whether a negative or positive relationship would emerge. Kobrin (1977) postulated a positive influence of the foreign-investment stock on growth because avenues of progress are provided to non-elite nationals, and social modernization and progressive cultural borrowings are promoted. Numerous indicators of economic and social modernization for 57 LDCs were reduced by means of factor analysis to three components. There was no simple correlation between these factors (summarizing the degree of modernization) and the incidence of foreign investment. However, when Kobrin (1977, chapter 7) took account of the interaction between industrialization and foreign investment, he reached the conclusion that foreign investment "intensifies the relationship between social modernization and industrialization." But the methodology provided no control for the positive influence that modernization could well have on the prevalence of direct investment, so that Kobrin's association (if we accept it) proves nothing about causation.

Research methods come off no better when we turn to the doubters, such as Chase-Dunn (1975) and Bornschier (1980). Both accepted "dependency theory," which is a catchall term for all possible ways in which foreign investment can reduce host-country welfare and growth. Chase-Dunn related income per capita in 1970 (and several other measures of the level of development) across a number of LDCs to those countries' GNP levels per capita in 1950 and proxies for stocks of foreign capital per capita as of 1950–5. He indeed secured a positive relationship to 1950 income and a negative relationship to the stock of foreign investment. However, the levels of foreign investment and income per capita in 1950 were positively related to one another, and therefore this apparent negative relationship of subsequent development to foreign investment would emerge statistically even if there were no behavioral relationship between them at all. In short, the methodology was biased to produce the expected relationship. Bornschier (1980) recognized that an inflow of foreign investment produces an increase in real capital formation, but he expected that the established stock of foreign investment would negatively affect subsequent growth. His cross-sectional regression analysis, like that of Chase-Dunn, built in a statistical bias that tended to produce a negative relationship between nations' rates of growth of national income per capita (1965–75) and their stocks of foreign direct investment in 1965.[21] We conclude from the existing studies that the relationship between a LDC's stock of foreign investment and its subsequent economic growth is a matter on which we totally lack trustworthy conclusions.

9.3. Summary

This chapter has addressed both the causes and effects of foreign investments in LDCs. The foreign subsidiaries found in

---

[21] Bornschier included among his independent variables a measure of the cumulative inflow of direct investment (1967–73) relative to 1967 gross domestic product. But that inflow must have been positively correlated with the initial stock of foreign investment (also normalized by a variable closely related to national income). The growth rate of national income per capita was positively related to the growth of foreign investment, as Bornschier (and conventional analysts) expected. But, given that positive relationship between the growth of income and the foreign-investment inflow, the statistical method tends to produce a negative relationship between the growth rate and the initial foreign-investment stock, even if no behavioral relationship exists.

LDCs tend to divide sharply into those producing primarily for export and those serving the domestic market – a reflection of the small sizes of most LDC economies. MNEs are active in sectors where marketing entry barriers would otherwise limit LDCs' manufactured exports, as well as in sectors that undertake labor-intensive stages of processing. Subsidiaries that serve LDCs' domestic markets are found in about the same sectors as their developed-country counterparts. Export-oriented subsidiaries and domestic-market subsidiaries differ in various ways: The former are more likely to be wholly owned by the parents and less reliant on local capital markets; as expected, there are no systematic or average differences in their profitabilities.

Despite hostile rhetoric, LDC governments often offer substantial inducements to MNEs – tax holidays and infrastructure investments for the export-oriented, tariff protection for the import-competing. Economic theory casts a skeptical eye at LDCs' benefits from some of these concessions. If MNEs are lured into a small national market by an "inefficient" tariff, the investment inflow can reduce national welfare. But considerations of employment and host-country tax revenue may supply reasons for offering such inducements.

Systematic evidence on MNEs' effects on developing economies is not abundant. MNEs' relationships to surrounding market structures generally are similar to those found in industrialized countries. Although MNEs tend to be found in concentrated sectors, they do not enjoy universal advantages over native entrepreneurs, nor do they always claim commanding market shares. National enterprises in the more advanced LDCs may do more R&D (if they do any at all), and native entrepreneurs who cannot compete successfully in sectors where MNEs are advantaged do flourish in other sectors. LDC enterprises are starting to become multinational themselves, usually relying on distinctive advantages of technological adaptation to LDC conditions; they also may deal more successfully with risks in the LDC environment.

Some MNEs pay higher wages in LDCs than do domestic enterprises, and they may provide some training for which the benefits accrue partly to nationals who receive it. But the evidence does not suggest that either the training or the extra wages provide a large stream of rents to LDC nationals.

LDC spokesmen voice concern that the technology of industrial countries may not be adapted sufficiently to the labor-abundant conditions of most LDCS. Survey evidence indicates that MNEs do some adapting, but not a great deal, and it appears that the costs of adaptation may be high relative to the benefits expected by individual companies. Much adaptation takes inexpensive forms, such as the use of second-hand machinery, or occurs incidental to designing facilities for operation on a small scale. Foreign subsidiaries have been found in some studies to use less labor-intensive techniques than their national competitors. They may adapt less where product quality depends on use of the parent's home technology, or where the market structure provides a less competitive spur.

MNEs may import more of their inputs than competing local enterprises and therefore generate weaker linkages in the host economy. Export-oriented subsidiaries seem to be weaker sources of linkage than those serving the domestic market.

MNEs' operations do not turn mainly on moving capital from where it is cheap to where it is dear; accordingly, bringing finance to the capital-scarce LDC economy is not one of their main functions. Foreign direct investments, like other funds from abroad, tend to go partly into expanded consumption (reduced saving) in the host country, only partly into enlarging the host's capital stock.

Some researchers have tried to identify the overall effects of MNEs' presence in developing countries on the LDCs' subsequent rates of economic growth. The possible causal connections are numerous but speculative and ill-defined in terms of economic models. Empirical investigations, whether by those disposed to think good or ill of the MNE, have employed inadequate research procedures and have yielded no trustworthy conclusions.

10

Public policy

The literature on public policy toward MNEs compels an approach different from that of previous chapters. To describe the policy issues and conflicts arising in each country touched by MNE activities would be a hopeless task. Therefore, we retreat to a telescopic approach that emphasizes not the substantive details of these issues but the behavioral context in which they arise. This chapter follows a two-pronged strategy proven fruitful in other areas of economics, such as the study of government regulation of domestic business. First, the apparatus of neoclassical welfare economics supplies conclusions about what economic policies will maximize real income. Most of the relevant results were reported in the preceding chapters; they will be recapitulated in the first section of this chapter. Second, economic models of political behavior help us to understand why governments adopt the policies they do. In the following sections we shall attempt to apply them to the actual dialogue over public policy toward MNEs.

10.1. National and international welfare

The preceding chapters set forth the neoclassical welfare economics of MNEs on the following assumptions: First, each national government seeks to maximize the real incomes of its citizens. Second, decisions about distributing that income get made separately from decisions about maximizing the pie to be divided. (We did, however, note some theoretical connections between MNE activities and the functional distribution of income.) Third, each enterprise is assumed to have an unambiguous national citizenship, so that it maximizes its profits (or optimizes its profits and risks) in terms of one national currency and price set, and the nation's government can regard its maximized profit as a component of national income.[1] Fourth, in order to bring out the richest aspects of the analysis, it is assumed that the MNE's unique assets lead it typically to face downward-sloping demand curves for its outputs (this assumption is sometimes applied to the source nation's competing MNEs as a group), and the host nation faces an upward-sloping supply curve of MNE resource commitments (in a sense that varies from model to model). Fifth, each country is assumed to make policy decisions on MNEs in its role as either source or host. The cross-hauling of direct investments makes many countries play both roles, but a country generally can treat policies toward domestic and foreign MNEs independently (subject to the constraining threat of retaliation by other countries).

These assumptions have generally been shared by the normative analyses presented in several of the preceding chapters. Their results will be reviewed after a few preliminaries. Foreign investment indicates arbitraged resources. To the extent that the arbitragers seek profits, and market prices are undistorted, arbitrage is a productive activity, intramarginally if not at the margin. On that simple basis rests any general presumption that the actual allocation of MNE resources is efficient. The same conclusion flows in more qualified form from the transactional model of the MNE. Where alternative

---

[1] The third assumption has not been defended explicitly in this book. All the evidence indicates that the great bulk of MNEs clearly keep their legal and administrative headquarters in single national locations where most of their beneficial shareholders also reside. The lack of international diversification of securities portfolios, mentioned in Chapter 6, supports this view. A few well-known binational MNEs are exceptions. So are some individual proprietors of LDC-based MNEs, in that the entrepreneur may move with his capital when a foreign subsidiary is started.

methods of allocation – administrative or market – can compete freely, the resulting distribution of activity between MNEs and single-nation companies can make some claim to efficiency. We need qualifications for the institutional arrangements that should first be optimized so as to minimize the extent of "market failure," and also for the possibility of small-numbers gaming among the market rivals.

We have a useful starting point in these conditions under which MNEs generate efficient allocations of resources, but one needing qualification. A general cavil is implicit in the many writings that have weighed the MNE's welfare significance by evaluating its benefits and costs (or at least have vouchsafed the rightness of this approach). If one assumes no equality between shadow and market prices, then the benefit–cost techniques of development planning can claim some usefulness for weighing the appropriateness of any allocation induced by market prices. However, the approach ususally dwindles into list making, the listed items running to poorly defined economic benefits and politically determined costs.[2]

A second qualification addressed the transition from our assumptions to the prescription of economic policy. Optimal policy for the nation involves setting various instruments that relate directly to MNEs' allocations. Bhagwati and Brecher (1980) pointed out that the presence of MNEs also qualifies the proper choice of many policies ostensibly unrelated to foreign investment, because the policy instruments redistribute income between domestic income recipients and foreign suppliers of equity capital. To take their simplest case, suppose that national policy aims to maximize national income, that the nation exports capital-intensive goods, that all workers are citizens, but that all capital is supplied by foreigners. Moving from autarky (no trade) to free trade will maximize domestic product, but it will reduce national income because the real wage falls while the real return to capital rises.

[2] Of course, those favoring Marxian and radical approaches to the MNE would have no use for neoclassical welfare analysis, start or finish. No attempt is made to present their views.

Now we turn to a review of the normative conclusions from preceding chapters.

Taxation

Surely the most important case for positive government action toward MNEs lies in the field of taxation. Corden (1967), for example, stressed the density of assumptions needed to warrant a zero tax in a host country. If governments' revenue needs demand the taxation of profits, global-welfare maximization generally requires that all countries apply the same rate and that it apply to both foreign and domestic investments (see Chapter 8). For global welfare, it matters not which country, source or host, taxes the foreign investment income so long as the common effective rate applies. The divergence of national welfare from global welfare stems from two sources. The first grows from the host country's prior claim to tax the profits of resident subsidiaries. When investment flows to the host nation, tax revenue (and national income) is therefore transferred from source to host country. Optimal tax arrangements for the source require marginal equality between pretax returns to capital at home and returns abroad after payment of foreign taxes. Optimal policy for the host depends on the tax policies of source countries, but it generally involves setting a tax rate no lower than that (assumed common) of the source countries. One important qualification applies if the source country lets its MNEs defer taxes on foreign profits until they are repatriated. Then the host optimally lowers its tax rate below the source's, but imposes a withholding tax on the dividends when they are paid to the parent.

The tax rules laid down thus far do not depend on small-numbers conditions – countries being large enough for their policies to affect the yield on their own capital placed abroad or the supply price of foreign capital to them. Opportunities for exploiting monopoly/monopsony power in world capital markets promote another set of policies. Maximum national welfare demands higher taxes than the rules already reviewed. These taxes are globally inefficient and can give rise to Stackelberg equilibria (Feldstein and Hartman, 1979).

Taxes on capital interact importantly with tariffs on trade. Without the opportunity to annex tax revenue from abroad, the small nation (unable to improve its terms of trade) may lower its real income by putting on a tariff that tempts a capital inflow from abroad, unless the capital inflow shifts its production structure enough to extinguish international trade (Brecher and Diaz Alejandro, 1977). If all countries do tax capital, then the tariff becomes attractive for a small host country as a way to ingest tax-paying capital,[3] although if capital is sector-specific, a particular tariff may fail by repelling more foreign investment from some industries than it attracts to others (Corden, 1967). Finally, in the general-equilibrium context of the Heckscher-Ohlin model, the capital stock in a (large) country influences its terms of trade, and the individual country may either tax or subsidize foreign investment because of the indirect effect on the terms of trade (Jones, 1967). All these tax applications aim to improve national welfare at the expense of global welfare.

Transfer-pricing decisions by MNEs seek (among other things) to minimize the burden of taxes and tariffs paid by the company. These minimization efforts redistribute real income between countries and will be condoned by one, condemned by another (their effect on global welfare depends on the optimality of the underlying taxes being avoided). A country whose taxes and tariffs create incentives for adverse transfer pricing makes an optimal outlay on policing transfer prices in relation to the extra revenue captured.

Natural-resource rents

The economics of natural resources indicates that world welfare is maximized by the competitive extraction of nonrenewable natural resources by well-informed owners. Neither the owning country nor using country gains from any different long-run program for extracting natural resources (although either would benefit from springing an unexpected monopoly or monopsony on the other). The efficient program for extracting resources leaves their owner with the maximum (present value of) scarcity rents. If the resource deposits are heterogeneous in quality or location, this same efficient alloca-

---

[3] The tariff is clearly just an example of small profit-increasing market distortions that could play this role.

tion also yields differential rents to those deposits of better quality or more favorable location (than the worst in actual use). MNEs enter the picture as bargainers with owning governments over the terms of extraction (see Section 4.4). The MNEs have no general interest (barring global monopoly power) in departing from the efficient program for extracting the resource. But they gain from any rents they can capture from the resource-owning nation (as will the resource-using countries if they are the homes of the MNEs). For the resource owners, if the extracting MNEs are not their citizens, the problem is to capture all rents imputable to the resource, leaving only a normal rate of return for the MNE. A predetermined royalty rate is not efficient for this purpose because it distorts the operating firm's output decision. Other instruments include demanding a "free" equity share for the government at the outset, requiring a local joint-venture partner, taxing, or nationalizing the project once in place. Shifting rates of taxation – the "obsolescing bargain" – may offer the highest yield by annexing not just the rents but also the quasi rents (depreciation allowances) from the project. Even without the host-government opportunism involved in the obsolescing bargain, appropriate tax schedules probably are the host country's most effective instrument.[4]

Competition policy

In Section 4.3 we saw that competition policy, like tax policy, encounters the dilemma of discordant national and international interests. At least under "clean" neoclassical conditions, maximum world welfare requires competitive markets. National welfare is similarly maximized by competitive domestic markets. However, each nation gains if it can monopolize its sales abroad (exports, or through foreign subsidiaries) and monopsonize its foreign purchases

---

[4] The source country without monopsony power lacks any instruments to help its MNEs to capture rents overseas. We can note the discussion over what the source can do to avert the obsolescing bargain. In the United States this issue has related to the Overseas Private Investment Corporation and to the use of various threats and punishments against countries treating U.S. MNEs in ways deemed unacceptable to the United States. See Bergsten et al. (1978, Chapters 9 and 13) and Haendel (1979).

(including those by its MNEs' foreign subsidiaries). Private-sector monopoly is as good for this purpose as taxes and tariffs, barring a positive shadow price on government revenue. However, the country may lack policy instruments to make an industry behave monopolistically in its foreign sales or purchases but competitively in domestic transactions. An intermediate degree of competition in both foreign and domestic markets is then optimal.

The nation similarly has an interest in fighting off exactions by foreign monopolists (monopsonists). A tax on monopolized imports is helpful even if the foreign monopolist produces subject to constant costs; authorities should pay attention to whether or not the tariff induces the foreign seller to invest behind the tariff wall, which may or may not be desirable. If foreign subsidiaries take part in noncompetitive domestic industries, and competition policy is confined to high-priority situations, it should first attack MNE-dominated sectors if monopoly leads mainly to excess profits, but sectors dominated by domestic sellers if monopoly leads mainly to inflated costs (technical inefficiency).

Technology creation and transfer

This area of policy toward the MNE may be regarded as either very simple or very complex. To make it simple, dwell on the analogy to the economics of the patent system. The outlays on innovation and the dissemination of innovative results that will maximize social surplus diverge from what profit-seeking firms will expend. The terms of the patent system can be adjusted to minimize the discrepancy, but a discrepancy will remain. Buyers of innovative goods can, in principle, form a coalition to pay up as a lump sum the cost of investment in innovation, but the free-rider problem induces each to try to avoid payment. In relation to MNEs, the source country hopes to collect monopoly rents on technology sent abroad, the host country hopes to pay as little as possible, and no arrangement emerging from this interaction is likely to maximize world welfare. The presence of many source and host countries worsens the problem by amplifying the free-rider elements.

The complexities enter via the theoretical models described in Chapter 7, thus suggesting the following points: (1) The source country has a self-interest in establishing property rights in new industrial knowledge, which the free-riding host will tend to resist. (2) The source country should cheapen the dissemination of its knowledge stock if the resulting production changes will improve its terms of trade. (3) The source country may command the same innovative rents whether it exports the innovation embodied in goods, lets its MNE monopolize the host's market, or licenses the technology; if production is subject to diminishing returns, however, using more than one of these instruments becomes attractive. (4) The source country can trust its national MNEs to maximize the foreign rents to the nation's technology unless (a) they compete as suppliers of technology or (b) they value incorrectly the probability of technology leaking from proprietary control when licensed abroad or used by a foreign subsidiary. (5) The level of foreign investment optimal for the host country is increased if the MNE's proximity raises the rate at which its technology leaks into natives' hands.

The preceding subsections certainly do not cover every normative issue bearing on MNEs; any close study of the questions affecting a particular country (e.g., Bergsten et al., 1978) will uncover many more. But they bring out the form that those issues take and the prevailing divergence among global welfare, source-country welfare, and host-country welfare. This divergence, long a staple in the theory of tariffs, proves widely relevant, especially because the market structures congenial to MNEs favor the assumption that market participants may be few in number.

10.2 National policies: a behavioral approach

Traditional welfare economics assumes that the government wishes to maximize real income for its citizens and merely needs help with the technical details of its policies. The behavioral approach to public policy assumes, instead, that governmental decisions result from self-interest agents interacting in a political setting. This positive treatment of policy decisions has not led to a single all-purpose model like that of neoclassical welfare economics, but the specific applications to date share a coherence of general approach. Policy toward MNEs has not generally attracted a behavioral treatment, and so the following subsections will offer only tentative suggestions.[5]

Host countries

We shall concentrate on host countries because policy toward resident foreign subsidiaries attracts more attention in most countries than policy toward overseas activities of the country's own MNEs. The policies implemented by industrialized host countries or urged on them prove particularly suggestive. Many are not easily reconciled with the prescriptions of neoclassical welfare economics, and so they cry out for some other explanation.[6] They suggest two models:

1. *National preference.* The first of these models follows the research tradition by assuming a democratic political system in which the elected government, seeking to remain in power, proposes packages of measures expected to appeal to a majority of voters. Each individual votes for the package among those offered expected to yield the most utility. The voters as producers may hold various equities in factor services that they supply, but one set of factor services, by assumption, yields income flows not reaching domestic voters: equities in the local subsidiaries of foreign MNEs. The government's package of measures may include various devices for redistributing income from the political minority to the majority, and these are expected generally to win approval up to a point: where expected losses of income to the median voter due to any inefficien-

---

[5] Writers such as Vernon (1977) would object that the following models overrationalize the political process and the coherence and consistency of government policy toward MNEs. The point is well taken for limiting one's expectations about how much policy toward MNEs can be explained from purposive models, but it does not rule out some systematic patterns.

[6] Useful descriptions of these policies have been provided: Kindleberger (1969); Behrman (1970); Vernon (1971, Chapters 5–7, 1977, Chapters 6 and 8); Parry (1973); Hodges (1974); Safarian (1978); Organization for Economic Cooperation and Development (1978, 1980).

cies built into the redistributive devices offset that voter's gains from the redistributions. Because foreigners do not vote in national elections, redistributions away from foreign equity holders by themselves cause no negative votes and thus should proceed further than redistributions adverse to the interests of enfranchised minorities.

The model so far does not require any nationalistic preference on the part of the voters, but that can, of course, be appended. The preference might take various forms. In one formulation, voters may experience disutility from perceiving that resource allocations in the national economy are influenced by foreigners (e.g., a foreign-subsidiary plant closes, costing workers their jobs). Freedom from perceived foreign influence thereby becomes a collective consumption good. The national electorate will then favor measures to reduce or regulate this influence, again subject to the condition that real-income costs of the restriction do not outweigh the utility of the gain in perceived independence. In a slightly different formulation, nationals may experience disutility when they see fellow nationals suffer losses from decisions made by foreigners, so that they will vote to reverse or regulate such decisions even when their welfare is not affected directly. Two arbitrary-sounding features of the model are in fact chosen advisedly. First, subjective perception of foreign influence is what matters; an adjustment emanating from an industry with many sellers, half foreign subsidiaries, may arouse less fuss than the same one stemming from a duopoly with one foreign firm. Second, disutility from foreign decision making may apply asymmetrically to decisions that impose losses on some nationals, decisions that confer gains being ignored. This asymmetry draws on a general proposition that political decisions often seem to aim at preserving existing allocations (maintaining perceived equities) rather than maximizing the utility of the politically powerful.

A different formulation of national preference holds that voters themselves prefer to deal with nationals and experience disutility from economic transactions with foreigners. National preference in this version involves xenophobia, but not the factor of collective goods invoked earlier. This form of preference could explain, say, a political decision to exclude foreigners from sectors bringing them into contact with large numbers of voters as stylers and sellers of consumer goods and services.

The national-preference model naturally leads into a consideration of interest groups, which provide an alternative way to think about political choice. One need not travel far to find assertions that MNEs (perhaps large companies in general) influence political decisions beyond their weight in voters' preferences. Careful models of the basis for this influence are not abundant. In an inversion of this view, Hirschman (1969) argued that the political impotence of foreign entrepreneurs (undone by national preference) displaces the interest-group equilibrium from what would prevail if untainted native entrepreneurs sat in the same executive chairs. In this spirit, interest groups of domestic entrepreneurs may seek regulation or exclusion of MNEs as undesired competitors or, alternatively, may promote their expansion for rent-increasing effects on supply or demand in adjacent markets.

2. *Government policy.* The second model need not diverge grossly from the national-preference model, but we shall develop it differently in order to illustrate the analytical possibilities. Shift the focus from utility-maximizing electoral behavior to the utility of a coalition of government officials whose tenure in office is not explained within the model. Assume that the government pursues numerous policy objectives but that it lacks policy instruments that are reliably sufficient to attain them. Perhaps powerful interest groups prohibit or restrict policies that unavoidably (if perhaps incidentally) harm their welfare. Perhaps norms of convention or constitution keep the government from imposing or fully enforcing policies that theoretically could suffice for the intended objective. The government periodically desires to change the economic allocations that result from market transactions. But the insufficiency of instruments leaves the government constantly uncertain about whether or not it can make its allocative preferences stick. Private economic agents then become odious to the government in proportion to their ability to dodge its allocative designs. If MNEs enjoy better alternatives than nationals (they can spread the transaction cost of dealing with the government over more business, or they can credibly threaten to

cut back their local activities sharply), they draw unfavorable glances from the government and invite overall restriction or special regulation of their activities.

The national-policy model can take on an electoral flavor if we suppose that the median voter holds a preference that the government's bidding be done, whatever its effect on the median voter's welfare. Put more simply, the median voter may believe that allocative preferences announced by the government are intrinsically superior to those cast up by the market. In that case, any proposal to restrict or regulate MNEs will receive approval, because the median voter's restraining concern with effects on real income from private-sector transactions (present in the national-preference model) is defined away.

These models of political behavior call for a systematic empirical test. Unfortunately, writers on policy toward the MNE generally have not considered the issue in this positivistic framework. Some have simply offered description. Others, writing from normative commitments of their own, typically have proceeded without making their premises explicit.[7] Hence, the following remarks on the fit of these models are entirely tentative and impressionistic.

Both models seem to enjoy some explanatory power. The national-preference model accords particularly well with the cases in which a source government uses its MNEs to influence resource allocations within a host country. The invasion of sovereignty typically evokes a popular response in the host country that is quite disproportionate to the real income at issue, suggesting a preference for sovereignty per se. Similar resentment surrounds the MNE's decision to, say, reallocate production facilities from host A to host B; A's sensation of being had by alien decision makers may grossly exceed the political reaction that would occur if, instead, one independent national firm were contracting in A and another expanding in B. The national-preference model also explains restrictions in

---

[7] A well-known example is that of Barnet and Müller (1974), whose views seem quite fully in accord with the government-policy model. That model also represents fairly the whole sovereignty-at-bay school, given to comparing national incomes to the leading MNEs' gross sales and concluding therefrom that the MNEs can overpower the governments.

some hosts (especially LDCs) on the foreign nationals employed by the MNE or the presence of MNEs in "nonessential" activity. Exclusion of MNEs, however, can also respond to the preference of certain interest groups (local entrepreneurs) for shunning the competitive pressure of MNEs' rivalry in the market.[8]

The government-policy model also seems to hold a good deal of explanatory force. This fit is rather obvious for socialist governments openly disinclined to accept market allocations of resources. The model more interestingly explains behavior patterns of less interventionist governments that periodically find themselves short of policy instruments. One evidence is the exclusion of MNEs from policy-sensitive sectors: defense, obviously, but also finance and public utilities. Another lies in the preference of some governments for using informal suasion on economic agents rather than laying down clear rules – a logical compromise when the policy goal in question is controversial or is in conflict with more general policies or precepts. The government then grows fearful that the foreign subsidiary may enjoy better alternatives than national firms to profit-reducing adherence to the policy, or that the MNE may simply hear the whispered hint less clearly. Still another support for the government-policy model lies in the practice of some hosts to capture surplus from the MNE not as revenue but in the form of policy commitments – exports, training or promotion of nationals, etc. These policy commitments imply (via the excess-burden theorem) that the government finds itself short of instruments to respond to some discrepancies between market and shadow prices (see Section 9.2). Finally, the government-policy model may explain some nations' decisions to regulate MNEs' entry, especially when the regulation aims not to enforce explicit policies (such as inclusion of local partners) but rather to give government officials an opportunity to bargain with incoming MNEs to favor whatever preferences the government may currently hold.[9]

[8] Japan's highly restrictive policies seem to contain both strands (Henderson, 1973).
[9] This pattern may characterize Canada's regulation in comparison with that employed by many developing countries. Compare Safarian (1978) and Robinson (1976). Also see Lombard's (1979) study of Colombia.

One good test of the national-preference and government-policy models is their ability to explain a widespread host-country policy such as incentives or requirements that the MNE take on local partners in its subsidiary, or ultimately surrender control to nationals. The policy is seldom consistent with maximizing national income by the host country, because nationals are allowed to bid for their equity shares in the subsidiary, letting the MNE capitalize any rents it is earning.[10] Imposing a requirement of 50 percent or more control by nationals is consistent with the national-preference model. Requiring local minority shareholding or participation, however, is hard to explain, because it neither maximizes the incomes of nationals nor mitigates foreign control. Perhaps governments believe that it sensitizes the subsidiary to informal suasion, thus serving the government-policy interest. In short, the policy of national equity participation seems more consistent with the political-behavior models than with the straight maximization of national income.

The national-preference model does not necessarily conflict with the assumption of neoclassical welfare economics that host governments maximize national income. Therefore, the extent of inconsistency between host policies and income maximization provides some evidence on the political-behavior models. To hazard a bold generalization, LDCs' policies run toward consistency with income maximization, whereas developed hosts are more likely to pursue noneconomic goals (Negandhi and Baliga, 1979). The evidence on the rationality of LDCs' policies was presented mainly in Chapter 4 (the obsolescing bargain), Chapter 8 (maximum exploitation of source countries' tax-credit policies), and Chapter 9 (use of policy commitments).[11] Developed-country policies that seem best explained by collective preferences for nonmarket goals include pressures for local minority ownership and local performance of R&D

---

[10] Sometimes the government itself demands a minority shareholding, but this is simply an alternative to taxation. See Section 8.3.

[11] Hawkins et al. (1976) argued that nationalizations of MNEs' subsidiaries in LDCs during 1946–73 resulted from a left-wing shift of government in about half the cases, but otherwise displayed considerable (and increasing) economic rationality. Also see Diaz Alejandro (1970), Truitt (1974), Williams (1975), Sigmund (1980), and the discussion in Chapter 4.

and support for competing national firms ("national champions") in sectors deemed nationally important.[12] Such a difference between developed and less-developed hosts would be consistent with collective nationalistic preferences for the economy's mixture of activities being an income-elastic good that is consumed in greater proportions by wealthier societies.

Surveying companies' reactions to host-government policies is as impossible as surveying the policies themselves. Copious evidence cited in previous chapters suggests that the MNE as a global profit maximizer tends to react to host-government policies so as to minimize their impairment of expected profits. Some may shun entirely countries imposing policies with a significant chance of leaving no positive return (see Grosse, 1980, on the effect of the Andean Foreign Investment Code). Others adapt in various ways that may affect quite intimately their corporate organizations and strategies (Doz, 1980).[13]

Source countries

Models of political behavior can also be applied to countries' policies toward their own MNEs. The basic voting model implies that a policy benefiting the nation's MNEs at the expense of foreigners will win favor with the median voter. If property income (including equity shareholdings) is more concentrated than labor income, however, a voting model does imply that under some conditions source-country voters will approve of restricting foreign in-

[12] Obviously there is ground for doubt whether market failures are involved. Governments often seem convinced that high-technology industries are important for the overall growth of real income, or that goals of growth and full employment are served by pushing resources toward fast-growing world industries. But economists perceive no general reason why the private sector (MNEs or others) should underallocate resources to such activities.

[13] Doz found that companies that have rationalized their production internationally resist national intrusion more than those serving closed local markets. Competitive position influences the MNE's adaptation. A firm with unique assets attractive to host governments can take a tougher line, and the MNE without close international rivals tries to do so. The less advantaged MNE, however, may follow a policy of close cooperation with the host government in order to secure a local-market position from which stronger rivals cannot dislodge it.

vestment in order to redistribute income from capital to labor (see Chapter 5). This issue aside, source countries will also approve measures to invoke public authority to assist national MNEs in maximizing their rents from foreign markets, subject to conditions relating to the costs of these policies and how they are financed. It is not obvious that a nationalistic preference to avoid dealings with foreigners will lead the median voter to curb the MNE from dealing with them abroad, and so the national-preference model seems to predict no restrictions on the nation's MNEs and some basis for public assistance if needed to increase their overseas rents.

The government-policy model seems potentially more symmetrical between host and source countries than the national-preference model. A government acting to curb hard-to-control economic agents will find domestic MNEs no more appetizing than foreign ones. However, rational voters with a preference for public-sector allocations should appreciate that the national MNE itself provides the government with an instrument usable to affect resource allocations abroad, or that MNEs' rents from abroad should compensate for some disutility from any weakening of the government's ability to control. Therefore, the government-policy model predicts that limits on MNEs' foreign activities will be subject to some constraint.

We shall not pursue these suggestions in more detail because countries recently have acted so much more passively as sources than as hosts.[14] The sporadic policies of the United States toward its MNEs have been consistent with a willingness to let nationals earn rents abroad so long as no obvious incidental costs result,[15] and gov-

---

[14] The debate over imperialism as a possible front for foreign investment will not be reviewed here.

[15] Bergsten et al. (1978, Chapter 9). Once more, thresholds of perception may be important. The costs of allowing favorable tax treatment to foreign-source income have received less attention from the voting public than issues on which much less real income rides. The same holds for the possible redistributive effects of MNEs, although these resist easy quantification even by subtle economic research (see Chapter 5). These patterns might suggest a model in which MNEs and other large corporations have privileged or cost-efficient access to political favor. (Helleiner, 1977, argued from U.S. trade policy for such a model.) However, U.S. companies have not sought or secured protection against entry by foreign MNEs, even if they have scored repeated successes at repelling competition from imports.

ernment resources have at times been committed to increase or preserve these rents. Sigmund (1980) characterized the main line of U.S. policy, holding that because the market allocation of MNE activities yields benefit to both source and host, the host country should not act to increase its share of the pie. Such a posture seems stronger in its consistency with rational behavior by source-country voters than in its logical consistency. The United States and other source countries have on random occasions sought to use their MNEs to influence allocations abroad, usually in support of objectives of foreign policy. This practice may connote some positive support for MNEs explained by the government-policy model. However, the increasing incidence of conflict between MNEs and host countries points to a rapid erosion of the MNE's usefulness on a policy instrument.

10.3. **International regulation**

Economic analysis points to a number of divergences between source and host countries' national interests in the MNE, and the increasing intervention of host countries (both developed and LDCs) has stirred these latent conflicts to the surface of the political waters. The cry has gone up from many quarters that the MNEs' power vis-à-vis governments calls for international regulation. Is there an economic case for collective international commitments on policy toward MNEs? If so, does it bear any relation to the actual dialogue over international regulation?

Global and national interests

The analysis summarized in Section 10.1 made clear that the national policies consistent with maximum global welfare from MNEs' activities diverge from those that appear to maximize national welfare. This proposition holds if countries fail to recognize the interdependent effects of their policies, and there is no guarantee in the theory of bargaining and retaliation that recognition will bring consensus on policies that maximize joint (global) welfare. The problem is highlighted by comparison to the General Agreement on Tariffs and Trade (GATT) as a forum for mutual reduction of barriers to trade. One possible interpretation of GATT is that each nation acting independently imposes excessive tariff protection for some combination of two reasons: It thinks it can thereby improve its terms of trade, and it gives in to domestic special interests for lack of any general principle or commitment for holding them at bay. The GATT attacks both problems. By bringing about general rounds of coincident tariff reduction, it tends to assume that the global gains are spread fairly evenly among the participating nations (because no country's terms of trade undergo much change when calculated at ex-tariff prices). And it gives the national government that really wants to maximize national welfare a commitment with which to stand off domestic pressure groups.

One can imagine a similar international forum that would bargain toward global-welfare-maximizing arrangements toward MNEs. These would include corporation income-tax treatments consistent with capital-import and -export neutrality, internationally efficient competition policies (through the coordination of national policies), commitments to keep the bargain over natural-resource rents from "obsolescing," and internationally efficient policies toward the creation and dissemination of technology.[16] They would also include arrangements to mediate or arbitrate cases in which the MNE is perceived to serve as the instrument for incursions by one country on another's sovereignty. These conflicts differ importantly from the economic ones emphasized earlier, because conflicting interests in international political or military (power) arrangements usually are intrinsically zero-sum and provide no basis for bargaining toward a global optimum.

This idealized agenda for international coordination of policy toward MNEs contains some intrinsic difficulties of execution that are also revealed by the comparison to GATT. Countries' interests in efficient arrangements for international trade are made similar by the (at least approximate) balance that must prevail between exports and imports (they can differ only through a persistent net international flow of capital). That balance permits a general tariff reduction to

---

[16] The substance of such policies cannot easily be summarized because of the complexity and failure-proneness of the market for proprietary intangible assets. See Chapter 7.

distribute its benefits fairly evenly among the participants without any complicating side payments. But there is no comparable balance condition for a country's interests as source and host of MNEs. Therefore, no globally efficient change in policy that is not neutral between source and host can claim to spread its benefits equitably without side payments being made. The trend for more and more countries to play significant roles as both sources and hosts improves the prospect, but not at a supersonic speed. One notes that a package of globally optimal policy changes would likely contain some providing net benefits to source countries, others shifting gains to hosts; the result could be declared to balance, as an act of faith, but there is no reason whatever why it should approximately do so.

Moves toward international regulation

The preceding scenario bears little relation to actual discussion of international control of the MNE. Scholarly treatments have largely ignored the economic issues in favor of those of sovereignty and diplomacy.[17] The popular campaign has sought not so much international regulation as resolutions from international organizations urging national governments to enlarge their efforts to regulate the activities of MNEs (Roberts and Liebhaberg, 1977, have provided a convenient account). Much of the push comes from trade unions in the industrial countries and from LDCS. In Chapter 5 we examined why national trade unions have reason to seek international sanction for their efforts to coalesce their bargaining power against MNEs – otherwise the intrinsic clash of interest among unions in different countries comes to the fore. The LDCs similarly seek international support for their own regulatory efforts, perhaps partly to stifle competition among themselves in the terms offered to entering and footloose MNEs, partly for help in minimizing the MNEs' opportunities to evade regulations already in force or to summon source-country aid.

Whatever the future trajectory of the trend toward more restrictive

---

[17] See Wallace (1976), Hellmann (1977), and Keohane and Ooms (1975). An exception is Vernon (1977, Chapter 8), who did appreciate the conflict between national welfare and global welfare.

regulation of MNEs, international regulation in a form deducible from welfare economics does not seem a likely occurrence.

10.4. **Summary**

Traditional welfare economics supplies rules for policies in the many markets affected by the presence of MNEs. These policies are derived on the assumption that policy's goal is to maximize real income. A dilemma immediately highlighted by the analysis is that policies maximizing the incomes of source countries, host countries, and the world as a whole are not identical. Conflict can therefore be expected, and in the important case of taxation policy, the conflict does not depend on countries being "large" in world markets or on the MNEs themselves enjoying monopoly power. The principal areas of policy, besides taxation (explored in earlier chapters and summarized in this one), are natural-resource rents, competition policy for industrial markets, and the creation and transfer of industrial knowledge. These policy conclusions are qualified by the existence of multiple market distortions, which forces the analyst into second-best prescriptions not dissimilar to the benefit–cost analyses often proposed for MNEs (but never applied rigorously). The presence of MNEs also colors the formation of policy on matters ostensibly unrelated to MNEs, because the distributional effects of the policies between nationals and foreign investors can alter a policy's effect on national income.

Policy toward MNEs also calls for a behavioral approach, especially to explain the policies used in or urged on host countries. Two lines of analysis seem fruitful. One addresses national (nationalistic) preferences in the context of democratic government, emphasizing the consequences of votes being denied to investors domiciled abroad (inappropriate, perhaps, if interest groups influence decisions). The national preference itself may take several forms, such as a collective distaste for perceived influence by foreign companies on the nation's resource allocation. Another model concentrates on the means–end relationship in policy and the constriction of a government's policy options that may result from the superior alternatives open to MNEs. If the government's preferences for allocating resources are axiomatically superior to the market's, or if the median voter believes them superior, discriminatory restrictions on MNEs follow from their superior alternatives. No systematic empirical research has followed up these policy models, but casual evidence suggests that both command some explanatory power. The national-preference model holds few implications for source countries' policies, but the government-policy model does call attention to the home-based MNE's possible usefulness as a policy instrument for influencing allocations abroad.

International regulation of MNEs has sometimes been urged. A logical case can be built on the conflict between policies maximizing national welfare and global welfare, but a comparison to the GATT stresses the improbability that such regulation could be realized. Actual international moves toward regulating MNEs grow largely from the efforts of host countries to legitimize and coordinate their own national regulations.

BIBLIOGRAPHIC ESSAY

Both students and professional economists using this volume will often want to know "But what should I read?" In a survey of this type one cannot constantly award gold stars and assign demerits. Therefore, this brief essay will identify what I consider the good stuff on a simple in-or-out basis. Because some, though not all, of the most original scholarly contributions are beyond easy access to the undergraduate student, I shall use an asterisk (*) to indicate those references that may be suitable for undergraduate use. In some cases I have assigned them in my own undergraduate course on MNEs. The following paragraphs first address general studies of MNEs, then proceed chapter by chapter through the topics covered in this book.

Of general volumes on the MNE, those of Bergsten et al.* (1978) and Vernon* (1971) stand out, and a number of chapters in Kindleberger* (1970) and Dunning* (1974*a*) remain useful. Much can be learned from historical studies such as those of Southard* (1931) and Wilkins* (1970, 1974), although they receive only passing attention in this volume. Much of our knowledge of the modern MNE stems from a series of country-study volumes that begin with Dunning* (1958) and continue with Brash* (1966) and Tsurumi* (1976) as notable examples; Franko* (1976) was broader in coverage. These books uniformly lack an analytical framework, but they do organize a good deal of evidence. Although basic statistical sources

300

will not be covered here, both data and analytical material of some interest can be found in official and semiofficial studies such as those of Reddaway* (1967, 1968), United Nations* (1974), U.S. Tariff Commission* (1973), and U.S. Department of Commerce* (1976). Gray* (1972), Hood and Young* (1979), and Parry* (1980) are in essence literature surveys.

Many writers have provided fuller accounts of the transactional models of Chapter 1. Dunning* (1977a) called them "eclectic theory" of foreign investment. Buckley and Casson* (1976) and Rugman* (1981) emphasized the "internalization" by the MNE of what would otherwise be arm's-length transactions. Of the many statistical tests of the transactional approach to "horizontal" MNEs, that of Swedenborg (1979) is the most impressive. Horst (1972b) also offered a valuable perspective, and Wells* (1983, Chapter 7) provided arresting case-study evidence on the transactional basis for MNEs. Grubel* (1977) offered a usefully comprehensive view of foreign investment in banking. Kaserman* (1978) provided a brief survey of the many models of vertical integration that may be relevant to vertical MNEs. The best empirical evidence is that of McKern* (1976), and Helleiner* (1973) provided a compact analysis of offshore procurement. The work of Jacquillat and Solnik (1978) is a good example of inquiries into the diversification effects of MNEs' multicountry operations, and Kopits* (1979) reported on the extent of product-market diversification in MNEs.

In relation to Chapter 2, Hymer's* (1960, published 1976) critique of the capital-arbitrage hypothesis is worth reading. The relationship between exporting and direct investment was worked out by Horst (1971), and Horst* (1973) provided an excellent simple account. None of the statistical studies of the influence of tariff changes on foreign investment is really satisfactory, although that of Schmitz and Bieri (1972) comes closest; Goldsbrough's (1979) research on exchange-rate changes is more impressive. Of the cross-sectional studies of how tariffs and other actors affect the choice between exporting and foreign investment, those of Swedenborg (1979, Chapter 5) and Buckley and Pearce* (1979) merit attention. The exposition of general-equilibrium trade models in Section 2.3 is meant to serve as a review rather than a full-fledged primary exposition for the average student, and resort will be needed to a standard textbook such as that of Caves and Jones* (1981). Neary (1978) provided a theoretical development of the specific-factors model, and Jones (1980) explored the role of absolute advantage. Nankani (1979) provided the most ambitious study of what determines the international distribution of direct investment. Davidson* (1980) showed how information costs affect the international spread of MNEs.

The principal study of the internal organization of the MNE is that of Stopford and Wells* (1972), and Aharoni* (1966) provided an interesting discussion of the initiating decision to become multinational. Horst* (1974*a*) provided an intensive study of the growth of MNEs in one sector. Interesting monographs on joint ventures in international business are those of Tomlinson* (1970) and Franko* (1971).

The conjunction between the factors promoting MNEs and those supporting high seller concentration was pointed out by Caves (1971) and was developed extensively by Vernon* (1977, Chapters 3–5). Knickerbocker (1973 and 1976*) provided interesting empirical studies of the relationship between foreign investment and market structure, and Graham* (1978) developed evidence of oligopolistic reaction among MNEs between source countries. Wilkins* (1970, 1974) gathered a good deal of historical evidence on noncompetitive conduct among MNEs; Kudrle* (1975) and Sciberras* (1977) provided more contemporary case studies. Bergsten et al. (1978, Chapter 7) made an interesting if controversial study of foreign investment and market performance. Bergsten et al.* (1978, Chapter 5) made a convenient survey of the "obsolescing bargain," and Moran* (1974) provided a good case study. Williams* (1975) dealt analytically with expropriation. Adelman* (1972) addressed rivalry among vertically integrated oil MNEs.

The effect of foreign investment on the distribution of income was studied in general equilibrium by Musgrave* (1975) and Frank and Freemen (1978), although both of their models left out potentially important mechanisms of adjustment. The literature involving the concepts of investment substitution and export substitution displays a high confusion content, but Hufbauer and Adler* (1968) merit attention, and Bergsten et al.* (1978, Chapters 3 and 4) have clarified many issues. Lipsey and Weiss (1981) provided a valuable statistical study. On the MNE's labor relations, Hershfield* (1975) and Jedel and Kujawa* (1976) described organizational patterns and their consequences, and Gunter* (1975) discussed their effects on national systems of labor relations.

The literature on the MNE's financial and investment decisions is particularly treacherous territory. Of scholarly studies of foreign-investment and asset decisions, those of Stevens (1969, 1972) and Goldsbrough (1979) merit the most attention. Hartman (1979) explored formally the MNE's financing decisions in the face of a varying exchange rate, and Shapiro (1978) explored leverage considerations. Agmon and Lessard* (1977) established interesting conclusions about the value to investors of the MNE's international diversification. Robbins and Stobaugh* (1973) offered a good deal of useful descriptive information on MNEs' short-term financing, although some of it is dated to conditions in the 1960s. Rodriguez (1980) provided the most interesting study of MNEs' efforts to cope with varying exchange rates; also see Evans and Folks* (1979) on MNEs' responses to the problem of currency translation, and a discussion of the conceptual issues by Aliber (1978). Most of the policy discussion of MNEs' effects on the balance of payments predates the present era of floating exchange rates, but some microeconomic research of continuing interest resulted – Prachowny and Richardson (1975) and Hawkins and Macaluso (1977).

Mansfield, Romeo, and Wagner* (1979) provided valuable evidence on the effects of firms' international opportunities on their R&D activities. For statistical investigations of the MNEs' international decentralization of R&D, see Mansfield, Teece, and Romeo* (1979) and Hirschey and Caves (1981). Unfortunately for our purposes, most of the literature on the arm's-length market for technology stresses normative issues (such as policies affecting transfer to the LDCs) rather than the market's behavioral properties. The work of Teece* (1977) is important for establishing the transaction costs, and Telesio* (1979) exposed many of the factors determining the trade-off between licensing and direct investment. The product cycle (Vernon,* 1966, 1979) is related to MNEs' activities and arm's-length licensing by Vernon and Davidson* (1979). Perhaps the most interesting theoretical models of technology transfer are those of Rodriguez (1975), Findlay (1978), and Krugman (1979). Mansfield and Romeo* (1980) presented evidence on the leakage of proprietary technology from MNEs, and Globerman (1979*a*) and Saunders (1980) provided alternative approaches to the relationship of MNEs to technological diffusion and productivity levels.

The basic relationship between taxation of profits and MNEs was set forth by Musgrave* (1969), and Macdougall* (1960) and Corden* (1967) made important contributions to the welfare economics of taxes on MNEs. Hartman (1980) developed the problem in general equilibrium, and Feldstein and Hartman (1979) explored international strategic aspects. Horst (1977) worked out the theoretical effects of source-country tax systems, and Grubel (1974) and Jenkins (1979) estimated their empirical consequences. Snoy* (1975) and Kopits (1972) provided empirical studies of MNEs' reactions to taxation. Horst (1971) made the main theoretical contribution on transfer pricing. Plasschaert* (1979) and Burns* (1980) described firms' actual transfer-pricing practices, and Jenkins and Wright (1975) and Vaitsos* (1974) investigated their effects.

Reuber et al.* (1973) provided the best study of the determinants and patterns of MNEs' activities in developing countries, and Helleiner* (1973) treated their relationships to LDCs' exports of manufactures. On LDCs' inducements, Brecher and Diaz Alejandro (1977) made an important contribution; a descriptive treatment of duty-free zones was provided by Fröbel et al.* (1980, Part III). Lall's* (1978*a*) survey of MNEs and LDC industrial organization is useful, and the work of Evans* (1979) stands out among the country studies. The works of Lecraw* (1977) and Wells* (1983) on third-world LDCs are recommended. Of the large literature on adaptation of technology, Wells* (1973), Courtney and Leipziger (1975), and Morley and Smith (1977*b*) provided perhaps the most interesting contributions. Weisskopf (1972) and Areskoug (1976) addressed the effects of MNEs' capital transfers on the LDCs' capital stocks. Although no studies of MNEs and LDCs' growth rates can be commended for scientific quality, those of Kobrin* (1977) and Bornschier (1980) represent the dubious state of the art.

The theory of public policy toward MNEs has many facets; a few not stressed in earlier chapters have been brought out by Bhagwati and Brecher (1980), Corden* (1967), and Jones (1967). Good overviews of policy issues have been provided by Vernon* (1977, Chapters 6–9) and Bergsten et al.* (1978, Chapters 2, 9–11, and 13). Barnet and Müller* (1974) presented a distinctive and coherent view but did not make its premises explicit. The works of Safarian* (1978) and Hodges* (1974) are interesting on policy in other industrial countries. Roberts and Liebhaberg* (1977) described the campaign for international regulation of MNEs.

BIBLIOGRAPHY

Adams, J. D. R., and J. Whalley (1977). *The International Taxation of Multinational Enterprises in Developed Countries*. Westport, CT: Greenwood Press.

Adelman, M. A., (1972). *The World Petroleum Market*. Baltimore: Johns Hopkins University Press.

Adler, M. (1974). "The Cost of Capital and Valuation of a Two-Country Firm," *J. Finance*, 29 (March), 119–32.

Adler, M., and B. J. Dumas (1975). "The Long-Term Financial Decisions of the Multinational Corporation." In E. Elton and M. Gruber (eds.), *International Capital Markets*, Chapter 9.1., Amsterdam: North-Holland.

(1977). "The Microeconomics of the Firm in an Open Economy," *Amer. Econ. Rev.*, 67 (February), 180–9.

Adler, M., and G. V. G. Stevens (1974). "The Trade Effects of Direct Investment," *J. Finance*, 29 (May), 655–76.

Aggarwal, R. (1980a). "Capital Market Evaluation of Foreign Operations: A Study of U.S. Multinationals," *De Economist*, 128 (No. 2), 251–4.

(1980b). "Investment Performance of U.S.-Based Multinational Companies: Comments and a Perspective on International Diversification of Real Assets," *J. Int. Bus. Stud.*, 11 (Spring/Summer), 98–104.

Agmon, T., and C. P. Kindleberger (eds.) (1977). *Multinationals from Small Countries*. Cambridge, MA: M.I.T. Press.

Agmon, T., and D. Lessard (1977). "Investor Recognition of Corporate International Diversification," *J. Finance*, 32 (September), 1049–55.

Aharoni, Y. (1966). *The Foreign Investment Decision Process*. Boston: Division of Research, Graduate School of Business Administration, Harvard University.

Aliber, R. Z. (1970). "A Theory of Direct Foreign Investment." In C. P. Kindleberger (ed.), *The International Corporation: A Symposium*, Chapter 1. Cambridge, MA: M.I.T. Press.

(1978). *Exchange Risk and Corporate International Finance*. Somerset, NJ: Halsted Press.

Alsegg, R. J. (1971). *Control Relationships between American Corporations and*

Their European Subsidiaries. AMA Research Study No. 107. New York: American Management Association.

Amano, A. (1977). "Specific Factors, Comparative Advantage, and International Investment," *Economica*, 44 (May), 131–44.

Andrews, M. (1972). "A Survey of American Investment in Irish Industry." Senior honors thesis, Harvard College.

Areskoug, K. (1976). "Foreign Direct Investment and Capital Formation in Developing Countries," *Econ. Devel. Cult. Change*, 24 (April), 539–47.

Ariga, M. (ed.) (1975). *International Conference on International Economy and Competition Policy*. Tokyo: Council of Tokyo Conference on International Economy and Competition Policy.

Arpan, J. S. (1971). *International Intracorporate Pricing*. New York: Praeger.

Arrow, K. J. (1975). "Vertical Integration and Communication," *Bell J. Econ.*, 6 (Spring), 173–83.

Arthur D. Little, Inc. (1976). "The Reasons and Outlook for Foreign Direct Investment in the United States." In U.S. Department of Commerce, *Foreign Direct Investment in the United States: Report of the Secretary of Commerce to the Congress in Compliance with the Foreign Investment Study Act of 1974*, Appendix G. Washington: U.S. Government Printing Office.

Auquier, A. A., and R. E. Caves (1979). "Monopolistic Export Industries, Trade Taxes, and Optimal Competition Policy," *Econ. J.*, 89 (September), 559–81.

Baba, M. (1975). "Foreign-Affiliated Corporations and Concentration in Japanese Manufacturing Industry." In M. Ariga (ed.), *International Conference on International Economy and Competition Policy*, pp. 172–82. Tokyo: Council of Tokyo Conference on International Economy and Competition Policy.

Baerresen, D. W. (1971). *The Border Industrialization Program of Mexico*. Lexington, MA: Lexington Books, D. C. Heath.

Baglini, N. A. (1976). *Risk Management in International Corporations*. New York: Risk Studies Foundation.

Bandera, V. N., and J. T. White (1968). "U.S. Direct Investments and Domestic Markets in Europe," *Econ. Int.*, 21 (February), 117–33.

Banks, R. F., and J. Stieber (eds.) (1977). *Multinationals, Unions, and Labor Relations in Industrialized Countries*. Cornell International Industrial and Labor Relations Report No. 9. Ithaca, NY: New York State School of Industrial and Labor Relations, Cornell University.

Baranson, J. (1970). "Technology Transfer through the International Firm," *Amer. Econ. Rev.*, 60 (May), 435–40.

(1978a). *Technology and the Multinationals: Corporate Strategies in a Changing World Economy*. Lexington, MA: Lexington Books, D. C. Heath.

(1978b). "Technology Transfer: Effects on U.S. Competitiveness and Employment." In U.S. Department of Labor, Bureau of International Labor Affairs, *The Impact of International Trade and Investment on Employment*, pp. 177–203. W. Dewald (ed.). Washington: U.S. Government Printing Office.

Barlow, E. R., and I. T. Wender (1955). *Foreign Investment and Taxation*. Englewood Cliffs, NJ: Prentice-Hall.

Barnet, R. J., and R. E. Müller (1974). *Global Reach: the Power of the International Corporations*. New York: Simon & Schuster.

Batra, R. N., and J. Hadar (1979). "Theory of the Multinational Firm: Fixed versus Floating Exchange Rates," *Oxford Econ. Pap.*, 31 (July), 258–69.

Batra, R. N., and R. Ramachandran (1980). "Multinational Firms and the Theory of International Trade and Investment," *Amer. Econ. Rev.*, 70 (June), 278–90.

Baum, D. J. (1974). *The Banks of Canada in the Commonwealth Caribbean: Economic Nationalism and Multinational Enterprises of a Medium Power.* New York: Praeger.

Baumann, H. G. (1975). "Merger Theory, Property Rights, and the Pattern of U.S. Direct Investment in Canada," *Weltwirtsch. Arch.*, 111 (No. 4), 676–98.

Beenstock, M. (1977). "Policies Towards International Direct Investment: A Neoclassical Reappraisal," *Econ. J.*, 87 (September), 533–42.

Behrman, J. N. (1969). *Some Patterns in the Rise of the Multinational Enterprise.* Research Paper No. 18. Chapel Hill, NC: Graduate School of Business Administration, University of North Carolina.

(1970). *National Interests and the Multinational Enterprise: Tensions among the North Atlantic Countries.* Englewood Cliffs, NJ: Prentice-Hall.

Behrman, J. N., and W. A. Fischer (1980). *Overseas R&D Activity of Transnational Companies.* Cambridge, MA: Oelgeschlager, Gunn and Hain.

Bergsten, C. F., T. Horst, and T. H. Moran (1978). *American Multinationals and American Interests.* Washington: Brookings Instituion.

Berry, A. (1974). "Static Effects of Technological Borrowing on National Income: A Taxonomy of Cases," *Weltwirtsch. Arch.*, 110 (No. 4), 580–606.

Bhagwati, J. N., R. W. Jones, R. A. Mundell, and J. Vanek (eds.) (1971). *Trade, Balance of Payments and Growth: Papers in International Economics in Honor of Charles P. Kindleberger.* Amsterdam: North-Holland.

Bhagwati, J. N., and R. A. Brecher (1980). "National Welfare in an Open Economy in the Presence of Foreign-Owned Factors of Production," *J. Int. Econ.*, 10 (February), 103–15.

Biersteker, T. J. (1978). *Distortion or Development: Contending Perspectives on the Multinational Corporation.* Cambridge, MA: M.I.T. Press.

Biger, N. (1979). "Exchange Rate Implications of International Portfolio Diversification," *J. Int. Bus. Stud.*, 10 (Fall), 64–74.

Blake, D. H. (1972). "The Internationalization of Industrial Relations." *J. Int. Bus. Stud.*, 3 (Fall), 17–32.

Boatwright, B. D., and G. A. Renton (1975). "An Analysis of United Kingdom Inflows and Outflows of Direct Foreign Investment," *Rev. Econ. Statist.*, 57 (November), 478–86.

Bond, E. (1981). "Tax Holidays and Industry Behavior," *Rev. Econ. Statist.*, 63 (February), 88–95.

Booth, E. J. R., and O. W. Jensen (1977). "Transfer Prices in the Global Corporation under Internal and External Constraints," *Can. J. Econ.*, 10 (August), 434–46.

Bornschier, V. (1980). "Multinational Corporations and Economic Growth: A Cross-National Test of the Decapitalization Thesis," *J. Devel. Econ.*, 7 (June), 191–210.

Bos. H. C., M. Sanders, and C. Secchi (1974). *Private Foreign Investment in Developing Countries: A Quantitative Study on the Evaluation of the Macroeconomic Effects.* Dordrecht: D. Riedel.

Bower, J. L. (1970). *Managing the Resource Allocation Process: A Study of Corporate Planning and Investment.* Boston: Division of Research, Graduate School of Business Administration, Harvard University.

Brandt, W. K., and J. M. Hulbert (1976). "Patterns of Communications in the Multinational Company: An Empirical Study," *J. Int. Bus. Stud.*, 7 (Spring), 57–64.

Brash, D. T. (1966). *American Investment in Australian Industry.* Cambridge, MA: Harvard University Press.

Brecher, R. A., and C. F. Diaz Alejandro (1977). "Tariffs, Foreign Capital and Immiserizing Growth," *J. Int. Econ.*, 7 (November), 317–22.

Brewster, K. (1958). *Antitrust and American Business Abroad.* New York: McGraw-Hill.

Brooke, M. Z., and H. L. Remmers (1970). *The Strategy of Multinational Enterprise: Organisation and Finance.* New York: American Elsevier.

Buckley, P. J. (1974). "Some Aspects of Foreign Private Investment in the Manufacturing Sector of the Economy of the Irish Republic," *Econ. Soc. Rev.*, 5 (April), 301–21.

Buckley, P. J., and M. Casson (1976). *The Future of the Multinational Enterprise.* London: Macmillan.

Buckley, P. J., and H. Davies (1979). "The Place of Licensing in the Theory and Practice of Foreign Operations." Discussion Paper No. 47, University of Reading.

Buckley, P. J., and J. H. Dunning (1976). "The Industrial Structure of US Direct Investment in the UK," *J. Int. Bus. Stud.*, 7 (Fall/Winter), 5–13.

Buckley, P. J., J. H. Dunning, and R. D. Pearce (1978). "The Influence of Firm Size, Industry, Nationality, and Degree of Multinationality on the Growth of the World's Largest Firms, 1962–1972," *Weltwirtsch. Arch.*, 114 (No. 2), 243–57.

Buckley, P. J., and R. D. Pearce (1979). "Overseas Production and Exporting by the World's Largest Enterprises: A Study in Sourcing Policy," *J. Int. Bus. Stud.*, 10 (Spring), 9–20.

Burgess, D. F. (1978). "On the Distributional Effects of Direct Foreign Investment," *Int. Econ. Rev.*, 19 (October), 647–64.

Burns, J. M. (1976). *Accounting Standards and International Finance, with Special Reference to Multinationals.* Washington: American Enterprise Institute.

Burns, J. O. (1980). "Transfer Pricing Decisions in U.S. Multinational Corporations," *J. Int. Bus. Stud.*, 11 (Fall), 23–39.

Business International (1981). *New Directions in Multinational Corporate Organization.* New York: Business International.

Casson, M. (1979). *Alternatives to the Multinational Enterprise.* London: Macmillan.

Caves, R. E. (1971). "International Corporations: The Industrial Economics of Foreign Investment," *Economica*, 38 (February), 1–27.

  (1974*a*). "Multinational Firms, Competition, and Productivity in Host-Country Industries," *Economica*, 41 (May), 176–93.

  (1974*b*). "Causes of Direct Investment: Foreign Firms' Shares in Canadian and United Kingdom Manufacturing Industries," *Rev. Econ. Statist.*, 56 (August), 279–93.

(1974*c*). "Industrial Organization." In J. H. Dunning (ed.), *Economic Analysis and the Multinational Enterprise*, pp. 115–46. London: George Allen & Unwin.

(1975). *Diversification, Foreign Investment, and Scale in North American Manufacturing Industries*. Ottawa: Economic Council of Canada.

(1980*a*). "Productivity Differences among Industries." In R. E. Caves and L. B. Krause (eds.), *Britain's Economic Performance*, pp. 135–98. Washington: Brookings Institution.

(1980*b*). "Investment and Location Policies of Multinational Companies," *Schweiz. Z. Volkswirtsch. Statist.*, 116 (No. 3), 321–38.

Caves, R. E., and R. W. Jones (1981). *World Trade and Payments: An Introduction*, 3rd ed. Boston: Little, Brown.

Caves, R. E., M. E. Porter, and A. M. Spence, with J. T. Scott (1980). *Competition in the Open Economy: A Model Applied to Canada*. Cambridge, MA: Harvard University Press.

Caves, R. E., and T. A. Pugel (1980). *Intraindustry Differences in Conduct and Performance*. Monograph Series in Finance and Economics, 1980–2. New York: Graduate School of Business Administration, New York University.

Chandler, A. D. (1980). "The Growth of the Transnational Industrial Firm in the United States and the United Kingdom: A Comparative Analysis," *Econ. History Rev.*, 2nd series, 33 (August), 396–410.

Chase-Dunn, C. (1975). "The Effects of International Economic Dependence on Development and Inequality: A Cross-National Study," *Amer. Soc. Rev.*, 40 (December), 720–38.

Chipman, J. S. (1971). "International Trade with Capital Mobility: A Substitution Theorem." In J. N. Bhagwati et al. (eds.), *Trade, Balance of Payments and Growth: Papers in International Economics in Honor of Charles P. Kindleberger*, pp. 201–37. Amsterdam: North-Holland.

Chudson, W. A., and L. T. Wells, Jr. (1974). *The Acquisition of Technology from Multinational Corporations by Developing Countries*. New York: United Nations.

Chung, B. S., and C. H. Lee (1980). "The Choice of Production Techniques by Foreign and Local Firms in Korea," *Econ. Devel. Cult. Change*, 29 (October), 135–40.

Chung, W. K., and G. C. Fouch (1980). "Foreign Direct Investment in the United States in 1979," *Surv. Curr. Bus.*, 60 (August), 38–51.

Coase, R. H. (1937). "The Nature of the Firm," *Economica*, 4 (November), 386–405.

Cohen, B. I. (1972). "Foreign Investment by U.S. Corporations as a Way of Reducing Risk." Discussion Paper No. 151, Economic Growth Center, Yale University.

(1973). "Comparative Behavior of Foreign and Domestic Export Firms in a Developing Economy," *Rev. Econ. Statist.*, 55 (May), 190–7.

(1975). *Multinational Firms and Asian Exports*. New Haven, CT: Yale University Press.

Connor, J. M. (1977). *The Market Power of Multinationals: A Quantitative Analysis of U.S. Corporations in Brazil and Mexico*. New York: Praeger.

Contractor, F. J. (1980). "The 'Profitability' of Technology Licensing by U.S. Multinationals: A Framework for Analysis and an Empirical Study," *J. Int. Bus. Stud.*, 11 (Fall), 40–63.

Copithorne, L. W. (1971). "International Corporate Transfer Prices and Government Policy," *Can. J. Econ.*, 4 (August), 324–41.

Corden, M. (1967). "Protection and Foreign Investment," *Econ. Record*, 43 (June), 209–32.

Courtney, W. H., and D. M. Leipziger (1975). "Multinational Corporations in LDCs: The Choice of Technology," *Oxford Bull. Econ. Statist.*, 37 (November), 297–304.

Creamer, D. B. (1976). *Overseas Research and Development by United States Multinationals, 1966–1975*. New York: Conference Board.

Creigh, S. W., and P. Makeham (1978). "Foreign Ownership and Strike-Proneness: A Research Note," *Brit. J. Ind. Relat.*, 16 (November), 369–72.

Crispo, J. (1967). *International Unionism: A Study in Canadian-American Relations*. Toronto: McGraw-Hill.

Curhan, J. P., W. H. Davidson, and R. Suri (1977). *Tracing the Multinationals: A Sourcebook on U.S.-Based Enterprises*. Cambridge, MA: Ballinger.

Curtin, W. J. (1973). "The Multinational Corporation and Transnational Collective Bargaining." In D. Kujawa (ed.), *American Labor and the Multinationals*, Chapter 9. New York: Praeger.

d'Arge, R. (1969). "Note on Customs Unions and Foreign Direct Investment," *Econ. J.*, 79 (June), 324–33.

Davidson, W. H. (1976). "Patterns of Factor-Saving Innovation in the Industrialized World," *Eur. Econ. Rev.*, 8 (October), 207–17.

(1980). "The Location of Foreign Direct Investment Activity: Country Characteristics and Experience Effects," *J. Int. Bus. Stud.*, 11 (Fall), 9–22.

Davidson, W. H., and D. G. McFetridge (1981). "International Technology Transactions and the Theory of the Firm." Unpublished manuscript, Carleton University.

Davies, H. (1977). "Technology Transfer through Commercial Transactions," *J. Ind. Econ.*, 26 (December), 161–75.

Davis, S. M. (1976). "Trends in the Organization of Multinational Corporations," *Columbia J. World Bus.*, 11 (Summer), 59–71.

Deane, R. S. (1969). "Import Licensing: A Stimulus to Foreign Investment," *Econ. Record*, 45 (December), 526–43.

(1970). *Foreign Investment in New Zealand Manufacturing*. Wellington, N.Z.: Sweet and Maxwell.

de Bodinat, H. (1975). "Influence in the Multinational Corporation: The Case of Manufacturing." D.B.A. thesis, Graduate School of Business Administration, Harvard University.

De la Torre, J., Jr. (1972). "Marketing Factors in Manufactured Exports from Developing Countries." In L. T. Wells, Jr. (ed.), *The Product Life Cycle and International Trade*, pp. 223–57. Boston: Division of Research, Harvard Business School.

De la Torre, J., Jr., R. B. Stobaugh, and P. Telesio (1973). "U.S. Multinational Enterprises and Changes in the Skill Composition of U.S. Employment." In D.

Kujawa (ed.), *American Labor and the Multinationals*, Chapter 7. New York: Praeger.

Diaz Alejandro, C. F. (1970). "Direct Foreign Investment in Latin America." In C. P. Kindleberger (ed.), *The International Corporation: A Symposium*, Chapter 13. Cambridge, MA: M.I.T. Press.

(1979). "International Markets for Exhaustible Resources, Less Developed Countries, and Multinational Corporations." In R. G. Hawkins (ed.), *Research in International Business and Finance: An Annual Compilation of Research. Vol. I. The Economic Effects of Multinational Corporations*, Chapter 8. Greenwich, CT: JAI Press.

Dietermann, G. J. (1980). "Evaluating Multinational Performance under FAS No. 8," *Manage. Account.*, 61 (May), 49–55.

Donsimoni, M.-P., and V. Leoz-Arguelles (1980). "Profitability and International Linkages in the Spanish Economy." Unpublished manuscript, Université Catholique de Louvain.

Doz, Y. L. (1980). "Strategic Management in Multinational Companies," *Sloan Manage. Rev.*, 21 (Winter), 27–46.

Dubin, M. (1976). "Foreign Acquisitions and the Spread of the Multinational Firm." D.B.A. thesis, Graduate School of Business Administration, Harvard University.

Dukes, R. E. (1980). "Forecasting Exchange Gains (Losses) and Security Market Response to FASB Statement Number 8." In R. M. Levich and C. G. Wihlborg (eds.), *Exchange Risk and Exposure: Current Developments in International Financial Management*, Chapter 8. Lexington, MA: Lexington Books, D. C. Heath.

Dunning, J. H. (1958). *American Investment in British Manufacturing Industry*. London: George Allen & Unwin.

(1970). *Studies in International Investment*. London: George Allen & Unwin.

(ed.) (1971). *The Multinational Enterprise*. London: George Allen & Unwin.

(1973a). "Multinational Enterprises and Domestic Capital Formation," *Manchester Sch. Econ. Soc. Stud.*, 40 (September), 283–310.

(1973b). "The Determinants of International Production," *Oxford Econ. Pap.*, 25 (November), 289–336.

(ed.) (1974a). *Economic Analysis and the Multinational Enterprise*. London: George Allen & Unwin.

(1974b). "Multinational Enterprises, Market Structure, Economic Power and Industrial Policy," *J. World Trade Law*, 8 (November/December), 575–613.

(1977a). "Trade, Location of Economic Activity and the MNE: A Search for an Eclectic Approach." In B. Ohlin, P.-O. Hesselborn, and P. M. Wijkman (eds.), *The International Allocation of Economic Activity: Proceedings of a Nobel Symposium Held at Stockholm*, pp. 395–418. London: Macmillan.

(1977b). *European Industry in the U.S.* London: Wilton House.

(1979). "Explaining Changing Patterns of International Production: In Defence of the Eclectic Theory," *Oxford Bull. Econ. Statist.*, 41 (November), 269–95.

(1980). "Toward an Eclectic Theory of International Production: Some Empirical Tests," *J. Int. Bus. Stud.*, 11 (Spring/Summer), 9–31.

(1981). "Explaining the International Direct Investment Position of Countries:

Towards a Dynamic or Developmental Approach," *Weltwirtsch. Archiv.*, 117 (No. 1), 30–64.

Dunning, J. H., and P. J. Buckley (1977). "International Production and Alternative Models of Trade," *Manchester Sch. Econ. Soc. Stud.*, 45 (December), 392–403.

Dunning, J. H., and E. J. Morgan (1980). "Employee Compensation in U.S. Multinationals and Indigenous Firms: An Exploratory Micro/Macro Analysis," *Brit. J. Ind. Relat.*, 18 (July), 179–201.

Dunning, J. H., and R. D. Pearce (1977). *U.S. Industry in Britain.* Boulder, CO: Westview Press.

Eastman, H. C., and S. Stykolt (1967). *The Tariff and Competition in Canada.* New York: St. Martin's Press.

Eden, L. A. B. (1978). "Vertically Integrated Multinationals: A Microeconomic Analysis," *Can. J. Econ.*, 11 (August), 534–46.

Edstrom, A., and J. R. Galbraith (1977). "Transfer of Managers as a Coordination and Control Strategy in Multinational Organizations," *Admin. Science Q.*, 22 (June), 248–63.

Engwall, L., and J. Johnson (eds.) (1980). *Some Aspects of Control in International Business.* Acta Universitatis Upsaliensis, Studia Oeconomiae Negotiorum No. 12, Uppsala.

Erland, O. (1980). "International Take-overs and Technology Intensity." In L. Engwall and J. Johnson (eds.), *Some Aspects of Control in International Business,* Chapter 2. Acta Universitatis Upsaliensis, Studia Oeconomiae Negotiorum No. 12, Uppsala.

Evans, P. (1979). *Dependent Development: The Alliance of Multinational, State and Local Capital in Brazil.* Princeton, NJ: Princeton University Press.

Evans, T. G., and W. R. Folks, Jr. (1979). *Contemporary Foreign Exchange Risk Management Practices at U.S. Multinationals: Implications for Exchange Markets.* Occasional paper No. 10. Washington: Center for Multinational Studies.

Feldstein, M. S., and D. G. Hartman (1979). "The Optimal Taxation of Foreign Source Investment Income," *Quart. J. Econ.*, 93 (November), 613–30.

Findlay, R. (1978). "Relative Backwardness, Direct Foreign Investment, and the Transfer of Technology: A Simple Dynamic Model," *Quart. J. Econ.*, 92 (February), 1–16.

Fishwick, F. (1981). *Multinational Companies and Economic Concentration in Europe.* Report submitted to Institute for Research and Information on Multinationals, Paris.

Flanagan, R. J., and A. R. Weber (eds.) (1974). *Bargaining without Boundaries: The Multinational Corporation and International Labor Relations.* Chicago: University of Chicago Press.

Flowers, E. B. (1976). "Oligopolistic Reactions in European and Canadian Direct Investment in the United States," *J. Int. Bus. Stud.*, 7 (Fall/Winter), 43–55.

Forsyth, D. J. C. (1972). *U.S. Investment in Scotland.* New York: Praeger.
    (1973). "Foreign-owned Firms and Labour Relations: A Regional Perspective," *Brit. J. Ind. Relat.*, 11 (March), 20–8.

Forsyth, D. J. C., and R. F. Solomon (1977). "Choice of Technology and Nationality of Ownership in Manufacturing in a Developing Country," *Oxford Econ.*

Pap., 29 (July), 258–82.

Frank, R. H., and R. T. Freeman (1978). *Distributional Consequences of Direct Foreign Investment*. New York: Academic Press.

Franko, L. G. (1971). *Joint Venture Survival in Multinational Corporations*. New York: Praeger.

(1976). *The European Multinationals: A Renewed Challenge to American and British Big Business*. Stamford, CT: Greylock.

Friedmann, W. G., and J.-P. Beguin (1971). *Joint International Business Ventures in Developing Countries*. New York: Columbia University Press.

Fröbel, F., J. Heinrichs, and O. Kreye (1980). *The New International Division of Labour: Structural Unemployment in Industrialised Countries and Industrialisation in Developing Countries*. Cambridge University Press.

Gale, B. T. (1972). "Market Share and Rate of Return," *Rev. Econ. Statist.*, 54 (November), 412–23.

Garnaut, R., and A. Clunies Ross (1975). "Uncertainty, Risk Aversion and the Taxing of Natural Resource Projects," *Econ J.*, 85 (June), 273–89.

Gennard, J., and M. D. Steuer (1971). "The Industrial Relations of Foreign-Owned Subsidiaries in the United Kingdom," *Brit. J. Ind. Relat.*, 9 (July), 143–59.

Germidis, D. (ed.), (1977). *Transfer of Technology by Multinational Corporations. Vol. I. A Synthesis and Country Case Study*. Development Centre Studies. Paris: Organization for Economic Cooperation and Development.

Gershenberg, I., and T. C. I. Ryan (1978). "Does Parentage Matter? An Analysis of Transnational and Other Firms: An East African Case," *J. Devel. Areas*, 13 (October), 3–10.

Ghertman, M., and J. Leontiades (eds.) (1978). *European Research in International Business*. Amsterdam: North-Holland.

Gillis, M., and R. E. Beals, in collaboration with G. P. Jenkins, L. T. Wells, and U. Peterson (1980). *Tax and Investment Policies for Hard Minerals: Public and Multinational Enterprise in Indonesia*. Cambridge, MA: Ballinger.

Gilman, M. (1981). *The Financing of Foreign Direct Investment: A Study of the Determinants of Capital Flows in Multinational Enterprises*. London: Frances Pinter.

Glejser, H. (1976). "The Respective Impacts of Relative Income, Price and Technology Changes, U.S. Foreign Investment, the EEC and EFTA on the American Balance of Trade." In H. Glejser (ed.), *Quantitative Studies of International Economic Relations*, pp. 133–71. Amsterdam: North-Holland.

Globerman, S. (1975). "Technological Diffusion in the Canadian Tool and Die Industry," *Rev. Econ. Statist.*, 57 (November), 428–34.

(1979a). "Foreign Direct Investment and 'Spillover' Efficiency Benefits in Canadian Manufacturing Industries," *Can. J. Econ.*, 12 (February), 42–56.

(1979b). "A Note on Foreign Ownership and Market Structure in the United Kingdom," *Appl. Econ.*, 11 (March), 35–42.

Goedde, A. G. (1978). "U.S. Multinational Manufacturing Firms: The Determinants and Effects of Foreign Investment." Ph.D. dissertation, Duke University.

Goldsbrough, D. J. (1979). "The Role of Foreign Direct Investment in the External Adjustment Process," *IMF Staff Pap.*, 26 (December), 725–54.

Gordon, L., and E. L. Grommers (1962). *United States Manufacturing Investment in Brazil: The Impact of Brazilian Government Policies, 1946–1960*. Boston: Division of Research, Graduate School of Business Administration, Harvard University.

Gorecki, P. K. (1976). "The Determinants of Entry by Domestic and Foreign Enterprises in Canadian Manufacturing Industries: Some Comments and Empirical Results," *Rev. Econ. Statist.*, 58 (November), 485–8.

(1980). "The Determinants of Foreign and Domestic Enterprise Diversification in Canada: A Note," *Can. J. Econ.*, 13 (May), 329–39.

Grabowski, H. G., and D. C. Mueller (1978). "Industrial Research and Development, Intangible Capital Stocks, and Firm Profit Rates," *Bell J. Econ.*, 9 (Autumn), 328–43.

Graham, E. M. (1978). "Transatlantic Investment by Multinational Firms: A Rivalistic Phenomenon?" *J. Post-Keynes. Econ.*, 1 (Fall), 82–99.

Grauer, F., R. H. Litzenberger, and R. Stehle (1976). "Sharing Rules and Equilibrium in an International Capital Market under Uncertainty," *J. Finan. Econ.*, 3 (June), 233–56.

Gray, H. P. (1972). *The Economics of Business Investment Abroad*. New York: Macmillan.

Greenberg, E., W. J. Marshall, and J. B. Yawitz (1978). "The Technology of Risk and Return," *Amer. Econ. Rev.*, 68 (June), 241–51.

Greene, J., and M. G. Duerr (1970). *Intercompany Transactions in the Multinational Firm: A Survey*. Managing International Business No. 6. New York: Conference Board.

Greenhill, C. R., and E. O. Herbolzheimer (1980). "International Transfer Pricing: The Restrictive Business Practices Approach," *J. World Trade Law*, 14 (May/June), 232–41.

Greening, T. S. (1976). "Oil Wells, Pipelines, Refineries and Gas Stations: A Study of Vertical Integration." Ph.D. dissertation, Harvard University.

Grosse, R. E. (1980). *Foreign Investment Codes and Location of Direct Investment*. New York: Praeger.

Grubel, H. G. (1968). "International Diversified Portfolios: Welfare Gains and Capital Flows," *Amer. Econ. Rev.*, 58 (December), 1299–314.

(1974). "Taxation and Rates of Return from Some U.S. Asset Holdings Abroad, 1960–1969," *J. Polit. Econ.*, 82 (May/June), 469–87.

(1977). "A Theory of Multinational Banking," *Banca Naz. Lavoro Quart. Rev.*, No. 123 (December), 342–63.

Gruber, W., D. Mehta, and R. Vernon (1967). "The R&D Factor in International Trade and International Investment of U.S. Industries," *J. Polit. Econ.*, 75 (February), 20–37.

Gunter, H. (1975). "Labor and Multinational Corporations in Western Europe: Some Problems and Prospects." In D. Kujawa (ed.), *International Labor and the Multinational Enterprise*, Chapter 7. New York: Praeger.

Haendel, D. (1979). *Foreign Investments and the Management of Political Risk*. Boulder, CO: Westview Press.

Hamada, K. (1966). "Strategic Aspects of Taxation on Foreign Investment Income," *Quart. J. Econ.*, 80 (August), 361–75.

(1974). "An Economic Analysis of the Duty-Free Zone," *J. Int. Econ.*, 4

(August), 225–41.

Hamilton, C., and L. E. O. Svensson (1980). "Duty-Free Zones and the Choice between Capital Import and Labor Export." Discussion paper, Institute for International Economic Studies, University of Stockholm.

Hartman, D. G. (1977). "Foreign Investment Taxation and Factor Returns in the Host Country." Unpublished manuscript, Harvard University.

(1979). "Foreign Investment and Finance with Risk," *Quart. J. Econ.*, 93 (May), 213–32.

(1980). "The Effects of Taxing Foreign Investment Income," *J. Pub. Econ.*, 13 (April), 213–30.

(1981). "Domestic Tax Policy and Foreign Investment: Some Evidence." National Bureau of Economic Research, Working Paper No. 784.

Hawkins, R. G. (ed.) (1979). *Research in International Business and Finance: An Annual Compilation of Research. Vol. I. The Economic Effects of Multinational Corporations.* Greenwich, CT: JAI Press.

Hawkins, R. G., and D. Macaluso (1977). "The Avoidance of Restrictive Monetary Policies in Host Countries by Multinational Firms," *J. Money, Credit, Banking,* 9 (November), 562–71.

Hawkins, R. G., N. Mintz, and M. Provissiero (1976). "Government Takeovers of U.S. Foreign Affiliates," *J. Int. Bus. Stud.*, 7 (Spring), 3–16.

Hay, G. A., and D. Kelley (1974). "An Empirical Survey of Price-Fixing Conspiracies," *J. Law Econ.*, 17 (April), 13–38.

Hayden, E. W. (1976). *Technology Transfer to East Europe: U.S. Corporate Experience.* New York: Praeger.

Heenan, D. A., and W. J. Keegan (1979). "The Rise of Third World Multinationals," *Harvard Bus. Rev.*, 57 (January/February), 101–9.

Helleiner, G. K. (1973). "Manufactured Exports from Less Developed Countries and Multinational Firms," *Econ. J.*, 83 (March), 21–47.

(1977). "Transnational Enterprises and the New Political Economy of U.S. Trade Policy," *Oxford Econ. Pap.*, 29 (March), 102–16.

(1979). "Transnational Corporations and Trade Structure: The Role of Intra-Firm Trade." In H. Giersch (ed.), *On the Economics of Intra-Industry Trade: Symposium 1978*, pp. 159–81. Tübingen: J. C. B. Mohr (Paul Siebeck).

Helleiner, G. K., and R. Lavergne (1979). "Intra-Firm Trade and Industrial Exports to the United States," *Oxford Bull. Econ. Statist.*, 41 (November), 297–311.

Hellmann, R. (1970). *The Challenge to U.S. Dominance of the International Corporation.* New York: Dunellen.

(1977). *Transnational Control of Multinational Corporations.* New York: Praeger.

Henderson, D. F. (1973). *Foreign Enterprises in Japan: Laws and Policies.* Chapel Hill, NC: University of North Carolina Press.

Herring, R., and T. D. Willett (1972). "The Capital Control Program and United States Investment Activity Abroad," *Southern Econ. J.*, 39 (July), 58–71.

Hershfield, D. C. (1975). *The Multinational Union Faces the Multinational Company.* Conference Board Report No. 658. New York: Conference Board.

Herskovic, S. (1976). *The Import and Export of Technological Know How Through Licensing Agreements in Israel, 1966–1974.* Jerusalem: Office of the Prime Minister, National Council for Research and Development.

Hewitt, G. (1980). "Research and Development Performed Abroad by U.S. Manu-facturing Multinationals," *Kyklos*, 33 (No. 2), 308–26.

Hirsch, S. (1976). "An International Trade and Investment Theory of the Firm," *Oxford Econ. Pap.*, 28 (July), 258–69.

Hirschey, M. (1981). "R&D Intensity and Multinational Involvement," *Econ. Let-ters*, 7 (No. 1), 87–93.

Hirschey, R. C., and R. E. Caves (1981). "Internationalization of Research and Transfer of Technology by Multinational Enterprises," *Oxford Bull. Econ. Sta-tist.*, 42 (May), 115–30.

Hirschman, A. O. (1969). *How to Divest in Latin America, and Why*. Essays in International Finance No. 76. Princeton, NJ: International Finance Section, Princeton University.

Hodges, M. (1974). *Multinational Corporations and National Governments: A Case Study of the United Kingdom's Experience, 1964–1970*. Lexington, MA: Lex-ington Books, D. C. Heath.

Hone, A. (1974). "Multi-National Corporations and Multi-National Buying Groups: Their Impact on the Growth of Asia's Manufactured Exports," *World Devel.*, 2 (February), 145–9.

Hood, N., and S. Young (1976). "U.S. Investment in Scotland—Aspects of the Branch Factory Syndrome," *Scot. J. Polit. Econ.*, 23 (November), 279–94.

(1979). *The Economics of Multinational Enterprise*. London: Longmans Group.

Horst, T. (1971). "The Theory of the Multinational Firm: Optimal Behavior under Different Tariff and Tax Rules," *J. Polit. Econ.*, 79 (September/October), 1059–72.

(1972a). "The Industrial Composition of U.S. Exports and Subsidiary Sales to the Canadian Market," *Amer. Econ. Rev.*, 62 (March), 37–45.

(1972b). "Firm and Industry Determinants of the Decision to Invest Abroad: An Empirical Study," *Rev. Econ. Statist.*, 54 (August), 258–66.

(1973). "The Simple Analytics of Multinational Firm Behaviour." In M. B. Con-nolly and A. K. Swoboda (eds.), *International Trade and Money*, pp. 72–84. London: George Allen & Unwin.

(1974a). *At Home Abroad: A Study of the Domestic and Foreign Operations of the American Food-Processing Industry*. Cambridge, MA: Ballinger.

(1974b). "The Theory of the Firm." In J. H. Dunning (ed.), *Economic Analysis and the Multinational Enterprise*, Chapter 2. London: George Allen & Unwin.

(1977). "American Taxation of Multinational Firms," *Amer. Econ. Rev.*, 67 (June), 376–89.

(1980). "A Note on the Optimal Taxation of International Investment Income," *Quart. J. Econ.*, 93 (June), 793–8.

Hu, Y. S. (1973). *The Impact of U.S. Investment in Europe: A Case Study of the Automotive and Computer Industries*. New York: Praeger.

Hufbauer, G. C. (1966). *Synthetic Materials and the Theory of International Trade*. Cambridge, MA: Harvard University Press.

(1975). " The Multinational Corporation and Direct Investment." In P. B. Kenen (ed.), *International Trade and Finance: Frontiers for Research*, pp. 253–319. Cambridge University Press.

Hufbauer, G. C., and F. M. Adler (1968). *Overseas Manufacturing Investment and the Balance of Payments.* Tax Policy Research Study No. 1. Washington: U.S. Treasury Department.

Hughes, H., and P. S. You (eds.) (1969). *Foreign Investment and Industrialisation in Singapore.* Canberra: Australian National University Press.

Hughes, J. S., D. E. Logue, and R. J. Sweeney (1975). "Corporate International Diversification and Market Assigned Measures of Risk and Diversification," *J. Financial Quant. Anal.*, 10 (November), 627–37.

Hymer, S. H. (1960). "The International Operations of National Firms: A Study of Direct Foreign Investment." Ph.D. dissertation, M.I.T. (published by M.I.T. Press, 1976).

Ingham, K. P. D. (1976). "Foreign Ownership and the Regional Problem: Company Performance in the Mechanical Engineering Industry," *Oxford Econ. Pap.*, 28 (March), 133–48.

International Labour Organization (1976*a*). *Multinationals in Western Europe: The Industrial Relations Experience.* Geneva: International Labour Organization.

  (1976*b*). *Wages and Working Conditions in Multinational Enterprises.* Geneva: International Labour Organization.

Itagaki, T. (1979). "Theory of the Multinational Firm: An Analysis of Effects of Government Policies," *Int. Econ. Rev.*, 20 (June), 437–48.

  (1981). "The Theory of the Multinational Firm under Exchange Rate Uncertainty," *Can. J. Econ.*, 14 (May), 276–97.

Jacquillat, B., and B. Solnik (1978). "Multinational Firms' Stock Price Behavior: An Empirical Investigation." In M. Ghertman and J. Leontiades (eds.), *European Research in International Business*, pp. 215–37. Amsterdam: North-Holland.

Jarrett, J. P. (1979). "Offshore Assembly and Production and the Internalization of International Trade within the Multinational Corporation." Ph.D. dissertation, Harvard University.

Jedel, M. J., and D. Kujawa (1976). "Management and Employment Practices of Foreign Direct Investors in the United States." In U.S. Department of Commerce, *Foreign Direct Investment in the United States: Report of the Secretary of Commerce to the Congress in Compliance with the Foreign Investment Study Act of 1974*, Appendix I. Washington: U.S. Government Printing Office.

Jenkins, G. P. (1979). "Taxes and Tariffs and the Evaluation of the Benefit from Foreign Investment," *Can. J. Econ.*, 12 (August), 410–25.

Jenkins, G. P., and B. D. Wright (1975). "Taxation of Income of Multinational Corporations: The Case of the United States Petroleum Industry," *Rev. Econ. Statist.*, 57 (February), 1–11.

Jilling, M. (1978). *Foreign Exchange Risk Management in U.S. Multinational Corporations.* Research for Business Decisions No. 6. Ann Arbor: UMI Research Press.

Joachimsson, R. (1980). "Taxation of International Corporations." In L. Engwall and J. Johnson (eds.), *Some Aspects of Control in International Business*, Chapter 3. Acta Universitatis Upsaliensis, Studia Oeconomiae Negotiorum, No. 12, Uppsala.

Johanson, J., and J.-E. Vahlne (1978). "A Model for the Decision Making Process Affecting the Pattern and Pace of the Internationalization of the Firm." In M.

Ghertman and J. Leontiades (eds.), *European Research in International Business*, pp. 9–27. Amsterdam: North-Holland.

Johnson, H. G. (1968). *Comparative Cost and Commercial Policy Theory for a Developing World Economy*. Wicksell Lectures. Stockholm: Almqvist & Wiksell.

(1970). "The Efficiency and Welfare Implications of the Multinational Corporation." In C. P. Kindleberger (ed.), *The International Corporation: A Symposium*, Chapter 2. Cambridge, MA: M.I.T. Press.

Jones, R. W. (1967). "International Capital Movements and the Theory of Tariffs and Trade," *Quart. J. Econ.*, 81 (February), 1–38.

(1970). "The Role of Technology in the Theory of International Trade." In R. Vernon (ed.), *The Technology Factor in International Trade*, pp. 73–92. Universities-National Bureau Conference Series No. 22. New York: National Bureau of Economic Research.

(1971). "A Three-Factor Model in Theory, Trade, and History." In J. N. Bhagwati et al. (eds), *Trade, Balance of Payments and Growth: Papers in International Economics in Honor of Charles P. Kindleberger*, pp. 3–21. Amsterdam: North-Holland.

(1979). *International Trade: Essays in Theory.* Amsterdam: North-Holland.

(1980). "Comparative and Absolute Advantage," *Schweiz. Z. Volkswirtsch. Statist.*, 116 (No. 3), 235–60.

Jorgenson, D. W. (1963). "Capital Theory and Investment Behavior," *Amer. Econ. Rev.*, 53 (May), 247–59.

Juhl, P. (1979). "On the Sectoral Patterns of West German Manufacturing Investment in Less Developed Countries: The Impact of Firm Size, Factor Intensities and Protection," *Weltwirtsch. Arch.*, 115 (No. 3), 508–19.

Kardasz, S. W. (1979). "The Capital-Stock Decision of Subsidiaries," *Econ. Inquiry*, 17 (January), 114–24.

Kaserman, D. L. (1978). "Theories of Vertical Integration: Implications for Antitrust Policy," *Antitrust Bull.*, 23 (Fall), 483–510.

Kassalow, E. M. (1978). "Aspects of Labour Relations in Multinational Companies: An Overview of Three Asian Countries," *Int. Lab. Rev.*, 117 (May/June), 273–87.

Katrak, H. (1977). "Multi-national Monopolies and Commercial Policy," *Oxford Econ. Pap.*, 29 (July), 283–91.

Katz, J. M. (1969). *Production Functions, Foreign Investment and Growth: A Study Based on the Argentine Manufacturing Sector, 1946–1961.* Contributions to Economic Analysis No. 58. Amsterdam: North-Holland.

Keddie, J. (1976). "Adoption of Production Technique in Indonesian Industry." Ph.D. dissertation, Harvard University.

Kemp, M. C. (1966). "The Gains from International Trade and Investment: A Neo-Heckscher-Ohlin Approach," *Amer. Econ. Rev.*, 56 (September), 788–809.

Keohane, R. O., and V. D. Ooms (1975). "The Multinational Firm and International Regulation." In C. F. Bergsten and L. B. Krause (eds.), *World Politics and International Economics*. Washington: Brookings Institution.

Kindleberger, C. P. (1969). *American Business Abroad: Six Lectures on Direct Investment.* New Haven, CT: Yale University Press.

(ed.) (1970). *The International Corporation: A Symposium.* Cambridge, MA: M.I.T. Press.

Klein, B. (1974). "The Role of U.S. Multinational Corporations in Recent Exchange Crises." Occasional Paper No. 6. Washington: Center for Multinational Studies.

Knickerbocker, F. T. (1973). *Oligopolistic Reaction and Multinational Enterprise.* Boston: Division of Research, Graduate School of Business Administration, Harvard University.

(1976). "Market Structure and Market Power Consequences of Foreign Direct Investment by Multinational Companies." Occasional Paper No. 8. Washington: Center for Multinational Studies.

Kobrin, S. J. (1977). *Foreign Direct Investment, Industrialization and Social Change.* Contemporary Studies in Economic and Financial Analysis No. 9. Greenwich, CT: JAI Press.

Koizumi, T., and K. J. Kopecky (1977). "Economic Growth, Capital Movements and the International Transfer of Technical Knowledge," *J. Int. Econ.,* 7 (February), 45–65.

(1980). "Foreign Direct Investment, Technology Transfer and Domestic Employment Effects," *J. Int. Econ.,* 10 (February), 1–20.

Kojima, K. (1975). "International Trade and Foreign Investment: Substitutes or Complements," *Hitotsubashi J. Econ.,* 16 (June), 1–12.

(1978). *Direct Foreign Investment: A Japanese Model of Multinational Business Operations.* New York: Praeger.

Kopits, G. F. (1972). "Dividend Remittance Behavior within the International Firm: A Cross-Country Analysis," *Rev. Econ. Statist.,* 54 (August), 339–42.

(1976a). "Taxation and Multinational Firm Behavior: A Critical Survey," *IMF Staff Pap.,* 23 (November), 624–73.

(1976b). "Intrafirm Royalties Crossing Frontiers and Transfer Pricing Behaviour," *Econ. J.,* 86 (December), 791–805.

(1979). "Multinational Conglomerate Diversification," *Econ. Int.,* 32 (February), 99–111.

Krainer, R. E. (1967). "Resource Endowment and the Structure of Foreign Investment," *J. Finance,* 22 (March), 49–57.

Krause, L. B., and K. W. Dam (1964). *Federal Tax Treatment of Foreign Income.* Washington: Brookings Institution.

Kravis, I. B., and R. E. Lipsey (1980). "The Location of Overseas Production and Production for Export by U.S. Multinational Firms." Working Paper No. 482, National Bureau of Economic Research.

Krugman, P. (1979). "A Model of Innovation, Technology Transfer, and the World Distribution of Income," *J. Polit. Econ.,* 87 (April), 253–66.

Kudrle, R. T. (1975). *Agricultural Tractors: A World Industry Study.* Cambridge, MA: Ballinger.

Kujawa, D. (1971). *International Labor Relations Management in the Automotive Industry: A Comparative Study of Chrysler, Ford, and General Motors.* New York: Praeger.

(ed.) (1973). *American Labor and the Multinationals.* New York: Praeger.

(ed.) (1975). *International Labor and the Multinational Enterprise.* New York: Praeger.

(1979). "Collective Bargaining and Labor Relations in Multinational Enterprise: A U.S. Public Policy Perspective." In R. G. Hawkins (ed.), *Research in International Business and Finance: An Annual Compilation of Research. Vol. I. The Economic Effects of Multinational Corporations*, Chapter 2. Greenwich, CT: JAI Press.

Kumar, K. (ed.) (1980). *Transnational Enterprises: Their Impact on Third World Societies and Cultures*. Boulder, CO: Westview Press.

Kumar, K., and M. G. McLeod (eds.) (1981). *Multinationals from Developing Countries*. Lexington, MA: Lexington Books, D. C. Heath.

Kwack, S. Y. (1972). "A Model of U.S. Direct Investment Abroad: A Neoclassical Approach," *Western Econ. J.*, 10 (December), 376–83.

Kyrouz, M. E. (1975). "Foreign Tax Rates and Tax Bases," *Nat. Tax J.*, 28 (March), 61–80.

Ladenson, M. L. (1972). "A Dynamic Balance Sheet Approach to American Direct Foreign Investment," *Int. Econ. Rev.*, 13 (October), 531–43.

Lake, A. W. (1979). "Technology Creation and Technology Transfer by Multinational Firms." In R. G. Hawkins (ed.), *Research in International Business and Finance: An Annual Compilation of Research. Vol. I. The Economic Effects of Multinational Corporations*, pp. 137–77. Greenwich, CT: JAI Press.

Lall, S. (1973). "Transfer Pricing by Multinational Manufacturing Firms," *Oxford Bull. Econ. Statist.*, 35 (August), 179–95.

(1978*a*). "Transnationals, Domestic Enterprises, and Industrial Structure in Host LDCs: A Survey," *Oxford Econ. Pap.*, 30 (July), 217–48.

(1978*b*). "The Pattern of Intra-Firm Exports by US Multinationals," *Oxford Bull. Econ. Statist.*, 40 (August), 209–22.

(1979*a*). "Multinationals and Market Structure in an Open Developing Economy: The Case of Malaysia," *Weltwirtsch. Arch.*, 115 (No. 2), 325–50.

(1979*b*). "The International Allocation of Research Activity by U.S. Multinationals," *Oxford Bull. Econ. Statist.*, 41 (November), 313–31.

(1980). "Monopolistic Advantages and Foreign Involvement by U.S. Manufacturing Industry," *Oxford Econ. Pap.*, 32 (March), 102–22.

Lall, S., and P. Streeten (1977). *Foreign Investment, Transnationals and Developing Countries*. London: Macmillan.

Lapan, H., and P. Bardhan (1973). "Localized Technical Progress and Transfer of Technology and Economic Development," *J. Econ. Theory*, 6 (December), 585–95.

Lecraw, D. (1977). "Direct Investment by Firms from Less Developed Countries," *Oxford Econ. Pap.*, 29 (November), 445–57.

Lee, W. Y., and K. S. Sachdeva (1977). "The Role of the Multinational Firm in the Integration of Segmented Capital Markets," *J. Finance*, 32 (May), 479–92.

Lees, F. A. (1976). *Foreign Banking and Investment in the United States: Issues and Alternatives*. New York: Halsted Press.

Leftwich, R. B. (1974). "U.S. Multinational Companies: Profitability, Financial Leverage, and Effective Income Tax Rates," *Surv. Curr. Bus.*, 54 (May), 27–36.

Lent, G. E. (1977). "Corporation Income Tax Structure in Developing Countries," *IMF Staff Pap.*, 24 (November), 722–55.

Leroy, G. (1976). *Multinational Product Strategy: A Typology for Analysis of World-wide Product Innovation and Diffusion*. New York: Praeger.

Lessard, D. G. (1979). "Transfer Prices, Taxes, and Financial Markets: Implications of Internal Financial Transfers within the Multinational Corporation." In R. G. Hawkins (ed.), *Research in International Business and Finance: An Annual Compilation of Research, Vol. I. The Economic Effects of Multinational Corporations*, pp. 101–25. Greenwich, CT: JAI Press.

Levy, H. and M. Sarnat (1970). "International Diversification of Investment Portfolios," *Amer. Econ. Rev.*, 60 (September), 668–75.

Lim, D. (1976). "Capital Utilisation of Local and Foreign Establishments in Malaysian Manufacturing," *Rev. Econ. Statist.*, 58 (May), 209–17.

(1977). "Do Foreign Companies Pay Higher Wages than Their Local Counterparts in Malaysian Manufacturing," *J. Devel. Econ.*, 4 (March), 55–66.

Lindert, P. H. (1970). "The Payments Impact of Foreign Investment Controls," *J. Finance*, 26 (December), 1083–99.

Lipsey, R. E., and M. Y. Weiss (1981). "Foreign Production and Exports in Manufacturing Industries," *Rev. Econ. Statist.*, 63 (November), 488–94.

Little, J. S. (1981). "The Financial Health of U.S. Manufacturing Firms Acquired by Foreigners," *New England Econ. Rev.*, (July/August), 5–18.

Litvak, I. A., and C. J. Maule (1977). "Transnational Corporations and Vertical Integration: The Banana Case," *J. World Trade Law*, 11 (November/December), 537–49.

Lombard, F. J. (1979). *The Foreign Investment Screening Process in LDCs: The Case of Colombia*. Boulder, CO: Westview Press.

Lubitz, R. (1971*a*). "Direct Investment and Capital Formation." In R. E. Caves and G. L. Reuber, *Capital Transfers and Economic Policy: Canada 1951–62*, Chapter 4. Cambridge, MA: Harvard University Press.

(1971*b*). "A Note on United States Direct Investment and Human Capital," *J. Polit. Econ.*, 79 (September/October), 1171–5.

Lunn, J. (1980). "Determinants of U.S. Direct Investment in the E.E.C.: Further Evidence," *European Econ. Rev.*, 13 (January), 93–101.

Lupo, L. A., A. Gilbert, and M. Liliestedt (1978). "The Relationship between Age and Rate of Return of Foreign Manufacturing Affiliates of U.S. Manufacturing Parent Companies," *Surv. Curr. Bus.*, 58 (August), 60–6.

Macdougall, G. D. A. (1960). "The Benefits and Costs of Private Investment from Abroad: A Theoretical Approach," *Econ. Record*, 36 (March), 13–35.

Machlup, F., W. S. Salant, and L. Tarshis (eds.) (1972). *The International Mobility and Movement of Capital*. Universities-National Bureau Conference Series No. 24. New York: Columbia University Press for National Bureau of Economic Research.

Magee, S. P. (1977*a*). "Information and Multinational Corporations: An Appropriability Theory of Direct Foreign Investment." In J. Bhagwati (ed.), *The New International Economic Order*, pp. 317–40. Cambridge, MA: M.I.T. Press.

(1977*b*). "Application of the Dynamic Limit Pricing Model to the Price of Technology and International Technology Transfer." In K. Brunner and A. H. Meltzer (eds.), *Optimal Policies, Control Theory and Technology Exports*, Amsterdam: North-Holland.

(1979). "Jobs and the Multinational Corporation: The Home-Country Perspective." In R. G. Hawkins (ed.), *Research in International Business and Finance: An Annual Compilation of Research. Vol. 1. The Economic Effects of Multinational Corporations*, pp. 1–16. Greenwich, CT: JAI Press.

Makin, J. H. (1974). *Capital Flows and Exchange-Rate Flexibility in the Post-Bretton Woods Era*. Essays in International Finance No. 103. Princeton, NJ: International Finance Section, Princeton University.

Makinen, G. E. (1970). "The 'Payoff' Period of Direct Foreign Investment by the United States Automobile Industry," *J. Bus.*, 43 (October), 395–409.

Mansfield, E. (1974). "Technology and Technological Change." In J. H. Dunning (ed.), *Economic Analysis and the Multinational Enterprise*, Chapter 6. London: George Allen & Unwin.

Mansfield, E., and A. Romeo (1980). "Technology Transfer to Overseas Subsidiaries by U.S.-Based Firms," *Quart. J. Econ.*, 95 (December), 737–50.

Mansfield, E., A. Romeo, and S. Wagner (1979). "Foreign Trade and U.S. Research and Development," *Rev. Econ. Statist.*, 61 (February), 49–57.

Mansfield, E., D. J. Teece, and A. Romeo (1979). "Overseas Research and Development by US-Based Firms," *Economica*, 46 (May), 187–96.

Mantel, I. M. (1975). "Source and Uses of Funds for a Sample of Majority-Owned Foreign Affiliates of U.S. Companies, 1966–72," *Surv. Curr. Bus.*, 55 (July), 29–52.

Markensten, K. (1972). *Foreign Investment and Development: Swedish Companies in India*. Scandinavian Institute of Asian Studies Monograph No. 8. Lund: Studentlitteratur.

Markusen, J. R., and J. R. Melvin (1979). "Tariffs, Capital Mobility, and Foreign Ownership," *J. Int. Econ.*, 9 (August), 395–409.

Marshall, H., F. A. Southard, Jr., and K. W. Taylor (1936). *Canadian-American Industry: A Study in International Investment*. New Haven, CT: Yale University Press.

Mason, R. H. (1973). "Some Observations on the Choice of Technology by Multinational Firms in Developing Countries," *Rev. Econ. Statist.*, 55 (August), 349–55.

Mathewson, G. F., and G. D. Quirin (1979). *Fiscal Transfer Pricing in Multinational Corporations*. Toronto: University of Toronto Press for Ontario Economic Council.

Mauer, L. J., and A. E. Scaperlanda (1972). "Remittances from United States Direct Foreign Investment in the European Economic Community: An Exploratory Estimate of Their Determinants," *Econ. Int.*, 25 (February), 3–13.

McAleese, D., and M. Counahan (1979). "'Stickers' or 'Snatchers'? Employment in Multinational Corporations during the Recession," *Oxford Bull. Econ. Statist.*, 41 (November), 345–58.

McAleese, D., and D. McDonald (1978). "Employment Growth and the Development of Linkages in Foreign-Owned and Domestic Manufacturing Enterprises," *Oxford Bull. Econ. Statist.*, 40 (November), 321–39.

McClain, D. S. (1974). "Foreign Investment in United States Manufacturing and the Theory of Direct Investment." Ph.D. dissertation, Massachusetts Institute of Technology.

McCulloch, R., and J. L. Yellen (1976). "Technology Transfer and the National Interest." Discussion Paper No. 526, Harvard Institute of Economic Research, Harvard University.

McKern, R. B. (1976). *Multinational Enterprise and Natural Resources*. Sydney: McGraw-Hill.

McManus, J. C. (1972). "The Theory of the International Firm." In G. Paquet (ed.), *The Multinational Firm and the Nation State*, pp. 66–93. Don Mills, Ontario: Collier-Macmillan.

McQueen, D. L. (1975). "Learning, the Multinational Corporation and the Further Development of Developed Economies." In M. Ariga (ed.), *International Conference on International Economy and Competition Policy*, pp. 118–34. Tokyo: Council of Tokyo Conference on International Economy and Competition Policy.

Michalet, C.-A., and M. Delapierre (1976). *The Multinationalization of French Firms*. Chicago: Academy of International Business.

Mikesell, R. F. (1962). *US Private and Government Investment Abroad*. Eugene, OR: University of Oregon Press.

(1971). *Foreign Investment in Petroleum and Mineral Industries: Case Studies of Investor-Host Country Relations*. Baltimore: Johns Hopkins Press for Resources for the Future.

(1975). *Foreign Investments in Copper Mining: Case Studies of Mines in Peru and Papua, New Guinea*. Baltimore: Johns Hopkins Press for Resources for the Future.

Miller, J. C., and B. Pras (1980). "The Effects of Multinational and Export Diversification on the Profit Stability of U.S. Corporations," *Southern Econ. J.*, 46 (January), 792–805.

Moran, T. H. (1974). *Multinational Corporations and the Politics of Dependence: Copper in Chile*. Princeton, NJ: Princeton University Press.

Morley, S. A., and G. W. Smith (1971). "Import Substitution and Foreign Investment in Brazil," *Oxford Econ. Pap.*, 23 (March), 120–35.

(1977a). "The Choice of Technology: Multinational Firms in Brazil," *Econ. Devel. Cult. Change*, 25 (January), 239–64.

(1977b). "Limited Search and the Technology Choices of Multinational Firms in Brazil," *Quart. J. Econ.*, 91 (May), 263–88.

Moxon, R. W. (1979). "The Cost, Conditions, and Adaptation of MNC Technology in Developing Countries," In R. G. Hawkins (ed.), *Research in International Business and Finance: An Annual Compilation of Research. Vol. I. The Economic Effects of Multinational Corporations*, pp. 189–222. Greenwich, CT: JAI Press.

Mueller, D. C. and J. E. Tilton (1969). "Research and Development Costs as a Barrier to Entry," *Can. J. Econ.*, 2 (November), 570–9.

Müller, R., and R. Morgenstern (1974). "Multinational Corporations and Balance of Payments Impacts in LDCs: An Econometric Analysis of Export Pricing Behavior," *Kyklos*, 27 (No. 2), 304–21.

Mundell, R. A. (1957). "International Trade and Factor Mobility," *Amer. Econ. Rev.*, 47 (June), 321–35.

Musgrave, P. B. (1969). *United States Taxation of Foreign Investment Income: Is-*

sues and Arguments. Cambridge, MA: International Tax Program, Harvard Law School.

(1975). *Direct Investment Abroad and the Multinationals: Effects on the United States Economy.* U.S. Senate, Committee on Foreign Relations, Subcommittee on Multinational Corporations, Committee Print, 94th Congress, first session. Washington: U.S. Government Printing Office.

Nankani, G. T. (1979). *The Intercountry Distribution of Direct Foreign Investment in Manufacturing.* New York: Garland.

Naumann-Etienne, R. (1974). "A Framework for Financial Decisions in the Multinational Corporations: Summary of Recent Research," *J. Financial Quant. Anal.*, 9 (November), 859–74.

Nayyar, D. (1978). "Transnational Corporations and Manufactured Exports from Poor Countries," *Econ. J.*, 88 (March), 59–84.

Neary, J. P. (1978). "Short-Run Capital Specificity and the Pure Theory of International Trade," *Econ. J.*, 88 (September), 488–510.

(1980). "International Factor Mobility, Minimum Wage Rates and Factor Price Equalization: A Synthesis." Seminar Paper No. 158, Institute for International Economic Studies, University of Stockholm.

Negandhi, A. R. (1975). *Organization Theory in an Open System: A Study of Transferring Advanced Management Practices to Developing Nations.* New York: Dunellen.

Negandhi, A. R., and B. R. Baliga. (1979). *Quest for Survival and Growth: A Comparative Study of American, European, and Japanese Multinationals.* New York: Praeger.

Ness, W. L., Jr. (1975). "U.S. Corporate Income Taxation and the Dividend Remittance Policy of Multinational Corporations," *J. Int. Bus. Stud.*, 6 (Spring), 67–77.

Newbould, G. D., P. J. Buckley, and J. C. Thruwell (1978). *Going International: The Experience of Smaller Companies Overseas.* Somerset, NJ: Halsted Press.

Newfarmer, R. S. (1979). "TNC Takeovers in Brazil: The Uneven Distribution of Benefits in the Market for Firms," *World Devel.*, 7 (January), 25–43.

(1980). *Transnational Conglomerates and the Economics of Dependent Development: A Case Study of the International Electrical Oligopoly and Brazil's Electrical Industry.* Contemporary Studies in Economic and Financial Analysis No. 23. Greenwich, CT: JAI Press.

Newfarmer, R. S., and W. F. Mueller, (1975). *Multinational Corporations in Brazil and Mexico: Structural Sources of Economic and Noneconomic Power.* U.S. Senate, Committee on Foreign Relations, Subcommittee on Multinational Corporations, 94th Congress, first session. Washington: U.S. Government Printing Office.

Newman, H. H. (1978). "Strategic Groups and the Structure-Performance Relationship," *Rev. Econ. Statist.*, 60 (August), 417–28.

Nieckels, L. (1976). *Transfer Pricing in Multinational Firms: A Heuristic Programming Approach and a Case Study.* Stockholm: Almqvist & Wiksell.

Northrup, H. R., and R. L. Rowan (1979). *Multinational Collective Bargaining Attempts: The Record, the Cases, and the Prospects.* Multinational Industrial Relations Series No. 6. Philadelphia: Industrial Research Unit, The Wharton School,

University of Pennsylvania.

O'Loughlin, B., and P. N. O'Farrell (1980). "Foreign Direct Investment in Ireland: Empirical Evidence and Theoretical Implications," *Econ. Soc. Rev.*, 11 (April), 155–85.

Organization for Economic Cooperation and Development (1974). *Export Cartels.* Paris: OECD.

(1977). *Restrictive Business Practices of Multinational Enterprises: Report of the Committee of Experts on Restrictive Business Practices.* Paris: OECD.

(1978). *National Treatment for Foreign-Controlled Enterprises Established in OECD Countries.* Paris: OECD.

(1980). *International Direct Investment: Policies, Procedures and Practices in OECD Member Countries, 1979.* Paris: OECD.

Orr, D. (1975). "The Industrial Composition of U.S. Exports and Subsidiary Sales to the Canadian Market: Comment," *Amer. Econ. Rev.*, 65 (March), 230–4.

Owen, R. F. (1979). "Inter-industry Determinants of Foreign Direct Investments: A Perspective Emphasizing the Canadian Experience." Working Papers in International Economics No. G-79-03, International Finance Section, Princeton University.

Ozawa, T. (1979*a*). "International Investment and Industrial Structure: New Theoretical Implications from the Japanese Experience," *Oxford Econ. Pap.*, 31 (March), 72–92.

(1979*b*). *Multinationalism, Japanese Style: The Political Economy of Outward Dependency.* Princeton, NJ: Princeton University Press.

Pack, H. (1976). "The Substitution of Labour for Capital in Kenyan Manufacturing," *Econ. J.*, 86 (March), 45–58.

Papanek, G. F. (1973). "Aid, Foreign Private Investment, Savings, and Growth in Less Developed Countries," *J. Polit. Econ.*, 81 (January/February), 120–30.

Parker, J. E. S. (1978). *The Economics of Innovation: The National and Multinational Enterprise in Technological Change*, 2nd ed. London: Longmans.

Parry, T. G. (1973). "The International Firm and National Economic Policy," *Econ. J.*, 83 (December), 1201–21.

(1974*a*). "Size of Plant, Capacity Utilization and Economic Efficiency: Foreign Investment in the Australian Chemical Industry," *Econ. Rec.*, 50 (June), 218–44.

(1974*b*). "Technology and the Size of the Multinational Corporation Subsidiary: Evidence from the Australian Manufacturing Sector," *J. Ind. Econ.*, 23 (December), 125–34.

(1978). "Structure and Performance in Australian Manufacturing, With Special Reference to Foreign-Owned Enterprises." In W. Kasper and T. G. Parry (eds.), *Growth, Trade and Structural Change in an Open Australian Economy*, pp. 173–99. Kensington, Australia: Centre for Applied Economic Research, University of New South Wales.

(1980). *The Multinational Enterprise: International Investment and Host-Country Imports.* Contemporary Studies in Economic and Financial Analysis No. 20. Greenwich, CT: JAI Press.

Parry, T. G., and J. F. Watson (1979). "Technology Flows and Foreign Investment in the Australian Manufacturing Sector," *Australian Econ. Papers*, 18 (June),

103–18.

Pastré, O. (1981). *Multinationals: Bank and Corporate Relationships.* Contemporary Studies in Economic and Financial Analysis No. 28. Greenwich, CT: JAI Press.

Peck, M. J. (1976). "Technology." In H. Patrick and H. Rosovsky (eds.), *Asia's New Giant: How the Japanese Economy Works*, Chapter 8. Washington: Brookings Institution.

Pennie, T. E. (1956). "The Influence of Distribution Costs and Direct Investments on British Exports to Canada," *Oxford Econ. Pap.*, 8 (October), 229–44.

Penrose, E. T. (1956). "Foreign Investment and the Growth of the Firm," *Econ. J.*, 66 (June), 220–35.

(1959). *The Theory of the Growth of the Firm.* Oxford: Basil Blackwell.

(1968). *The Large International Firm in Developing Countries: The International Petroleum Industry.* London: George Allen & Unwin.

(1973). "International Patenting and the Less-Developed Countries," *Econ. J.*, 83 (September), 768–86.

Pindyck, R. S. (1978). "Gains to Producers from the Cartelization of Exhaustible Resources," *Rev. Econ. Statist.*, 60 (May), 238–51.

Plasschaert, S. (1974). "Multinational Companies and International Capital Markets." In J. S. G. Wilson and C. F. Scheffer (eds.), *Multinational Enterprises—Financial and Monetary Aspects*, Chapter 7. Leiden: A. W. Sijthoff.

(1979). *Transfer Pricing and Multinational Corporations: An Overview of Concepts, Mechanisms and Regulations.* Farnborough: Saxon House.

(1981). "The Multiple Motivations for Transfer Pricing Modulations in Multinational Enterprises and Governmental Counter-Measures: An Attempt at Clarification," *Management International Rev.*, 21 (No. 1), 49–63.

Prachowny, M. F. J., and J. D. Richardson (1975). "Testing a Life-Cycle Hypothesis of the Balance-of-Payments Effects of Multinational Corporations," *Econ. Inquiry*, 13 (March), 81–98.

Prindl, A. R. (1976). *Foreign Exchange Risk.* New York: John Wiley.

Pugel, T. A. (1978). *International Market Linkages and U.S. Manufacturing: Prices, Profits, and Patterns.* Cambridge, MA: Ballinger.

(1980a). "Profitability, Concentration and the Interindustry Variation in Wages," *Rev. Econ. Statist.*, 62 (May), 248–53.

(1980b). "Endogenous Technical Change and International Technology Transfer in a Ricardian Trade Model." International Finance Discussion Papers No. 167, Board of Governors of the Federal Reserve System, Washington, D.C.

(1981). "Technology Transfer and the Neoclassical Theory of International Trade." In R. G. Hawkins and A. J. Prasad (eds.), *Technology Transfer and Economic Development.* Greenwich, CT: JAI Press.

Purvis, D. D. (1972). "Technology, Trade and Factor Mobility," *Econ. J.*, 82 (September), 991–9.

Radetzki, M. (1980). "Has Political Risk Scared Minerals Investments Away from the Deposits in Developing Countries?" Seminar Paper No. 169, Institute for International Economic Studies, University of Stockholm.

Ragazzi, G. (1973). "Theories of the Determinants of Direct Foreign Investment," *IMF Staff Pap.*, 20 (July), 471–98.

Ray, E. J. (1977). "Foreign Direct Investment in Manufacturing," *J. Polit. Econ.*, 85 (April), 283–97.

Reddaway, W. B. (1967). *Effects of U.K. Direct Investment Overseas: An Interim Report*. University of Cambridge, Department of Applied Economics, Occasional Papers No. 12. Cambridge University Press.

(1968). *Effects of U.K. Direct Investment Overseas: Final Report*. University of Cambridge, Department of Applied Economies, Occasional Papers No. 15. Cambridge University Press.

Reuber, G. L., with H. Crookell, M. Emerson, and G. Gallais-Hamonno (1973). *Private Foreign Investment in Development*. Oxford: Clarendon Press.

Reuber, G. L., and F. Roseman (1972). "International Capital Flows and the Takeover of Domestic Companies by Foreign Firms: Canada, 1945–61." In F. Machlup, W. S. Salant, and L. Tarshis (eds.), *The International Mobility and Movement of Capital*, pp. 465–503. Universities-National Bureau Conference Series No. 24. New York: Columbia University Press for National Bureau of Economic Research.

Richardson, J. D. (1971*a*). "Theoretical Considerations in the Analysis of Foreign Direct Investment," *Western Econ. J.*, 9 (March), 87–98.

(1971*b*). "On 'Going Abroad': The Firm's Initial Foreign Investment Decision," *Quart. Rev. Econ. Bus.*, 11 (Winter), 7–22.

Richman, P. B. (1963). *Taxation of Foreign Investment Income*. Baltimore: Johns Hopkins Press.

Riedel, J. (1975). "The Nature and Determinants of Export-Oriented Direct Foreign Investment in a Developing Country: A Case Study of Taiwan," *Weltwirtsch. Arch.*, 111 (No. 3), 505–28.

Robbins, S. M., and R. B. Stobaugh (1973). *Money in the Multinational Enterprise: A Study of Financial Policy*. New York: Basic Books.

Roberts, B. C. (1972). "Factors Influencing the Organization and Style of Management and Their Effect on the Pattern of Industrial Relations in Multi-national Corporations." In H. Günther (ed.), *Transnational Industrial Relations*, Chapter 6. London: Macmillan.

(1973). "Multinational Collective Bargaining: A European Prospect?" *Brit. J. Ind. Relat.*, 11 (March), 1–19.

Roberts, B. C., and B. Liebhaberg (1977). "International Regulation of Multinational Enterprises: Trade Union and Management Concerns," *Brit. J. Ind. Relat.*, 15 (November), 356–73.

Roberts, B. C., and J. May (1974). "The Response of Multi-National Enterprises to International Trade Union Pressures," *Brit. J. Ind. Relat.*, 12 (November), 403–16.

Robinson, R. D. (1976). *National Control of Foreign Business Entry: A Survey of Fifteen Countries*. New York: Praeger.

Rodriguez, C. A. (1975). "Trade in Technological Knowledge and the National Advantage," *J. Polit. Econ.*, 83 (February), 121–35.

Rodriguez, R. M. (1980). *Foreign-exchange Management in U.S. Multinationals*. Lexington, MA: Lexington Books, D. C. Heath.

Ronstadt, R. (1977). *Research and Development Abroad by U.S. Multinationals*. New York: Praeger.

Root, F. R., and A. A. Ahmed (1978). "The Influence of Policy Instruments on Manufacturing Direct Foreign Investment in Developing Countries," *J. Int. Bus. Stud.*, 9 (Winter), 81–93.

Rosenblatt, S. M., and T. W. Stanley (1978). *The Multinational Enterprise in North-South Technology Transfer.* Occasional Paper No. 9. Washington: Center for Multinational Studies.

Rosenbluth, G. (1970). "The Relation between Foreign Control and Concentration in Canadian Industry," *Can. J. Econ.*, 3 (February), 14–38.

Rowthorn, R., with S. Hymer (1971). *International Big Business, 1957–1967: A Study of Comparative Growth.* University of Cambridge, Department of Applied Economics, Occasional Paper No. 24. Cambridge University Press.

Rubin, P. H. (1973). "The Expansion of Firms," *J. Polit. Econ.*, 81 (July/August), 936–49.

Rugman, A. M. (1979). *International Diversification and the Multinational Enterprise.* Lexington, MA: Lexington Books.

(1980*a*). "Internalization as a General Theory of Foreign Direct Investment: A Re-appraisal of the Literature," *Weltwirtsch. Arch.*, 116 (No. 2), 365–79.

(1980*b*). *Multinationals in Canada: Theory, Performance, and Economic Impact.* Boston: Martinus Nijhoff.

(1981). *Inside the Multinationals: The Economics of Internal Markets.* New York: Columbia University Press.

Rutenberg, D. P. (1970). "Maneuvering Liquid Assets in a Multi-National Company: Formulation and Deterministic Solution Procedures," *Management Science*, 16 (June), B-671–84.

Safarian, A. E. (1966). *Foreign Ownership of Canadian Industry.* Toronto: McGraw-Hill.

(1969). *The Performance of Foreign-Owned Firms in Canada.* Washington and Montreal: Canadian-American Committee.

(1978). "Policy on Multinational Enterprises in Developed Countries," *Can. J. Econ.*, 11 (November), 641–55.

Saham, J. (1980). *British Industrial Investment in Malaysia, 1963–1971.* Kuala Lumpur: Oxford University Press.

Sato, M., and R. M. Bird (1975). "International Aspects of the Taxation of Corporations and Shareholders," *IMF Staff Pap.*, 22 (July), 384–455.

Saunders, R. S. (1978). "The Determinants of the Productivity of Canadian Manufacturing Industries Relative to That of Counterpart Industries in the United States." Ph.D. dissertation, Harvard University.

(1980). "The Determinants of Productivity in Canadian Manufacturing Industries," *J. Ind. Econ.*, 29 (December), 167–84.

Scaperlanda, A. E., and L. J. Mauer (1969). "The Determinants of U.S. Direct Investment in the E.E.C.," *Amer. Econ. Rev.*, 59 (September), 558–68.

(1972). "The Determinants of U.S. Direct Investment in the E.E.C.: Reply," *Amer. Econ. Rev.*, 62 (September), 700–4.

Scherer, F. M. (1980). *Industrial Market Structure and Economic Performance*, 2nd ed. Chicago: Rand-McNally.

Scherer, F. M., A. Beckenstein, E. Kaufer, and R. D. Murphy, with F. Bougeon-Maassen (1975). *The Economics of Multiplant Operation: An International*

Comparisons Study. Harvard Economic Studies No. 145. Cambridge, MA: Harvard University Press.

Schmitz, A. (1970). "The Impact of Trade Blocs on Foreign Direct Investment," *Econ. J.*, 80 (September), 724–31.

Schmitz, A., and J. Bieri (1972). "E.E.C. Tariffs and United States Direct Investment," *Europ. Econ. Rev.*, 3 (October), 259–70.

Schnitzer, M. (1980). *U.S. Business Involvement in Eastern Europe: Case Studies of Hungary, Poland, and Romania.* New York: Praeger.

Sciberras, E. (1977). *Multinational Electronic Companies and National Economic Policies.* Contemporary Studies in Economic and Financial Analysis No. 6. Greenwich, CT: JAI Press.

Sebenius, J. K. (1980). "Anatomy of Agreement: Negotiation Analysis and the Law of the Sea." Ph.D. dissertation, Harvard University.

Sekiguchi, S. (1979). *Japanese Direct Foreign Investment.* Atlantic Institute for International Affairs Series No. 1. Montclair, NJ: Allenheld, Osmun & Co.

Senbet, L. W. (1979). "International Capital Market Equilibrium and the Multinational Firm Financing and Investment Policies," *J. Financial Quant. Anal.*, 14 (September), 455–80.

Servan-Schreiber, J. J. (1968). *The American Challenge.* New York: Atheneum.

Severn, A. K. (1972). "Investment and Financial Behavior of American Direct Investors in Manufacturing," In F. Machlup, W. S. Salant, and L. Tarshis (eds.), *The International Mobility and Movement of Capital*, pp. 367–96. Universities-National Bureau Conference Series No. 24. New York: Columbia University Press for National Bureau of Economic Research.

(1974). "Investor Evaluation of Foreign and Domestic Risk," *J. Finance*, 29 (May), 545–50.

Severn, A. K., and M. M. Laurence (1974). "Direct Investment, Research Intensity, and Profitability," *J. Financial Quant. Anal.*, 9 (March), 181–90.

Shank, K. S., Jesse F. Dillard, and Richard J. Murdock (1979). *Assessing the Economic Impact of FASB No. 8.* New York: Financial Executives Research Foundation.

Shapiro, A. C. (1975a). "Exchange Rate Changes, Inflation and the Value of the Multinational Corporation," *J. Finance*, 30 (May), 485–502.

(1975b). "Evaluating Financing Costs for Multinational Subsidiaries," *J. Int. Bus. Stud.*, 6 (Fall), 25–32.

(1978). "Financial Structure and Cost of Capital in the Multinational Corporation," *J. Financial Quant. Anal.*, 13 (June), 211–26.

Sharpston, M. (1975). "International Sub-contracting," *Oxford Econ. Pap.*, 27 (March), 94–135.

Sigmund, P. E. (1980). *Multinationals in Latin America: The Politics of Nationalization.* Madison: University of Wisconsin Press.

Singer, H. W. (1950). "The Distribution of Gains between Investing and Borrowing Countries," *Amer. Econ. Rev.*, 40 (May), 473–85.

Smith, D. N., and L. T. Wells, Jr. (1975). *Negotiating Third World Mineral Agreements.* Cambridge, MA: Ballinger.

Snoy, B. (1975). *Taxes on Direct Investment Income in The EEC: A Legal and Economic Analysis.* New York: Praeger.

Soenen, L. A. (1979). "Efficient Market Implications for Foreign Exchange Exposure Management," *De Economist*, 127 (No. 2), 330–9.

Solnik, B. H. (1974). "An Equilibrium Model of the International Capital Market," *J. Econ. Theory*, 8 (August), 500–24.

Solomon, R. F., and D. J. C. Forsyth (1977). "Substitution of Labour for Capital in the Foreign Sector: Some Further Evidence," *Econ. J.*, 87 (June), 283–9.

Solomon, R. F., and K. P. D. Ingham (1977). "Discriminating between MNC Subsidiaries and Indigenous Companies: A Comparative Analysis of the British Mechanical Engineering Industry," *Oxford Bull. Econ. Statist.*, 39 (May), 127–38.

Southard, F. A., Jr. (1931). *American Industry in Europe*. Boston: Houghton Mifflin.

Sprietsma, H. B. (1978). "International Subcontracting and Developing Countries," *De Economist*, 126 (No. 2), 220–42.

Steuer, M. D., et al. (1973). *The Impact of Foreign Direct Investment on the United Kingdom*. London: Her Majesty's Stationery Office.

Steuer, M., and J. Gennard. (1971). "Industrial Relations, Labour Disputes and Labour Utilization in Foreign-Owned Firms in the United Kingdom." In J. H. Dunning (ed.), *The Multinational Enterprise*, Chapter 4. London: George Allen & Unwin.

Stevens, G. V. G. (1969). "Fixed Investment Expenditures of Foreign Manufacturing Affiliates of United States Firms: Theoretical Models and Empirical Evidence," *Yale Econ. Essays*, 9 (Spring), 137–206.

(1972). "Capital Mobility and the International Firm." In F. Machlup, W. S. Salant, and L. Tarshis (eds.), *The International Mobility and Movement of Capital*, pp. 323–53. New York: Columbia University Press for National Bureau of Economic Research.

(1974). "The Determinants of Investment." In J. H. Dunning (ed.), *Economic Analysis and the Multinational Enterprise*, Chapter 3. London: George Allen & Unwin.

Stigler, G. J. (1951). "The Division of Labor Is Limited by the Extent of the Market," *J. Polit. Econ.*, 59 (June), 185–93.

Stobaugh, R. B. (1970). "Financing Foreign Subsidiaries of U.S. Controlled Multinational Enterprises," *J. Int. Bus. Stud.*, 1 (Summer), 43–64.

(1972). "The Neotechnology Account of International Trade: The Case of Petrochemicals." In L. T. Wells (ed.), *The Product Life Cycle and International Trade*, pp. 81–105. Boston: Division of Research, Graduate School of Business Administration, Harvard University.

Stobaugh, R. B., et al. (1976). *Nine Investments Abroad and Their Impact at Home: Case Studies on Multinational Enterprises and the U.S. Economy*. Boston: Division of Research, Harvard Business School.

Stonehill, A. (1965). *Foreign Ownership in Norwegian Enterprises*. Samfunnsokonomiske Studier No. 14. Oslo: Central Bureau of Statistics.

Stopford, J. M. (1976). "Changing Perspectives on Investment by British Manufacturing Multinationals," *J. Int. Bus. Stud.*, 7 (Fall/Winter), 15–27.

Stopford, J. M., and K. O. Haberich (1978). "Ownership and Control of Foreign Operations." In M. Ghertman and J. Leontiades (eds.), *European Research in*

International Business, pp. 141–67. Amsterdam: North-Holland.

Stopford, J. M., and L. T. Wells, Jr. (1972). *Managing the Multinational Enterprise: Organization of the Firm and Ownership of the Subsidiaries*. New York: Basic Books.

Strassmann, W. P. (1968). *Technological Change and Economic Development: The Manufacturing Experience of Mexico and Peru*. Ithaca: Cornell University Press.

Stubenitsky, R. (1970). *American Direct Investment in the Netherlands Industry*. Rotterdam: Rotterdam University Press.

Stuckey, J. A. (1981). "Vertical Integration and Joint Ventures in the International Aluminum Industry." Ph.D. dissertation, Harvard University.

Svedberg, P. (1977). *Foreign Investment and Trade Policies in an International Economy with Transnational Corporations: A Theoretical and Empirical Study with References to Latin America*. Stockholm: privately printed.

(1979). "Optimal Tariff Policy on Imports from Multinationals," *Econ. Record*, 55 (March), 64–7.

(1981). "Colonial Enforcement of Foreign Direct Investment," *Manchester Sch. Econ. Soc. Stud.*, 48 (March), 21–38.

Swann, D., D. P. O'Brien, W. P. J. Maunder, and W. S. Howe (1974). *Competition in British Industry: Restrictive Practices Legislation in Theory and Practice*. London: George Allen & Unwin.

Swedenborg, B. (1979). *The Multinational Operations of Swedish Firms: An Analysis of Determinants and Effects*. Stockholm: Industrial Institute for Economic and Social Research.

Taira, K., and G. Standing (1973). "Labor Market Effects of Multinational Enterprises in Latin America," *Nebr. J. Econ. Bus.*, 12 (Autumn), 103–17.

Tang, R. Y. W. (1979). *Transfer Pricing Practices in the United States and Japan*. New York: Praeger.

Taylor, C. T., and Z. A. Silberston (1973). *The Economic Impact of the Patent System: A Study of the British Experience*. University of Cambridge, Department of Applied Economics, Monograph No. 23. Cambridge University Press.

Teece, D. J. (1976). *Vertical Integration and Vertical Divestiture in the U.S. Oil Industry*. Stanford, CA: Institute for Energy Studies, Stanford University.

(1977). "Technology Transfer by Multinational Firms: The Resource Cost of Transferring Technological Knowhow," *Econ. J.*, 87 (June), 242–61.

(1981). "The Market for Know-How and Efficient International Transfer of Technology," *Ann. Amer. Acad. Pol. Soc. Sci.*, 458 (November), 81–96.

Telesio, P. (1979). *Technology Licensing and Multinational Enterprises*. New York: Praeger.

Terrell, H. S., and S. J. Key (1978). "U.S. Offices of Foreign Banks: The Recent Experience." International Finance Discussion Papers No. 124. Washington: Board of Governors of the Federal Reserve System.

Thoman, G. R. (1973). *Foreign Investment and Regional Development: The Theory and Practice of Investment Incentives with a Case Study of Belgium*. New York: Praeger.

Thurow, L. C. (1976). "International Factor Movements and the American Distribution of Income," *Intermountain Econ. Rev.*, 2 (Spring), 13–24.

Tilton, J. E. (1971). *The International Diffusion of Technology: The Case of Semi-*

conductors. Washington: Brookings Institution.

Tomlinson, J. W. C. (1970). *The Joint Venture Process in International Business: India and Pakistan*. Cambridge, MA: M.I.T. Press.

Tourneden, R. L. (1975). *Foreign Disinvestment by U.S. Multinational Corporations, with Eight Case Studies*. New York: Praeger.

Truitt, J. F. (1974). *Expropriation of Private Foreign Investment*. International Business Research Series No. 3. Bloomington, IN: Graduate School of Business, Indiana University.

Tsurumi, Y. (1976). *The Japanese Are Coming: A Multinational Spread of Japanese Firms*. Cambridge, MA: Ballinger.

Tyler, W. G. (1978). "Technical Efficiency and Ownership Characteristics of Manufacturing Firms in a Developing Country: A Brazilian Case Study," *Weltwirtsch. Arch.*, 114 (No. 2), 360–79.

United Nations, Department of Economic and Social Affairs (1974). *Multinational Corporations in World Development*. New York: Praeger.

U.S. Department of Commerce (1976). *Foreign Direct Investment in the United States: Report of the Secretary of Commerce to the Congress in Compliance with the Foreign Investment Study Act of 1974*. Washington: U.S. Government Printing Office.

U.S. Department of Labor, Bureau of International Labor Affairs (1978). *The Impact of International Trade and Investment on Employment*, W. Dewald (ed.). Washington: U.S. Government Printing Office.

U.S. Senate, Foreign Relations Committee, Subcommittee on Multinational Corporations (1975). *Multinational Corporations in the Dollar-Devaluation Crisis: Report on a Questionnaire*. Washington: U.S. Government Printing Office.

U.S. Tariff Commission (1973). *Implications of Multinational Firms for World Trade and Investment and for U.S. Trade and Labor*. Washington: U.S. Government Printing Office.

Vaitsos, C. V. (1974). *Intercountry Income Distribution and Transnational Enterprises*. Oxford: Clarendon Press.

Van Loo, F. (1977). "The Effect of Foreign Direct Investment on Investment in Canada," *Rev. Econ. Statist.*, 59 (November), 474–81.

Vendrell-Alda, J. L. M. (1978). *Comparing Foreign Subsidiaries and Domestic Firms: A Research Methodology Applied to Efficiency in Argentine Industry*. New York: Garland.

Verlage, H. C. (1975). *Transfer Prices for Multinational Enterprises*. Rotterdam: Rotterdam University Press.

Vernon, R. (1966). "International Investment and International Trade in the Product Cycle," *Quart. J. Econ.*, 80 (May), 190–207.

(1971). *Sovereignty at Bay: The Multinational Spread of U.S. Enterprises*. New York: Basic Books.

(1974a). "Competition Policy toward Multinational Companies," *Amer. Econ. Rev.*, 64 (May), 276–82.

(1974b). "The Location of Industry." In J. H. Dunning (ed.), *Economic Analysis and the Multinational Enterprise*, pp. 89–114. London: George Allen & Unwin.

(1976a). *The Oil Crisis*. New York: W. W. Norton.

(1976b). "Multinational Enterprises in Developing Countries: Issues in Dependency and Interdependence." In D. E. Apter and L. W. Goodman (eds.), *The Multinational Corporation and Social Change*, pp. 40–62. New York: Praeger.

(1977). *Storm Over the Multinationals: The Real Issues.* Cambridge, MA: Harvard University Press.

(1979). "The Product Cycle Hypothesis in a New International Environment," *Oxford Bull. Econ. Statist.*, 41 (November), 255–67.

Vernon, R., and W. H. Davidson (1979). "Foreign Production of Technology-Intensive Products by U.S.-Based Multinational Enterprises." Working Paper No. 79-5, Division of Research, Graduate School of Business Administration, Harvard University.

Vernon, R., and B. Levy (1980). "State-owned Enterprises in the World Economy: The Case of Iron Ore." Working Paper No. 80-24, Division of Research, Graduate School of Business Administration, Harvard University.

Wagner, K. (1980). "Competition and Productivity: A Study of the Metal Can Industry in Britain, Germany and the United States," *J. Ind. Econ.*, 29 (September), 17–35.

Wall, D. (1976). "Export Processing Zones," *J. World Trade Law*, 10 (September/October), 478–89.

Wallace, D., Jr. (ed.) (1976). *International Control of Investment.* New York: Praeger.

Weinberg, P. J. (1978). *European Labor and Multinationals.* New York: Praeger.

Weisskopf, T. E. (1972). "The Impact of Foreign Capital Inflow on Domestic Savings in Under-developed Countries," *J. Int. Econ.*, 2 (February), 25–38.

Wells, L. T. (ed.) (1972). *The Product Life Cycle and International Trade.* Boston: Division of Research, Graduate School of Business Administration, Harvard University.

Wells, L. T. (1973). "Economic Man and Engineering Man: Choice in a Low-Wage Country," *Public Policy*, 21 (Summer), 319–42.

(1983). *Third World Multinationals.* Cambridge, MA: M.I.T. Press.

Westphal, L. E., Y. W. Rhee, and G. Pursell (1979). "Foreign Influences on Korean Industrial Development," *Oxford Bull. Econ. Statist.*, 41 (November), 359–88.

Whichard, O. G. (1978). "Employment and Employee Compensation of U.S. Affiliates of Foreign Companies, 1974," *Surv. Curr. Bus.*, 58 (December), 23–34, 58.

White, L. J. (1976). "Appropriate Technology and a Competitive Environment: Some Evidence from Pakistan," *Quart. J. Econ.*, 90 (November), 575–89.

Wilkins, M. (1970). *The Emergence of Multinational Enterprise: American Business Abroad from the Colonial Era to 1914.* Cambridge, MA: Harvard University Press.

(1974). *The Maturing of Multinational Enterprise: American Business Abroad from 1914 to 1970.* Cambridge, MA: Harvard University Press.

Williams, M. L. (1975). "The Extent and Significance of the Nationalization of Foreign-owned Assets in Developing Countries 1956–1972," *Oxford Econ. Pap.*, 27 (July), 260–73.

Williamson, O. E. (1970). *Corporate Control and Business Behavior.* Englewood Cliffs, NJ: Prentice-Hall.

(1971). "The Vertical Integration of Production: Market Failure Considerations," *Amer. Econ. Rev.*, 61 (May), 112–23.

(1973). "Markets and Hierarchies: Some Elementary Considerations," *Amer. Econ. Rev.*, 63 (May), 316–25.

Willmore, L. (1976). "Direct Foreign Investment in Central American Manufacturing," *World Devel.*, 4 (June), 499–517.

Wilson, B. D. (1980). "The Propensity of Multinational Companies to Expand Through Acquisitions," *J. Int. Bus. Stud.*, 11 (Spring/Summer), 59–65.

Wilson, R. W. (1977). "The Effect of Technological Environment and Product Rivalry on R&D Effort and Licensing of Inventions," *Rev. Econ. Statist.*, 59 (May), 171–8.

Wolf, B. N. (1975). "Size and Profitability Among U.S. Manufacturing Firms: Multinational versus Primarily Domestic Firms," *J. Econ. Bus.*, 28 (Fall), 15–22.

(1977). "Industrial Diversification and Internationalization: Some Empirical Evidence," *J. Ind. Econ.*, 26 (December), 177–91.

Wonnacott, R. J., and P. Wonnacott (1967). *Free Trade Between the United States and Canada: The Potential Economic Effects*. Cambridge, MA: Harvard University Press.

Yeoman, W. A. (1976). *Selection of Production Processes for the Manufacturing Subsidiaries of U.S.-Based Multinational Corporations*. New York: Arno Press.

Yoshihara, K. (1976). *Foreign Investment and Domestic Response: A Study of Singapore's Industrialization*. Singapore: Eastern Universities Press.

(1978). *Japanese Investment in Southeast Asia*. Monographs of the Center for Southeast Asian Studies, Kyoto University, No. 11. Honolulu: University Press of Hawaii.

Yoshino, M. Y. (1976). *Japan's Multinational Enterprises*. Cambridge, MA: Harvard University Press.

Zenoff, D. B. (1966). "The Determinants of Dividend Remittance Practices of Wholly-Owned European and Canadian Subsidiaries of American Multinational Corporations." D.B.A. thesis, Graduate School of Business Administration, Harvard University.

NAME INDEX

Adams, J. D. R., 238
Adelman, M. A., 125
Adler, F. M., 139–41, 146, 171, 173, 190
Aggarwal, R., 176
Agmon, T., 176
Aharoni, Y., 70–1
Ahmed, A. A., 59, 243, 256
Aliber, R. Z., 176, 181, 186
Alsegg, R. J., 77, 78, 198
Amano, A., 52
Andrews, M. E., 254
Areskoug, K., 273
Arpan, J. S., 246–7
Arrow, K. J., 18, 19
Arthur D. Little, Inc., 43, 106
Auquier, A. A., 115

Baba, M., 97
Baerresen, D. W., 258
Baglini, N., 75
Baliga, B. R., 292
Bandera, V. N., 35
Banks, R. F., 153
Baranson, J., 203, 219, 220
Bardhan, P. K., 260
Barlow, E. R., 27, 123, 167
Barnet, R. J., 104, 191, 290
Batra, R. N., 42, 53, 182, 236
Baum, D. J., 12
Baumann, H. G., 10, 97
Beenstock, M., 235
Beguin, J. P., 90

Behrman, J. N., 12, 109, 177, 198, 199, 202, 287
Bergsten, C. F., 9, 111–12, 121, 136, 143, 145, 146, 155, 191, 238, 241, 284, 286, 294
Berry, A., 260
Bhagwati, J. N., 281
Bieri, J., 42
Biersteker, T. J., 253, 262, 269, 270, 271, 274
Biger, N., 171
Bird, R. M., 238
Blake, D. H., 156
Boatwright, B. D., 164, 165, 189
Bond, E., 258
Booth, E. J. R., 244
Bornschier, V., 275–6
Bos, H. C., 274
Bower, J. L., 70
Brandt, W. K., 79
Brash, D. T., 40, 143, 222, 223
Brecher, R. A., 214, 259, 281, 283
Brewster, K., 117
Brooke, M. Z., 71, 77, 167, 177, 178, 183, 247
Buckley, P. J., 6, 17, 44, 108, 164, 165, 204, 254, 271
Burgess, D. F., 53–4
Burns, J. M., 186
Burns, J. O., 247
Business International, 78

Casson, M., 6, 17, 202, 244

Caves, R. E., 6, 10, 11, 14, 27, 28, 44, 46, 52, 57, 94, 97, 99, 109, 115, 117, 197, 199, 221, 222
Chandler, A. D., 79
Chase-Dunn, C., 275–6
Chipman, J. S., 134
Chudson, W. A., 267
Chung, B. S., 43, 269
Clunies Ross, A., 122
Coase, R. H., 1
Cohen, B. I., 27, 258, 262, 266, 269, 271, 272
Connor, J. M., 97, 110–11
Contractor, F. J., 200, 203
Copithorne, L. W., 36, 244
Corden, W. M., 115, 232, 282, 283
Counahan, M., 267
Courtney, W. H., 268
Creamer, D. B., 199
Creigh, S. W., 153
Crispo, J., 157
Crookell, H., 202
Curhan, J., 82, 87
Curtin, W. J., 155, 156

Dam, K. W., 227
d'Arge, R., 35
Davidson, W. H., 60, 62, 63, 73, 210–12
Davies, H., 204, 206, 219
Davis, S. M., 76
Deane, R. S., 40, 44, 64, 86, 96
de Bodinat, H., 77
Delapierre, M., 64, 71, 82, 90–91, 205
De la Torre, J., 255
Diaz Alejandro, C. F., 124, 259, 265, 283, 292
Dietermann, G. J., 187
Donsimoni, M. P., 109
Doz, Y. L., 293
Dubin, M., 27, 72, 83–4, 102
Duerr, M. G., 247
Dukes, R. E., 187
Dumas, B., 171, 173
Dunning, J. H., 6, 10, 15, 27, 57, 59, 91, 96, 101, 105, 151, 157, 173, 222, 223, 256

Eastman, H. C., 6, 11
Eden, L. A. B., 245
Edstrom, A., 79
Erland, O., 85

Evans, P., 256, 262, 263, 264
Evans, T. G., 182, 184–7

Feldstein, M. S., 236–7, 282
Findlay, R., 214–15
Fischer, W. A., 198, 199
Fishwick, F., 96, 97, 101
Flowers, E. B., 100
Folks, W. R., 182, 184–7
Forsyth, D. J. C., 15, 152, 222, 223, 269, 270, 271
Fouch, G. C., 43
Frank, R. H., 136–7, 143, 144–5
Franko, L. G., 11, 60, 79, 80, 86–7, 90, 105, 106, 107, 108, 209
Freeman, R. T., 136–7, 143, 144–5
Friedmann, W. G., 90
Fröbel, F., 23, 258

Galbraith, J. A., 79
Gale, B. T., 111
Garnaut, R., 122
Gennard, J., 152–3
Germidis, D., 199
Gershenberg, I., 262, 264
Gilman, M., 167, 173
Glejser, H., 146
Globerman, S., 97, 210, 221
Goedde, A. G., 9
Goldsbrough, D. J., 164, 166, 189
Gordon, L., 266
Gorecki, P. K., 29, 100
Grabowski, H., 96
Graham, E. M., 106–7
Grauer, F., 171
Greenberg, E., 26
Greene, J., 247
Greenhill, C. R., 248
Greening, T. S., 19–20, 125, 126
Grommers, E. L., 266
Grosse, R. E., 293
Grubel, H. G., 12, 240
Gruber, M. H., 9, 209
Gunter, H., 153, 157

Haberich, K. O., 88, 89
Hadar, J., 42, 182
Haendel, D., 284
Hamada, K., 236, 258
Hamilton, C., 259
Hartman, D. G., 136, 173, 233–5, 236–7, 242, 244, 282
Hawkins, R. G., 192, 292

Hay, G. A., 106
Hayden, E. W., 220
Heenan, D. A., 265
Helleiner, G. K., 21, 23, 254–5, 294
Hellmann, R., 98
Henderson, D. F., 291
Herbolzheimer, E. O., 248
Herring, R., 189
Hershfield, D. C., 148, 157
Herskovic, S., 200, 202
Hewitt, G., 199
Hirsch, S., 36
Hirschey, M., 198
Hirschey, R. G., 199
Hirschman, A. O., 289
Hodges, M., 287
Hone, A., 255
Hood, N., 200, 253
Horst, T., 9, 13, 14, 29, 36–9, 41, 43,
  44, 63, 112, 162, 173, 229, 232,
  241–2, 244
Hu, Y. S., 98, 105
Hufbauer, G. C., 34, 139–41, 164,
  190, 210, 221–2
Hughes, H., 240, 254, 268
Hughes, J. S., 176
Hulbert, J. M., 79
Hymer, S. H., 6, 32–3, 164

Ingham, K. P. D., 222
International Labour Organization, 150,
  152, 153
Itagaki, T., 179, 232, 245

Jacquillat, B., 27
Jarrett, J. P., 10, 21–22, 23, 64, 100,
  255
Jedel, M. J., 79, 148, 153
Jenkins, G. P., 239, 248
Jensen, O. W., 244
Jilling, M., 179–81
Joachimsson, R., 248
Johanson, J., 72
Johnson, H. G., 6, 208
Jones, R. W., 46, 53, 55, 206, 215–6,
  235, 283
Jorgenson, D. W., 162
Juhl, P., 65, 254

Kaserman, D. L., 16
Kassalow, E., 148, 153
Katrak, H., 115, 233
Katz, J., 222

Keddie, J., 270
Keegan, W. J., 265
Kelley, D., 106
Kemp, M. C., 235
Keohane, R. O., 297
Key, S. J., 12
Killing, H. P., 202
Kindleberger, C. P., 6, 33, 72, 122,
  287
Klein, B., 183
Knickerbocker, F. T., 98–100, 101,
  102, 106
Kobrin, S. J., 275
Koizumi, T., 137, 214, 218
Kojima, K., 216
Kopecky, K. J., 137, 214, 218
Kopits, G. F., 28, 178, 238, 243, 245–
  6
Krainer, R. E., 60
Krause, L. B., 227
Kravis, I. B., 63, 64
Krugman, P. K., 212–13, 215
Kudrle, R. T., 105
Kujawa, D., 79, 148, 149, 153, 155,
  156
Kumar, K., 253, 265
Kwack, S. Y., 163, 165, 189
Kyrouz, M. E., 226, 238

Ladenson, M. L., 166, 243
Lake, A. W., 210
Lall, S., 9, 23, 44, 98, 101, 199, 244,
  249, 253, 261–2, 264, 267, 274
Lapan, H., 260
Laurence, M. M., 112, 197
Lavergne, R., 23
Lecraw, D., 265, 269
Lee, C. H., 269
Lee, W. Y., 175
Lees, F. A., 12
Leftwich, R. B., 177, 264
Leipziger, D. M., 268
Lent, G., 238
Leoz-Arguelles, V., 109
Leroy, G., 210, 212
Lessard, D. G., 176, 247
Levy, H., 20, 171
Liebhaberg, B., 297
Lim, D., 265, 266
Lindert, P. H., 190
Lipsey, R. E., 63, 64, 146
Little, J. S., 84

Litvak, I. A., 126
Lombard, F. J., 291
Lubitz, R., 59, 147
Lunn, J., 164
Lupo, L. A., 35, 73

McAleese, D., 267, 271
Macaluso, D., 192
McClain, D. S., 62, 166
McCulloch, R., 213–14, 216
McDonald, D., 271
Macdougall, G. D. A., 230
McFetridge, D. G., 211
McKern, R. B., 18, 124
McLeod, M. G., 265
McManus, J. C., 6
McQueen, D. L., 220
Magee, S. P., 6
Makeham, P., 153
Makin, J., 42
Makinen, G. E., 190
Mansfield, E., 196, 197, 199, 200, 220–1
Mantel, I. M., 189
Markensten, K., 266, 269
Markusen, J. R., 259
Marshall, H., 40
Mason, R. H., 269, 270
Mathewson, G. F., 244
Mauer, L. J., 41–2, 178
Maule, C. J., 126
May, J., 148, 157
Melvin, J. R., 259
Michalet, C. A., 64, 71, 82, 90–1, 205
Mikesell, R. F., 124
Miller, J. C., 27
Morgan, E. J., 151, 157
Morgenstern, R., 246
Morley, S. A., 254, 268, 269, 270
Moxon, R., 267
Mueller, D. C., 96
Müller, R. E., 104, 191, 246, 290
Mueller, W. F., 97
Mundell, R. A., 50–1, 135
Musgrave, P. B., 136, 137, 227, 229, 231, 238, 240, 245

Nankani, G., 58–9, 60, 62, 254, 256
Naumann-Etienne, R., 172
Nayyar, D., 255
Neary, J. P., 52, 55
Neghandi, A. R., 265, 292

Ness, W. L., 238, 239, 241, 243, 245
Newbould, G. D., 72, 73, 89
Newfarmer, R. S., 97, 105, 262
Newman, H. H., 109
Nieckels, L., 244
Northrup, H. C., 155, 156

O'Farrell, P. N., 44, 64, 65, 271–2
O'Loughlin, B., 44, 64, 65, 271–2
Ooms, V. D., 297
Organization for Economic Cooperation and Development, 115, 117, 287
Orr, D., 41
Owen, R. F., 10, 44
Ozawa, T., 61, 254

Pack, H., 269
Papanek, G. F., 275
Parker, J. E. S., 9
Parry, T. G., 10, 96, 199, 200, 222, 223, 287
Pastré, O., 12
Pearce, R. D., 44, 91, 222, 223
Peck, M. J., 201, 219
Pennie, T. E., 6
Penrose, E. T., 6, 13, 19, 125, 127, 190, 220
Pindyck, R., 120
Plasschaert, S., 172, 245, 248
Prachowny, M. F. J., 190–1
Pras, B., 27
Prindl, A., 184
Pugel, T. A., 9, 10, 14, 18, 97, 100, 147, 212, 217–18
Purvis, D. D., 51, 55, 133

Quirin, G. D., 244

Radetzki, M., 124
Ragazzi, G., 6
Ramachandran, R., 53, 236
Reddaway, W. B., 73, 146, 190
Remmers, E. L., 71, 77, 167, 177, 178, 183, 247
Renton, G. A., 164, 165, 189
Reuber, G. L., 41, 85, 90, 151, 165, 256, 257–8, 266, 268, 271, 275
Richardson, J. D., 72, 162, 190–1
Richman, P. B., 227
Riedel, J., 65, 255, 262, 269
Robbins, S. M., 167, 177, 179, 180
Roberts, B. C., 148, 155, 156, 157, 297

Robinson, R. D., 291
Rodriguez, C. A., 216–17
Rodriguez, R. M., 180–1, 182, 183
Romeo, A., 197, 199, 200, 220–1
Ronstadt, R., 199, 200
Root, F. R., 59, 243, 256
Roseman, F., 85, 165
Rosenblatt, S. M., 200
Rosenbluth, G., 97, 101
Rowan, R. L., 155, 156
Rowthorn, R., 108, 164
Rubin, P. H., 6
Rugman, A. M., 6, 26, 27, 36, 240, 248
Rutenberg, D. P., 179
Ryan, T. C. I., 262, 264

Sachdeva, K. S., 175
Safarian, A. E., 12, 27, 80, 143, 199, 271, 287, 291
Saham, J., 27, 40, 89
Sarnat, M., 171
Sato, M., 238
Saunders, R. S., 10, 11, 222
Scaperlanda, A., 41–2, 178
Scherer, F. M., 7, 120
Schmitz, A., 42
Sciberras, E., 109
Sebenius, J., 121
Sekiguchi, S., 207
Senbet, L. W., 171
Servan-Schreiber, J. J., 10, 11
Severn, A. K., 112, 164, 165–6, 167, 171, 197
Shank, K. S., 187
Shapiro, A. C., 173, 175, 183, 187, 257
Sharpston, M., 21, 255
Sigmund, P. E., 123, 292, 295
Silberston, Z. A., 201, 202, 203
Singer, H. W., 271
Smith, D. N., 121–2
Smith, G. W., 254, 268, 269, 270
Snoy, B., 238, 243
Soenen, L. A., 173
Solnik, B. H., 27, 171
Solomon, R. F., 222, 269, 270
Southard, F. A., 6, 91
Sprietsma, H. B., 255
Standing, G., 152
Stanley, T. W., 200

Steuer, M. D., 75, 91, 96, 97, 101, 152–3
Stevens, G. V. G., 146, 160, 162, 163, 164, 165–6, 167
Stieber, J., 153
Stigler, G. J., 21
Stobaugh, R. B., 145, 167, 174, 177, 179, 180, 210
Stonehill, A., 192
Stopford, J. M., 63–4, 75, 76–7, 83, 86, 87–8, 89
Strassmann, W. P., 268, 270
Streeten, P., 249, 253, 264, 274
Stubenitsky, F., 23, 85
Stuckey, J. A., 18–19, 88, 127–8
Stykolt, S., 6, 11
Svedberg, P., 58, 116, 259, 260, 266
Svensson, L. E. O., 259
Swann, D., 106
Swedenborg, B., 10–11, 14, 41, 43, 58, 59–60, 62, 146

Taira, K., 152
Tang, R. Y. W., 247
Taylor, C. T., 201, 202, 203
Teece, D. J., 19, 96, 125, 199, 200, 201, 206, 207, 212, 240
Telesio, P., 204–6
Terrell, H. S., 12
Thurow, L. C., 136
Tilton, J. E., 96, 209, 219
Tomlinson, J. W. C., 86, 89
Tourneden, R. L., 71
Truitt, J. F., 123, 292
Tsurumi, Y., 20, 23, 61, 64, 65, 82, 89, 107, 198, 207, 209, 254
Tyler, W. G., 264

U.S. Senate, 183
U.S. Tariff Commission, 23, 65, 144, 145, 151, 168, 249

Vahlne, J. E., 72
Vaitsos, C., 244, 248–9
Van Loo, F., 147
Vendrell-Alda, J. L. M., 223, 264
Verlage, H. C., 244
Vernon, R., 20, 61–2, 72, 89, 101, 104, 106, 110, 121, 127, 207–9, 210–12, 249, 253, 263, 287, 297

Wagner, K., 105

Wagner, S., 197
Wall, D., 258
Wallace, D., 297
Watson, J. F., 199, 200
Weinberg, P. J., 156
Weiss, M. Y., 146
Weisskopf, T. E., 273
Wells, L. T., 73, 75, 76–7, 86, 87–8, 121–2, 208, 265, 267, 269, 270
Wender, I. T., 27, 123, 167
Westphal, L. E., 272
Whalley, J., 238
Whichard, O. G., 150
White, J. T., 35
White, L. J., 270
Wilkins, M., 40, 72, 105–6, 117, 125–6
Willett, T. D., 189

Williams, M. L., 123, 292
Williamson, O. E., 4, 16
Willmore, L., 96, 264
Wilson, B. D., 83, 84
Wilson, R. W., 201, 211
Wolf, B. N., 9, 14, 28
Wonnacott, P. W., 40
Wonnacott, R. J., 40
Wright, B. D., 248

Yellen, J. L., 213–14, 216
Yeoman, W. A., 268, 270
Yoshihara, K., 64, 89, 254, 264, 265
Yoshino, M. Y., 61, 80, 89
You, P. S., 240, 254, 268
Young, S., 200, 253

Zenoff, D. B., 178

SUBJECT INDEX

accelerator relation, 163, 164
acquisition: effect on competition, 102;
  MNE market entry by, 81–5, 165
advertising outlays, 9, 10, 94–5, 99,
  100
aluminum industry, 18–19, 105, 124,
  127–8
American Tobacco Co., 104
Andean Foreign Investment Code, 293
arbitrage: capital, 32–5, 65, 165, 168,
  172, 206, 280; commodity, 39, 232
Argentina, 246
Australia, 18, 40, 63, 64, 124, 221

balance of payments policy, 180, 188–
  91
banking sector, 11–12
bankruptcy, 170, 174
Belgium, 151
Benelux, 44
benefit-cost analysis, 281
bilateral monopoly, 15, 18, 19, 84, 119
borrowing, foreign, 161, 166–7, 172–
  3, 174, 176–7, 234, 257, 272
Brazil, 63, 97, 110–11, 262, 264

Canada: capital formation, 147; corporate diversification, 29; foreign subsidiaries in, 10, 11, 14, 44, 63, 72,
  99–100, 109, 221; gains from foreign
  investment, 239–40; imports, 44; industrial relations, 148, 151, 157;

seller concentration, 101; tariffs, 40,
  41
capacity utilization, 15, 165
capital asset pricing model, 169–72,
  176
capital cost: diversification, 171, 176;
  entry barrier, 75; investment determinant, 165–8, 205; MNE advantage,
  263, 270; tax effect, vertical integration, 19
cartels, 12, 105–6, 115, 118, 155
chemicals industry, 9, 23
Chile, 149
collective bargaining, 147, 149–50,
  156–7
Colombia, 248–9
colonialism, 58, 121
commitment, market, 20, 22, 142
communication costs, intracorporate,
  74, 76, 78, 80
competition policy: application to
  MNEs, 105–6, 107; global vs. national welfare, 113–14, 117, 284–5;
  optimal rules, 113–18
conglomerate mergers, 28–9
contracts, long-term, 16–17, 19, 20,
  21, 86, 121
control, market for corporate, 26, 81–2,
  84–5; *see also* acquisition
credits, tax, 228–9, 230–2, 234, 241,
  260–1
cross-hauling, foreign investment, 32,

53, 62, 106–7, 235, 280, 297

debt, intracorporate, 174–5, 177, 241
deferral, tax, 238, 241–2, 245, 260–1, 282
denomination, currency, 177, 180, 183
dependency theory, 276
devaluation, 42, 182–3
disinvestment, 71, 82
distribution systems, 9, 22
diversification of MNEs: corporate organization, 74, 76; joint ventures, 87, 88; MNE market entry, 83–4, 101; MNE objectives, 24–9; MNE risk-taking, 112; product market, 2, 6, 27–9; research and development, 197
diversification of portfolios, 169–71, 175, 280
dividend remittance: controls on, 28; MNE behavior, 165–6, 167, 177–8; tax effects, 238, 241, 243–4, 245–6
domestic content requirements, 41, 271
duty-free zones, 258–9, 260

electrical equipment industry, 23
entry barriers, 94–7, 200–1, 204–5, 206, 255
essential sectors, 291, 293
Eurocurrency market, 12
European Community, 41–2, 78, 80, 107, 157, 164
exchange-rate variations: financial portfolios, 171–2; MNE finance, 166, 172–4, 176–7, 179–83; MNE location, 42–3; *see also* devaluation
expatriates, 59, 73, 207, 270, 291
export substitution, 138, 141–7
exports, alternative to MNE, 36–40, 43–4; *see also* intracorporate trade
expropriation; *see* nationalization

factor-price equalization, 49
Financial Accounting Standards Board, 185–8
Fisher "open" hypothesis, 186
food processing industry, 9
foreign exchange market: efficiency, 181–2; forward market, 180; *see also* exchange-rate variations
France, 63, 64, 91, 96, 101, 151
functional organization, 74

gains from trade, 49
gambler's earnings, 167
General Agreement on Tariffs and Trade, 295–6
Germany, West, 23, 63, 96, 101, 147, 151, 254, 258, 270
Ghana, 269, 270
going-concern value, 7, 82
green-field entry, 81–5
growth process, MNEs: changing activity pattern, 12–15, 68–73, 83; organizational changes, product cycle, 61–2; 74–5; relation to national base, 108, 164–5
growth rates, of less developed countries, 274–6
Guatemala, 96

Heckscher-Ohlin model, 46–9, 55, 132–5, 141, 235, 259
Hong Kong, 65

impacted information, 5, 18
Imperial Tobacco Co., 104
India, 207
Indonesia, 269
information costs, 13–14, 18, 25, 63, 71, 83, 89, 95
infrastructure investments, 257–8
innovations, labor relations, diffusion of, 153
innovations, organizational, diffusion of, 74, 79–80
innovations, product and process, diffusion of: evidence on welfare effects, 218–23: role of MNEs, 85, 207–12; theoretical models, 55, 212–18
intangible assets, 3–6, 8–10, 11, 33, 86, 142
international regulation, MNEs, 298–9
intracorporate trade: bases for, 23–4, 37; complementary with foreign investment, 143, 145–6; corporate organization, 75–6, 77; joint ventures, 87, 257; transfer pricing, 246
investment decisions: capital cost, 165–8; demand conditions, 160–5; organizational factors, 68–73; stability, 191–2
investment substitution, 138–41, 147
Ireland, 64, 267, 271–2

iron ore market, 20
Italy, 101

Japan: foreign subsidiaries in, 63, 291; MNEs based in, 20, 60–1, 64, 65, 80, 82, 89–90, 198, 216, 254
Joint ventures: competitive effects, 105, 107, 118, 125–6; MNE participation, 19, 85–90, 265; public policy, 90, 207, 256

Korea, 272

leads and lags, international payments, 180
leverage, financial, 165–6, 170, 177
licensing, technology: competitive effects, 105, 206; distribution of rents, 202–3; relation to foreign investment, 45, 72, 204–7, 211, 217, 219; terms of agreement, 200–2
linkages, 270–2
liquidity, corporate, 85–5, 165, 166
Luxembourg, 151

Malaysia, 89, 101, 261, 265, 266
matrix organization, 77
Mexico, 63, 72, 97, 110–11, 151, 258, 268, 269
minority shareholdings, 90–1, 292
Modigliani-Miller theorem, 170
multidivisional organization, 74, 80
multiplant operation, 2, 7–8, 11, 24, 72

nationalistic preferences, 287–9, 290–1, 292–5
nationalization, 122–3, 284, 292
Netherlands, The, 23, 63, 85
neutrality, tax, 227–9, 238–9
New Zealand, 44, 64, 96
Nigeria, 262, 269, 271
nontraded goods, 54, 87

objectives, managerial, 26, 69–70, 162, 170
obsolescing bargain, 123–5, 284
offshore fabrication, 21–2, 64–5, 254–5; *see also* intracorporate trade
oligopoly: competition policy, 116; cross-hauling, foreign investment, 106–7; MNE patterns, 103–8; parallel behavior, 98–100; sizes of rivals, 108, 110
Organization of Petroleum Exporting Countries, 19, 120, 126
Overseas Private Investment Corporation, 284

patents, 4, 5, 197–8, 200, 203, 219–20, 285–6
payback period, 190
petroleum industry, 19–20, 125–7, 248
pharmaceutical industry, 9, 264
Philippines, 269
policy instruments, scarcity, 289–95
portfolios, financial, 25–6, 168–72, 176
predatory conduct, 108
product cycle, 61–2, 207–9
product differentiation, 4, 106, 255
productivity: labor relations, 150; MNEs and domestic competitors, 221–2, 264–5
productivity bargaining, 153
profit centers, 74, 246
profit rates: age of subsidiary, 35, 73; corporate organization, 76–7; location of subsidiary, 257, 264; market shares, 111; market structure, 110–12; MNEs and domestic competitors, 109, 223; size of subsidiary, 73
public goods, 5, 6, 288, 292–3
purchasing power parity, 186

quotas, import, 41

rents: natural resources, 118–25, 283–4; Ricardian, 119, 124
research and development: affected by foreign investment, 196–7; basis for MNEs, 9, 10, 197–8; diversification, 28, 197; entry barrier, 95–6; less developed countries, 263–4; MNE organization, 76, 198–200; scale economies, 200
risk aversion: basis for MNEs, 19, 24–7; foreign investment decisions, 71–2; joint ventures, 88, 89; MNE diversification, 29, 112; technology licenses, 202, 205–6; vertical integration, 19, 122, 125
royalty payments: intracorporate, 246, 257; natural resources, 121; technology licenses, 201, 203, 217, 240
rules of thumb, 69

saving behavior, 137, 140, 227, 272–4

scale economies: administration, 84; advertising, 95; production, 7–8, 39, 41, 43–4, 88, 95, 99, 253; research and development, 196, 200

sector-specific capital, 51–5, 135–6, 236, 259

seller concentration: affected by foreign investment, 100–2, 261–3; common causes, foreign investment, 94, 96–7; competition policy, 117; effects on foreign investment, 98–100; trend in, 106

semiconductor industry, 109, 209, 210

service industries, 11

Singapore, 264

Singer Sewing Machine Co., 72

size of market, 40, 41, 44, 59, 84, 253

small-numbers bargaining, *see* bilateral monopoly

sovereignty, 290, 296–7

Spain, 63, 109

specific factors of production, *see* sector-specific capital

speculation, foreign exchange market, 180–1, 182–3

steel industry, 20

Stolper-Samuelson theorem, 135

strategic groups, 108–9

strikes, 149, 152–3

suboptimization, 75–6

Sweden: exports, 41, 43, 60; foreign subsidiaries in, 85; MNEs based in, 10, 14, 41, 43, 60, 64

switching costs, 17, 19, 22

Switzerland, 44

Taiwan, 255

tariffs: corporate organization, 80, 87; effect on MNE location, 39, 40–1, 58, 107, 257–8; general equilibrium, 50–1, 53, 135; rebates, 257–8; relation to optimal tax on capital, 232, 235–6, 283; transfer pricing, 244–5

tax credits, *see* credits, tax

tax deferral, *see* deferral, tax

tax holidays, 240, 257–8, 261

tax neutrality, *see* neutrality, tax

tax treaties, bilateral, 238

taxes, corporation income: conditions for neutrality, 226–9, 238–9; effect on dividend remittance, 238–9, 243–4; effect on MNE location, 238–9,

242–3; global and national welfare, 136, 170, 229–32, 282–3; strategic aspects, 260–1; transfer pricing, 175, 177, 241, 244–9

taxes, monopoly/monopsony gain: global and national welfare, 282–3; methods, 232–6; strategic aspects, 236–7

taxes, natural-resource rents, 121, 123–4

taxes, personal income, 178

taxes, withholding, 238, 239, 240, 282

team production, 10

technology, choice of, 267–70

technology policy, 198, 215–8, 219–20; *see also* patents

Thailand, 269

tobacco industry, 104

trade unions, 131, 147, 149–50, 152–6, 297

trademarks, 4, 77, 86, 205, 277

training, labor, 265–7

transfer pricing: intercountry income distribution, 248–9; organizational problems, 246–8; tax avoidance, 241, 244–6

transfer process, 189–90

transformation curve, 46–7

translation, balance sheet, 183–8

transportation costs, 8, 21–2, 58–9, 103, 124

transportation equipment industry, 23

turnover, labor, 266

unemployment, 137–8, 260, 267

United Kingdom: foreign subsidiaries in, 10, 11, 63, 91, 96, 101; industrial relations, 152–3; MNEs based in, 63–4, 79, 88–9, 148, 157, 166

United States: antitrust policy, 105–6, 117–8; controls on direct investment, 189; corporate diversification, 28; exchange rate, 42–3; exports, 42, 44, 145; foreign subsidiaries in, 12, 65, 148, 150–1, 198; functional distribution, 131, 136–7, 144; gains from foreign investment, 240; intra-corporate trade, 23, 24; MNEs based in 9, 10, 14, 18, 42, 44, 99–100, 157; organizational innovation, 79; tax system, 241–2; trade policy, 21, 294

valuation reserves, 185
vertical integration: basis for MNEs, 2, 15–18; competitive processes, 125–8; intracorporate trade, 20–4; nationalization, 123; natural-resource rents, 119–25
voting behavior, 287–8, 290

wages, location determinant, 22, 255, 258; MNE levels, 150–3, 266
welfare, global vs. national: competition policy, 113–14, 117, 284–5; conditions for divergent national interests, 279–82; international regulation, 295–7; natural-resource rents, 283–4; taxation, corporate income, 282–3; technology creation, transfer, 284–5